GREECE SINCE 1945

Politics, Economy and Society

The Postwar World
General Editors: A.J. Nicholls and Martin S. Alexander

As distance puts events into perspective, and as evidence accumulates, it begins to be possible to form an objective historical view of our recent past. *The Postwar World* is an ambitious series providing a scholarly but readable account of the way our world has been shaped in the crowded years since the Second World War. Some volumes will deal with regions, or even single nations, others with important themes; all will be written by expert historians drawing on the latest scholarship as well as their own research and judgements. The series should be particularly welcome to students, but it is designed also for the general reader with an interest in contemporary history.

GREECE SINCE 1945

Politics, Economy and Society

DAVID H. CLOSE

An imprint of **Pearson Education**

London · New York · Toronto · Sydney · Tokyo · Singapore · Hong Kong · Cape Town
New Delhi · Madrid · Paris · Amsterdam · Munich · Milan · Stockholm

Pearson Education Limited

Head Office:
Edinburgh Gate
Harlow CM20 2JE
Tel: +44 (0)1279 623623
Fax: +44 (0)1279 431059

London Office:
128 Long Acre
London WC2E 9AN
Tel: +44 (0)20 7447 2000
Fax: +44 (0)20 7240 5771
Website: www.history-minds.com

First published in Great Britain in 2002

© Pearson Education Limited 2002

The right of David H. Close to be identified as Author
of this Work has been asserted by him in accordance
with the Copyright, Designs and Patents Act 1988.

ISBN 0 582 35667 9

British Library Cataloguing-in-Publication Data
A CIP catalogue record for this book can be obtained from the British Library

Library of Congress Cataloging-in-Publication Data
A CIP catalog record for this book can be obtained from the Library of Congress

All rights reserved; no part of this publication may be reproduced, stored
in a retrieval system, or transmitted in any form or by any means, electronic,
mechanical, photocopying, recording, or otherwise without either the prior
written permission of the Publishers or a licence permitting restricted copying
in the United Kingdom issued by the Copyright Licensing Agency Ltd,
90 Tottenham Court Road, London W1P 0LP. This book may not be lent,
resold, hired out or otherwise disposed of by way of trade in any form
of binding or cover other than that in which it is published, without the
prior consent of the Publishers.

10 9 8 7 6 5 4 3 2 1

Typeset in Baskerville MT 11/13pt by Graphicraft Limited, Hong Kong
Printed in Malaysia

The Publishers' policy is to use paper manufactured from sustainable forests.

CONTENTS

LIST OF TABLES

LIST OF MAPS

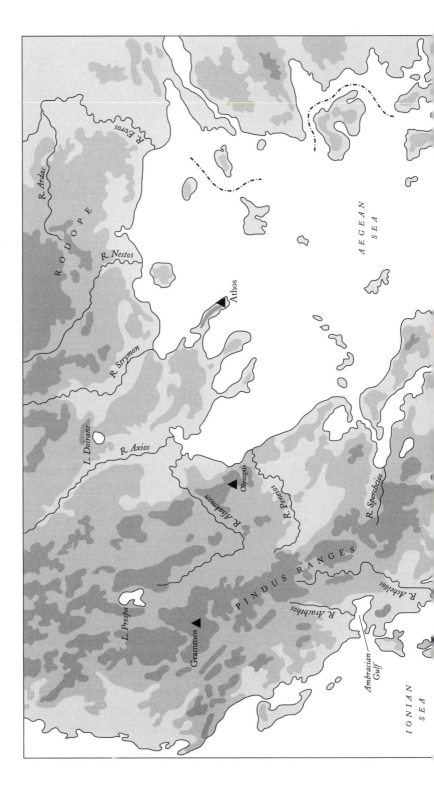

R. Alpheios

N

	25	50 miles
0	50	100 km
0		

■ Land over 1000 metres

■ 200–1000 metres

□ Under 200 metres

Map 1   Greece: physical features

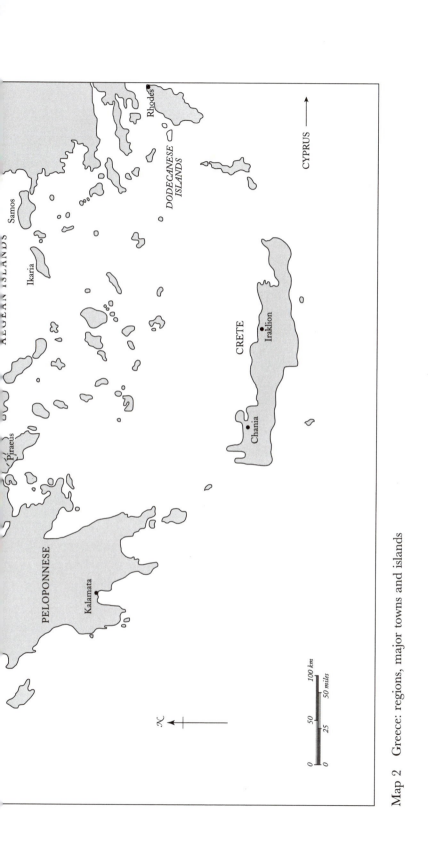

Map 2   Greece: regions, major towns and islands

ABBREVIATIONS

ADEDY	Supreme Directorate of Civil Servants' Unions
ASEP	Supreme Council for the Selection of Personnel
CIA	Central Intelligence Agency (of the United States)
DEI	Public Electricity Corporation
EAM	National Liberation Front
EDA	United Democratic Left
EENA	Union of Young Greek Officers
EEC	European Economic Community (until 1992, whenceforth it was the European Union)
ERM	Exchange Rate Mechanism
ESA	National Military Security
EK	Centre Union
EKKE	National Centre of Social Research
ELIAMEP	Hellenic Foundation of Defence and Foreign Policy (later, Hellenic Foundation for European and Foreign Policy)
EMU	Economic and Monetary Union (of the EU, popularly known as the euro-zone)
EOKA	National Organisation of Cypriot Fighters
ERE	National Radical Union
ESA	National Military Security
EU	European Union (the name of the EEC from the Treaty of Maastricht in 1992)
GSEE	General Confederation of Greek Workers
GDP	Gross Domestic Product
GNP	Gross National Product
IDEA	Sacred Union of Greek Officers
IDIS	Institute of International Relations
IKA	Social Insurance Foundation
IOVE	Foundation for Economic and Industrial Research
KKE	Communist Party of Greece
KYP	Central Intelligence Service
NATO	North Atlantic Treaty Organisation
ND	New Democracy

OAED   Organisation for the Employment of the Labour Force
OGA   Organisation for Farmers' Insurance
OTE   Organisation for Telecommunications
PASEGES   Panhellenic Confederation of Unions of Agricultural
                 Cooperatives
PASOK   Panhellenic Socialist Movement
PR   proportional representation
SDOE   Corps for the Pursuit of Economic Crime
SEV   Federation of Greek Industries
TAXIS   Integrated Programme of Tax Information
TEA   National Defence Battalions
USA   United States of America
UN   United Nations
VAT   value-added tax
WWF   World Wide Fund for Nature

PREFACE

This book is an introduction to recent developments in Greek history, written for those new to the subject and interested in seeing sources of information in endnotes. I have tried to develop important themes, rather than give a mere catalogue of events, names and dates; but this aim has made it necessary to be selective. As the title and table of contents should show, the aspects of Greek history that have been selected are interrelated and central to most historians' interest; but much has been unavoidably omitted.

Some justification is needed for starting in 1945, because this year is in effect an interval in a civil conflict. Yet the choice of date makes sense. As in many other countries immediately after the Second World War, it was 'Year Zero', in which the country had to rebuild from the foundations its political system, economy and society in a new international environment. In this year, moreover, Greece began to be drawn into American tutelage, which profoundly shaped its later development. From 1947 the Americans reinforced massively the support for the government given by the British in the previous three years, and so ensured defeat of the communist side in the civil war. Thus they confirmed Greece's membership of the capitalist zone of western Europe and its isolation until the 1990s from the communist-dominated remainder of the Balkans. Anglo-American intervention propelled the Greek people to unprecedented levels of physical wellbeing and, in the longer term, placed them on the road to unprecedented prosperity. But it also left them with a powerful monarchy and a politicised army, operating in a political system warped by the civil war. This system ended in an anachronistic military dictatorship in 1967–74. From the mid-1950s to the mid-1970s, America's economic and political influence declined steadily, while its military influence remained strong.

Meanwhile the country's wealth grew at an extraordinary rate, thanks largely to unprecedented investment in communications, in construction, and in agricultural and industrial production; to mass migration from low-productivity agriculture to higher-productivity activities in cities or overseas; and to participation, within the pax Americana, in the long boom of the western economies. Thus an economic miracle was achieved, though at the expense of great social inequality and cancerous growth of the metropolis.

While America remained a major external source of investment, the countries of the European Economic Community (EEC) came to form the country's dominant trading partner. Most of the population began to pursue prosperity together with the material and moral values of western countries, with the result that the structure of rural society crumbled. This period also saw the steady decline of tension with the Soviet satellites in eastern Europe, and the beginning, with the Cyprus issue, of the military confrontation with Turkey which still continues, requiring burdensome defence expenditure.

The collapse of military dictatorship in 1974 marked the start of a new era. In reaction against the post-civil war regime, the electorate supported a comprehensive process of democratisation and decentralisation which still continues. An immediate and decisive step was the legalisation of the Communist Party, and much later stages were the strengthening of local government and the proliferation of voluntary associations. Other parts of the process were a rapid rise in wages and social expenditure, and the enactment of legal equality for women. At the same time, the international economic environment changed after the first postwar recession in 1974. Foreign investment declined, discouraged partly by the lurch towards economic democracy. Economic growth slowed down during the following twenty years, and did not recover until 1994. From a country of emigration, Greece changed in 1974 to a country of immigration, which has continued at an increasing rate. An expansion of the state and public sector – in response to voters' demand for political patronage and social services – burdened the budget, restricted economic competition and caused double-digit inflation which lasted from 1973 until 1994. In 1975, the government sought full membership of the EEC. After this was attained in 1981, Greece enjoyed the benefits in growing subsidies, but paid a stiff price in commercial competition. Then, so as to qualify for entry into the EEC's projected Economic and Monetary Union (EMU) with its common currency, the country endured budgetary austerity from 1990 onwards. This caused extensive hardship, but helped to bring about a combination of low inflation with strong economic growth. This achievement enabled Greece in 2000 to become a proud member of EMU. Another change in 1973–74 was further heightening of tension with Turkey, which started to challenge Greek sovereignty in the Aegean and seized by force part of Cyprus, which was inhabited predominantly by ethnic Greeks.

In important respects, 1989 marked another turning point. The general disillusionment with socialism – inside and outside Greece – rendered increasingly irrelevant an ideological confrontation between left and right which originated in the early twentieth century and had dominated politics since the 1940s. Governments of both major parties had thenceforth to tackle the same structural reforms – economic and political – aimed at convergence with the developed countries of the EEC. Governments also had to satisfy the demand of increasingly critical and demanding voters for more efficient social services. The crumbling of the Iron Curtain led to closer engagement with the rest of the Balkans, and also to a swelling torrent of illegal immigrants. The collapse of the Soviet Union from the late 1980s initially strengthened Turkey and enabled it to become more aggressive.

The termination of this history, and chronological vantage-point of this book, is December 2000. I realise the risks of interpreting trends so close to the time of writing; but feel that it is necessary to try.

In this book, there are certain themes which run from the origins of the modern state in the 1820s to the present. One is the tension between widespread admiration for the developed countries of western Europe, and strong devotion to traditional values represented primarily by the Orthodox Church of Greece. Another theme is the tension between a general desire to exploit state institutions for private benefit, and an equally widespread realisation that they must be made more efficient in order to achieve national strength and prosperity. A third theme is the conflict between universal loyalty to the primary social group (the family and its network of personal friends) and a generally reluctant recognition of the public interest, represented by the national government and the apparatus of law. It will be argued that in recent years, the traditional gulf between primary and public loyalties has been narrowed in various ways. In all three dichotomies, modernisers have been pitted against traditionalists. In recent years, the conflict between them has possibly been more intense than ever before; and the modernisers, strengthened by a feeling of inevitability, seem to be gaining ground.

To turn to a few mundane, stylistic matters: unless stated otherwise the place of publication of books in English is London, and of books in Greek, Athens. In references to Greek newspapers, the author is sometimes omitted because authorship is not clear in the source, and page numbers are unavailable on some Internet editions. On economic matters, I have had to refer in some places to Gross Domestic Product (preferred by foreign analysts) and in others to the somewhat greater Gross National Product (preferred by Greek analysts).

Anything but mundane is my debt to the academic editors of this series, Anthony Nicholls and Martin Alexander, for their patient and helpful comments on drafts of this text. Among the authorities on modern Greece who have been generous with their time and advice over many years – although they may not care to be associated with this book – are Nicos Alivizatos, Richard Clogg, Hagen Fleischer, John Iatrides, Thanos Veremis and Susannah Verney. I also owe a debt of a different kind to Elizabeth for tolerating the mess in the house.

David Close

EDITORIAL FOREWORD

The aim of this series is to describe and analyse the history of the world since 1945. History, like time, does not stand still. What seemed to many of us only recently to be 'current affairs' or the stuff of political speculation, has now become material for historians. The editors feel that it is time for a series of books which will offer the public judicious and scholarly, but at the same time readable, accounts of the way in which our present-day world has been shaped since the Second World War. The period which began in 1945 has witnessed political events and socio-economic developments of enormous significance for the human race, as important as anything which happened before Hitler's death or the bombing of Hiroshima. Ideologies have waxed and waned, the developed economies have boomed and bust, empires of various types have collapsed, new nations have emerged and sometimes themselves fallen into decline. While we can be thankful that no major armed conflict occurred between the so-called superpowers, there have been many other wars, and terrorism emerged as an international plague. Although the position of ethnic minorities improved in some countries, it worsened dramatically in others. As communist tyrannies relaxed their grip on many areas of the world, so half-forgotten national conflicts re-emerged. Nearly everywhere the status of women became an issue which politicians were unable to avoid. The same was true of the natural environment, apparent threats to which have been a recurrent source of international concern. These are only some of the developments we hope will be illuminated by this series as it unfolds.

The books in the series will not follow any set pattern; they will vary in length according to the needs of the subject. Some will deal with regions, or even single nations, and others with themes. Not all of them will begin in 1945, and the terminal date may vary; as with the length, the time-span chosen will be appropriate to the question under discussion. All the books, however, will be written by expert historians drawing on the latest research, as well as their own expertise and judgement. The series should be particularly welcome to students, but it is designed also for the general reader with an interest in contemporary history. We hope that the books will stimulate scholarly discussion and encourage specialists to look beyond their own particular interests to engage in wider controversies.

History, and especially the history of the recent past, is neither 'bunk' nor an intellectual form of stamp-collecting, but an indispensable part of an educated person's approach to life. If it is not written by historians it will be written by others of a less discriminating and more polemical disposition. The editors are confident that this series will help to ensure the victory of the historical approach, with consequential benefits for its readers.

A.J. Nicholls
Martin S. Alexander

CHAPTER ONE

Introduction

The development of the new nation, 1821–1940

People and territory

The modern Greek state came into being in 1821–33, when part of the Greek people won independence from the Ottoman empire in their 'national revolution'. This was an early stage in the emancipation of the Balkan peoples from Ottoman rule, and Greeks were the first of them to win internationally recognised sovereignty. Like the other Balkan states which thus emerged during the nineteenth and early twentieth centuries, Greece derived legitimacy from a sense of identity which was based on deep-rooted ethnic characteristics and then cultivated by intellectuals and patriotic insurgents from the late eighteenth century onwards, before being inculcated by a national government in its subjects. Among the characteristics of the Balkan nations, religion was especially influential, a fact which led, except in Muslim-dominated areas, to close association between church and nation.

In the Greek case the historical foundations of ethnic identity were particularly compelling in their appeal, consisting of descent – attested by linguistic as well as geographical continuity – from classical Greek civilisation and the subsequent Byzantine empire, which had expired after over a millennium of existence with the fall of Constantinople to the Ottoman Turks in 1453. An institutional link with the Byzantine empire was the Greek Orthodox Church, which could claim a direct line of continuity including language with the earliest Christian communities. From the late seventeenth century, Greek families – many of them wealthy and cultivated – played a major role in the administration and commerce of the Ottoman empire.[1] The Ecumenical Patriarch of the Orthodox Church, who was in effect chosen by some of those families, was acknowledged as spiritual leader by the empire's millions of Orthodox Christian subjects, who formed the majority of the Balkan peoples. Greeks therefore had reason to see their cultural heritage as exceptionally valuable.

It is only recently that most Greeks came to inhabit national territory, as a result both of its expansion and also of immigration. Later in the nineteenth century, the new state acquired the Ionian Islands and Thessaly. In the Balkan wars of 1912–13, it wrested Epirus, Macedonia, Crete and many eastern Aegean islands from the Ottoman empire, so expanding its territory by 70 per cent, and increasing its population from 2,800,000 to 4,800,000. The First World War added western Thrace, acquired from Bulgaria. Under the Treaty of Lausanne of 1923, Greek boundaries took almost their present form, enclosing large new territories and populations which then had to be assimilated. The only territory to be added thereafter consisted of Rhodes and the other Dodecanese Islands, acquired from Italy in 1947, and inhabited by 121,000 people.

During the spasms of ethnic reorganisation which occurred during the twentieth century, most of the Greek diaspora that existed in the nineteenth century immigrated to the new state. The years 1913–23 saw 1,300,000–1,400,000 Greeks arrive from what is now Turkey, most of them expelled by the armies of Kemal Atatürk in the 'Asia Minor Catastrophe' of 1922. Another 100,000 arrived in these years from Bulgaria and the Soviet Union. Thus in 1940 the national population of 7,345,000 was nearly ten times that of 1833. Thereafter the national population was increased by the further contraction of the old diaspora, with the arrival in the 1950s and 1960s of tens of thousands of Greeks from Constantinople (now Istanbul) and Egypt; since the late 1980s of 163,000 more from the former Soviet Union and tens of thousands from Albania.

The new frontiers were for a long time vulnerable to challenge, and were indeed changed by Bulgaria and Italy, as satellites of Nazi Germany, during the joint military occupation by the three countries in 1941–44. Bulgaria reclaimed western Thrace, and Italy annexed part of Epirus to its protectorate of Albania. These territories returned to Greece with liberation in 1944. Thereafter the slav-Macedonian speakers of Macedonia tried to secede to the Macedonian Republic of the new federation of Yugoslavia. During civil conflict in 1944–49, about 86,000 or more speakers of Albanian, slav Macedonian and Vlach (a Romanian dialect) fled abroad or were killed, because they were accused of supporting the occupation forces or the communists. In addition, during the enemy occupation in 1942–44, 67,000 Jews (making up 87 per cent of their prewar numbers) were deported to their deaths. Thus by 1950, and until the 1990s, the country was ethnically homogeneous by Balkan standards, with about 95 per cent of the population being both Greek-speaking from preference and Greek Orthodox in religion, and under 2 per cent diverging in both language and religion.[2]

Dependency, political and economic

Like other Balkan countries, Greece looked to great powers for political models and military backing. The movement for independence from the late eighteenth century was inspired by the western Enlightenment, and particularly by the western cult of classical civilisation. The entourage of the first monarch Otto (a Roman Catholic Bavarian selected by Britain, France and Russia in 1832) imposed on the country a mixture of German and Napoleonic concepts of government. After Otto was deposed by a revolt in 1862, his successor George was selected by the same powers from the Danish royal family, but he at least converted to Orthodoxy. When from 1910 the Prime Minister Elevtherios Venizelos – the Greek counterpart to Bismarck – sought to reform the navy, army and police, he entrusted the task to foreign missions – British, French and Italian respectively. In a later era of intensive modernisation – from 1990 onwards – governments as a matter of course consulted foreign specialists: for example the British about reforming state broadcasting, the civil service and social insurance, Americans about reforming the tax department, and both about reforming the police.

Greece was always dependent on foreign military backing, partly because an extraordinarily long coastline exposed the country to pressure from naval powers – the five largest cities in the mid-twentieth century being coastal – and partly because of a recurring need both for protection against territorial threats and support for territorial claims. In the late 1930s, the dictator Ioannis Metaxas drew closer for protection to Britain – which since the early nineteenth century had been the leading naval power in the Mediterranean – against threats by Fascist Italy and Nazi Germany. Thus the national custom of seeking patrons was extended by governments beyond the frontiers.

The Balkan countries also became increasingly dependent, from the late nineteenth century, on the great powers for loans and investment. Their economic development was hindered by, among other things, lack of credit, poor internal communications, and competition with their own products by the developed countries' manufactured exports, which since the eighteenth century had ruined or discouraged native industries. The public utilities that were constructed before the 1940s, like railways, power stations and reservoirs, were meagre by northern European standards, and were mainly built by foreign firms and financed by foreign credit. In Greece, the railway network, being built to suit the needs of foreign creditors, never reached

Epirus in the north-west; and perhaps the majority of the population in the 1930s was still accessible only by rough tracks or infrequent boats.

Like much of Mediterranean Europe Greece is relatively poor in mineral resources, fisheries and arable land. Most of the surface area consists of rocky mountains and only 28 per cent of the area after 1947 can be cultivated; so that the area of arable land per head in the 1940s was 1.3 acres (compared with 5.4 in Britain); while the general quality of grazing land was poor. Part of the better arable and grazing land lay beside malarial marshes. Through lack of investment, productivity was low by northern European standards: for example, iron ploughs were used by only one-quarter of farmers in 1935, and production of wheat per acre was little over half the Italian level. For the sizeable proportion of the population living among mountains or on small islands, there was little hope of economic improvement save by migration to cities or abroad.[3] Lacking the resources to pay for a top-heavy bureaucracy and army, the government became so indebted that from 1897 until the 1950s – and again in the 1990s – its finances were supervised by successive commissions representing foreign creditors.

But Greece benefited from location on major maritime routes. Largely for this reason, economic ties with other countries, and especially with the industrialised powers of northern Europe and the United States of America, were stronger and more varied than those of other Balkan nations. With the improvement of internal communications from the late nineteenth century, more and more villages were drawn into a national or international economy. One-quarter of the country's food – and one-third of the staple item of diet, wheat – before 1940 were imported, and paid for in part by exports of a limited range of primary products (consisting largely of tobacco, raisins and currants), which were vulnerable to fluctuations in foreign demand.

Another link with western commerce was the Greek-owned merchant fleet, which in the 1930s was the world's ninth largest. Like other maritime peoples, Greeks were especially ready to travel and emigrate. Consequently, a different source of foreign exchange – and of personal ties with western countries – consisted of remittances from emigrants, of whom there were 445,000 in the United States by the early 1930s, besides nearly 200,000 who had returned from there. By then there must have been thousands of villages thus linked by personal ties with America. Ties of various kinds were especially close with all the maritime democracies: Britain, America and France. On them the merchant fleet depended heavily for its viability and existence; while in the first two were placed much of the savings of the wealthy.

Economic dependency was reflected in a generally low level of material wellbeing, even by Balkan standards.[4] The general level of health was also low, so that the proportion of the population suffering from malaria was always at least one-sixth, while average life expectancy at birth in 1928 was 46.3 – lower than in Britain in 1901. There prevailed a sense of backwardness in relation to the developed countries of the west. From the 1820s onwards, the most influential of the ruling elites strove to catch up with them, their specific aim being to establish effective government in place of the anarchic misrule of the Ottoman empire.[5] In time the westernisers would predominate. In the later twentieth century, they were chiefly preoccupied with adapting all institutions and practices to the goal of producing wealth more efficiently so as to promote human welfare and national power – a process which we usually refer to as modernisation.

Economy, society and political system

The main form of landholding in this largely agrarian economy was the small family farm. In the 1820s this already had a long and respected history, there being virtually no landed aristocracy, and limited incentives for businessmen to invest in agriculture. Meanwhile the rapid growth of population, with little economic development, led – as in the rest of the Balkans – to widespread land hunger. For these reasons, successive governments until the 1950s distributed in small allotments the extensive agricultural lands which they acquired from former Turkish owners, monasteries or Greek landowners. The chief phase in this process was stimulated by the mass influx of refugees from Asia Minor, and occurred in 1917–23. Thereafter four-fifths of farms in Greece were under ten acres, and most farms were owner-occupied. There was still much variation in the size of holdings, and village communities varied in social composition; but there were no extensive class divisions in the countryside.[6] As in the rest of Mediterranean Europe, farmers lived in compact villages, typically clustered near a water source. In the 1930s, most landholders were heavily indebted and incapable of investing in improved productivity. But in the long run, the widespread distribution of land protected most of the population against total destitution. The great majority of the nation's householders owned their dwellings; and much of the urban population still have land or close relatives in the country, where they return to celebrate Easter.

There was little industrial activity in the nineteenth century; and industrial development did not take off until the 1920s, even this being earlier than in the rest of the Balkans. In 1939, after more than doubling in value in the previous fifteen years, industrial production satisfied most of domestic demand, and with mining accounted for 18 per cent of GNP and 15 per cent of employment. The mercantile and shipowning element of the population had traditionally been large. Associated with it were comparatively numerous professional and administrative classes, trained in schools and universities. These institutions were for much of the nineteenth century paid for by mercantile communities abroad, which until the early twentieth century far outnumbered their counterparts within the country.[7] Thus Greece differed from other Balkan countries in 1940 in that the farming population was smaller, at about 54 per cent of the population, while the city population was larger. The latter consisted overwhelmingly of people engaged in small-scale businesses and workshops, in state administration, commerce and retailing. Like the farming population, most of those engaged in construction, industry, commerce and transport worked in small family enterprises. By 1940 the metropolis, consisting of Athens and its adjacent port of Piraeus, formed the largest conurbation in the Balkans, with 1,124,000 inhabitants: 15 per cent of the national population, a large proportion of whom had immigrated recently from villages.[8] Altogether, 24 per cent of the national population lived in cities with over 50,000 people. The two biggest cities – Athens–Piraeus and Salonika – formed enclaves of western tastes and consumption habits, contrasting with the more conservative villages and market towns where most people lived.

There existed then a cultural division between city and country, and another between natives and refugees. But in general Greek society was distinguished by its relative homogeneity. It was closely knit by religion, language and national myths, and by the prevalence in town and country of small family businesses. Moreover it lacked the aristocratic and anti-clerical traditions, and the hereditary class divisions, that were widespread in western Europe. An important reason for social cohesion was the fluidity of social lines, of which one example was the varied background of industrialists.[9]

Greece also diverged from other Balkan countries in its political system, characterised from early in its modern history by vigorous parliamentary politics combined with a highly centralised administration. Under Ottoman rule, Greek notables consisting of landowners, merchants, bishops and military chiefs, wielded local power and were represented in consultative assemblies. The movement for national independence was suffused with western liberal ideas, which were expressed in a series of revolutionary assemblies and a flourishing newspaper press. Community leaders, who were joined by some of the wealthy and educated Greeks from Constantinople known as Phanariots, therefore regarded parliament based on a broad suffrage as a natural part of the new state, and consequently forced the autocratic King Otto to accept one in 1843–44.[10] Thenceforth the great majority of men had the vote,[11] and parliamentary life continued with little interruption until 1936, with democratic local politics closely associated with it. An upper house existed only under two short-lived constitutions (1844–63 and 1924–35). After 1875, the principle was established that governments, while appointed by the king, should be based on a parliamentary majority. A form of two-party system became the norm from the 1880s. From at least as early as 1920 it was possible for a ruling party – despite its extensive patronage – to lose a general election. Thus from the late nineteenth century, the legislature was the expression of popular sovereignty and the basis of governmental legitimacy, although it never acquired the same corporate power as in Anglo-Saxon countries. Such a long-established tradition of political participation and competition makes it understandable why the dictatorships which appeared at intervals in the twentieth century were short-lived and unpopular.

Politics were distinguished from the 1820s onwards by vigorous competition between parties for control of the national administration, a contest in which much of the public, especially journalists, took a lively interest. The contest for power and spoils was not marked by respect for civil liberties or electoral legality. Even in the 1930s, much of the rural population was so poor that it responded to the crudest bribery or coercion. But at least public debate could normally flourish. In consequence, corruption, although widespread, was frequently exposed and its proceeds widely distributed. It is characteristic of this political tradition that the Communist Party – while illegal for much of the period from 1929 to 1974 – was still able for most of these years to participate in parliamentary politics either in its own right or through a front party. Focusing on competition for the metropolitan power base, the major parties were more successful than their counterparts in other Balkan countries in winning the support of a range of regions, and of diverse social and ethnic groups, thus preventing for example the rise of large ethnically based or peasant parties.

The centralised administration was built up by successive governments from the 1820s onwards, encroaching on local autonomies. This trend continued until the 1970s. The original architects of the administration were imbued with the Germanic ideal of the state as the source of national identity and civil rights. The need to define the claims of this exotic organisation over local communities – and to settle disputes among myriad small-scale proprietors and businesses – gave rise to a legal profession which was extraordinarily large relative to population. Submission to civil authority had always been exhorted by the Orthodox Church. At the outset this was made an integral part of the national state, and until 1925 the government appointed the members of its ruling body the Holy Synod. Thus the Church's jurisdiction expanded with the state's boundaries. In 1909 its clergy became in effect dependent on state salaries, funded from the administration of church property.

From 1844 the growth of the state was also promoted by parliamentary politicians, who without inhibition treated the administration and its budget as a source of spoils with which to recruit their clienteles – hence the general use of the term clientelism to describe a basic feature of parliamentary politics until the present. For this reason, parties penetrated the state machine, so hindering the civil service and police from acquiring professional cohesion.[12] The resulting ineffectiveness of the public administration accounted for the chronic tendency of politicians to indulge in wish-fulfilment, or in other words to neglect, in their speeches and legislation, the problem of implementing grandiose intentions.

When in the twentieth century national parties became more extensively organised, the state machine came to be identified with the ruling party. A later driving force behind state growth was the relatively large urban population, which required an extensive administration for its governance and for employment outlets. As a result of all these pressures the national administration was from the start large and costly by northern European and even by Balkan standards: thus in the 1870s the number of civil servants in relation to population was about seven times higher than in Britain. Employment in it for their sons was the goal of many upwardly mobile families.[13]

Politicians won influence among voters by mediating between them and this administration which used the official form of the language, *katharevousa* – prestigious because closer to classical Greek – which was obligatory also in politics, journalism, scholarship and the law, but comprehensible only to those – fewer than 10 per cent of the population in 1940 – who completed secondary schooling. Among the majority of the population, political behaviour patterns dating from the Ottoman period persisted. The primary object of loyalty was the family which was seen as competing with other families, through a network of friends, in a context of scarcity or limited good. The voter saw it as his duty to promote his family's fortunes by seeking the mediation of the powerful, especially politicians, each of whom had to seek favours for thousands of voters. For this reason, the number of MPs in relation to population was high.[14]

The scope of political patronage tended to expand with the powers of the state, and partly for this reason the influence of national leaders during the late nineteenth and twentieth centuries grew at the expense of local notables. Some of the politicians' power derived from the great increase in state leverage over various branches of the economy, leverage which in the twentieth century became extraordinarily far-reaching by the standards of other parliamentary democracies.[15] Thus the state-controlled National Bank (established in 1841) provided the main source of finance for industry, while the state-owned Agricultural Bank (established in 1929) was the main source of banking credit for farmers. The allocation of this credit was the chief function of the growing agrarian cooperative movement. The state regulated the structure and purpose of chambers of commerce, trade unions and agricultural cooperatives, licensed new businesses and entry into occupations, and ratified collective agreements between employers and workers. Most parties when in power established great influence over the main trade union confederation, the General Confederation of Greek Workers (GSEE, formed in 1918), and over the agricultural cooperatives (united in the Panhellenic Confederation of Unions of Agricultural Cooperatives, PASEGES, in 1935). Thus the economy was moving towards a corporatist organisation, in the sense that major sectors of it were hierarchically organised under state control or influence. The socio-political system was bourgeois in bias, because politicians in power were on cosy terms with leading bankers and businessmen, and habitually used the police on employers' behalf against striking workers.

The police forces, consisting of the gendarmerie, the city police and the agricultural constabulary, extended state power over society.[16] Their authority increased considerably in the early twentieth century; so that by about 1930 the city police had asserted their authority over the formerly crime-ridden port of Piraeus, while the semi-military gendarmerie had gone far towards suppressing banditry and sheep-stealing even in the most inaccessible areas. The police issued licences for all manner of businesses, while a special branch, the market police, supervised retail prices. As parties when in power permeated the state machine, their interests were promoted by the police, especially during elections.

While extending its power over the population, the state did little to earn its respect or cultivate a sense of citizenship. Governments changed or flouted laws as it suited them, and were readier to demand sacrifices from citizens than provide benefits to them. Universal military conscription was established by the early twentieth century; but primary education was still unavailable for many people in 1940; and a state social insurance system was still available to very few. The state did little to help farmers, and promoted industrial development by means such as high tariffs and easy credit for favoured businessmen, so making life harder for the great majority of the population.

The National Schism

Party competition reached new heights in 1915, when the prime minister Elevtherios Venizelos quarrelled with King Constantine over the country's orientation in the First World War. As was usually the case in this dependent country, international alignments were very divisive. Venizelos wanted Greece to ally with the maritime democracies of the Entente, Britain and France, so as to win their backing for the traditional 'Great Idea' of union with the Greek peoples beyond the frontiers, who lived mainly in present-day Turkey and were ruled by the Ottoman empire. Britain encouraged this hope by offering its colony of Cyprus as a reward. As the Great Idea had provided much of the *raison d'être* of the state since its origins, Venizelos's policy seemed inspiring to many. Constantine – asserting the monarch's traditional claim to control foreign policy and the army – preferred a cautious stance of neutrality towards the Central Powers and and their allies Bulgaria and the Ottoman empire, and was influenced by his family ties with the Kaiser. This policy required abandonment of the Greeks of Asia Minor. So the issues at stake were not only the boundaries and orientation of the new state, but the power – and eventually the existence – of the monarchy.

The National Schism, as it became known, between Venizelists and anti-Venizelists, raged intermittently for over twenty years, during which coups and counter-coups led to repeated purges of the whole state machine, including the public service, judiciary, army, police and Church.[17] After the Asia Minor catastrophe in 1922, the Great Idea lay dormant until the end of the German occupation in 1944. But the National Schism continued, based on support by the natives of the older southern territories for the anti-Venizelists and of the refugee population for the Venizelists. After Venizelists attained power by a bloody military coup in 1922, a republic was proclaimed in 1924. Then, after another spasm of violent conflict in 1935, anti-Venizelists restored the monarchy by means of a rigged plebiscite, and dominated the army and police. These events made it possible for an anti-Venizelist general-turned-politician who was a friend of the royal family, Ioannis Metaxas, to establish a dictatorship in 1936.

Meanwhile a different schism arose in the 1920s: between bourgeois society of both parties and the small but active Communist Party of Greece (KKE). The latter dominated the infant socialist movement and took a prominent role in organising industrial workers. Over time it grew in size and cohesion, even though successive governments mobilised the police and judiciary with increasing determination against it. Just before Metaxas's coup, the party had about 15,000 full members (selected, according to Comintern requirements, for their dogmatic faith and organisational ability), and seemed poised for rapid advance among industrial workers and farmers.

Both types of schism strengthened two political trends: firstly the centralisation of power in the executive, and secondly the politicisation of the whole state machine.[18] Metaxas took advantage of these trends in constructing his dictatorship. He also used the Communist bogy as his pretext for seizing power; and utilised the experience of the police to destroy that party's organisation and jail nearly all its cadres. As his regime suppressed by thorough police terror all other dissenters, including anti-Venizelist politicians, it became extremely unpopular, and had little prospect of surviving the dictator's death in January 1941, even if it had not been destroyed by German invasion three months later.

The collapse of this regime left a vacuum of legitimacy. Monarchy and republic were each advocated by powerful factions; and politicians were accustomed to struggling for power with no holds barred. Nevertheless dominant institutions were now rooted in tradition: a national parliament based on manhood suffrage; a centralised administration derived originally from the Napoleonic model, within which partisan influence competed with professional spirit; elected municipalities and communes supervised by government-appointed prefects; an educational system subjected to the needs of the prevalent regime, but always with a strong emphasis on teaching *katharevousa*, theology and law. All these institutions were challenged by the Communists; yet they, too, felt themselves to be members of an ethnically cohesive nation.

Total devastation, 1941–44

Enemy occupation

After the German invasion, the occupying forces – German, Italian and Bulgarian – plundered the country ruthlessly and showed no interest in distributing relief. Meanwhile, a British blockade intercepted food shipments, so that a terrible famine ensued over the winter of 1941–42. Although this was eventually alleviated by the International Red Cross, virtually all the necessities of life remained scarce for most people for the rest of the occupation. The government lost its authority because it was coerced by the occupation authorities into collaboration, and was deprived of resources. Traditional leaders of society, such as politicians and army officers, were slow to organise either welfare or resistance activities.

In these circumstances, there was a vacuum of authority which was gradually filled by the National Liberation Front (EAM), organised from the first weeks of the occupation by Communist cadres, several hundred of whose members managed to escape from Metaxas's jails and prison islands. The initial welfare groups of EAM developed into a confederation of diverse organisations, based on mass participation and covering as best they could most of the population's needs. The culmination of this movement was a provisional government formed in March 1944. While professedly democratic, and certainly inspiring mass enthusiasm, EAM was covertly directed by the Communist Party, which provided its leading members and imbued the whole movement with its ruthlessly intolerant spirit. Through its guerrilla army and its terroristic local chieftains, EAM drove most other resistance groups either into joining itself or else into collaboration with the enemy.

During 1943–44 the possibility loomed that EAM would take power after the Germans withdrew. The approach of the Soviet army was welcomed by Communists in August–September 1944; while EAM extended its authority over most of the population.[19]

In response to this danger of revolution, the defenders of traditional values assumed the label of *ethnikofron* (meaning 'of national opinions') and tried without much success to organise their forces. Those within Greece either formed resistance groups or joined armed units under German leadership. Those in exile sought British patronage in Egypt, and joined either the king's government there or the exiled armed forces which the British, who were strongly anti-communist, purged of their many EAM sympathisers. All sections of the national camp saw the British as their sole hope of salvation after the Germans withdrew. During the last year of the occupation, fighting between EAM and its varied opponents spread to most regions and was frequently marked by atrocities. This fighting intensified in the wake of the German withdrawal in September–November 1944.

Liberation and civil conflict

Thus Greece was politically as well as economically in ruins at the time of liberation. The total number of civilian deaths from hunger, disease and violence during the Axis occupation seems to have been about 450,000. Roads, railways, ports and bridges had been devastated; one-quarter of all housing was destroyed; three-quarters of the once vast merchant fleet and four-fifths of coastal shipping had been sunk; nearly all railway rolling stock and most motor vehicles had gone.[20] Output of nearly all agricultural products was less than half the prewar level, and industrial output less than a quarter. The national currency, the drachma, was worthless. Devastation on this scale gave great power to the British, to whom most of the population looked either for protection against EAM or just in hope of desperately needed supplies of all necessities, which had to be brought by British ships and distributed by British troops.[21] Many people saw that Greece also needed British backing against claims by Albania, Yugoslavia and Bulgaria on northern territories. The British forces, building on the goodwill as allies which they had won by fighting alongside Greeks against the invading Germans in 1941, were therefore welcomed even by the EAM rank and file.

The Communists could not challenge British power without support from their patron the Soviet Union or its new satellites, which now included the other Balkan countries. But the British and Soviet governments had moved towards tacit agreement on spheres of influence, whereby Stalin accepted that Greece, because of its maritime position, was beyond his reach, while Churchill more reluctantly conceded Soviet dominance of Bulgaria and Romania – and eventually of Yugoslavia and Albania also. The question of influence over Turkey and the Straits of Constantinople remained unresolved. These understandings, which included the famous percentages agreement of October, were concluded without the knowledge of the Greek people. What the Greek Communists did know was that Soviet representatives warned them, obliquely, against quarrelling with the British. An immediate result of the percentages agreement was a Soviet order to Bulgarian forces, now under Communist control, to withdraw from what had been Greek territory before the occupation.[22]

The Greek Communists were forced therefore in August to acknowledge the government in exile under British patronage, and even send representatives to join it. This government, under the leadership of an experienced Venizelist politician of left-liberal views, Georgios Papandreou, was brought to liberated Athens in a British warship on 18 October. But outside the capital, most of the population for the next few months was administered by EAM, which acted like the communist-led movements which were at this time taking power in other Balkan countries: suppressing rival political groups, jailing masses of alleged collaborators with the occupation forces, and massacring armed ex-collaborators (except, in Greece, for those protected by British troops). EAM exercised extensive influence over the population even of Athens, where the British headquarters were based.

The relationship between EAM and the British-dominated government collapsed and turned into armed conflict early in December. The cause of rupture was the British demand that the Communists demobilise EAM's army, which would have meant exposing themselves to annihilation by anti-communist Greek forces armed by the British. The Communists refused, and tried to overawe Papandreou's government through a mass demonstration and a general strike. This pressure escalated into fighting that raged throughout the metropolis, and in large areas of the west and north of the country, between early December 1944 and early January 1945. In the metropolis the protagonists were, on the one side, the EAM forces and, on the other, Greek anti-communists backed by British troops using tanks, artillery, aircraft and warships. The British denied food to EAM-occupied areas of the country; bombarded districts of Athens and Piraeus; and armed many thousands of former collaborators keen for revenge against the left-wing resisters who had recently terrorised them. One of the most savage phases in the civil conflict of the 1940s, causing thousands of deaths on each side, this became known as the *Dekemvrianá*.

Having been driven out of the capital, the Communist forces faced the reality that the national population depended for survival on British relief supplies, and that they themselves had been abandoned by other Communist parties. They were driven therefore to surrender to British representatives in the Varkiza agreement of February, and undertook to dissolve their army. In return the British promised an amnesty for political crimes, free elections and civil liberties – promises which they did not have the power, or resolve, to implement. The Communists could not hope now for mercy from all the people whom they had persecuted or alarmed during the previous two years.

The Varkiza agreement confirmed that Greece belonged to the western capitalist sphere of Europe rather than the Soviet communist sphere. The basic factors leading to this outcome were the country's vulnerability to British maritime blockade, and dependence on western aid which was distributed by British troops, though largely financed by the United States. During the following 45 years, Greece would diverge in its economic, social and political development from the Balkans and move parallel to the developing countries further west. So thenceforth the countries with which comparison is most fruitful are Italy, Portugal and Spain.

Notes

1 Richard Clogg, *A Short History of Modern Greece* (Cambridge 1979), 32, 45, 78.

2 Dimitri Constas and Charalambos Papasotiriou, 'Greek policy responses to the post-Cold War Balkan environment', in Van Coufoudakis, Harry J. Psomiades and André Gerolymatos (eds), *Greece and the New Balkans. Challenges and Opportunities* (New York 1999), 219.

3 Seraphim Seferiades, 'Small rural ownership, subsistence agriculture, and peasant protest in interwar Greece: the agrarian question recast', *Journal of Modern Greek Studies* 17 (1999), 292.

4 Nicolas Spulber, 'Changes in the economic structures of the Balkans, 1860–1960', in Barbara and Charles Jelavich (eds), *The Balkans in Transition. Essays on the Development of Balkan Life and Politics since the Eighteenth Century* (Hamden, CT 1974), 359.

5 John A. Petropulos, *Politics and Statecraft in the Kingdom of Greece* (Princeton, NJ 1968), 40–1; Nicos P. Mouzelis, *Modern Greece: Facets of Underdevelopment* (1978), chs 3–5.

6 William W. McGrew, *Land and Revolution in Modern Greece, 1821–71* (Kent, OH 1986), *passim*; Diane O. Bennett, ' "The poor have much more money": changing socio-economic relations in a Greek village', *Journal of Modern Greek Studies* 6 (1988), 217–20.

7 Konstantinos Tsoucalas, *Social Development and the State. The Composition of the Public Sphere in Greece* (in Greek, 2nd ed. 1986), 100, 145–63; Mouzelis, *Modern Greece*, 145.

8 Lila Leontidou, *The Mediterranean City in Transition. Social Change and Urban Development* (Cambridge 1990), 104, 181, 218.

9 Maria Nassiakou, 'The tendency towards learning in the Greek countryside', *Journal of the Hellenic Diaspora* 8 (1981), 64–5; Alec P. Alexander, *Greek Industrialists. A Social and Economic Analysis* (Athens 1964), 86–7.

10 Petropulos, *Politics and Statecraft*, 23–6, 48–50, 434–52.

11 The qualifying age for voting was 25 until 1877, 21 until 1981, and then 18. By stages from 1930 to 1956, women gained the vote on the same terms.

12 Dimitrios A. Sotiropoulos, 'A colossus with feet of clay: the state in post-authoritarian Greece', in Harry J. Psomiades and Stavros B. Thomadakis (eds), *Greece, the New Europe, and the Changing International Order* (New York 1993), 50.

13 Mouzelis, *Modern Greece*, 11, 16–17, 101; Nicos P. Mouzelis, *Politics in the Semi-Periphery. Early Parliamentarism and Late Industrialisation in the Balkans and Latin America* (1986), 10–12; Tsoucalas, *Social Development*, 153.

14 Adamantia Pollis, 'The impact of traditional cultural patterns on Greek politics', *Review of Social Research* 29 (1977), 4–5; Richard Clogg, *Parties and Elections in Greece. The Search for Legitimacy* (1987), 4.

15 Alkis Rigos, *The Second Greek Republic, 1924–35. Social Dimensions of the Political Scene* (in Greek, 1988), 89–90.

16 David H. Close, *The Origins of the Greek Civil War* (1995), 25–6; Lee Sarafis, 'The policing of Deskati, 1942–6', in Mark Mazower (ed.), *After the War Was Over. Reconstructing the Family, Nation, and State in Greece, 1943–60* (Princeton, NJ 2000), 211–12.

17 George T. Mavrogordatos, *Stillborn Republic. Social Coalitions and Party Strategies in Greece, 1922–36* (Berkeley, CA 1983), 27, 55–64, 72–3, 127–9, 284–5.

18 Nicos C. Alivizatos, 'The difficulties of "rationalization" in a polarized political system: the Greek Chamber of Deputies', in Ulrika Liebert and Maurizio Cotta (eds), *Parliament and Democratic Consolidation in Southern Europe. Greece, Italy, Portugal, Spain and Turkey* (1990), 132.

19 Close, *Origins*, chs 3–5.

20 Wray O. Candilis, *The Economy of Greece, 1944–66. Efforts for Stability and Development* (New York 1968), 4–5.

21 Angeliki Laiou-Thomadakis, 'The politics of hunger: economic aid to Greece, 1943–5', *Journal of the Hellenic Diaspora* 7 (1980), 27–42.

22 Jordan Baev, *The Greek Civil War. A View from Outside* (in Greek, 1996), 55–6.

CHAPTER TWO

Civil war and Reconstruction, 1945–1950

Troubled peace, February 1945–March 1946

Want and disorder

After the Varkiza agreement, desperate want and anarchic disorder prevailed in most areas outside the metropolis.[1] The want was gradually alleviated by western aid of many kinds: food, clothing, medical supplies, as well as raw materials and equipment to rebuild houses, reconstruct communications and revive economic activity. The rehabilitation of liberated peoples was a proclaimed Allied war aim for which systematic preparations had been made by the British and American governments. They worked at first through British troops, and then from April 1945 to June 1947 through the United Nations Relief and Rehabilitation Administration (UNRRA), substantially supplemented by the British army and by voluntary organisations in which American Greeks were especially important. In eighteen months during 1945–46, official aid alone was worth 70 per cent of national income in 1939, and at one point – April 1945 – it provided most of the food consumed in the country.[2] During 1945, the recovery of economic production and living standards was held back by the sheer extent of the destruction and chaos left by the enemy occupation followed by the *Dekemvrianá*. To add to these disasters, drought wrecked the grain harvest in 1945.

Meanwhile government authority was too feeble and partisan to restore order or ensure the equitable distribution of relief supplies. Greek officials assumed the prime responsibility for distribution, being rather ineffectively supervised by the mainly British and American staff of UNRRA, until this supervision lapsed in September 1946 with the spread of civil war. The

Greek officials diverted what seems to have amounted to the greater part of food supplies to friendly merchants or local anti-communists. This malpractice characterised the demoralisation of the state administration, which had been abused by successive regimes – quisling, EAM and now anti-communist – to benefit their own supporters and penalise those of the preceding regime. State officials and their political superiors were freed by their dependence on foreign supplies from any need to win public support. Also corrupted were businessmen and investors, who for many years thereafter felt little confidence in the country's future, and so concentrated on making quick profits which they could convert into foreign exchange.[3]

During 1946, there was some economic improvement. Inflation declined sharply, thanks largely to a British loan to the government. There was a good cereal harvest; government authority strengthened in the cities and coastal plains; and speculators had to sell hoarded goods as these lost their scarcity value. By 1948 the calorific content per capita of supplies available nationally was above the prewar level; but statistics make no allowance for the continuing privations of left-wing civilians, especially in rural areas where there were no trade unions to protect them. GNP reached its prewar level in 1950. This recovery was mainly due to the growth of industrial output in the cities, which by 1950 was more than twice in value what it had been in 1946, while electricity consumption was over three times its prewar level. Agriculture recovered more slowly, mainly because it suffered from delay in replacing livestock slaughtered during the enemy occupation.

Thus there persisted a contrast – which had also existed during the occupation – between those who could seek relief supplies and physical security in the cities and rich agricultural plains, and the mountain villagers exposed to deprivation and persecution. Most politicians and senior public officials, with the wealthier bourgeoisie, stayed in the cities. After January 1945 these were untouched by civil war, although the restoration of order took time. As late as December 1945, the American diplomat, William H. McNeill, reported that 'gunfire can be heard almost nightly' in Athens.[4] In rural areas, however, villagers were exposed for several years thereafter to vindictive and predatory attacks by rival gangs, and in consequence many, especially left-wingers, fled to cities; so that the percentage of the national population living in towns of 10,000+ increased between 1940 and 1951 from 32.8 to 37.7. As for the inequality in distribution of wealth and income, this became greater even than before the war. The runaway inflation in the years 1941–45 favoured those who controlled the supply of scarce necessities, and impoverished those depending on cash incomes or cash savings. The wealthy were also favoured by the weakness of postwar governments which found it difficult to levy direct taxation, and found it easiest to promote development by channelling credits and licences, as well as raw materials, food and equipment imported under aid programmes, to a few favoured businessmen.

In other ways the ravages of war persisted. The destruction during the enemy occupation was followed by sabotage by Communist guerrillas during the renewed civil war in 1946–49. Attacks in this later period, according to government figures, destroyed 11,788 houses, at least 54 schools, 100 railway stations, at least 375 railway bridges and 423 road bridges. It was not until 1948–49 that some arterial communications destroyed during the enemy occupation – notably the Corinth Canal and the Athens–Salonika railway – were restored. In the Peloponnese – a region probably better than average – the state of all except the main roads was reported by an American diplomat in May 1949 to vary 'from bad to terrible'.[5]

Polarisation

The disorder which prevailed in 1945 was thereafter brought under control by opposed forces between which the country was increasingly polarised: on the right the defenders of traditional values and on the left the Communist Party. The right was spearheaded by the official army and police, equipped by the British. Anti-communists included those politicians, Venizelist and anti-Venizelist, who upheld all or most features of the traditional political and social system, and so could be termed bourgeois. In opposition to them were the socialist forces associated with EAM, which had attracted the enthusiastic participation of much of the population in all regions. It was now obvious (as it had not generally been during the enemy occupation) that the Communist Party was its directing force; but the influential and quite numerous left-wingers who distrusted or feared the Communists were driven by persecution into alliance with them. The overriding aims of the right were, firstly, to smash the authority which EAM still wielded over much of the population and, thereafter, to dissolve the Communist Party's organisation. The resulting persecution soon made the Communist Party doubt the feasibility of working, like its French and Italian counterparts, within a parliamentary system.

In the capital, in Salonika, and in some larger towns, EAM and the Communist Party continued to operate legally for some time, being protected by the British; but only in the capital could it organise large public meetings in safety. The prewar leader of the Communist Party, Nikos Zachariadis (1903–73), was actually brought back to Greece in May 1945 in a British military plane, having spent four years in a German concentration camp, preceded by over four in Metaxas's jails. Born and brought up in the Ottoman empire, he had travelled to the Soviet Union as a seaman and become active in the Communist Party there in 1921, distinguishing himself later as a student in the Moscow college for foreign party workers. Selected by Stalin in 1931 to lead the strife-torn Greek party, he built it up in the following years, emulating Stalin's brutality towards dissidents and thorough methods of organisation. He thus attracted a personality cult of his own, and was now welcomed back by his party. He reassembled around himself a leadership group which shared his dogmatic and ruthless mentality.[6] He also reimposed strict discipline and selective recruitment policies on a party which during the occupation had been ruled collectively and enlarged by mass recruitment. Consequently, membership fell from several hundred thousand in 1944 to 45,000 in September 1946, flanked however by tens of thousands more candidate members and fellow-travellers, and hundreds of thousands of members of EAM organisations.

The Communist Party in its press exposed the weaknesses of successive governments in 1945–46 and, as a way of putting pressure on them, instigated industrial unrest and resistance by civil servants to attempts at stabilising prices. It denounced the close association between ministers, the main banks and a few wealthy businessmen. It benefited from growing public resentment of social inequality and right-wing intimidation. It emphasised the prosperity of wartime profiteers, and pointed to the immunity enjoyed by prominent ex-collaborators with the Germans, while left-wing resisters were being persecuted.

As in all formerly occupied countries, the culpability of collaborators with the occupation forces was a matter of controversy for decades afterwards. There was a strong public demand for the punishment of the worst of them, many of whom were guilty of atrocities. Many were in fact tried and sentenced to death or imprisonment, which is more than happened in Italy. Nevertheless – in the anti-communist atmosphere of 1945 – police, soldiers and public officials were much more interested in persecuting the left than they were in persecuting collaborators, who usually pleaded in self-defence that they had been motivated by anti-communism. So collaborators formed a small proportion of those thrown in jail. There were 2,900 alleged collaborationists in jail in September 1945; and the total who were executed was eventually 29. Admittedly, as in Italy, many others had been killed by the left without official trial as the German forces withdrew in 1944. Moreover, some people who had cooperated or fought with Germans against resisters held prominent positions in the army, police and even in politics between 1945 and 1974. Meanwhile, participation in the wartime resistance tended to be viewed by the authorities as prima facie evidence of subversive intentions, even though there had been many conservative resisters. This inversion of patriotic values gave the left a potent and enduring grievance.[7]

The organised might of the left survived for some time after the Varkiza agreement. The left continued until early 1946 to dominate the trade unions and mobilise demonstrations far larger and more enthusiastic than those of their opponents.[8] In rural areas however left-wing forces by that time had been generally crushed by the heterogeneous forces of the right.

The right forces were at first led by a militia supervised by army officers, known as the National Guard which, having been hastily recruited and equipped by British troops from former collaborators during the *Dekemvrianá*, recruited tens of thousands more people whose grudges against EAM dated from the occupation. Their fury was fanned by the discovery of mass graves of EAM victims, and hit lists of intended victims. All over the country, the National Guard and unofficial thugs wrecked EAM offices and printing presses, bashed, raped or murdered masses of EAM supporters, freed those whom EAM had jailed for collaboration and replaced them with left-wingers. Thus they turned the tables in the localised civil wars which had broken out in most regions during the occupation.[9] At the end of 1945 the total number of left-wingers in jail reached about 49,000, by which time 80,000 people had been prosecuted, according to figures collected by British officials. Most seem to have been imprisoned in wretched conditions, where they were receptive to the well organised propaganda and recruiting activities of Communists.

Later in 1945 the National Guard was replaced by the more disciplined gendarmerie. They too excluded former left-wing resisters from their ranks and accepted former collaborators in prominent positions. Having suffered fearful losses from EAM during the occupation and *Dekemvrianá*, they now sought revenge. Like the smaller city police they were authorised by the British to increase their numbers fast – much faster than training pro-grammes demanded – in the vain hope that they would create conditions orderly enough for a general election and a plebiscite on the monarchy, as provided for by the Varkiza agreement. Their officers consisted largely of monarchist veterans of the Metaxas dictatorship, which had renewed the officer corps of the two police forces and the army by running large-scale training programmes. These veterans aimed to repeat Metaxas's achieve-ment of destroying the Communist Party. Thus they reassembled files on left-wingers so as to be prepared, when instructed, to arrest them *en masse*.

Army officers were likewise dominated by monarchist veterans of Metaxas's regime who were embittered by recent struggles against EAM. They were favoured by the British because many of them had acquired combat experience in the war against Italy in 1940–41, and then, under British leadership, against German troops in Italy in 1944. They now formed a determined nucleus of the armed forces, many of whom bound them-selves by oath in political organisations of which the most important was the Sacred Union of Greek Officers (IDEA). They ensured that 'democratic' (i.e. left-wing or left-liberal) officers were sidelined in insignificant posts or retired from active service.

The bias of the security forces was further guaranteed by the British military mission and the British police mission, which were responsible for their supervision and training. British officials assumed that monarchists were sound people and communists were a bad lot, and did not prevent – or fully comprehend – the monarchists' political mission.

Until late in 1946, the official forces were outnumbered in many places by gangs led by anti-communist chieftains, each wielding personal sway in some locality. The gangs terrorised EAM sympathisers and operated protection rackets. Benefiting from the collusion of the official forces, some continued their activities for several years, although most by 1949 had been persuaded to regularise their status by, for example, accepting militia armbands.

The right exploited in its propaganda the atrocities committed by the Communists and EAM in the *Dekemvrianá*, and the known friendliness between the Communist Party and Greece's territorial enemies: the Macedonian nationalists of the new Yugoslav federation, and the rising Communist parties of other Balkan countries. Behind the right were class interests, chiefly those of many thousands of businessmen, large and small, who for the past few years had hoarded scarce necessities and bought cheaply the property which many people had sold to buy food. The profitability of these activities is shown by the establishment of several thousand new business enterprises since the start of the occupation. The profiteers had during the occupation been attacked by EAM, which had periodically raided their stores and organised a more equitable distribution of goods.[10] So they now had reason to fear the left or any government bold enough to increase direct taxation.

As the right-wing forces destroyed EAM, the civil administration was reconstructed. Prefects reopened their offices and appointed municipal and communal administrations. Law courts grappled with a vast backlog of cases, most of which consisted at first of charges against recently jailed left-wingers. Country gendarmerie stations were reopened. Taxation started to be collected, although state revenues did not return to prewar levels until 1951–52. During 1945–46 thousands of sympathisers with EAM were purged from probably all branches of public employment, and replaced by people with anti-communist credentials. However, administrative reconstruction in many provincial areas was soon delayed – or thrown into reverse – by left-wing rebellion.

It was not till after the civil war in 1950 that politicians regained the power which they had before the suspension of parliament by the Metaxas dictatorship in August 1936. Indeed, until parliament had been revived by the first postwar election in March 1946, politicians were so dependent on British patronage as to have little relevance. Those who had participated in the Metaxas regime or the occupation regime were now too discredited to be serious players. The rest had been prevented by their enforced inactivity since 1936 from cultivating the goodwill of voters or recruiting clients by patronage, and so could claim little public support. Until the general election, five successive prime ministers were nominated by the British who, in the hope of preventing polarisation, favoured governments which were non-party or drawn from the prewar centrist groups, which were dominated by the old Liberal (or Venizelist) Party. While disliking the violent methods and monarchist aims of the security forces, Liberals depended on those forces for protection against the Communist Party which had been terrorising them until January 1945 and might quite conceivably recover. So they lacked the self-confidence and cohesion to pursue a clear policy. Furthermore, most bourgeois politicians of all shades were bankrupt of ideas for the postwar world,[11] and could not be expected to provide decisive leadership in the prevailing conditions of foreign tutelage and domestic chaos.

The Liberals were led by that aged doyen of politics Themistocles Sophoulis (1860–1949), who had succeeded his patron Elevtherios Venizelos as leader of the party on his death in 1936. Liberals favoured republicanism and democratic institutions, unlike the security forces, most of which favoured monarchy with authoritarian government like that of their hero Metaxas. The latter option was ruled out by the British and later the Americans, who realistically saw parliamentary democracy – with or without a monarchy – as offering better hope of stability. Restoration of the monarchy therefore became the objective of the army and police, who to that end favoured politicians consisting chiefly of anti-Venizelists centred around the prewar People's Party. The political right was not inspired by affection for the person of the Anglophile monarch, Metaxas's patron George II, a vacillating and aloof character. Rather their motive was that monarchy symbolised conservative values, and offered a guarantee against a communist coup.

Policies with general public appeal, that were common to Liberal and People's Party politicians, were to support the alliance with Britain, and call for territorial gains at the expense of recent enemies, Albania, Bulgaria and Italy, while denouncing the secessionist aspirations of slav Macedonians. Most Greeks felt that territorial gains were a just reward for sacrifices on behalf of the Allies in the Second World War. But at the peace conference held in Paris, in July–October 1946, the extravagant claims made by the People's Party government, and their inept presentation, provoked contempt from Allied governments.[12] The only claim to be satisfied was that on Rhodes and the other Dodecanese Islands in the south-eastern Aegean, which were inhabited entirely by 121,500 ethnic Greeks and held by Italy since 1912. A larger territory inhabited mainly by ethnic Greeks – Cyprus – bourgeois politicians could not claim, because it had been occupied by Britain since 1878. The Communists had no such inhibition, but were in turn embarrassed by claims against their allies Albania, Bulgaria and the slav Macedonians.

Thus the left and the right presented the public with opposed visions, as they prepared for an election and plebiscite. EAM appealed to workers, farmers and small-scale business and professional people, whom it called 'the popular masses'. It saw its opponents as big business and prewar elites consisting largely of bankers, politicians, senior professionals and higher public officials. This anti-plutocratic bias was expressed in attacks on alleged collaborators with the Germans, because during the occupation the wealthy had more to offer to and gain from the enemy. EAM relied on modern methods of organisation, which other parties did not adopt until thirty years later, characterised by centralised discipline, mass participation through geographical and occupational branches, and a detailed programme based on an explicit ideology. The bourgeois parties, consisting chiefly of the Liberals and the People's Party, were similar to each other in social composition (see below, p. 100), and they and their successors would remain so until the 1970s. They relied for electoral support on their leaders' popularity, and on MPs' personal influence and patronage, and they differed relatively little in their vague programmes.

As in other countries emerging from the Second World War, most voters were especially interested in social equity and economic development. Here EAM excelled with a programme characteristic of eastern European Communist Parties. It promised state intervention which would prevent entrepreneurs from making exorbitant profits at the expense of consumers, and would construct a comprehensive welfare state funded from equitable taxation, something which has not been fully achieved in Greece to this day. EAM also promised that the state would promote systematic economic development – with special attention to electricity and heavy industry – which would be pursued and financed in a way which would promote the country's independence from the advanced industrialised countries. Economic development was a subject to which the left devoted strenuous thought and preparation, contrasting with the nonchalant tendency by most of their opponents to await foreign aid and then channel it to their friends. The recent practice of EAM promised vigorous local government based on mass participation, which contrasted with the prewar model of local authorities subservient to ministries in Athens. Equal rights for women, and their full participation in the labour force on equal terms with men, were also based on EAM practice, and contrasted with their opponents' defence of the patriarchal family, with women confined to domestic activities and responsibilities. The adoption as the language of power of vernacular demotic, in place of the official *katharevousa*, would remove a social barrier against most of the population. A cheap and accessible system of justice would remove another social privilege in a traditionally litigious society. Foreign policy would be characterised by independence and non-alignment, rather than the long-standing subservience to certain capitalist powers.

An ugly aspect of EAM policy was its identification with a supposedly homogeneous 'people', and its view of all dissidents as the people's enemies. 'People's rule' claimed to be democratic, but would be so only in the sense that it required regimented mass participation: there would be little or no place in it for pluralism, still less civil liberties. EAM did however differ from its opponents in avoiding discrimination against ethnic and religious minorities.

Thus EAM's concept of the people (*laos*) confronted the conservative concept of the nation (*ethnos*): each seen as an ideologically homogeneous society which excluded dissidents from effective citizenship. The contrast was reflected in the self-ascribed titles of the opposed armies in the next phase of the civil war that was imminent: democratic and national. As conflict intensified, the antagonists became more ruthless in demanding the total loyalty of all citizens within their reach. On each side, masses of people believed fervently that they were risking their lives in a noble cause, which won the loyalty of large sections of society.[13] The ideological confrontation between the two sides would continue, with modifications, until it eventually lost relevance in the late 1980s. Although EAM faded away as the civil war intensified in 1947, it was replaced in 1951, after peace had returned, by the United Democratic Left. This in turn would give way, in the mid-1970s, to diverse left-wing parties. The EAM programme held considerable appeal in the late 1940s to intellectuals, professional people, and students, as well as to industrial workers. EAM appealed more successfully than any other political group to the intense preoccupation of most politically aware people with the wrongs of prewar society, and with the high hopes – fanned both by US and Soviet propaganda during the war – of a world in which governments would cooperate to secure economic development and promote their peoples' welfare.

EAM commanded support in all regions and diverse social groups. In the towns, there was a strong class component in its support, though only in some agricultural communities could it exploit class divisions. EAM was especially powerful and well organised among industrial and clerical workers, although its opponents also attracted followers in both groups. There was also an ethnic factor. EAM had formed an alliance during the occupation with the majority of slav Macedonians: a nexus deriving originally from prewar policy imposed on the Greek Communist Party by the Comintern, and cemented now by affinity with the Yugoslav Communist leader Tito. This alliance tended in northern regions to alienate the many Greek refugees from Asia Minor who had acquired their land from slavs who emigrated in the 1920s, and had been deliberately settled by the Greek government in areas where slavs were numerous. These refugees naturally feared dispossession if slavs won the right of secession. But Greek Asia Minor refugees in northern industrial towns, and in all southern regions, tended to support EAM because they had been radicalised by social discrimination since the 1920s.

Because they were integrated with the communities among whom they lived, many parish priests participated on each side of the schism of the 1940s.[14] Although some (perhaps most of) the leading Communists were atheists, their party's policy was not anti-clerical, and did not authorise the disrespectful treatment of clergy and churches inflicted by, it seems, many guerrilla fighters. Because EAM had identified itself during the Axis occupation with the cause of patriotic resistance, at least five bishops and hundreds of priests sympathised passively or actively with it. Now they were persecuted by right-wing thugs, and disciplined by the ecclesiastical hierarchy. Three bishops were deprived of their sees; possibly scores of parish priests were defrocked; and some were murdered. Opposed to them were the great majority of bishops who rejected Marxist–Leninist ideology and so had always distrusted the Communist Party. From now on, they became increasingly militant. In June 1946 the assembled bishops condemned the Communist 'rebellion', and thenceforth many of them gave their fervent blessing to the government cause. Bishops openly attacked Communism as hostile to the family and to the nation's territorial integrity – the latter being an issue on which the Church was always prepared to speak out. At least nine chaplains in the national army later became bishops. For their part, senior officers of the national army emphasised Orthodox Christianity in their ideological pronouncements; while those officers active in political conspiracy valued the Church's support for their ideals.

As the civil war revived in 1946, parish priests found themselves caught between the two sides. Many worked in areas controlled for long periods by the Communist army, and participated in the local administration which this army established; while some even fought in its ranks. Those who were captured were executed by the national army after being defrocked by the Church. On the national side, about 250 priests were killed by left-wing combatants (on the Archbishop's estimate).

There were in addition myriad personal or geographical reasons why people favoured one side or the other. Thus there were regions where pro-EAM and anti-EAM villages were intermingled; while some villages were divided within themselves on family, ethnic, party or other lines. In the anarchic conditions of the years 1943–46, these local animosities intensified, and they would continue to be reflected in electoral alignments for several decades thereafter.

However, the ideological confrontation did not occur in a free election in the 1940s. This is because the armed supporters of the right rigged the registration process, and terrorised voters and candidates, in 1945–46. As the polling date approached, politicians opposed to, or merely neutral on, the restoration of the monarchy could not safely campaign in rural areas; while left-wing activists were killed or driven into jail, hiding or exile. The British government, impatient to withdraw from Greece and so rejecting reports of these abuses, insisted that the election be held, which it was on 31 March 1946. Rather than legitimise it, EAM as well as many centrist politicians publicly abstained, and something like 25 per cent of the registered electorate followed their example. Thus the monarchist groups, dominated by the People's Party, won a great majority of seats, whereas in fair conditions they might have lost the election.

The white terror therefore gave power to the small minority of parliamentary politicians who had remained faithful to the monarchy since 1936, without participating either in the Metaxist regime or the collaborationist governments. As the monarchy had made itself extremely unpopular by its association with Metaxas, and tended to attract unthinking conservatives, most of these people were characterised by reactionary views and mediocrity.

Descent into war, April 1946–December 1947

Reconstructing anti-communist institutions

After the general election, the victorious People's Party under Konstantinos Tsaldaris formed a government. This and its successors in the following two years restored important features of Metaxas's dictatorship, partly by giving the police extra powers through decrees based on prewar measures, decrees which would remain in force until 1974. Tsaldaris's government promptly revived the practice of deporting political suspects to prison islands after summary hearings by regional Security Commissions (each comprising a prefect, a judge and a judicial prosecutor) which usually accepted without much question the recommendations of police officers. Deportations continued at the rate of several hundred a year during the civil war in 1946–49. The police were given summary powers to search houses, arrest people and impose curfews. They revived the prewar practice – designed to discredit

Communists with their own party – of forcing suspects into signing retractions of subversive opinions, retractions which were widely publicised. Standing courts martial were established in most prefectures, and by summary procedures they tried alleged offences against public security during the following three years, sentencing over 2,000 people to be executed, and several thousand more to be jailed for offences as trivial as the reported slandering of prominent public figures. By 'Law 509' of December 1947 any attempt, or alleged intention, to detach part of the national territory (a reference to the Communists' suspected support for slav Macedonian secession), or to overthrow 'the prevailing social system' was banned, in order to defend 'country, family, and religion'. In practice police had discretionary power to decide whether someone was guilty of such intentions. Soon afterwards, the prewar requirement was reintroduced for 'certificates of lawful opinions', issued at police discretion, as a prerequisite for such necessities as a passport, a driving licence, public employment, a contract with a public body or entry to university. The police also exploited the state's power to license the smallest business activity, and to grant loans to farmers. The owner of a newspaper kiosk or café might thus be obliged to divulge names of suspects. As a result, left-wingers found it difficult to make a living, especially in rural areas, although in cities they derived some protection from anonymity and mutual support. From 1946 until 1974, a system of apartheid was in force which turned much of the population into second-class citizens.[15]

Through the law courts and the police, governments destroyed EAM domination of trade unions, and reasserted the control once imposed on them by Metaxas. Consequently real wages fell during the late 1940s. By the same methods, EAM domination of agricultural cooperatives was also destroyed, and with it the ability of farmers to defend their interests.[16]

The centralised character of the Metaxist state was also restored. Metaxas had for example repressed the vigorous and widespread attempts at autonomous organisation, whereby farmers responded to the economic hardships of the Great Depression, through electing local assemblies, and establishing voluntary associations, newspapers and even 'popular' courts of justice. The democratic procedures, normal in the Orthodox world, enabling lay people to participate in the administration of their parishes, were abolished and have never been restored.[17] In the same way, governments from 1945 suppressed the local organisations established over most of the country by EAM. But there was a significant difference in the spirit of postwar centralisation. Metaxas had at least tried to inculcate a sense of public obligation among the socially privileged, and to provide greater security for the underprivileged. Governments of the late 1940s showed little interest in such goals, and indeed expressed no ideology apart from a vague defence of traditional values and visceral anti-communism based on exploitation of recent EAM atrocities. They displayed class bias in their construction of an economic system favouring a small group of businessmen, while treating as evidence of communist sympathies any attempt to secure a fairer distribution of resources.

Revival of war

By intensified persecution of left-wingers, the government forced increasing numbers of them into outlawry and armed rebellion. This result was predicted by British diplomats, who yet – because of their anti-communist prejudice, confusion of purpose and limited powers – did little to prevent it. Under the new government, the white terror was increasingly directed by senior officials rather than merely instigated by junior officials. Thus for villagers accused of supporting EAM, the gendarmerie was a scourge as terrible as the unofficial gangs.

In response, armed left-wing gangs, continuously augmented by refugees from the white terror, became increasingly aggressive from late 1945. The government found itself unable to curb this menace, leaving the brunt of the work to gendarmerie patrols which were severely over-stretched. In addition, several anti-communist chieftains were given arms to equip followers. One of them was a guerrilla chief who had been a British protégé during the enemy occupation, Napoleon Zervas. He had since turned into a politician, and as Minister of Public Security in 1947 reorganised much of the police into battalions which operated in the Peloponnese. In a real sense, counter-guerrilla operations were for some time conducted by politicians, who preferred persecuting unarmed villagers to pursuing guerrilla fighters.

The suppression of widespread guerrilla warfare required a professional army, because this alone could undertake nationally coordinated operations with overwhelming manpower, a range of armaments and plentiful transport, in cooperation with aircraft for reconnaissance and ground support. Unfortunately for the government, the army was still in the basic stages of reconstruction in 1946. The experience and cohesion of its officer corps had been lost during the repeated upheavals since 1935. The British military mission, which had been training and equipping the army since mid-1945, had worked slowly, through lack of resources or of apparent urgency. Thus the army lacked nearly everything that it needed, including trained officers and NCOs, mules and mountain artillery.

Most troops were psychologically unready for their new task. For officers, counter-guerrilla operations were a novel and dispiriting form of warfare which needed time to learn. The privates consisted for a long time of older men who had already done one or more spells of military service (because they needed less training than raw recruits). These conscripts resented being taken from their families, for whom the government made little provision, while younger men, as well as those with wealth and influence, were spared. Morale was also weakened by the rottenness of the political system. There was at first no effective leadership of the war effort. Politicians hampered military operations by clamouring for protection of their supporters' villages, and damaged military discipline by interfering in appointments and pro-motions of officers. The majority of privates had no stomach for fighting their fellow countrymen, especially on behalf of a government which was encouraging thuggery. What further damaged morale was the prominence among officers of the army and gendarmerie, as well as among politicians, of former collaborators with the Axis occupation, contrasting with the dis-tinguished resistance record of many left-wingers. Because of the general demoralisation of the state machine, governments could not curb the glar-ing social privileges on their own side.[18]

For all these reasons the army failed, in its two summer campaigns in 1946 and 1947, to prevent the expansion of guerrilla activity, and was not yet disciplined enough to pursue the guerrillas in winter when they were more vulnerable because of hard weather and lack of food. Late in 1947, the army was reduced again to static defence of scattered settlements and lines of communication.

This failure was especially remarkable in view of its opponents' weak-ness. The transition of left-wing supporters from passive endurance of the white terror to full-scale war took nearly two years, from late 1945 to late 1947. In December 1945 or earlier, Zachariadis decided to prepare for armed resistance, and embarked on a quest for the necessary support from foreign communist parties. From March 1946 onwards, communist-led guer-rillas periodically attacked small government forces in northern regions. Meanwhile the party maintained its vast legal organisation in the cities.

This contradictory strategy had disastrous results. When the Communist leaders committed themselves fully to war during 1947, many thousands of their city followers had been arrested, and nearly all the rest were prevented by police surveillance from going to the mountains even if they wanted to. By late 1947, the national army had introduced effective measures to segre-gate and 're-educate' left-wing conscripts. So the communist army had to rely for recruits on poor mountain villagers of both sexes.

Yet Zachariadis had reasons for this delay. Commitment to military rebellion was a drastic step, which when taken cost the support of most allies in Greece, and led to the destruction of the party's urban organisa-tion. A military strategy could not succeed until foreign communist regimes sent supplies – and these did not arrive in bulk until well into 1947, most coming from Yugoslavia. Aid of some sort was eventually received from several or all other communist states of eastern Europe.[19] But supplies of any substance from the Soviet Union were awaited in vain, because Stalin never showed any interest in the Greek Communists. The supplies which the Soviet Union sent were so meagre that they seem to have been designed merely to prevent the Greek Communist Party from falling too far under the control of the Yugoslav Tito, whose expansionist ambitions were distrusted by both the Soviet Union and Bulgaria.

It was impossible for guerrilla bands to raise any supplies within Greece before nation-wide destitution was alleviated by the summer wheat harvest of 1946 and the cumulative effect of foreign relief. Thereafter, supplies were meagre, but sufficient to sustain guerrilla fighters over the ensuing winter. Arms had to be bought on the black market, or seized from government forces, because few were inherited from the resistance army. Thus the guerrillas in late 1946 were poorly armed and wretchedly clothed. Many went barefoot in freezing and rocky conditions. When supplies did arrive from Yugoslavia, Bulgaria and Albania, they had to be transported by pack animals along mountain paths, and across roads patrolled by the enemy. So they were hard to distribute far south of the frontiers. Until the end of the war it was mainly near the frontiers that the Communists' artillery was deployed. It was light and poor in quality, but included some quite effective anti-aircraft guns. Mortars and heavy machine guns were even there rationed to about two per battalion (which numbered about 400 combatants); while further south these arms were still more limited.

Even under these limitations, the Communist leadership built up its guerrilla army from July 1946, a month when one of its number, Markos Vafeiadis, was appointed military commander, and despatched fellow-resistance veterans to different regions to command political refugees. In October Markos established a national headquarters of what was soon called the Democratic Army of Greece. This was in effect the military wing of the Communist Party; and probably all its senior commanders were party members. In time, commanders were selected increasingly on ideological rather than military criteria, and never during the course of the war learnt fully how to command large bodies of troops in positional warfare, which was a prerequisite of victory.

From April 1946 onwards, several thousand communist veterans of the resistance returned from exile in Yugoslavia, with limited armaments. From September Markos's forces were making attacks with forces numbered no longer in scores but in hundreds. Among them were slav Macedonian secessionists who had originally fled from Greece, and were now supported by the governments of Albania, Yugoslavia and Bulgaria. Towards the end of 1946, Tito agreed that the slav Macedonians' National Liberation Front in Greece be placed under Greek Communist command. Concentrated in western parts of the Greek province of Macedonia, the followers of this organisation henceforth constituted a large part of the Communist forces.[20] Politically however they were a handicap, because they showed that a Communist victory would facilitate the secession of the slav Macedonians to the neighbouring Socialist Republic of Macedonia, which was part of federal Yugoslavia. This was Tito's obvious intention. The Bulgarian government also encouraged Macedonian secession; but could not compete with Yugoslavia's asset of an autonomous Macedonian republic, with its own church and official language.[21]

The total number of leftist combatants increased until – according to the national army's estimate – it just exceeded 10,000 in January 1947, being most numerous in the mountains of northern Thessaly and Macedonia, but one thousand strong also in Thrace, and scattered through other mainland regions.[22] During 1947–48 guerrilla forces became numerous in Epirus and the Peloponnese as well. In the latter, they grew to about three thousand and came to control most of that province.

These combatants inflicted serious damage on the government's authority, because many were skilled in guerrilla tactics in terrain which was rugged and mountainous, and extensively wooded in the north. They could still rely on networks of support from sympathisers in nearby villages, and from masses of civilians suffering from the white terror. Throughout 1947 and 1948, hit-and-run raids by guerrilla groups occurred frequently in many regions, either to commit sabotage, or else to secure supplies or recruits. They usually succeeded in evading government forces, and could as a last resort escape across the rugged northern frontiers into Albania, Yugoslavia or Bulgaria. Although small government units quite frequently crossed these borders for short distances, any thought of large-scale invasion was quashed by the United States, which did not want an international crisis. What the Greek and American governments did not realise for some time was how much the communist states also feared escalation of the war.[23] The initial willingness of the latter to support the Democratic Army was encouraged by their realisation in 1946–47 that the British were about to pull out, without clear signs that the Americans would take their place.

American intervention

The Truman Doctrine

The government's persecution of the left was made possible by British backing. This was a precarious asset, because Britain was an over-stretched imperial power, which had never intended to commit forces or finances to

Greece for long, and could not change its intentions, even when it became obvious that the government which emerged from the general election of March 1946 would not become self-sufficient.

Meanwhile it started to appear to the British and American governments, during 1946, that Greece was a domino threatened by an expansionist Soviet bloc. Their belief was derived in part from Soviet backing for the client communist dictatorships that were being established throughout eastern Europe, and partly from Soviet pressure on Turkey. In March 1945 the Soviet Union pressed Turkey to cede joint control of the Straits of Constantinople, as well as territory close to the Soviet frontier; and in August 1946 repeated the request concerning the Straits. At the end of the year, there were Soviet troop concentrations and exercises along the frontier. In February 1946, the Soviet Union also asked Greece for a naval base in the Dodecanese Islands, in return for aid. All these requests were declined by the Greek and Turkish governments, with American support; but the threat remained of renewed Soviet pressure. Meanwhile, late in 1946, the British government despaired of its ability to protect the Greek government from the rebellion which it had provoked. Through sheer lack of resources the British were forced to set a deadline to their Greek commitment: 31 March 1947 – the end of a hegemony which dated from the 1820s and in some ways earlier.

By that time, however, the United States government had reached the conclusion that the defeat of communism in Greece was strategically vital. Since the end of the war against Germany, the makers of US policy had become strongly opposed to the Soviet Union's method of extending its influence through totalitarian and terroristic communist parties. They believed that the withdrawal of British support from Greece would result in the accession to power of the Greek Communist Party, so giving the Soviet bloc access to large and strategically sited ports in the Aegean and the Mediterranean. They shared the Greek government's alarm at the open Yugoslav and Bulgarian support for the secession of Greek Macedonia. Moreover the Americans, like the British, recognised that any power controlling Greece could interdict the trade routes through both the Straits of Constantinople and the Suez Canal, and considered that Greece with Turkey formed part of a 'northern tier' of states shielding the oil-rich regions of the Middle East from the Soviet Union. The revolt of the Greek Communists was therefore seen as a dangerous example of Soviet expansionism which had to be stopped – a view which was understandable but as we have seen unfounded.[24] President Truman therefore secured the passage through Congress, in May 1947, of a measure authorising massive aid to Greece, and lesser aid to Turkey which seemed strategically still more important but less immediately threatened. To justify this reversal of traditional

American isolationism, the President proclaimed in March what came to be known as the Truman Doctrine: America's mission to protect freedom-loving peoples anywhere in the world against totalitarian communism.[25]

American aid

This event made almost inevitable the defeat of the Greek Communists, because the US government was prepared to take whatever measures were needed to secure this end, and had the necessary resources. By the end of 1949, military aid alone to Greece amounted to $353.6 million and included 159,922 small arms weapons and 4,130 mortar and artillery pieces. Economic aid in the years 1948–52 was worth $976 million, about half of it being spent on economic reconstruction, so that it accounted for the bulk of gross fixed capital investment. US aid of all kinds averaged 6.6 per cent of Greece's annual GNP in the years 1948–56, though by the latter date it had declined to a relatively low level. In the twenty years from 1947, economic and military aid totalled $3,749 million.[26] While other countries of this region received massive American aid in these years – Italy, Spain, Turkey and, to a lesser extent, Portugal – Greece received by far the most per capita. Even during the civil war, economic aid was as important as military, because it thwarted the Communist aim of undermining the government's authority. The government could invest funds in economic recovery; and it received the resources with which it provided the livelihood of a large proportion – possibly a majority – of the population, through direct employment, welfare benefits, contracts and credits, as well as licences of various sorts. The Communists could not convince sympathisers that they had much chance of success, when all could see that for every mule-load of supplies reaching them from eastern Europe, a shipload was reaching the government side from mythically wealthy America.

But in March 1947, all this lay in the future. The Greek Communists now had no option but to press on with military rebellion, while constantly promising themselves that Soviet help was on its way. Foreign communist governments were secretly dismayed by the prospect of American military intervention in the Balkans, but continued their cautious support for the Greek Communists. Presumably they intended to withdraw it if American intervention proved too threatening.[27]

American aid began to arrive in August; and after several months the reconstruction of roads, railways, bridges and ports accelerated under American direction. In importance this work far outweighed the Communist campaign of economic sabotage. Invigorated by American supplies, civilians in areas sheltered from the war increased their efforts to rebuild houses and secondary roads. The work continued steadily after the civil war; so that, as early as 1951, the network of unsealed minor roads, which connected remote villages to the outside world, was 2.4 times as extensive as before 1941 while, thanks also to American aid, the number of vehicles of all types in the country was about 2.5 times as great.[28] American aid also resulted in an especially large expansion of the merchant fleet, and of the use of fertilisers and tractors in agriculture.[29]

American agencies, with officials of the World Health Organisation, expanded the medical work of UNRRA after it withdrew in June 1947. Medical aid from these sources included diverse vaccines; X-ray machines for detection of tuberculosis; penicillin and sulphonamides for treating infections; disinfectants; chlorine for purifying mains water and large quantities of pipes to convey it; and DDT for combating lice which spread typhus and the anopheles mosquito which spread malaria. Many of these items had first gone into mass production – and at least one, penicillin, had actually been discovered as a medication – during the Second World War. The Americans also financed training programmes for doctors, nurses and technicians. Engineers helped reconstruct or build urban sewerage systems. The proportion of the population reached by sewerage systems and clean piped water increased greatly in the late 1940s and early 1950s.

The results of these efforts are shown by an impressive fall in the national death rate of 43 per cent between 1939 and 1949, the first year in which mortality statistics became available after the German occupation. Causes of death were recorded in 1949 in towns of 10,000+ people, which contained 37 per cent of the population. There the fall in deaths from infections, contagious diseases and their consequences, between 1939 and 1949, was nearly thrice the increase in deaths from violence and accidental causes resulting from the civil war. Meanwhile, national death rates in the communist countries of south-eastern Europe in the late 1940s remained at about the same level as in the late 1930s.[30] As most historical studies published in the last twenty-five years have condemned the national humiliation and social oppression resulting from British and American intervention, it is worth emphasising that many people in these years were alive and healthy who, but for this intervention, would have been seriously ill or dead. As in other respects, the expectations of the population, and the expertise of professional experts, were raised by their experience of western aid. Foreign medical staff took care to cooperate with Greek medical staff and government medical officers.[31] In consequence, the new health measures were largely continued by Greek agencies after American aid almost ceased in 1954.

While never committing their own forces to combat, the Americans tried to ensure that their Greek clients in every governmental and military activity gave American taxpayers their money's worth. To this end, they assumed the right to appoint the heads of governments and of the armed forces, and to order reforms in many spheres of government policy. In practice, they were often forced to accept Greek ways of doing things.[32] An especially striking example was that politicians continued to treat appointments to public office as a means of rewarding masses of friends and supporters. Something that the Americans did achieve, almost immediately, was to take the conduct of the war out of the inept hands of politicians, and place it in the hands of the army command, which they gradually insulated from political interference. Thereafter the army gathered into its hands the complete control of operations, as well as command of the police and militia units behind the lines. From late 1948 to late 1949 most of the mainland was under martial law, and the Commander-in-Chief of the armed forces wielded semi-dictatorial powers.

In an equally direct fashion, Americans changed the government. In August 1947, they forced Konstantinos Tsaldaris to resign just after returning to the prime ministership, and made him join a coalition with the Liberals under their leader Sophoulis as prime minister. The Liberals had distinguished themselves from the People's Party by calling for amnesty for Communist supporters who surrendered. Unlike the governments dominated by the People's Party since April 1946, the new coalition ministry seems to have been reasonably representative of the anti-communist public. The eloquent Sophoulis (until his death in June 1949), the conscientious King Paul (who had succeeded his brother George in April 1947) and his forceful consort Frederica, gave leadership to the government cause, and made suitably publicised visits to front-line troops.

Defeat of the Communists

The Democratic Army at its zenith

In about March 1948, the left-wing guerrillas reached the peak of their strength, which was estimated by various sources on both sides at 26,000, consisting overwhelmingly of active combatants, with perhaps a few thousand reservists across the frontiers. They were active now all along the northern frontiers from the Adriatic to near Turkey, as well as along the Pindus Ranges which form the mountain backbone of the Greek peninsula, south to Roumeli bordering the Gulf of Corinth, and also in much of the interior of the Peloponnese. They were also active in several islands to the east, south and west of the mainland: Lesbos, Samos, Ikaria, Crete and

Cephalonia. On the mainland their regional commands were coordinated by radio.

The national forces opposed to them eventually, at the beginning of 1949, reached a total of about 150,000 in the regular army, 100,000 in militia forces, 14,300 in the navy, 7,500 in the air force, and 32,500 in the gendarmerie and city police. The gendarmerie had by 1949 largely abandoned its combat role, and specialised instead in security and intelligence.

Even at the end of 1948 – when the national army was at last becoming effectively led – the Democratic Army impressed British and American officers as being superior in discipline and aggressive spirit. This superiority – all the more striking because of its massive inferiority in arms and supplies – can be attributed in part to the desperation instilled into the guerrillas by persecution, and the national ardour of the slav speakers. But by the end of 1947 it is probable that a majority of the combatants were conscripts, mainly from villages where EAM and the Communist Party had friends and relatives. They were effectively incorporated into the army by the methods of draconian discipline and intensive indoctrination better known from the People's Liberation Army of Mao Zedong in the same period. The Communist Party established a strong chain of command from top to bottom, relying on its members to guarantee discipline at all levels. Thus party commissars at platoon level reported frequently to their security service on their troops' loyalty, knowing that suspected dissent would be thoroughly investigated and savagely punished. By such organisation the party enabled the army to keep going despite its losses and shortage of resources. It organised a training school for officers, from which 3,640 people graduated; while its printing presses produced a daily news bulletin and an official gazette for its provisional government, which had been established in December 1947.

The Democratic Army continued to outmanoeuvre its opponents by skilful guerrilla tactics. Repeatedly, large forces filtered through national army lines, and made surprise attacks in force behind them. In the second half of 1948, the army also showed a limited capacity for positional warfare, by raiding some country towns in or near the Pindus Ranges, and holding the massif of Grammos, on the Albanian frontier, against about 50,000 national forces in June–August.

Government predominance

What the Democratic Army could not do was hold towns or attack strong garrisons. These weaknesses condemned its efforts to ultimate futility, and they were due primarily to lack of heavy armaments and the disappearance of potential recruits. Within Greece, sources of recruits and of provisions were drained by the national army's forced evacuation of mountain villagers to provincial towns in the plains. By the beginning of 1949 the evacuees totalled over 700,000, most of them transferred to wretched accommodation such as tents, and all dependent on government relief. To this total must be added the immense numbers – apparently over 40,000 – who were deported to prison islands, on orders from Security Commissions or military commanders. These were high figures in a national population of about 7,500,000. The mountainous regions north of the Gulf of Corinth, from which most of the evacuees came, must as a result have been extensivly depopulated. A part of this population movement which attracted special attention was the mass evacuation of children by both sides, in an attempt to rescue them from physical danger, starvation or indoctrination by the other side. Over 50,000 children were taken by the two sides, some being seized from their parents and some permanently separated from them.[33]

The leaders of each side impressed on their rank and file a demonised view of the enemy, and publicised their opponents' atrocities since the start of civil conflict in 1943. Communists portrayed their enemies as plutocratic interest-groups which had benefited from collaboration with the Germans, and then placed the country in thrall to British and American imperialists. The national leaders portrayed their enemy as 'Bulgaro-communism' – totalitarian barbarism in league with Greece's slav enemies. Hysteria about spies and saboteurs swept through both sides; but became especially intense in the Democratic Army, which depended for military success on surprising the enemy, and depended for internal morale on insulating its rank and file from the outside world.

In the competition for public support within Greece, and still more in the English-speaking world, the Communists suffered from their isolation in the mountains, and from the weakness of economic ties – then or before the war – between Greece and the rest of eastern Europe. Riddled as the government side was with corruption and privilege, most of the population could not approve of a war against it, particularly when the outcome seemed likely to be impoverishment and loss of territory. The Communists' international isolation was shown by their failure to secure recognition from any country for their provisional government. They were not even invited by the Soviet Union to the inaugural meeting of the Cominform, the revived Communist International, in September 1947.

By the end of 1948, the balance of power had changed decisively, because the national army had been building up manpower and equipment with American aid, and learning by experience the techniques of counter-guerrilla operations. Officers were establishing a strong chain of command, which was completed with Alexandros Papagos's assumption of the post of

Commander-in-Chief of the Armed Forces in January 1949. Like Metaxas, Papagos (1883–1955) acquired advanced military training in northern Europe at the start of the century and participated with distinction in the Balkan Wars of 1912–13. He took a leading role in overthrowing the republic and restoring the monarchy in 1935, and as Chief of the General Staff under Metaxas he reconstructed an army ravaged by the National Schism. When the Italians invaded in October 1940, Metaxas, while retaining responsibility for grand strategy, appointed Papagos as Commander-in-Chief of the Army, valuing him for his hold on the loyalty of monarchist officers. In this capacity, Papagos won prestige from the success of the war. During the German occupation he refused favours from the quisling administrations, and tried to organise the officer corps so as to resist EAM. Eventually the enemy thought him dangerous enough to deport him to Germany.

Under him in 1949 were experienced commanders who had likewise played a prominent role in resisting EAM during the occupation. In January 1949, the best-known, Thrasyvoulos Tsakalotos, began a whirlwind operation in the Peloponnese which within two months destroyed the guerrilla forces in that region. Key features of the campaign were the mass arrest or deportation of left-wing civilians in the area of operations; continuous pursuit of guerrilla fighters so as to allow them no respite; and where necessary encirclement by forces which had overwhelming numerical superiority and were echeloned in depth, so as to prevent their quarry from evading capture by lying low or doubling back. Similar operations followed north of the Gulf of Corinth, then moved by stages further north. Their success undermines the general assertion of historians that the Communists could have saved themselves by sticking to guerrilla tactics, because these proved no defence. By the end of August the remnants of the Democratic Army were ranged on ridges and peaks along the northern frontiers. The bulk of them, with much of the Communist Party leadership, made a last stand at Mount Grammos, from which, after intensive bombardment by artillery and aircraft, they retreated for the last time into Albania during the night of 29–30 August.

They were prevented from returning in force by a shift which had occurred in international alignments. The break between Tito and Stalin the previous year had provoked an economic blockade of Yugoslavia by the Soviet bloc. Needing US aid, Tito was forced to reduce steadily his support for the Greek Communists, and closed the frontier with Greece in July 1949. Meanwhile the Soviet bloc, and particularly the Bulgarian and Albanian regimes – still politically shaky and economically weak – were made nervous by the increasing strength and resolve of the western alliance, shown for example in the formation of the North Atlantic Treaty Organisation in April 1949, and the growing strength of the Greek national army.

Consequently they too reduced their aid to the Greek Communists. So the life-support system of the Democratic Army was cut by August 1949. Thereafter all that Zachariadis could do was to send small groups of fighters into Greece from Albania and Bulgaria, and these had difficulty even in surviving because they had lost their supply depots in Greece, and were exposed to the full might of the national forces. The scale of fighting diminished steadily; and the last sizeable group of guerrillas was hunted down early in January 1950.

Thus ended a civil war which was particularly tragic in nature, in that it was fought between people most of whom shared a strong sense of ethnic identity, and often too of local community.[34] The war had really been an intermittent process dating from the first conflicts between rival resistance groups at the start of 1943. It had broken out initially because the state and economy had been destroyed by enemy occupation, and because political consensus had disappeared during the profound divisions that occurred before it. Then each phase of civil war generated hatreds which inspired the next one. For most of this period the main dynamic force was the remarkable organising drive of the Communist Party of Greece; but from January 1945 an increasingly effective counter-force was formed by a nucleus of army and gendarmerie officers who had combated the Communists during the occupation.

There exist only rough indications of the extent of human losses during the eight years of conflict. The total number of casualties was probably over 100,000, and the total number of fatalities over 60,000, more than in any of the other five wars in which the country had engaged in the previous fifty years.[35] The disappearance through death or exile, between the census of 1940 and that of 1951, of 86,107 people whose mother tongues were Romanian, Albanian or slav Macedonian indicates the importance of conflict between rival ethnic communities in northern regions – conflict which had been encouraged by the occupation forces. According to the Central Committee of Greek Political Refugees in the 1980s, the number of exiles whose first language was Greek must have been more – perhaps considerably more – than 50,000, most of whom were separated for at least twenty-four years from their native villages and from relatives within Greece.[36] Many of them returned in the 1970s and 1980s; while some have stayed abroad until this day.

The police and military authorities cooperated to ensure that communist activity would not revive. Their aim was to prevent another guerrilla movement based on mountain villages; and to this end the army ensured that many villages were connected to the outside world by roads useable by motor vehicles, while preventing remoter villages from being resettled. The establishment of a comprehensive security system made possible the steady release of those held in some sort of detention towards the end of major fighting – nearly 50,000 on the government's admission, probably with thousands more in unofficial detention. Martial law was lifted in the last areas in February 1950, but courts martial remained to try those charged with communist activities, and were used extensively by the police.

Papagos overshadowed all other figures on the national side at the close of the civil war and retained a major voice in internal security policy. During the civil war villagers had been conscripted into militia forces organised by army officers. Known as Battalions of National Defence (TEA), which totalled over 50,000 in strength, these provided the gendarmerie and army with a means of imposing their authority on the rural population. Given that police also wielded extensive arbitrary powers, the atmosphere in villages was politically repressive.

Nevertheless, the regime was more lenient than others which followed major civil wars of this period, if one thinks for example of Tito's regime in Yugoslavia after 1944, Franco's in Spain after 1939, and Lenin's in the Soviet Union after 1920. Executions of political prisoners ceased in October 1949, in view of a coming session of the United Nations General Assembly. Although 2,877 people were still in prison under sentence of death in July 1950, only a few were executed thereafter, and their executions provoked an outcry inside and outside the country. The numbers in some kind of imprisonment or detention steadily declined after 1949. At American insistence, parliamentary elections were held in March 1950; and this time the army command exerted itself to ensure that there was no overt disorder or intimidation. During the election the covert pressure of the army and police remained strong in rural areas, but conditions in the towns and even in prison camps were relatively free, with the result that the right-wing parties (which the army and police favoured) lost their parliamentary majority to politicians of the Liberal Party and the centre (see Appendix 2), many of whom earned the security forces' distrust by preaching reconciliation with the left. This outcome can be attributed to the Americans' need to demonstrate to the United Nations that they were promoting democratic practices, a need which harmonised with the strong parliamentary tradition that existed in Greece. Thus the Americans prevented the outcome of other civil wars of this period, which was the gravitation of power to an extreme faction. The parliamentary politicians who controlled the system saw, for their part, no need for extreme measures, because American backing made them feel secure against a renewed Communist assault, domestic or exernal. Thus the political system thereafter allowed some degree of open debate and competition for power, which made it very different from the communist dictatorships which were consolidating their authority in the rest of the Balkans.

Notes

1 On conditions in this period, see especially Giorgos Margaritis, *History of the Greek Civil War* (in Greek, 2000), I, ch. 6; my *The Origins of the Greek Civil War* (1995), ch. 6; and the earlier work edited by myself, *The Greek Civil War. Studies of Polarization* (1993), ch. 7.

2 Stavros B. Thomadakis, 'Stabilization, development, and government economic authority in the 1940s', in John O. Iatrides and Linda Wrigley (eds), *Greece at the Crossroads. The Civil War and its Legacy* (University Park, PA 1995), 188, 223.

3 George Woodbridge, *UNRRA. The History of the United Nations Relief and Rehabilitation Administration*, 3 vols (New York 1950), II, 120, 130, 134; Margaritis, *History*, I, 97, 116–7, 191; Thomadakis in Iatrides and Wrigley, eds, *Greece*, 223.

4 Close, *Origins*, 177.

5 Close, 'Introduction', in Close (ed.), *Greek Civil War*, 11.

6 Petros Antaios, *Nikos Zachariadis. Persecutor and Victim* (in Greek, 1991), 395–6.

7 Close, 'The reconstruction of a right-wing state', in Close (ed.), *Greek Civil War*, 164; Mark Mazower, 'Three forms of political justice,1944–5'; Eleni Haidia, 'The punishment of collaborators in northern Greece, 1945–6'; Susanne Sophia-Spiliotis, '"An affair of politics, not justice:" the Merten trial (1957–9) and Greek–German relations', in Mark Mazower (ed.), *After the War Was Over. Reconstructing the Family, Nation, and State in Greece, 1943–60* (Princeton, NJ 2000), 38, 54, 294.

8 Close, *Origins*, 165–73.

9 Stathis N. Kalyvas, 'Red terror: leftist violence during the occupation', in Mazower (ed.), *After the War*, 175–7; Riki van Boeschoten, *Upside-down Years. Collective Memory and History in Ziaka, Grevena Prefecture* (in Greek, n.d.), 158.

10 Thomadakis, 'Stabilization', in Iatrides and Wrigley (eds), *Greece*, 180–6.

11 George T. Mavrogordatos, 'The 1940s between past and future', in Iatrides and Wrigley (eds), *Greece*, 37.

12 Basil Kondis, 'The Greek minority in Albania', *Balkan Studies* 36 (1995), 97–8.

13 For illustrations of these opposed beliefs, see Polymeris Voglis, 'Between negation and self-negation: political prisoners in Greece, 1945–50', and Tassoula Vervenioti, 'Left-wing women between politics and family', in Mazower (ed.), *After the War*, 76–8, 84–5, 110–12.

14 Giorgos N. Karagiannis, *The Church from the Occupation to the Civil War* (in Greek, 2001), 84–102, 129–141; Foivos N. Grigoriadis, *History of the Civil War. The Second Guerrilla War*, 6 vols (in Greek, n.d.), IV, 1358–9.

15 Nicos C. Alivizatos, *The Political Institutions of Greece during Crises, 1922–74* (in French, Paris 1979), 359–414; Voglis, 'Between negation and self-negation', in Mazower (ed.), *After the War*, 82.

16 Kostas Vergopoulos, 'The emergence of the new bourgeoisie, 1941–52', in John O. Iatrides (ed.), *Greece in the 1940s. A Nation in Crisis* (Hanover, CT 1981), 311.

17 Parmenion Avdelides, 'The role of cooperation in rural development' (in French), *Review of Social Research*, Special Issue, 1981, 42–8; Anna Collard, 'Researching "social memory" in the case of Greece', in Evthymios Papataxiarches and Theodoros Paradelles (eds), *Anthropology and the Past. Contributions to the Social History of Modern Greece* (in Greek, 1993), 371–2; *Vima*, 11 March 2001, A28, I.M. Konidari.

18 Close, 'The reconstruction of a right-wing state', in Close (ed.), *Greek Civil War*, 172.

19 Ivo Banac, 'The Tito–Stalin split and the Greek civil war', in Iatrides and Wrigley (eds), *Greece*, 266; Jordan Baev, *The Greek Civil War: a View from Outside* (in Greek, 1996), 187.

20 Evangelos Kofos, 'The impact of the Macedonian question on civil conflict in Greece, 1943–9', in Iatrides and Wrigley (eds), *Greece*, 299–302; David C. Van Meter, 'The Macedonian question and the guerrilla war in northern Greece on the eve of the Truman Doctrine', *Journal of the Hellenic Diaspora* 21 (1995), 80.

21 Baev, *Civil War*, 65.

22 Margaritis, *History*, I, 254.

23 Baev, *Civil War*, 193.

24 Peter J. Stavrakis, 'Soviet policy in areas of limited control: the case of Greece, 1944–9', in Iatrides and Wrigley (eds), *Greece*, 227–57.

25 Lawrence S. Wittner, *American Intervention in Greece, 1943–9* (New York 1982), 65–80.

26 A.F. Freris, *The Greek Economy in the Twentieth Century* (1986), ch. 4.

27 Elisabeth Barker, 'Yugoslav policy towards Greece, 1947–9', in Lars Baerentzen, John O. Iatrides and Ole L. Smith (eds), *Studies in the History of the Greek Civil War, 1945–9* (Copenhagen 1987), 267–8; Baev, *Civil War*, 123.

28 William H. McNeill, *Greece: American Aid in Action, 1947–56* (New York 1957), 51; C.A. Munkman, *American Aid to Greece* (New York 1958), 201.

29 Freris, *Greek Economy*, 134–48; J.R. Lampe and M.R. Jackson, *Balkan Economic History, 1550–1950* (Bloomington, IN 1982), 538, 587.

30 L.P. Morris, *Eastern Europe since 1945* (1984), 122; National Statistical Service of Greece, *Statistical Summary of Greece 1954* (in English and Greek, 1955), 26–7; US Mutual Security Agency. Mission to Greece, *Medical and Sanitary Data on Greece* (Washington, DC, 1952), 3–4, 41, 103; Munkman, *American Aid*, 188–9.

31 McNeill, *American Aid*, 183.

32 Theodore A. Couloumbis,. *The United States, Greece and Turkey. The Troubled Triangle* (New York 1983), 17–18; Hubert R. Gallagher, 'Administrative reorganization in the Greek crisis', *Public Administration Review* 8 (1948), 250–8.

33 Lars Baerentzen, 'The "Paidomazoma" and the Queen's Camps', in Baerentzen *et al.* (eds), *Studies*, 25–40, 141–3, 152–5; Helena Smith, 'Scandal over "political" adoptions', *Guardian Weekly*, 2 June 1996, 7.

34 Stanley Aschenbrenner, 'The civil war from the perspective of a Messenian village' in Baerentzen *et al.* (eds), *Studies*, 124–5.

35 Close, 'Introduction' in Close (ed.), *Civil War*, 8–9; Margaritis, *History*, I, 51.

36 Riki van Boeschoten, 'The impossible return: coping with separation and the reconstruction of memory in the wake of the civil war', in Mazower (ed.), *After the War*, 127–31.

CHAPTER THREE

Dependent Development: the Economy, 1950–1973

Economic recovery

The roles of America and the Greek government

American aid was, as we have seen, vital to economic recovery, and it was administered as part of a strategy for the rehabilitation of western Europe. In the international conditions after 1945, when the United States and the Soviet Union offered competing models of political and economic development, each tried to direct the countries in its sphere onto its chosen road. The underdeveloped countries of the Mediterranean region (Turkey, Greece, southern Italy, Spain and Portugal) were especially influenced by American aid, which was later largely replaced by private investment, domestic and foreign. Partly as a result of American influence, the governments of these countries addressed themselves in a more systematic and better-equipped way than ever before to the promotion of economic growth. The unprecedented scale of this growth can be accounted for by the fact that these countries tried, and cooperated, to realise the benefits of new technologies and international trade.[1] Governments must moreover have increased their peoples' productivity by programmes to improve their health.

Because the Soviet Union forbade its satellites to accept American aid, it was not extended to countries adjoining Greece except Turkey and Yugoslavia – the latter mainly after it was expelled from the Soviet bloc. In Greece, in 1947–57, American aid accounted for over half of state investment expenditure. Thereafter aid for civilian purposes declined and virtually ceased after 1962, although large-scale military aid continued, continuing to include at times grants besides the more usual sales and loans. Greek state investment increased with revenue-raising capacity, and made up 34 per cent of the total fixed capital of industrial enterprises in 1959, and 4.7 per cent of GNP in 1957, rising to 9.2 per cent in 1970. Thus the drive to economic development began with American aid and was taken up by the Greek state, which took a much greater role in the development process than it had in the past, and greater too than that taken by governments in the other Mediterranean countries referred to. Particularly influential in the economic ministries was a younger generation of officials who were promoted by American advisers.[2] In accordance with American wishes, barriers to American investments and exports were minimised, and trade was conducted as far as possible with capitalist countries.

The key year in the government's promotion of recovery was 1953. It was then that quotas and other quantitative restrictions on imports were virtually abolished as part of a long-term policy of trade liberalisation. Import tariffs still averaged just over 20 per cent, declining gradually to 14 per cent in 1973. The value of exports and imports, as a percentage of GNP, rose from 21.8 in 1950 to 36.5 in 1973, and did not tend to rise thereafter. There was a large though diminishing trade gap, with exports being worth 25.3 per cent of imports in 1950, rising to 58.7 per cent in 1973. The Bank of Greece, under British and then American supervision, maintained the viability of the drachma in the years 1946–52 by operating a gold exchange standard, which required it to sell to the public on demand vast quantities of gold sovereigns. This practice encouraged private investment in gold rather than in production of goods; and so, under American pressure, the government stopped it in 1952. Henceforth public confidence in the drachma was upheld by deflationary policies, including a steady increase of income tax during the first half of the 1950s to 27 per cent of total tax revenue. Another prerequisite to investor confidence, taken by the government in April 1953, was to devalue the drachma by 50 per cent, so encouraging exports and discouraging imports.[3]

These achievements were prerequisites to the revival of production and domestic investment. Inflation, which had been out of control until 1945 and a recurrent problem since 1946, was finally tamed; and stayed in single digits from 1955 to 1972, and at about 2 per cent in most of these years. After the high levels of the 1940s however, it would be many years before public confidence in the currency was restored; so that in the late 1950s prices of, for example, houses, land and dowries were still commonly quoted in gold sovereigns, which had been a widespread unit of exchange since the German occupation. But by tempting customers with high interest rates, the major banks stimulated a large increase in savings deposits in the latter half of the 1950s, and these became an important source of capital for investment. Thus the contribution of private households to financing net capital formation rose from 28 per cent in 1954 to 59 per cent in 1961;

while fixed capital investment in total accounted for about 25 per cent of GDP from the early 1960s onwards.

In 1953 a law granted extraordinary privileges and guarantees to externally based investors, including Greek shipowners. The latter, like foreigners, needed enticement to direct their investment into Greece and base their operations there, because for the most part their ships were registered and their operations based in other countries. The privileges, which were increased in time, and included tax exemptions and cheap energy, provoked much criticism from those who saw them as nationally demeaning. This strategy was the reverse of that of the international drive towards national autarchy in the 1930s. Now, within the pax Americana, the goal was to encourage foreign trade and welcome foreign investment.

The outcome of government policy was to concentrate wealth in a small circle of business magnates. A key part of it continued to be the maintenance of industrial peace and low wages through police control of trade unions and state intervention in industrial disputes. A good illustration of the prevalent bias was the cosy relationship between the Ministry of Merchant Marine and the Greek Shipowners' Union.[4] The government favoured the shipowners with low taxes, and with assistance in taming the seamen's union; while the shipowners reciprocated by giving ex-government employees jobs in shipping companies and giving preference in employment to Greeks.

The government also maintained extensive control of commercial credit – a traditional policy which was now accentuated.[5] By the 1960s, after a series of mergers, 95 per cent of the banking assets in the country were in the hands of three banks: primarily the state-controlled National Bank, and also the private Commercial and Ionic Banks. The first owned two-thirds of the commercial banking assets in the country; and in important ways the three banks behaved like a monopoly. Foreign banks were not allowed to establish branches until the 1960s, and then developed slowly. The lack of competition was not conducive to banking efficiency, and would become even more marked after 1974 when the Commercial and Ionic Banks would also come under state control. The government also owned the Agricultural Bank, which was more than ever before the main source of credit to farmers, and the Hellenic Industrial Development Bank, which was formed in 1964 from two institutions established in the previous ten years, and contributed much to fixed capital formation. The government also established institutions, in cooperation with American representatives and Greek industrialists, to lend money on easy terms to foreign investors and encourage joint ventures between them and Greek capitalists. In 1970 commercial banks owned 70 per cent of industrial assets; participated in the management of some industrial firms, and channelled credit to a limited number of large firms. This close relationship between banks and industry was due in part to the historic weakness of the stock market, which was characteristic of underdeveloped economies and was in Greece accentuated by memories of the disastrous collapse of the economy under German occupation. In general, the lack of competition between banks, and the government's tight control over credit policy, warped the processes for mobilising and allocating credit, at the expense probably of innovative industries, and certainly of small-scale manufacturers, who had to rely on their own savings.

Governments used their control of all prices to keep down that of food – so as to help keep labour costs low – and thus stimulated farmers to increase production in order to cover their costs. Farmers were helped by the Agricultural Bank with easy credit to buy fertilisers, tractors and new crop varieties.[6]

Social consequences of government policies

Thus the official policy of economic development relied heavily on a form of crony capitalism favoured with light taxation, tariff protection, state contracts, easy credit and a cheap and docile labour force. In the communist countries to the north, by contrast, the economies were largely state-owned and tightly planned, in the context of relatively egalitarian societies. In Greece, the government systematically transferred resources to large-scale capitalists from the bulk of the population by keeping down wages and agricultural prices, and relying on a system of taxation which remained regressive by the standards of northern – but not southern capitalist – Europe. The resulting concentration of income was high by the standards of advanced industrialised countries, though similar to that of at least some other developing economies.[7]

This policy required not only indifference to social consequences, but avoidance of any challenging administrative tasks. The socially fair alternative – levying more direct taxation from the higher professions and larger-scale businesses – was ruled out for various reasons. It was contrary to the prevalent social ideology; it risked scaring foreign and Greek investors; and it would have placed impossible demands on the inefficient state administration.

Governments nevertheless kept control over interest rates, credit, prices, wages and the location even of small enterprises. Being generally inefficient and overbearing, public officials habitually contravened government strategy by obstructing businessmen with complex regulations and unnecessary delays. Businessmen responded by seeking mediation by politicians, or hiring professional intermediaries to deal with public officials. Meanwhile politicians lacked the will, and the civil service lacked the capacity, to attempt some major and necessary tasks: indicative planning, which would for example promote balanced sectoral growth of high-technology manufacturing and also of tourism; effective regional planning which might curb the growing concentration of population and economic activity in the metropolis; the improvement of the educational and vocational training system to provide the human resources for modernising the economy; the provision of services such as insurance, legal advice, information exchange, or research; or the restructuring of agriculture, so as to consolidate farms and enable them to employ machinery more efficiently. Some effects of administrative weakness are indicated by a Bank of Greece report for the year 1963: 'government investment shows a tendency to stagnate. The causes can be traced to lack of adequate and methodical planning, the failure to exercise a proper supervision during the implementation of projects and the insufficient utilisation of completed projects'.[8] These kinds of defect were however compensated for in this period by other factors: the potential for expansion in a country which had suffered badly from underinvestment and political instability; the impetus of international growth; and within Greece the initiative, ingenuity and energy of countless private entrepreneurs, large and small.

Thus, having become integrated with the western economic world, Greece shared in the rapid and almost uninterrupted process of growth, known as the long boom, which lasted until 1973 in the capitalist west. This made the year 1974 a turning point in economic development in Greece. Before that the growth rate of Gross Domestic Product (GDP) was indeed the highest in the capitalist countries of southern Europe and perhaps in the whole western world, averaging 6.5 per cent a year in 1950–73. This of course was a cause for self-congratulation, because even in the late 1950s it was not at all clear that economic growth could be maintained without the crutch of American aid.

All major sectors contributed to Greece's economic growth, but to differing degrees, so that the composition of the economy changed greatly between 1951 and 1973. Agriculture declined from 29.1 per cent to 15.5 per cent of GDP, and manufacturing increased from 11.5 per cent to 21 per cent, while construction increased from 5.5 per cent to 9.7 per cent. The service sector (including commerce, banking, professional services and the government administration) remained relatively large, declining from 45.7 per cent to 41.4 per cent of GDP.[9]

Greece's record also compares well with that of the communist countries of the Balkans, given especially that their economic development was skewed towards heavy industry, and was achieved by methods which became disastrously unsustainable in the 1980s. Yugoslavia, which was the only one apart from Greece to receive American aid, achieved a growth rate almost as high – until here, too, production started to decline from the late 1970s.[10] Economic historians rightly emphasise the high growth rates of this period, because they indicate improvement in human welfare. But by other criteria Greece's record has been subjected to criticisms, the validity of which we will discuss later.

Agriculture

Increasing production

In terms of increased production, the record of agriculture was impressive: a more than two-fold increase in value in 1950–73 (122 per cent), while the rural population declined by about one-quarter, which meant of course that a greatly increased proportion of produce was sold rather than consumed by producers. Even in 1973, agriculture accounted for more than half the value of exports, with the old staples of raisins, currants and tobacco still being important.

Meanwhile the proportionate contribution of agriculture to employment and production was declining, as in the rest of Europe. The proportion of the working population employed in farming fell from 57 per cent to 36 per cent in 1950–73. These however were the official figures: the real fall was somewhat greater, and it was continuing steadily. There were tax benefits to be gained by declaring one's primary occupation to be agricultural, because most farming income was exempt from income tax. It was found in the early 1970s that 27 per cent of self-declared farmers actually derived their main income from a non-agricultural source, a practice facilitated by the spread of industry into rural areas.[11]

The reasons for the increase in production are easily found. Agriculture had suffered badly before the war from underinvestment; and this deficiency was made up steadily, at first under the stimulus of United Nations and American aid, later on the continuing initiative of the government which needed to save on foreign exchange by curbing imports and boosting exports. Advice on new investment was given by the official network of agronomists, which was reorganised and expanded at American urging in 1950, with at least some agronomists being trained in the United States. Government price support for wheat increased its production greatly, most of it being marketed through a state organisation; and the country became self-sufficient in it in 1957. The government establishment of processing works for sugar beet enabled this to become an important crop in the 1960s.

Urged on at first by agronomists, and helped by government aid and loans, followed later by state pressure to borrow, farmers from the late 1940s onwards increased rapidly the use of machinery and fertilisers, which were affordable for the first time.[12] Also important in increasing production were the extension of irrigation, the use of pesticides to control both crop pests and malaria, the purchase of improved crop varieties and the large-scale cultivation of hitherto neglected crops, like cotton, rice, citrus fruits and sugar beet. More effective crop rotations also increased productivity. Dramatic increases in crop production had been achieved within five years of American intervention in 1947: for example production of rice rose by twelve times, of potatoes by thrice, of citrus fruit by nearly thrice and of cotton by nearly twice.[13] Figures that illustrate the magnitude of continued investment were the doubling in use of fertilisers and the quadrupling of the number of tractors in the years 1956–66 alone.

Social obstacles to productivity

The increase in productivity was nevertheless retarded by social factors. One was the integral identification of the farm with the social status and moral worth of the family, and the importance in particular of agricultural land as currency in inheritance and dowries. This interweaving of agricultural tenure with family ties, and therefore with village society, seems to explain why progress towards consolidation of fragmented holdings was slow, and why governments failed to accelerate it. The government in fact encouraged small family farms by a law of 1952 redistributing 140,000 hectares of land in several thousand smallholdings. Thus in 1973 farms were one-quarter of their average size in the European Economic Community (EEC), and smaller even than in Italy, Portugal or Spain, or than in other Balkan countries before communist parties took power.[14] In Greece each farm consisted on average of six scattered pieces of land, and 80 per cent were twelve acres or less – only a little more concentrated than in the 1920s. Most of the agricultural labour force still consisted of the owners and their families, with only 10 per cent consisting of wage-earners.

Another impediment to productivity was the increasing orientation of farmers towards urban values of consumption. As a means of advancing their families' fortunes, farmers tended to invest their profits in city real estate or in educating a child for an urban job, rather than improved agricultural productivity.

The fragmentation of each farm in scattered pieces made the use of machinery, fertilisers and pesticides more laborious. The small size of farms might have mattered less had their owners cooperated effectively in buying capital equipment, production and marketing. But in most cases they failed to do so because of the individualism which characterised Greek family enterprises, rural and urban. This was shown in the limitations of the cooperative movement. In size this seemed impressive, being represented in the 1960s by 7,453 village organisations, linked to regional and national unions. Yet farmers were reluctant to participate in it because of its traditional association with the state bureaucracy. The head of the Panhellenic Confederation of Unions of Agricultural Cooperatives was a government appointee. While there were local variations in their functions, the cooperatives were preoccupied mainly with distributing credit and essential goods like fertilisers from the Agricultural Bank. In the mid-1960s one-third of farmers did not even belong to cooperatives; while in 1982 only one-fifth of produce was actually processed or marketed through them. Even when they belonged to a cooperative, farmers tended to prefer selling their best produce directly to merchants. Among the common results of this individualism was the exploitation of farmers by merchants, and the duplication among farmers of expensive machinery like tractors.[15]

Industry

Features of growth

The growth of industrial production in this period was also impressive, even by the standards of the communist Balkan countries, which took special pride in it.

We have noted the dramatic expansion of electricity generation in the early 1950s. Because of the American-inspired programme, the output of electricity in 1955 was five times the prewar level, and the number of communities connected to the grid was nine times as great.[16] Expansion

Table 3.1 *Industrial production (millions of drachmae, 1970 prices), 1951–71*[17]

	1951	1961	1971
Mining	0.59	1.67	4.03
Manufacturing	9.28	19.89	54.59
Construction	4.44	12.68	26.27
Electricity, gas, water, sewerage	0.47	1.63	5.91
Transport, storage, communications	5.49	9.47	21.86
Total output of the economy	80.51	143.77	278.55

continued steadily thereafter. Important for the balance of payments was the fact that the increased production depended on indigenous sources: lignite and hydro power.

As we see from Table 3.1, growth was also marked in other utilities and in construction, especially the latter. Construction absorbed over two-thirds of fixed capital investment in 1961–73, and was especially important as a motor of economic growth, because it relied heavily on domestic raw materials and provided scope directly and indirectly for small family enterprises. It also proved more labour-intensive than manufacturing, and so was valuable in reducing the high rate of unemployment and underemployment. Thus employment in construction grew from 2.4 per cent of the active population in 1951 to 9.7 per cent in 1981; and this did not take into account the massive employment in industries which supplied the needs of construction firms.[18]

From the beginning of this period, construction was a major area of state investment. As we saw, rural roads received special attention from the late 1940s because they were essential to the army. Major projects such as bridges and power stations, apart from their inherent usefulness, were also found by politicians to be effective for impressing voters. Consequently, governments tended to begin too many and take too long to complete them.

Construction also accounted for over 40 per cent of private fixed investment. The result of this investment from state and private sources was that, towards the end of this period, the sector became a bottleneck in the economy, with high wages and profits and expensive building materials. Housing accounted for over 40 per cent of the value of construction output throughout this period. By comparison with other developing countries, this proportion was remarkably high, and remarkable also in the extent to which it was financed by purchasers' savings rather than credit, which was restricted by government policy, so that – by contrast with northern Europe – the contribution of government was negligible. Here is one of several examples of the importance as a driving force in the economy of families' desire to improve their status and welfare. More specific reasons for the importance attached to housing – apart that is from the severe shortage of it after the occupation and civil war – seem to be the relatively egalitarian distribution of land in Greek society; the traditional tendency to identify the fortunes of the family with the land that it occupied; and villagers' ambition to establish their offspring in cities.

The weak point in economic development is generally considered by economic historians to be manufacturing, which might have had an important role in providing high-status jobs and ensuring self-sustaining growth of the whole economy. Investors in the 1950s, still nervous about monetary and political stability, were wary of novel forms of manufacturing; and, as we have seen, banks did not do enough to encourage handicrafts or, probably, innovative enterprises. The bulk of manufacturing production around 1960 consisted, as before 1940, of industries selling light consumer goods – such as textiles, clothing and food processing – to the domestic market.[19]

Private external investment

The necessary investment in other forms of manufacturing eventually came from externally based capitalists, consisting mainly of Americans or Greek-American shipowners. These started in the 1960s to take advantage on a big scale of the incentives provided by governments, and were presumably encouraged by the country's political and financial stability, and by governments' provision of necessary infrastructure such as roads and electricity. Thus during the 1960s, $630 million was invested by outsiders in Greece, most of it in petroleum refineries, chemical processing plants, basic metallurgical industries and shipyards. The outsiders received systematic help from government agencies, and were also joined by Greek-based investors who followed where they led. Industries producing transport components, rubber and electrical equipment also grew rapidly in the 1960s and early 1970s. In 1968, 36 per cent of the capital assets of industrial firms were directly controlled or owned by foreign or expatriate Greek firms. This external ownership was concentrated especially in larger firms.[20]

This investment certainly contributed greatly to economic growth, and created much employment. It increased particularly the numbers of skilled Greek workers. But certain features limited the contribution of this new investment to the reduction of the trade deficit and to future industrial development. It was directed chiefly to certain phases of production, such as the assembly of half-finished products or the initial processing of raw materials. The place among exports of high-technology goods, such as completed machinery, remained negligible. Thus the external investment was articulated with the needs of the American and northern European economies rather than the Greek economy, and the industries dependent on it created a need for imports which largely offset the contribution which they made to exports. Moreover, because they tended to be monopolistic, the new industries charged prices to Greeks which were higher than those prevailing overseas. Finally, much of the new industrial development depended on relatively high tariffs, which were scheduled to disappear by 1984 under the terms of associate membership of the European Economic Community (EEC).

The new industries, large and highly capitalised, continued to co-exist with a sea of small family workshops relying on primitive technology. Under one-third of workshops or factories used any machinery in 1959. In

1969 workshops with up to ten people continued to employ over half the workforce and accounted for about one-quarter of output in manufacturing. Even after the extraordinary growth of the 1960s, the investment per manufacturing worker in Greece was little over half that in the six western European countries of the EEC. These facts are striking evidence of the popular preference for self-employment and family businesses which, like farms, showed glacially slow tendency towards consolidation. The average number of people per industrial enterprise in 1969 was four, whereas in 1938 it had been three. Many businessmen were unwilling to seek credit for expansion, because they did not want to dilute family control of their firms.[21] They were helped to survive by low costs, political favours such as tax concessions, and personal ties with customers.

Even in most of the firms which were relatively large, ownership and management were combined as late as the 1960s. By then, however, a rapidly increasing proportion of large firms (those with over 50 employees) were going public; and these firms controlled 90 per cent of fixed industrial capital and employed 38 per cent of the labour force in industry in 1973. But even in them, authority tended to be centralised in a small group of powerful shareholders and a president who was also managing director.[22]

A flawed development strategy?

The scale of growth in this period was a striking achievement on the part of governments, American agencies and a multitude of private entrepreneurs. Nevertheless, one can speak of flaws in the prevailing strategy because they account in part for the persistence of widespread poverty in this period and the fall in the rate of economic growth after it. One flaw was a habit of dependence on foreign investment and imported technology. Largely as a result, total foreign indebtedness in 1976 amounted to $2.2 billion, and a fast-growing proportion of the national product and the government budget was therefore consumed by foreign debt service – income which might otherwise have been devoted to investment or consumption. The burden was constantly growing, with a current account deficit of nearly 7 per cent of GNP being the norm in the 1970s. Only a constantly increasing inflow of foreign capital could maintain a positive balance of payments; and this might dry up or be repatriated at any time. This deficit was large even by the standards of developing countries, and reflected the continuing backwardness of industry and agriculture.

Much of this deficit was paid for by immense growth in invisible earnings from shipping, tourism, and emigrants' remittances. The recovery of the

Greek-owned merchant fleet from almost scratch in 1945 was a tribute to the drive of the shipowners and the maritime tradition in the islands. The family and community loyalties of the islands were particularly important in accounting for the efficiency of shipping firms and crews. Shipowners seized advantage of the great increase in transport from the late 1940s, with the result that from 1970 onwards the Greek-owned fleet was the world's largest, most of it engaged in cross-trading between third countries. The majority of the ships were admittedly registered abroad; but the profits, and most of the wages, were earned by Greek citizens. In the 1970s, 8-10 per cent of the nation's labour force was employed in some occupation related to shipping.[23] Tourism, meanwhile, benefited from the growing prosperity of northern Europe, and the perennial attractions of Greece's climate, landscape and antiquities. The industry was based on what flourished in Greece: low-priced, hard-working family businesses running hotels and restaurants, with reasonably effective regulation by the police of price and quality. From a level in 1938 of 90,000 visitors, tourism more than quadrupled by 1960, and quadrupled again during the following decade. In the 1970s, shipping and tourist receipts covered 32 per cent of commercial imports. As for remittances from family-minded emigrants, they covered half the current account deficit in the 1970s.[24] But these invisible imports depended on the prosperity of developed economies, and so dipped during the recessions that recurred after 1973 in western economies.

Greek expenditure on research and development was still extraordinarily low by western European standards. It was only a small fraction of that in most countries of that club of industrialised and semi-industrialised countries, the Organisation for Economic Cooperation and Development (OECD), with the contribution of private enterprise being especially small.[25] It was as if most politicians, civil servants and businessmen were resigned to continuing dependency. As John Campbell observed, governments before 1974 tended to welcome foreign investment even on demeaning terms as evidence of international recognition rather than recognising it as evidence of Greek incapacity.[26] This deferential attitude was attacked by many within the country. Centrist and left-wing politicians campaigned against dependency by advocating large-scale increases in public educational expenditure, the low level of which was further evidence of resignation to peripherality. The public educational system was, as we will see later, under-resourced and archaic. The scarcity of people with technological, technical and managerial skills was worsened by emigration; so that, in 1971, the National Statistical Service recorded only 1.7 per cent of the labour force as having any formal technical education. Admittedly, such a mentality of dependency was evident to varying degrees as late as the 1970s in the other developing capitalist economies of the Mediterranean region.[27]

Another charge against the prevalent strategy of development before 1974 was its dependence on extremely low incomes for the great majority of the population, resulting in social inequality that was enforced by police repression. This was especially resented during the military dictatorship of 1967–74, because by 1967 the majority of voters had shown their desire for relaxation of police pressure. The state had done almost nothing to mitigate such inequalities (described later). Indirect taxation had been tending to increase in relation to direct taxation, and even direct taxation hit small and middling incomes harder.[28] Low wages made Greece attractive to foreign investors; but there was bound in time to be a revolt by wage earners and, when this occurred after 1974, it hampered further growth.

Notes

1 Giovanni Arrighi, 'Fascism to democratic socialism', in Giovanni Arrighi (ed.), *Semiperipheral Development. The Politics of Southern Europe in the Twentieth Century* (1985), 266–70.

2 Kostis Papadantonakis, 'Incorporation in peripheralization', in Arrighi (ed.), *Semiperipheral Development*, 90; Nicos Mouzelis, 'Capitalism and the development of the Greek state', in Richard Scase (ed.), *The State in Western Europe* (Beckenham 1980), 252–3; W.H. McNeill, *Greece: American Aid in Action, 1947–56* (New York 1957), 180.

3 James C. Warren Jr, 'Origins of the "Greek economic miracle": the Truman Doctrine and Marshall Plan development and stabilisation programs', in Eugene Rossides (ed.), *The Truman Doctrine for Aid to Greece. A Fiftieth Anniversary Appraisal* (Washington DC 1998), 97–100.

4 Kostas A. Lavdas, *The Europeanization of Greece. Interest Politics and the Crises of Integration* (1997), 79.

5 Lavdas, *Europeanization*, 75; D.J. Halikias, *Money and Credit in a Developing Economy. The Greek Case* (New York 1978), 15, 21,188–92, 232–9.

6 Sofia N. Antonopoulou, *The Postwar Transformation of the Greek Economy and the Construction Phenomenon* (in Greek, 1991), 56, 66–7; Mouzelis in Scase (ed.), *The State*, 252.

7 Nicos Mouzelis, *Politics in the Semi-Periphery. Early Parliamentarism and Late Industrialisation in the Balkans and Latin America* (1986), 121.

8 Cited in Nicholas Pirounakis, *The Greek Economy. Past, Present and Future* (1997), 32; Gelina Harlaftis, *Greek Shipowners and Greece, 1945–75* (1993), 169.

9 Persefoni V. Tsaliki, *The Greek Economy. Sources of Growth in the Postwar Era* (New York 1991), 1–6.

10 Harold Lydall, *Yugoslavia in Crisis* (Oxford 1989), 24, 41; John R. Lampe, *Yugoslavia as History. Twice There was a Country* (Cambridge 1996), 275, 289, 315–17.

11 Nikolaos Vernikos, *Greece Confronting the Decade of the 1980s* (in Greek, 1975), 116.

12 McNeill, *Greece*, 55, 101.

13 C. Evelpidis, 'Some economic and social problems in Greece', *International Labour Review* 68 (1953), 153.

14 J.R. Lampe and M.R. Jackson, *Balkan Economic History, 1550–1950* (Bloomington, IN 1982), 442–5, 542.

15 John Campbell and Philip Sherrard, *Modern Greece* (1966), 353–4; A.F. Freris, *The Greek Economy in the Twentieth Century (1986)*, 186.

16 W.H. McNeill, *Greece: American Aid in Action, 1947–56* (New York 1957), 72.

17 Tsaliki, *Greek Economy*, 5.

18 Antonopoulou, *Postwar Transformation*, 234–5.

19 Alec P. Alexander, *Greek Industrialists. An Economic and Social Analysis* (Athens 1964), 29.

20 Kostas Vergopoulos, 'Economic crisis and modernization in Greece', *International Journal of Political Economy* 17 (1987), 114; Antonopoulou, *Postwar Transformation*, 100; Freris, *Greek Economy*, 173–4.

21 Campbell and Sherrard, *Modern Greece*, 371–2; Vernikos, *Greece*, 121; Lavdas, *Europeanization*, 60.

22 Lavdas, *Europeanization*, 80–1; Lila Leontidou, *The Mediterranean City in Transition. Social Change and Urban Development* (Cambridge 1990), 175.

23 Harlaftis, *Greek Shipowners*, 1; Anna E. Bredima, 'The shipping sector', in Speros Vryonis, Jr (ed.), *Greece on the Road to Democracy. From the Junta to PASOK, 1974–86* (New York 1991), 237.

24 Fotopoulos, *Dependent Development*, 248–56; McNeill, *Metamorphosis*, 217.

25 Tsaliki, *Greek Economy*, 163; Jane Lambiri-Dimaki, *Social Stratification in Greece, 1962–82* (Athens 1983), 114.

26 *Modern Greece*, 317.

27 Papadantonakis, 'Incorporation as peripheralization', in Arrighi (ed.), *Semiperipheral Development*, 89; Constantine Tsoucalas, 'Some aspects of "over-education" in modern Greece', *Journal of the Hellenic Diaspora* 8 (1981), 121; Theodore K. Katsanevas, *Trade Unions in Greece. An Analysis of Factors determining their Growth and Present Structure* (Athens 1984), 43.

28 Mouzelis, *Modern Greece*, 122–3.

CHAPTER FOUR

Uneven Prosperity: Society, 1950–1973

Population, health and migration

Trends in population and health

During this period, there was a steady natural increase in population, offset in part by loss through emigration. The sharp fall in death rates among all age groups and especially infants – which, as we saw, occurred in the late 1940s and early 1950s – continued more slowly thereafter. In consequence, average life expectancy at birth rose dramatically from 52.9 in 1940 to 65 years in 1950, and then to 71.8 in 1970. Deaths of infants under one year old fell from 99.4 per thousand live births in 1938 to 41.9 in 1949, and then to 27.3 in 1972. Life expectancy for 65-year-olds rose from 13.7 years in 1950 to 14.6 in 1970. By the late 1960s, the infant mortality rate was far lower than in authoritarian Portugal or communist Yugoslavia, though a little higher than in Franco's Spain.[1]

Much of the improvement in physical well-being continued to be due to progress in the prevention and treatment of contagious diseases and infections. Official analyses of causes of death are available for towns of 10,000+ inhabitants in 1938, 1949 and 1953, and for the whole country in 1972. These show that the death rate from infections, contagious diseases and from bronchitis and pneumonia (which were probably, in most cases, the consequence of contagious diseases), was in 1953 less than one-third of that for 1938, much of this dramatic improvement having occurred by 1949. The decline in deaths from tuberculosis, influenza, malaria, diarrhoea and enteritis was especially great; and there were also big reductions in deaths from typhoid, measles, diphtheria and whooping cough. Malaria made people more susceptible to that outstanding killer tuberculosis; so the abrupt eradication of malaria after 1944 was especially significant. Then from 1953 to 1972, deaths from contagious diseases and infections fell by a further third as a proportion of all deaths. In 1972, no one died any more from malaria, typhoid, typhus or puerperal infection (the last affecting mothers after childbirth); although in contrast to wealthy countries tuberculosis was still an important killer – an indication of the widespread persistence of poverty and poor housing. But deaths from causes characteristic of developed countries – cardio-vascular diseases (e.g. heart attacks and strokes), cancer and traffic accidents – increased, so that, as a proportion of all deaths, those from cardio-vascular diseases rose almost thrice, those from cancer by more than thrice, and those from violence and accident (partly because of traffic accidents and, presumably, the booming construction industry) also by more than thrice.

The fertility rate declined between 1950 and 1975 from 2.6 to 2.3 children per woman. This decline was partially offset by a short-term increase in the fertility of younger age groups (15–29) during the 1960s and 1970s. This was Greece's limited counterpart to the postwar baby boom of developed countries, which may be accounted for by the growing prosperity of the 1960s, and the restoration of confidence in economic security, combined with the persistence of the traditional valuation of large families in a population still largely rural. On the other hand, during the whole period 1950–75 the fertility rate in older age groups (30+) fell, presumably because childbearing was thought less desirable at higher ages. The overall decline in fertility rates dated nationally from the 1920s and 1930s, and seems to have been due basically to changing social conventions about desirable family size, together with somewhat greater availability of contraceptives and abortion. The Second World War probably increased knowledge among soldiers about condoms in a society where the husband's views about the desirability and techniques of fertility control were still decisive in most families, especially among conservative country people. The changing conventions could be attributed in large part to aspirations for a higher standard of living, and a higher rate of school attendance, factors which made children more of an economic liability. These factors explain why the fertility rate fell faster in the cities, and among the wealthy.

There was also, because of mass emigration, a decline in the age groups most likely to have children. In summary, the rate of natural increase of the population fell greatly from 12.9 births per thousand in 1950–52 to 7.6 in 1970–72.[2]

Internal migration

Emigration was part of a complex process. Firstly, much of the rural population – and an especially high proportion of the inhabitants of mountains and small islands – moved permanently to cities. Secondly, much of both the rural and urban population moved abroad, temporarily or permanently.

There had as we saw been much internal migration during the occupation and civil war. Most of the forced evacuees from mountain villages in the civil war were allowed, or ordered, to return after the end of fighting, although many left their villages again later. The view remained general among villagers that city life was greatly preferable for its economic opportunities, material comforts and cultural attractions. The view was already quite widespread before 1940, but was disseminated by the first contact of many villagers with towns in the 1940s. Thereafter such acquaintance was facilitated by the extension of roads, the proliferation of radios, and the evidence in newspapers and magazines of western consumer goods flooding into the cities. As we have seen, the widespread ambition among farming families to invest in urban land and jobs contributed much to the building boom of this period, and was later fuelled to a considerable extent by emigrants' remittances. Because movement to cities was so often a planned investment in social ascent, those making it tended to be relatively well off, unlike many of the emigrants who went abroad. Thus unemployment among those newly arrived in the metropolis in the 1960s was less than among other residents; while the metropolitan population as a whole was relatively well off.

Villagers' attraction to city life was largely due to the deprivations and hardships of rural society. In the 1950s, and to a lesser extent the 1960s, there were far too many people on the land for farms to support, as a result of the high birth rates of the nineteenth and early twentieth centuries, and the traditional underinvestment in agricultural production. By law and custom, farmers' property was bequeathed equally to their children (the daughters' share in the form of dowries); and so many farmers inherited too little land to live on. The extent of rural underemployment seems impossible to estimate. There are no reliable statistics; and anyway in a country where families, not individuals, were the effective units of production and income, unemployment did not yet have the same meaning as in developed western countries. Attempted estimates of the national unemployment rate include one of an average 9.8 per cent in the years 1960–78 (twice the official rate); but other estimates put it as high as 22.4 per cent in the 1960s.[3] Partly because of rural overpopulation, and partly as an indirect consequence of government policy, the per capita income of the farming population was far below that of the urban workforce for much of this period, and the gap tended to widen. In 1951 it was 83.3 per cent of average national income, and in 1971 it was 51.1 per cent. In 1958, 64 per cent of households in Athens (where such amenities were best) had electricity and, in 1964, 35 per cent of urban households had running water. By contrast, only 13 per cent of rural households in 1961 had electricity; and only 11 per cent had running water.[4] It was partly because of the difficulty of ensuring reception in remote villages that the start of television broadcasting in Greece was delayed until 1966. Although villagers then took to this entertainment like ducks to water, many of those living in mountains suffered from poor reception. For villages, access to secondary education was still comparatively difficult. As secondary schools tended to be remote, many of the pupils had to find board and lodging during term time, something difficult for poor parents to finance. As in many other peripheral areas of western Europe, the disadvantages of rural life were especially obvious to the young, who did not share the older generation's attachment to ancestral ways, and were more readily impressed by modern technology and culture.

The total number who migrated from the countryside in 1950–73 was massive. Successive censuses show that it was 560,000 in the 1950s, 680,000 in the 1960s and 620,000 in the 1970s. These constituted about half the internal migrants during each of these decades, who amounted to 15 per cent of the national population in 1961, 17 per cent in 1971 and 17 per cent in 1981.[5] As the productivity of farming was very low, such an exodus to more productive activities, inside or outside the country, contributed to the high economic growth rates of this period, a contribution calculated by Persefoni Tsaliki as adding 1.1 percentage points a year to the growth of national income.[6] Another consequence was that Greece ceased to be largely rural and became largely urban. Defining towns as having over 10,000 people and villages as having under 2,000, the proportion of the national population living in towns rose between 1940 and 1991 from 33 per cent to 59 per cent, while the proportion living in villages fell from 52 per cent to 28 per cent. These however are the official figures. Because many townsfolk moved back to their native villages to be censused (so as to strengthen the villages' case for public expenditure), the true extent of the shift was greater. This trend contrasted with the slower movement from country to town before 1940. Consequently much of the city population consisted of people with a small-town or rural background in diverse regions. It was found for example in 1961 that 44 per cent of the population of the metropolis were newcomers from other (mostly rural) areas; and many more must have had relatives in them. The rate of intermarriage between people from different villages and regions must have increased greatly. So did the concentration of national population in certain zones: the two main cities of Athens and Salonika, the coastal strips along the northern Peloponnese and the eastern mainland, and a few large towns of Thessaly and western Macedonia. These trends, together with the rising proportion of people who tuned in to the same radio and television programmes, shared the problems of city life and followed the same high school curriculum, were uniting the national population culturally.

Emigration

Emigration was directed only in small part to the former main destination, the United States, and instead to Australia, Canada and, from 1960 onwards, West Germany also. Emigrants were attracted by the demand for labour created by high growth rates in these countries during the long boom. The flow of emigrants started as a trickle after the Second World War and gathered force from 1954 (when Australia began actively to recruit migrants), becoming a flood in the 1960s and early 1970s. Then with the recession of 1974, jobs for emigrants slumped in their countries of destination. Consequently the flow of migration went into reverse, causing a net return movement thenceforth. Demographically, as in other respects, 1974 was a turning point. The net emigration abroad in 1946–74 was 666,355, to which, for a gross total, one should add about 200,000 temporary emigrants who returned in these years.[7] There has always been considerable movement to and fro, so keeping diaspora populations in touch with their native communities.

The fact that much of the population was interested in emigrating needs no explanation, as this had for decades been a well-known means of material advancement. It is likely that in the late 1940s and 1950s the usual motive of emigrants was simply to escape from poor economic conditions. Probably then, as later, the overwhelming majority of emigrants were farmers or workers: the poorest strata. A government survey of 1962 found that 83.5 per cent of the rural emigrants declared that lack of work was their reason for going. Political persecution was also an important motive, although statistics on this point are lacking.[8] Later on, it is commonly agreed that the most common motive of emigrants was the desire to improve their families' status at home, by earning abroad the money needed for some goal in Greece like the accumulation of a dowry or the purchase of land. A survey published in 1978 found that those who claimed that their motives for emigration were to improve their existing situation, or save money for some investment, were three times the number who said that they were forced by the absence of alternative ways of making a living.[9] This was perhaps more true of the migrants to nearby countries like West Germany who formed a large proportion of the total in the 1960s. It follows that the majority of emigrants abroad, at least in the later periods, intended to return; and in this respect they presumably differed from most of those who migrated internally to cities.

The great majority of emigrants abroad were men, but the proportion of women tended over time to increase. While emigrants came from all regions, those from the north were much more numerous than those from the islands and the south.[10] In practice, most emigrants to other continents, and many emigrants to northern Europe – whatever their original intentions – found themselves eventually bonded to their country of destination by getting a good job, buying a house and, above all, by having children.

Consequences of migration

The scale of emigration naturally provoked prolonged discussion about its desirability on economic and other grounds.[11] After the war it was widely accepted that it was necessary to relieve rural overpopulation. But by the 1960s its extent provoked anxious questions, especially about the depletion of the economically active age groups, which declined by 11 per cent in the 1960s. Male farmers below 30 years old declined from 700,000 in 1961 to only 130,000 in 1989. Because so many rural people had been underemployed, most farms could for a long time survive this haemorrhage of people. Even so, by the mid-1960s, acute seasonal shortages of labour were apparent in some areas, and agricultural wages consequently rose steeply. As a result of migration (internal and overseas) the population in the poorer rural areas declined severely, especially in many smaller islands, in the mountainous interior, in Epirus and the north-east. The social life and cultural values of many villages collapsed,[12] and the inhabitants of some villages emigrated collectively. The resident population of regions above 600 metres declined officially from 14.9 per cent of national population in 1950 to 9.2 per cent in 1990. For reasons explained above, the latter figure was presumably swollen by people whose real home was urban. Little terraced fields around mountain villages became overgrown. Although arable land expanded in the plains, the nation's cultivated area fell by 3.5 per cent in the twenty years from 1961. The fact that many of the derelict villages were close to the frontiers of potential enemy states gave cause for concern about national security.

There were some undoubted benefits gained by the country from emigration, though whether the whole process was on balance beneficial is hard to resolve. One benefit was the quite substantial reduction of unemployment – by one estimate by 40 per cent during the 1960s. Another was the important positive contribution of remittances to the country's current account balance. There was a great gain in welfare for most emigrants. Coming as they did from the most deprived or persecuted social groups, most obtained a much better living for themselves. Moving to countries with relatively efficient systems of public education, and possessing the high esteem for educational qualifications that was traditional in Greece, they gave their children the opportunity to qualify for good jobs. Evidence that speaks for itself is the large number of professional and business people with Greek names in, for example, Australia and the United States.

Village life

Family structure

The bond between the patrimonial farm and the family was shown in the reluctance of migrants to part with title to their land or abandon ties with their villages. Many of the migrants to cities or abroad were heads of households whose families worked the farm on the assumption that they would return. Emigrating families tended to keep title to their house and land, usually leasing the land to someone else in the village. Many migrants to cities also kept their right to vote in their native villages, knowing that their villages' claims to state expenditure and political patronage were determined by the number of their voters. So they returned periodically to vote and for holidays.

In the villages in which 47 per cent of the population lived in 1951, the basic social unit was everywhere the extended family, including grandparents, uncles, aunts and first cousins and, more tenuously, second cousins.[13] The rural household commonly consisted of the nuclear family, perhaps with the inclusion of grandparents, unmarried grown-up children, or a married son and his wife. The family's claims on its members' loyalties was absolute, while within it the claims of the nuclear family took priority. People cared passionately about their family's prestige, which was based in part on the ownership of property, and also on compliance with social and moral conventions enforced by village opinion, and to a large degree sanctified by religion. So comprehensive was the family's claim on its members that individual friendships based solely on sentiment were rare or unknown, as distinct from friendships between families based on the exchange of favours. One common way in which a family sought an ally was through requesting a person of influence, such as an MP, to be a *koumbaros*: the best man at a marriage, who normally became the godfather of the children resulting from the marriage.

The parents in rural society usually arranged marriages for their daughters, and were obliged by custom and law to provide large dowries for them. As in the more conservative countries of western Europe – Ireland, Italy, Portugal, Spain – the dowry was still an important institution. As a good dowry enabled a daughter to secure a husband of high income and status who would be an asset to the family, it was an obligation to which parents, brothers and the daughters themselves were all expected to contribute. Thus marriage in rural society, and also among more conservative families in urban society, was a matter for negotiation between heads of household, in which a professional matchmaker might be needed.

The sons were obliged to find some sort of livelihood as a prerequisite for respectable marriage, and for this reason tended to marry later in life than the daughters. The double sexual standard still prevailed; so that it was acceptable for men to be promiscuous even after marriage, provided they were discreet, whereas women's chastity was vital to the good name of their own and their husbands' families. As wives tended to be younger than their husbands they could expect a long widowhood, during which of course chastity was also expected. As in much of the western world in the past, women's status depended primarily on maternity within marriage; so that they needed to marry early in life. Thus the terms of bargaining between prospective wives and prospective husbands were unequal. As men were allowed by convention to defer marriage, they had the upper hand in negotiations with the families of women who feared being left on the shelf.

Husbands were responsible for families' relations with the outside world, which required bargaining with other interest groups. It was men who participated in village politics and discussed national politics; so that women were excluded from the *kafeneion* which was the centre of public life. Wives kept company continuously with female neighbours, and in public treated their husbands with reserved deference so as to maintain the husbands' reputation for manliness. The separation of spheres did however ensure a respected role for women. They were responsible for domestic arrangements; so that, as a common saying had it, a husband was a guest in his own home. While rural women depended on their menfolk for their social identity, they seemed generally to have derived their sense of personal identity and self-worth from their domestic role. In fact, given the importance of the families and households to men's social prestige, wives exercised real power in their sphere.[14] Moreover, as wives retained title to their dowries, they might help provide dowries for their daughters. On the other hand, a gruelling burden was imposed on village women everywhere by the combined load of farm work, family care and housework.

The erosion of village values

The village values just described were in the 1950s on the brink of steady decline. They were undermined by the increasing familiarity of villagers with city values and through them with western mores. This familiarity was much accelerated by internal and external migration, and by the advent of television, through which villagers viewed the very different cultures and consumption habits of the affluent in the United States.

One agent of change was the appearance of paid work for women outside the rural household. Thus in the little country town of Megara in the 1950s, many young women started going out to work in a nearby cotton factory; and even though their purpose was to earn money for their dowries, they were much criticised at first for working outside the home. After several years the criticism died away. This was an instance where work outside the home had the effect – initially at least – of reinforcing old customs. But increasingly often the result was the opposite. For example, two neighbouring villages in Crete, in the late 1980s, differed in that in one of them work outside the home was freely available for women, and was the decisive factor in their greater independence and thus sexual liberation.[15]

Alternatively, young men and women could reject traditional values by leaving the village altogether. Young women were especially keen to escape both from farming and from village life, an urge which evidently grew over coming decades, because an investigator in the 1990s found it to be 'virtually universal' and even encouraged by mothers. At first, in the 1960s, young women seem to have been repelled especially by the drudgery and menial status of their traditional life. It was normal for example for newly married wives to live in the husbands' home, subject to their mothers-in-law, and serving on the men of the family. In the 1990s, when the exodus of women was far advanced, the survey just mentioned found that they were especially oppressed in the villages by social isolation and lack of entertainment. Nationally, by 1991, there was one unmarried girl to every 2.3 unmarried boys in farming households (presumably among people of marriageable age). In the 1990s, many male farmers had to find wives among immigrants from eastern Europe.[16]

In cities, family values were steadily changed, in ways that caused much tension between those who immigrated from villages and their offspring brought up in cities. The smaller size of accommodation, and the availability of diverse occupations in scattered localities, tended to reduce contact between family members and reduce the average size of household. Thus in 1971, the average rural household held 3.6 people (presumably reduced by emigration), and the average urban household 3.2. In consequence, paternal authority within the nuclear family was weakened, as wives and growing children found friends and incomes independently. The physical separation of households also made mothering and housekeeping more solitary occupations, and weakened the bonds of the extended family.

The rising educational level of women, and the increasing acceptability of women's work outside the home, led to a change in relationships between the sexes. The traditional view was still widespread that the proper basis for marriage was compatibility of status, combined with mutually acceptable terms between families, rather than romantic love. But, in all strata, families varied in their attachment to this convention, and it was becoming normal, especially among professional people, for men and women to decide first whether they wanted to marry each other, and then seek parental approval and work out dowry arrangements. There was towards the end of this period a fast-growing tendency among the young to see the legal institution of dowry as oppressive, because it restricted their choice of marriage partners and subjected their relationship to mercenary haggling between third parties. Economic modernisation seems to have been the decisive force behind this change, because increasing individual and occupational opportunity for both sexes was starting to deprive the dowry of its old functions. Economic modernisation was combined with an individualistic ideology which saw people's worth in terms of their personal qualities rather than their property. To an increasing extent women's education, earning power and personalities formed their dowry.

The scale of the change in values over about thirty years was expressed by Mariella Christea-Doumanis, author of a sociological study in the 1980s, who expressed a view by then commonplace among educated city people when she described as 'for us . . . incomprehensible' the iron family solidarity and absolute paternal authority that were still widespread in villages in the early 1950s.[17] But as we shall see, the pace of change allowed important elements of village values to persist in the cities.

Urban society

Social stratification

As was usual in developing countries which relied for economic growth on foreign investment and private enterprise, there were immense social inequalities, which in Greece were accentuated by right-wing dominance from 1946 onwards. Thus real wages remained below the pre-1940 level until 1956; and thereafter rose at a slower rate than industrial profits.[18]

In various ways, inequalities were increased once more by the military dictatorship of 1967–74.

Yet there had for a long time existed considerable opportunities for upward mobility, which presumably made inequalities less objectionable. Thus 40 per cent of the more important industrialists in about 1960 were sons of men of quite humble status such as craftsmen, peasants and small shopkeepers. Because teaching at the military academy had been free since 1916, the officer corps had long provided a social ladder for people of humble and provincial origin. Another such ladder was the monastic system through which poor farmers' sons might become bishops, such as the powerful figures Makarios, Archbishop of Cyprus from 1950 to 1977, and Serapheim, Archbishop of Greece from 1974 to 1998.

The most important social ladder was the public educational system. Many people of modest status, especially if they themselves had some education, placed sons (such as the future politician Konstantinos Karamanlis) on the educational ladder to high status. Social differentials in access to university education, although large, were far smaller than in Italy, Portugal and Spain, and smaller even than in Communist Yugoslavia. A survey of young people in 1962–64 found that 68 per cent of those with upper-class parents, 25 per cent of those with middle-class parents, 9 per cent of those whose parents were farmers and 7 per cent of those whose parents were workers went to university. Because farmers and workers were numerous, their children constituted a large proportion of university students: for example, 34 per cent of them in the early 1960s were farmers' children. The archaic methods of teaching which prevailed, with their emphasis on cramming and rote learning, actually had an egalitarian outcome in that they were accessible to people of deprived cultural background, by contrast with the skills of expression, and critical and creative thought, which came more easily to children from educated households.[19]

Of course family connections were important; and so there existed a patrician class of good families in the metropolis consisting largely of merchants, industrialists, bankers, shipowners, lawyers, doctors and politicians, whose values and culture were likely to be westernised. Their wives tended to be highly educated and independent in status, and many of their offspring were given an expensive education in elite private schools, followed by university in North America or western Europe. There was an immense and varied middle class – including much of the city population – consisting of businessmen, professional people, civil servants, business executives, shopkeepers and industrialists. They tended to be especially keen for the social success of their offspring, and so exhorted their sons to complete their university education, and tried to ensure that their daughters obtained husbands of suitably high status. Then there was a varied working class, about half the population of Athens and Salonika in 1971, and consisting of skilled workers, unskilled labourers, domestic servants, waiters and taxi drivers. Many of their wives and daughters worked outside the home, and so tended to be more independent of the male head of the household than women working in family enterprises, or than women whose husbands could afford to keep them at home.[20]

The span of earnings between strata in 1973 is indicated by these figures published by one sociologist.[21] In pounds sterling a month, building labourers earned 115; plasterers and carpenters 165; small-scale contractors 700; farm and factory workers 50; shop assistants 34; white-collar workers 55; senior civil servants 192; university professors 195; and colonels 190. The figures show the prosperity of the construction industry in the late 1960s, and the low pay of white-collar workers, which was offset however by job security, comparatively good working conditions and pension rights. As these figures indicate, inequalities remained great. Another illustration of them is a survey in 1958, which found that, in a large and apparently quite typical area of Athens, 57 per cent of households had only one room, and in most there were three or more people to a room. In 1955, a government survey of most of the farming population found that only 11 per cent of households had an income above what it considered to be subsistence level. The reduction of poverty by economic growth was only gradual. According to a national survey in 1974, which is supported by the results of other surveys, 31 per cent of households were still in poverty, by a definition which evidently put it close to subsistence level.[22]

Inequalities were however mitigated by the traditionally egalitarian distribution of land and therefore of housing. Thus 53 per cent of heads of household in large cities in the 1980s owned their homes, whereas in the whole country it was 75 per cent.[23]

Community life: strengths and limitations

There existed no strong tradition of city life or civic obligation. Athens had been a mere provincial town for most of the nineteenth century, although endowed by the royal family and by wealthy benefactors with some imposing and graceful public buildings, which still shine among a sea of drab cement boxes built in recent decades. The rapid growth of the modern city and port from the 1920s was basically unplanned and unlicensed, because official permits were not sought, or were corruptly acquired. Thus the layout of most of the city was the outcome of decisions by numerous small-scale property owners and developers; while construction firms were not subjected to systematic public regulation.

But urban society was quite cohesive, because the majority of the population of the metropolis lived in fairly self-contained districts, in which most people had relatives and did their shopping, and – in about one-third of cases – earned their living as well. One-third of industrial workers in the metropolis in the early 1960s walked to work. Many immigrants lived near others from their native regions or villages, forming community associations, frequenting the same *kafeneia* and participating in the same religious ceremonies. For example, the residential districts formed by Asia Minor refugees of the 1920s tended to acquire stereotypes associated with their main regions of origin; while the neighbourliness of village life was reproduced in their streets. It was normal for people to spend holidays in gatherings of their relatives. The transfer to cities of some of the sociability of villages was shown by the fact that in 2000 the percentage of people who claimed to speak to neighbours at least once a week was higher in Greece (95 per cent) than in any other country of the European Union.[24]

Another feature of village life which survived movement to cities was the absence of an effective notion of obligation to an overriding civic community to moderate the competitive rivalry for status between families. Also seriously lacking was overall regulation, or provision of essential amenities, by a national or municipal administration with a professional ethos. In fact, governments avoided building and planning regulations, so as to encourage construction work which would relieve the prevalent housing shortage.[25] Exemptions to those regulations which existed were a common form of political patronage. For this reason, Greece remains to this day the only country in the European Union without a national land register, which is desperately needed to check unlicensed building on public open space.

The consequences of this urban anarchy were illustrated by the relatively poor district of Kokkinia in Piraeus, which was first built over by Asia Minor refugees in the 1920s, but remained without a central sewerage system, or bitumen side streets with pavements, until the 1970s.[26] Public squalor was still widespread in the metropolis even in the 1990s: for example in wrecked pavements with cars parked all over them adjoining luxury shop fronts; and periodic floods resulting from unlicensed building on slopes and in natural water courses. In 1983 the area, per metropolitan inhabitant, of land not covered by roads and buildings was less than one-third of that in Rome; while from at least as early as 1978, the density of particulates in the air was extraordinarily high by northern hemisphere standards. An exception to the squalor is the picturesque old quarter of Plaka, enclosing exposed remnants of the ancient city, which was saved from increasingly garish development by the initiative of its inhabitants from the 1970s onwards.

The status of women

Widening opportunities

Gradually, women started to participate in political life. Although women over 30 gained the right to vote in municipal elections in 1930, very few exercised it before 1940. Then, during the enemy occupation of 1941–44, a large proportion of women participated actively in political life through the National Liberation Front, which gave rise to a mass women's movement. This however was crushed by the right-wing reaction of 1946 onwards.

The gradual extension thereafter of civil rights was stimulated by associations of upper-class women and by international organisations like the United Nations. Many voted in the municipal elections of 1951, and showed that they tended to be relatively conservative. Women were admitted to the civil service in 1953 and to the army in 1977. In 1952 women finally got the right to vote for parliament (at the age of 21 as for men), although they could not exercise it at a general election until 1956, in which a majority of them voted. Until the 1980s, women were shown by surveys as less likely to take an interest in politics and more likely to vote for the right. These characteristics may be attributed to their lower level of education; their limited participation in the labour force outside the home; and the lack of family encouragement to take an interest in politics.[27]

The legacy of past discrimination against women was still apparent in the educational system. Women were still only 32 per cent of university students in 1971, the gender gap being greater among the offspring of farmers and workers. Twenty-one per cent of all women over ten were illiterate in 1971 compared with 6 per cent of men. Discrimination was however being steadily reduced in practice by the rapid expansion of the higher educational system, and the removal of obstacles to access such as university fees. Educated women found more job opportunities because of the changing structure of the economy.

Women in the labour force

Thus the percentage of economically active women employed in professional and managerial jobs rose from 3.7 in 1961 to 5.6 in 1971; those employed in other white-collar jobs rose from 13.2 to 19.0 ; those employed in farming work declined from 65.5 to 61.9; and those employed in equally low-status manual work like house-cleaning or dressmaking remained at about 13 per cent. So an elite of middle-class women was leading the way in pursuing responsible and satisfying careers. Indeed there is reason to believe that, high in the social scale, relations between the sexes were more egalitarian in Greece than in the United States in the 1960s, with Greek women more likely to see themselves as equal partners of the husband, and American women more likely to define themselves as mothers and housewives.[28]

Continuing discrimination in the job market was shown in the low proportion of women in the workforce: 27.8 per cent of the whole female population in 1960 and 19.3 per cent in 1980, the majority at both dates being employed, as we have seen, in menial occupations. The overall decline in employment was part of a trend widespread in countries at an early stage of industrialisation, which resulted from a decline in the agricultural workforce (where women were traditionally numerous) which initially outweighed the increase of employed women in urban occupations.[29] It was still normal for city women – except perhaps for those in professional occupations – to leave the workforce when they married; and for that reason, employers were reluctant to pay them so well as men or even employ them at all. In all social strata, women's earnings were much less than men's for the same job – typically about two-thirds, with the differential surprisingly being somewhat wider in the upper strata. Moreover, economically active women were more vulnerable to unemployment. At least, though, most women in cities did not, like farming women, combine laborious work inside and outside the home.

Social services

Social insurance and health services

As in other developing countries, social services were stunted by lack of public funds, and hampered by the geographical inaccessibility of much of the population. For some time after the termination in 1954 of relief programmes financed largely by foreign aid, governments spent little on health and welfare. After the end of relief efforts for civil war refugees in the early 1950s, governments – as in Italy, Portugal and Spain – spent very little on housing either. Expenditure on health and welfare increased in the latter half of the 1950s, so that it reached 5.2 per cent of GNP in 1960, compared with 13.5 in France and 9.8 in Italy. However the Greek figure looked respectable by comparison with those of the Iberian dictatorships: 2.9 in Portugal and 2.3 in Spain.

Public expenditure on health alone in 1960, as a percentage of GNP, was 1.7 in Greece, compared with 3.2 in Italy and 2.5 in France. The percentage of Greek government expenditure devoted to health services was 4 in 1960 and 5.5 in 1965, leaving much of the shortfall to be made up by charitable organisations and by private individuals.[30] The ratio of hospital beds to population was improving steadily, so that in the 1960s it was higher than in Spain, although lower than in Italy. Public expenditure was much less effective than it could have been because of poor organisation of services and inefficient allocation of resources. Government responsiblity for health services was divided chaotically between several ministries, public organisations, and insurance funds. Little attempt was made by governments to coordinate services, or plan their development, in accordance with need. So there were too many hospitals in some regions and too few in others. Although the ratio of physicians to population was high by the standards of developing countries, there were too many specialists and far too few general practitioners, nurses and social workers. Medical practitioners of all types were concentrated in the metropolis, leaving desperately few in the country, especially in remoter areas. These imbalances were clearly due to differences in the pay and professional prospects of medical personnel, a problem that could be remedied only by government intervention. Some of the improvement in life expectancy in this period can nevertheless be attributed to public health services, for example the provision of free vaccination programmes and of hospital beds for maternity.

For social insurance, the population relied until the 1960s on a skimpy patchwork of private occupational schemes, or an actuarially based state scheme, the Social Insurance Institute (IKA), catering for private-sector employees in non-farming and especially in manual occupations. This began to operate in 1937, providing coverage against sickness, disability and old age; and its scope expanded to cover unemployment benefits in 1951. The government made no contribution to it before the 1960s – an omission gradually rectified from then on. In 1962 the social insurance system still had immense gaps: only one-third of the population over ten belonged to an insurance scheme, and only 41 per cent of the population over the age of 55 received a pension.

Governments went some way to reducing the gaps in the 1960s. The first measure of state social assistance was introduced in 1960, in the form of a means-tested benefit for destitute children. A major step was the establishment in 1961 of what became the second-largest insurance scheme after IKA, the Organisation for Farmers' Insurance (OGA), which provided farmers with pensions and cover against old age, disability, sickness and crop failure. OGA was state-financed, as most farmers had little or no cash income. Other insurance schemes expanded to cover remaining urban employees. In 1973, people on low incomes in towns became eligible for free medical cover. As a result of the extension of insurance coverage, its total cost rose from 8 per cent of GNP in 1962 to 12 per cent in 1968.[31]

Education

Although reverence for educational attainment has always been noteworthy in Greece, it illustrates the general poverty of state services that government expenditure on education – 2.1 per cent of GNP in the mid-1960s – was low not only by comparison with that in northern Europe, but even with that in other developing countries. This level could not satisfy the strong public demand for educational qualifications, nor the pressing need to modernise the curriculum, especially through the introduction of technical and vocational education. Successive governments worsened the problem by moving towards state monopoly of tertiary education, and so nationalised, one after another, those tertiary-level colleges which had been established by private initiative, while continuing to control in detail the curricula of all educational institutions. The control was, moreover, inspired by the ideology of the post-civil war regime. Primary and secondary education was also dominated by the state, with over 90 per cent of pupils attending government schools. The combination of tightly centralised control, seriously inadequate funding and mounting social demand goes far to explain why education has been an explosive issue from the 1950s to the present day.[32]

In itself, progress seemed impressive. The illiteracy rate fell steadily among those aged ten and over, being estimated as 32 per cent in 1951, and officially recorded as 18 per cent in 1961 and 14 per cent in 1971. Meanwhile the proportion of the economically active population with only primary education fell from 63.7 per cent in 1950 to 27.7 per cent in 1973, while those with completed secondary education increased from 4.7 per cent to 13.7 per cent. The population of university students increased rapidly from the 1950s; and it numbered 30,617 in 1961–62 and 70,161 in 1971–72 . In 1971 the educational participation rate was 69 per cent of the relevant age groups in secondary schools and 10 per cent in universities. But this was an era of rapid educational expansion throughout Europe; and by the 1970s the participation rates were greater in most or all other European countries. In fact the participation rate in tertiary education was ahead only of the Portuguese.

Nor do these figures take account of the generally poor quality of education. In part this could be blamed on the geographical dispersal of country people, which helps to explain why over half the primary schools had only one teacher and one or two class-rooms for the obligatory six grades. In part it was due to lack of funding, which explains why in 1961 the average staff/pupil ratio was 1:40 in primary schools and 1:38 in secondary schools, improving by 1967 to 1:35 and 1:32 respectively. Another problem was official ideology which viewed attempts to modernise curricula or teaching methods as subversive. In the curriculum nearly one-quarter of the compulsory *gymnasion* (or lower secondary) syllabus was devoted to Ancient Greek in 1964, and much additional time to the study of the official form of the language *katharevousa*; while there were at this time more secondary teachers of theology than of natural sciences. Although English had been by far the most useful foreign language since 1945, it still received low priority thirty years later. An awakening recognition of the need for technical education was shown by the government's establishment of a few special schools at secondary level in 1959. Subsequently, other institutions for technical and vocational education were established, but on private initiative. In the decade 1955–64, Greece had the highest proportion in the OECD of students enrolled in legal and social studies – adapted to entry into the civil service – and the lowest enrolled in technological subjects. Governments neglected disciplines of growing importance like psychology or sociology, as well as disciplines in technology or the natural sciences which required expensive equipment.[33]

The quality of education was also marred by authoritarian teaching methods, which were confined to rote-learning of textbooks prescribed by the government, and so designed to inculcate uncritical respect for authority. Meanwhile, emphasis on archaic grammar encouraged preoccupation with linguistic form rather than substance. As an eminent Greek sociologist wrote in the 1970s, the entire educational system was 'geared almost exclusively to testing of memory . . . and not to testing of ability to think critically and originally'. An expert on primary education in 1979 concluded that it was designed to suffocate critical and creative thinking.[34] A minister in a left-wing government in 1984 described the traditional school system as 'very authoritarian, oppressive and unrelated to real needs'. A professor of history added in 1983 that 'methods of teaching [in universities] are still largely based on oratory to huge audiences'. Students could succeed at university by mere memorisation of lecture notes and authorised textbooks, which made feasible a staff/student ratio which was the lowest in Europe (varying according to definition of teaching staff, but by one well-informed estimate about 1:81).[35]

The results of such education were reflected in the deficiencies of the chief occupational outlet for university graduates, the state administration (described in the next chapter). Other results are seen for example in politicians' speeches and quality newspapers, both marked all too often by attention to linguistic erudition and sonority rather than to substance and clarity. The children of the well-to-do bypassed the educational system by attending foreign universities preceded by Greek private schools (though even here the curricula were prescribed by the government). One-quarter of university students in the 1960s were enrolled abroad in foreign universities (a much higher proportion if equivalent full-time students could be estimated); and in the 1950s private expenditure on students abroad was 2.5 times the public provision for universities – an extraordinary ratio by international standards. Many of the best graduates stayed abroad, and from those who returned were recruited the majority of – and by the late 1970s all – university staff. They proved powerless, however, to change the basic features of the educational system.[36]

A success story?

Increasing material welfare

'If satisfaction of human wants and aspirations is taken as the criterion', wrote the celebrated historian William H. McNeill in 1977, 'then the development of Greece across the last thirty years must be viewed as an extraordinary success story'.[37] Does this evaluation still seem appropriate? The general answer is yes, but with reservations.

Improvements in welfare were certainly dramatic. Real per capita net income grew nearly threefold in 1950–73. In a village near Volos, farm labourers had to spend 88 per cent of their income on food in 1954 but only 17 per cent thirty years later. In the years 1961–77 alone, private consumption per capita increased by well over twice – 142 per cent – compared with 89 per cent in Italy, 114 per cent in Spain and 124 per cent in Portugal, in fact by more than in any other OECD country except Japan. Because Greece started from a comparatively low basis, such growth put the country, in per capita take-home earnings in 1971–72, at just over one-third of the West German level, 62 per cent of the Italian level, almost the Spanish level and well ahead of the Portuguese, according to one estimate. For a French authority, Guy Burgel, the most striking change in the human geography of Greece in the 1960s and 1970s was the increased accessibility to the outside world of villages, because of sealed roads, vehicles, telephones, radios, television and (in the case of islands) improved ports and boat services.[38]

During the 1970s, the effects of twenty years of rapid economic growth, combined with the growing flood of emigrants' remittances, made their effects felt in a marked improvement in housing conditions and a proliferation of consumer goods. Despite the damage to housing caused by periodic earthquakes, and despite the expenses caused by migration from country to town, the average number of people per room fell from 2.5 in 1940 to 1 in 1973.[39] Between 1970 and 1978, per capita domestic consumption of electricity doubled, vehicles per thousand people increased from 45 to 125 and telephones per thousand from 120 to 245. This was still mainly an urban trend; and, as late as 1974, 40 per cent of rural households possessed no consumer durables. How Greece compared with the rest of capitalist southern Europe in such measures of affluence is indicated by Table 4.1, which will approximately indicate ratio of consumer goods to household if one multiplies by three:

Table 4.1 *Ownership of consumer goods per thousand inhabitants in Greece, Italy, Portugal and Spain, in 1976–77*[40]

	Greece	Italy	Spain	Portugal
telephones	234	265	236	167
radios	355	not available	248	163
televisions	125	208	193	118
cars	55	283	148	108

The low rate of car ownership may have been due to Greece's large urban population, because cars were not very useful in densely populated cities. The general impression is that Greece was trailing far behind Italy and a little behind Spain, while well ahead of Portugal.

Between the early 1960s and the early 1980s, diet became much richer and more diverse, with an increase of twice or more in the consumption of meat, fruit, sugar, potatoes and green vegetables, and by 50 per cent or more in the consumption of milk and eggs. Meanwhile consumption of the traditional staples, bread and beans, diminished. From the early 1950s to the early 1990s there were also dramatic increases in expenditure on alcoholic drink and tobacco.[41]

With the growing scarcity of labour, the old relations of deference between social strata largely disappeared. In the early 1980s – by contrast with the early 1960s – domestic servants in the metropolis were Filipino not Greek, and customers were abandoning the habit of clapping for service in cheap restaurants. So by 1973, the majority of people enjoyed much higher incomes, better health, better housing, more pleasant lives and more dignity than in 1950.

Limitations: inequality, imbalances and quality of life

One reservation is that inequalities of income remained vast, largely because the prevalent political forces succeeded in curbing the incomes of lower socio-economic groups. It has been estimated that at the end of our period, 40 per cent of the lowest income groups received (after taxation and social benefits) 9.5 per cent of the national income, while 17 per cent in the top income brackets received 58 per cent.[42]

A consequence of underdevelopment, also apparent in other Mediterranean countries, was a shortage of jobs with high pay and status – for example, professional people, managers, or skilled workers. Governments created outlets for graduates of the educational system by overexpanding the public service, which in consequence became a burden on the economy. In part, too, the difficulties that many educated people experienced in finding suitable jobs was due to the traditional role in Greece of family or political connections in access to employment. People lacking connections had to accept poor jobs or emigrate.[43]

McNeill rightly emphasises the importance of family loyalty as a motive for economic improvement and social advancement. But this motive also led many people to work uneconomically, either on their own account or in small businesses. Largely for this reason, average working hours were extraordinarily long. State employment was sought after, partly because government offices closed early in the afternoon, allowing for casual self-employment after office hours. As a result the public sector helped to sustain an economy based on small family businesses.[44] As a visitor to Greece could see at a glance in many places of work, whether they were state-owned banks or family-owned shops, the long working hours of much of the population were relatively unproductive.

There were problems created by a combination of economic dependency with political overcentralisation. One was the increasing concentration of people and industry in Athens. Partly in response to government incentives and restrictions, some dispersal of industrial activity to the provinces began in the 1970s as a result of development in Kavalla, Volos, Larisa, Drama, Patras and Herakleion. Otherwise, regional planning by governments was virtually unknown before 1980. By 1971 well over one-third of the economically active population lived in Athens, and another 17 per cent in Salonika, with still higher percentages of professional people, or people in managerial or leadership positions. Per capita income in the greater metropolitan region in the 1960s was over twice that in most others, and over 50 per cent greater than in the most affluent provinces, which were central Macedonia (including Salonika) and the Peloponnese. The dominance of the metropolis was reflected in its press, the circulation of which in 1987 was nearly five times that of all provincial newspapers. The ratio of inhabitants to public libraries in the 1970s was three times better in the metropolitan region than the national average. Yet this regional inequality came at an increasing price, because urban growth brought with it in the 1970s the ills common in conurbations of poor countries, and attributable to a low level of civic consciousness, weak administrative systems and shortage of technical expertise: pollution, congestion and shortage of essential infrastructure and services. Meanwhile, provincial towns suffered from economic neglect and cultural stagnation. One of many examples of the problems caused by migration to cities was their critical shortage of school buildings; while many of the imposing primary schools built in thousands of villages earlier in the century became empty.

Notes

1 Michail Papadakis and Georgios Siambos, 'Demographic developments and prospects of the Greek population, 1951–2041', in Ioanna Lambiri-Dimaki and Nikos Kiriazis (eds), *Greek Society at the End of the Twentieth Century* (in Greek, 1995), 37; Richard A.H. Robinson, *Contemporary Portugal. A History* (1979), 158; *Vima*, 30 July 2000, A8–9, Elenas Fyntanidou.

2 National Statistical Service of Greece, *Statistical Summary of Greece 1954* (in Greek and English, 1955), 26–7; *Statistical Yearbook of Greece 1973* (1974), 38–9; Violetta Hionidou, 'The adoption of fertility control on Mykonos, 1879–1955: stopping, spacing, or both?' *Population Studies* 52 (1998), 67–83; Ernestine Friedl, *Vasilika. A Village in Modern Greece* (New York 1962), 56; C. Evelpidis, 'Some economic and social problems in Greece', *International Labour Review* 68 (1953), 152.

3 A.F. Freris, *The Greek Economy in the Twentieth Century* (1986), 163–6; Sofia N. Antonopoulou, *The Postwar Reconstruction of the Greek Economy and the Phenomenon of the Construction Industry, 1950–80* (in Greek, 1991), 83.

4 Christoforos Vernadakis and Giannis Mavris, *Parties and Social Alliances in Predictatorship Greece* (in Greek, 1991), 127–31.

5 Nikolaos Glytsos, 'Prospects of the Greek labour market in the year 2000', in Lambiri-Dimaki and Kyriazis (eds), *Greek Society*, 114.

6 *Greek Economy*, 146.

7 McNeill, *Metamorphosis*, 216.

8 Vernadakis and Mavris, *Parties*, 121; Iras Emke-Poulopoulou, 'Greece: a country of migrants', *Kathimerini*, 12 December 1999, Special Feature, 22–3 (in Greek).

9 Konstantinos Tsoucalas, *State, Society, Work in Postwar Greece* (in Greek, 1987), 123.

10 Papadakis and Siambos, in Lambiri-Dimaki and Kyriazis (eds), *Greek Society*, 38; Emke-Poulopoulou, 'A country of migrants', 22.

11 Demetrios G. Papademetriou, 'Illusions and reality in international migration: migration and development in post-World War II Greece', *International Migration* 23 (1985), 211–23.

12 Juliet du Boulay, 'The meaning of dowry: changing values in rural Greece', *Journal of Modern Greek Studies* 1 (1983), 261–2.

13 John K. Campbell, *Honour, Family, and Patronage. A Study of Institutions and Values in a Greek Mountain Community* (Oxford 1964), 38–48, 189–94; Mariella Christea-Doumani, *The Greek Mother. Formerly and Today* (in Greek, 1989, originally published in English in New York 1983, under the name Doumanis as *Mothering in Greece*), 54–64.

14 Jill Dubisch, 'Introduction', in Jill Dubisch (ed.), *Gender and Power in Rural Greece* (Princeton, NJ 1986), 18–20, 30.

15 Jane Lambiri-Dimaki, *Social Stratification in Greece, 1962–82* (Athens 1983), 143–56; Gabriella Lazarides, 'Sexuality and its cultural construction in rural Greece', *Journal of Gender Studies* 4 (1995), 281–95.

16 W.H. McNeill, *The Metamorphosis of Greece since World War II* (Oxford 1978), 171–2; Isabella Gidarakou, 'Young women's attitudes towards agriculture and women's new roles in the Greek countryside: a first approach', *Journal of Rural Studies* 15 (1999), 147, 152–3, 156.

17 Christea-Doumani, *Greek Mother*, 58; Roi Panayotopoulou, ' "Rational" individualistic practices in the context of an "irrational" political system', in Christos Lyrintzis, Ilias Nikolakopoulos and Dimitris Sotiropoulos (eds), *Society and Politics. Aspects of the Third Greek Republic, 1974–94* (in Greek, 1996), 154–5 ; James Georgas, 'Changing family values in Greece: from collectivist to individualist', *Journal of Cross-Cultural Psychology* 20 (1989), 81; Muriel Dimen, 'Servants and sentries – women, power, and social reproduction in Kriovrisi', *Journal of Modern Greek Studies* 1 (1983), 234–5.

18 Maria Petmesidou-Tsoulouvi, *Social Inequalities and Social Policy* (in Greek, 1992), 142; Vernadakis and Mavris, *Parties*, 121.

19 Lambiri-Dimaki, *Social Stratification*, 53; Constantine Tsoucalas and Roy Panagiotopoulou, 'Education in socialist Greece: between modernization and democratization', in Theodore C. Kariotis (ed.), *The Greek Socialist Experiment. Papandreou's Greece, 1981–9* (New York 1992), 313; Tsoucalas, *State, Society, Work*, 132.

20 Campbell and Sherrard, *Modern Greece*, 367–70; Christea-Doumani, *Greek Mother*, 146.

21 Margaret E. Kenna, 'Institutional and transformational migration and the politics of community', *Archives Européennes de Sociologie* 24 (1983), 279.

22 Vernadakis and Mavris, *Parties*, 119–20, 126–8.

23 Lefteris Tsoulouvis, 'Aspects of statism and planning in Greece', *International Journal of Urban and Regional Research* 11 (1987), 719–20.

24 McNeill, 232; Kenna , 'Institutional and transformational migration', 269–72; Renée Hirschon, *Heirs of the Greek Catastrophe. Social Life of Asia Minor Refugees in Piraeus* (Oxford 1998), 24–5, 172; European Commission, *Living Conditions in Europe. Statistical Pocketbook* (Luxembourg 2000), 114; Lila Leontidou, *The Mediterranean City in Transition. Social Change and Urban Development* (Cambridge 1990), 136.

25 *Vima*, 19 December 1999, Andreas Giakoumakatos, Supplement, 6; Leontidou, *Mediterranean City*, 148–50, 170.

26 Hirschon, *Heirs*, 53.

27 Tassoula Vervenioti, 'The women's vote', *Kathimerini*, 28 November 1999, Special Issue, 28; Maro Pantelidou Malouta, 'Greek political culture: the gender of the left and the right', in Christos Lyrintzis and Ilias Nikolakopoulos (eds), *Elections and Parties in the Decade of the 1980s. Developments and Prospects of the Political System* (in Greek, 1990), 104–5; Betty Dobratz, 'Sociopolitical participation of women in Greece', in Gwen Moore and Glenn Spitze (eds), *Research in Politics and Society* 2 (1986), 137.

28 Constantina Safilios-Rothschild, 'Some aspects of social modernization in the United States and Greece', *Sociologie et Société* 1 (1969), 36.

29 Susan Buck Sutton, 'Family and work: new patterns for village women in Athens,' *Journal of Modern Greek Studies* 4 (1986), 40–2.

30 Leontidou, *Mediterranean City*, 139; Vernadakis and Mavris, *Parties and Social Alliances*, 125; Petmesidou-Tsoulouvi, *Social Inequalities*, 141; Anne Wood-Ritsatakis, *An Analysis of the Health and Welfare Services in Greece* (Athens 1970), 42–4, 177.

31 Christos Andricopoulos, 'Farmers' social insurance in Greece', *International Social Security Review* 29 (1976), 18–48; Petmesidou-Tsoulouvi, *Social Inequalities*, 137; Ian Gough, 'Social assistance in southern Europe', *South European Society and Politics* 1 (1996), 6–7; Dimitrios N. Venieris, 'Dimensions of social policy in Greece', *South European Society and Politics* 1 (1996), 262–3.

32 Takis Fotopoulos, *Dependent Development: the Greek Case* (in Greek, 1985), 186; Harry A. Patrinos, 'The private origins of public higher education in Greece', *Journal of Modern Greek Studies* 13 (1995), 188–95.

33 Tsoucalas, *State, Society, Work*, 131; Henry Wasser, 'A survey of recent trends in Greek higher education', *Journal of the Hellenic Diaspora* 6 (1979), 85–6;

Theophrastes Yerou, 'Basic education today', *Journal of the Hellenic Diaspora* 8 (1981), 38; Campbell and Sherrard, *Modern Greece*, 384–5.

34 Lambiri-Dimaki, 107; Yannis Yannoulopoulos, 'On the university reform law', in Zafiris Tzannatos (ed.), *Socialism in Greece. The First Four Years* (Aldershot 1986), 186.

35 Theophrastis Yerou, 'Basic education today', *Journal of the Hellenic Dispora* 8 (1981), 38; Anna Frangoudakis, 'The impasse of educational reform in Greece: an introduction', *Journal of the Hellenic Diaspora* 8 (1981), 9; George Papandreou, 'Lifetime education in Greece', in Tzannatos (ed.) ibid., 181; Yannis Yannoulopoulos, 'On the university reform law', in Tzannatos, (ed.), ibid., 186.

36 Constantine Tsoucalas, 'Some aspects of "over-education" in modern Greece', *Journal of the Hellenic Diaspora* 8 (1981), 113.

37 *Metamorphosis*, 247.

38 Nicholas Michas, 'Economic development, social mobilization, and the growth of public expenditures in Greece', *American Journal of Economics and Sociology* 39 (1980), 44 ; Diane O. Bennett, ' "The poor have much more money": changing socio-economic relations in a Greek village', *Journal of Modern Greek Studies* 6 (1988), 233; Burgel, 'Rural Greece Revisited', *Review of Social Research*, special issue 1981, 11; Wood-Ritsatakis, *Health and Welfare*, 154.

39 Dimitris Oikonomou, 'Housing policy: current situation and prospects in the European Community and Greece', in Panagiotis Getimis and Dionisis N. Gravaris (eds), *Social State and Social Policy. The Current Debate* (in Greek, 1993), 336–8; Marios Nikolinakos, 'Transnationalization of production, location of industry, and the deformation of regional development in peripheral countries: the case of Greece', in Ray Hudson and Jim Lewis (eds), *Uneven Development in Southern Europe. Studies of Accumulation, Class, Migration, and the State* (1985), 200; McNeill, *Metamorphosis*, 162, 181–2, 201, 219.

40 Vasilis Karapostolis, *Consumer Behaviour in Greek Society, 1960–75* (in Greek, 1983), 332.

41 *Vima*, 27 June 1993, A55, K. Chalvatzakis.

42 Mouzelis, *Modern Greece*, 122–3.

43 Petmesidou-Tsoulouvi, *Social Inequalities*, 63; National Statistical Service of Greece, *Statistical Yearbook of Greece 1983* (Athens 1984), 451.

44 Tsoucalas, *State, Society, Work*, 126.

CHAPTER FIVE

The Post-Civil War Regime, 1950–1967

The right-wing establishment

After the general election of March 1950, the political system was in outward appearance a democracy, run by a government of politicians dependent on a majority in a parliament elected by secret ballot and male suffrage. In reality, power was shared between politicians and the monarchy, army officers and American representatives. Civilian governments worked through a highly centralised state machine. The resulting regime favoured relatively few – perhaps one or two hundred – business magnates and bank directors, many of whom were on friendly terms with influential political figures. This interlocking system of power centres could be described as the right-wing establishment, which included the government when it was run by the right. Such was the case from November 1952 to November 1963, a period when the government and the rest of the establishment were basically united by mutual confidence, even though different groups quarrelled as they jostled for power. The confidence broke down when a reformist party held power from November 1963 to July 1965; and this breach led indirectly to a military coup in 1967.

During the 1950s, all members of the establishment were nervously aware of the appeal of the exiled Greek Communist Party – directly through its radio broadcasts and indirectly through its front party within Greece – to the masses of poor workers, shopkeepers, clerical workers and farmers, who resented social inequality and bureaucratic corruption. As often happens, fear drove the ruling groups to exacerbate the causes of that fear; and so they reacted to the communist threat by maintaining social privilege and an apparatus of repression.

Army

The army officers felt that they were the guarantors of the regime, and gave their primary loyalty to extra-parliamentary sources of power. They did not forget that they had won the civil war with American resources and active support by their constitutional head the king, but with little help from politicians. Insulated from political life, army officers remained unanimously imbued with the values common in the national camp during the civil war, values which comprised ardent belief in the Orthodox Christian faith, private property, the patriarchal family and national greatness dependent on alliance with the United States and the North Atlantic Treaty Organisation (NATO). Binding all elements together was intense anti-communism, which was reproduced for example in army training manuals. The officers resembled the Communist Party in their incongruous combination of intense patriotism with submission to foreign patrons.

Officers' sense of political mission was encouraged by their special relationship with the crown and the American representatives. Expressive of this attitude was the persistence of political conspiracy, the best-known example being the activities of the Sacred Union of Greek Officers (IDEA). Periodically provoking much controversy – and even attempting a coup in May 1951 – IDEA exerted much influence on promotions and postings. At a higher level the general staff possessed a contingency plan for a coup, that was authorised by American representatives through NATO, to counter subversive activities if these coincided with an external threat. For many years, however, conspiratorial activities were kept in check by the high command, the king and the Americans.

The dominant influence in the army, from his appointment as Commander-in-Chief in January 1949 until his death in October 1955, was Papagos. He was realistic enough to comply with American wishes by expediting a prompt return after the civil war to parliamentary government, which required the nominal subjection soon afterwards of the armed forces to control by politicians. After resigning as Commander-in-Chief in May 1951, he entered politics as leader of his own political party, the Greek Rally, which won a large parliamentary majority in November 1952. For the following three years Papagos wielded extraordinary authority in army and state as prime minister, acting as custodian of the interests of the king and the Americans. After his death, the army continued to see its interests as linked with those of the political party which he had created, which was re-labelled the National Radical Union (ERE) by Papagos's successor Konstantinos Karamanlis. This perception was realistic, in that the officers' career prospects depended on the large military budget which was an essential feature of the political system.

The army's special status was embodied in various institutions. The police cooperated with it in tracking down most of the agents which the exiled Communist Party sent into Greece, and shadowing Communist cadres within the country. The police themselves employed tens of thousands of spies, and they with army officers encouraged numerous anti-communist vigilante groups – a legacy of the 1940s, which were useful because their activities could be disowned. These unofficial allies of the security system were notorious as the 'shadow state' or *parakratos*. From 1951, the army ran a national radio station with public 'enlightenment' as an objective. Because it catered more than civilian radio stations for popular tastes, it had a big audience, while being political and even partisan in its bias. Eventually, in 1967, it would be accompanied by an equally popular television station. During this period the village militia continued to intimidate political dissenters and intervened regularly in elections. The political views of conscripts were vetted; their reading matter was censored (Ernest Renan and Victor Hugo being among the prohibited authors); and they were subjected to political indoctrination. For these reasons it mattered greatly where soldiers voted; and at several elections in this period they (as well as all state officials) could vote wherever they were serving, to the benefit of right-wing parties. The army was also responsible for much of the extensive construction programme of the period, building roads, bridges, ports and airfields.[1]

The nerve centre of the security apparatus was the Central Intelligence Service (KYP), the supreme information-gathering body on all matters relating to communist subversion. It was established by Papagos as prime minister in 1953, and was equipped and trained by officials of the American Central Intelligence Agency, which maintained one of its largest stations in Greece. Staffed by officers of the armed forces and police, the KYP had informants and representatives in all branches of government as well as links with unofficial anti-communist groups, and answered directly to the prime minister. It tapped phone calls and opened mail, so establishing a practice which later prime ministers until the 1990s found hard to abandon. Even right-wing MPs in the 1950s feared that it would give the prime minister dictatorial powers.

Americans

After the 1950 election, the Americans ceased to appoint governments directly; but continued to convey their wishes about senior political and military appointments to the king and to prime ministers. By 1952 their political influence was under challenge: for example the ambassador provoked uproar in that year by publicly insisting on a change to a simple plurality electoral system (like the British) so as to enable the Greek Rally to gain a majority. This was the last time that foreigners dictated the electoral system; and the Americans could not prevent Papagos's new government from making unwelcome changes in the military high command.[2] Even in March 1950, Americans could not dictate to voters, as the election outcome showed. Eighteen former members of, or sympathisers with, EAM were elected; while a veteran Venizelist, Nikolaos Plastiras, became prime minister with a programme of reconciliation and amnesty which the Americans and the establishment distrusted. He nevertheless held power for much of the following 30 months of instability.

The Americans could allow voters such freedom because of their overwhelming economic power, which allowed little scope for manoeuvre in the early 1950s to governments of any complexion. The economic treaties of 1948 and 1953 ceded to American investors virtually colonial rights. For example the 1948 treaty allowed them first choice among foreign investors in exploitation of any mineral resources that might be discovered, a right of which they would take advantage in 1973 after oil was discovered in the Aegean.[3] American representatives played a major role from 1947 in promoting able staff in most ministries, and continued in the first half of the 1950s to supervise each department's expenditure. Americans exerted great and undiminished influence over the armed forces throughout this period.

Hemmed in as they were by the establishment, centrist governments like those of Plastiras could do little to oppose its wishes by leniency to the left in 1950–52. Although right-wing politicians, and American representatives, criticised these governments for freeing too many political prisoners, and for tolerating left-wing parties and newspapers, there was in these respects little break in continuity when Papagos came to power.

The right-wing governments of 1952–63 saw American favour as an important asset in competition with Greek political rivals.[4] Karamanlis was attentive to American interests in foreign policy. For example he diverged from all other western leaders in his unconditional support for the American blockade of Castro's Cuba in the early 1960s, even though it put Greek seamen out of work.

After Karamanlis's resignation in June 1963, American representatives again wished to influence the choice of prime minister. By now, however, their influence was much diminished by various factors: mainly the cessation in 1962 of their civilian aid, and also the decline in public fear of the Soviet bloc. Americans had abandoned attempts to influence election results by subsidising favoured groups. While trying, through advice to key players, to maintain stability (for example opposing drastic changes in the senior ranks of the armed forces by a reformist prime minister in 1964), they realised now that overt intervention in politics would provoke a damaging public outcry.[5]

Monarchy

The monarchy was flattered as a bastion of their values by the army, right-wing politicians and British and American representatives. Successive monarchs – Paul I and Frederica until March 1964, and then Paul's successor Constantine II – were thus encouraged to interpret their role audaciously; and in time accumulated formidable resources. The monarch's budget in the mid-1960s came to $650,000 a year; and the size of this sum was becoming very controversial. In addition a capital sum of $10 million was raised from certain earmarked taxes (including controversially one on cinema tickets) for 'The Foundation of the Queen', which spent about three-quarters as much as the Ministry of Health and Welfare and employed several thousand people. Although devoted to worthy purposes, such as sports centres for children and programmes of technical education, its allocation was entirely at the Queen's discretion. Successive monarchs gathered round themselves influential people – politicians, army officers, senior civil servants, businessmen – who constituted a palace party, which formed temporary governments to supervise elections, mobilised political support and negotiated agreements with politicians. Under the 1952 constitution the king was head of the armed forces, and so maintained a right to be consulted by governments over major military matters such as senior appointments, including, as he controversially maintained, the Ministry of National Defence.

For some time the monarchy's role was restricted by the power of the Americans and of Papagos as prime minister. Papagos's death removed one constraint, and the decline of US influence removed another. During the 1960s, the busybody Queen Frederica (widely thought to wield more influence than her husband), and her unstable son Constantine (23 years old in 1964 and under Frederica's influence), reacted to growing challenges in ill-judged and provocative ways. It was the Queen's activities which provoked the resignation at different points of key figures: Papagos as Commander-in-Chief in May 1951 and Karamanlis as Prime Minister in June 1963. The latter event weakened the respect which many army officers felt for the crown.[6] The monarchy thus departed from the explicit provision of the constitution that it should preside impartially over government but not usurp its role. In the process it did much to undermine the post-civil war system and eventually its own position. The successive monarchs relied especially on their power to appoint and dismiss prime ministers, on their patronage resources and on their special relationship with the army. A further source of power was the uncritical support which could be counted on from the Greek Rally and its successor the National Radical Union. The successive monarchs were biased against many centre politicians, including Plastiras and Georgios Papandreou, because of their republican associations before 1940. It is evident that the king and queen, because of their own links with the army and the political right, condoned or encouraged the wholesale intimidation practised in the general election of 1961 (discussed below, p. 104).

The institutions of controlled democracy, 1950–1961

Government

The structure of the state administration can best be understood by its traditionally clientelist goal, which was to allocate much of the national product to members of the ruling party and deny it to opponents. There was much irrational duplication or division of functions between departments; but rationalisation of structure was prevented by ministers' jealousy of their patronage. Each ministry was an empire, coordinated ineffectively with others, in overlapping policy areas, by standing ministerial committees. Ministers tried to undertake in person all responsibilities which might be used for patronage, and so spent much of their time interviewing applicants for jobs or favours, who might on occasion besiege them in hundreds. The result was over-centralisation of responsibility.

At lower levels, masses of clerical workers devoted themselves to unproductive paperwork. They thus created a bureaucratic labyrinth, which provided work for unofficial expeditors who guided ordinary citizens through, for example, the tax department, the customs service and even the post offices. Although most civil servants were poorly paid and low in status, their jobs were widely sought after because they were secure, undemanding and rewarded with privileged health insurance and pensions. The total number of civil servants employed by the national government in the 1949/50 financial year was 76,581, compared with 53,379 in 1938. About this number again was employed by government agencies and local authorities. In addition, about 140,000 people (including retired police and army officers) received public service pensions, even though many were still in the labour force. The total number of public employees was nearly the same as the 150,000 in Italy (with six times Greece's population) in 1948.

The proportion of the state budget devoted to the civil service and police became and remained even greater than it had been traditionally: for example in 1971 it was 37.5 per cent, nearly twice the proportion in, say, Spain.[7]

During their long rule from 1952 to 1963, right-wing forces – as well as the army and the police – became closely associated with the state machine. But there were periods (1945–52, and again in 1964–65) when centre parties had a chance to build up their clienteles within it. Although they could not dismiss officials without special legislation, they could transfer them to inconvenient places, while rewarding supporters with acceptably located posts. Most of the police – and quite possibly other members of the public service – were frequently shuffled around for such reasons. In addition, politicians had wide scope for favouritism in appointments of temporary staff. While many appointments were made on grounds of partisan preference, promotion depended in perhaps the majority of cases on seniority or formal qualifications. Promotion by merit alone was actually precluded by law until 1999.[8]

Because so much of the state budget was wasted on salaries and pensions, there was little to spare for buildings and equipment, or for adequately qualified staff. These faults led to shortcomings that characterise bureaucracies in many developing countries: shabby infrastructure, absurd formalism, lack of initiative, indifference to citizens' needs and arrogance towards citizens who lacked *mesa* (meaning influential contacts or intermediaries).

The control which this bureaucracy exercised over citizens' lives extended to minute details. For example, all citizens had to obtain from the police an identity card, showing among other things their religion, occupation and spouse's name, and this card was a prerequisite for every type of official permit and document, including the booklet required for compulsory voting at parliamentary elections. The police might deny a citizen an identity card for trivial or arbitrary reasons. Citizens had to be skilled in evading the tentacles of the bureaucracy or negotiating their way out of them when caught. How much more oppressive officialdom was in Greece than in many western countries is shown in Michael Herzfeld's study, *The Social Reproduction of Indifference. The Symbolic Roots of Western Bureaucracy*.[9] Among the exceptions were agronomists and medical officers who were more likely to show a professional sense of mission to help fellow citizens.

The combination of political patronage and poor training prevented the development of a corps of senior public servants, devoted to their profession and able to initiate policy and think strategically. The civil service was also incapable of giving independent advice to ministers or confronting powerful interest groups. In the late 1940s, weak and incompetent ministers, and prevailing economic scarcity, made these defects especially marked and conducive to widespread corruption. Thus the bureaucracy became a social pillar of the restored conservative regime from 1946 onwards, but not an effective instrument of government.[10]

By 1940 the scope of government included the main social insurance organisation, IKA, and several public utilities also run by the state in other European countries: the postal service, broadcasting authority, water supplies and harbour authorities. The state also controlled much of the banking system. Extension of the state sphere came after 1944 with the nationalisation of the railways, the establishment of the Organisation for Telecommunications (OTE) in 1949, and the Public Electricity Corporation (DEI) in 1950. The state-controlled sector of the banking system was to be further expanded, and state organisations were created for regulating other sectors of the economy: for example to the long-established organisation for exporting currants there were added organisations for running the vegetable markets of Athens and Salonika. The government also set up plants for refining oil, refining sugar and producing fertiliser. In all, the state sector accounted for 7 or 8 per cent of GNP around 1960.[11]

The sociologist Konstantinos Tsoucalas estimated that public employment of some sort, soon after 1945, began to absorb about a half of all non-manual workers, and one-third of wage and salary earners in towns.[12] While strong in formal powers, the state was weak in its low level of competence and lack of resources. Bearing also in mind its partisan character, we can understand why the state, and the legal system with which it identified itself, have remained dismally incapable until the present day of securing citizens' respect.

The requirements of the public services shaped the character of the educational system. The participation rate of the relevant age groups in the secondary and tertiary sectors of the education system was high by European standards in the early 1950s, though less so later. The public service absorbed over half the graduates of Greek universities in the post-civil war period, and these graduates formed an extraordinarily high proportion – nearly a half – of civil servants as well as all secondary school teachers and most primary school teachers. Given the high unemployment and severe economic insecurity of the 1940s and 1950s, state employment became more attractive than ever to people with some education and modest means. Systematic steps were taken to secure the ideological conformity of the public service, by measures which included police certificates of lawful opinions.

The judicial corps was in effect a branch of the state. It derived originally from the French model; so that judges followed a career path separate from that of lawyers. Criminal investigations were conducted by judicial prosecutors who formed departments of the judiciary at various levels. Because of the legalistic preoccupations of the state administration, judges were given extensive tasks by governments, including enquiries into diverse public problems. Responsibility for monitoring government finances fell to the Court of Auditors, which in practice enquired whether legal requirements were fulfilled rather than whether money was well spent.

As in western democracies, leading judges (who themselves influenced the selection of their juniors) were appointed by governments from the senior ranks of the judiciary. Governmental choices were assumed by informed observers to be politically biased, an assumption which persists even in the much more democratic conditions of today.[13] In the post-civil war period, judges saw themselves as servants of the state, rather than protectors of citizens' rights, and so administered with little question the special security measures against Communism, even though these measures conflicted with the guarantees of civil liberties in the constitution of 1952. Even the Council of State failed during this period to fulfil its intended role – when it was established by Elevtherios Venizelos in 1929 – as monitor of the constitutional legality of government actions. For example, until 1962 it maintained the fiction that a state of civil war continued, so as to validate emergency decrees. In general, when interpreting the law, judges habitually gave the government the benefit of any doubt. Reasons for their attitude were that, like the whole public service, they were educated to accept the political system and screened for ideological soundness. Another reason was that – as in France and other countries with a civil law rather than a common law tradition – they saw their role as restricted to the administration, rather than interpretion and creation, of the law.[14]

Elected institutions

Governments were responsible to a single-chamber parliament, in which most ministers held seats. From 1950, parliament regained its former role as a forum for conflict between the government and opposition parties. But, despite its long tradition, its effectiveness in controlling the executive – particularly by analysing current problems and scrutinising government legislation – remained limited. One example of this limitation was that the 1952 constitution reaffirmed the provision, established in the constitution of 1927, which enabled the government to legislate by decree.[15] Parliaments varied in size from 354 MPs in 1946–50 to 250 in 1950–51, but from 1952 onwards always numbered 300. The electoral system which produced them was regularly manipulated by governments, a practice which continued until 1990. In the 1950s, manipulation was directed against the United Democratic Left (EDA). For example, as late as 1961, the multitude of voters who had moved from villages to towns were disfranchised because the electoral register was based on the census of 1940. In the general elections of 1946 and 1950, the electoral system – dictated by the protector powers – was pure proportional representation (PR), presumably because this promised the fairest result, though predictably it gave no single party a majority of seats. In the 1951 election was adopted the system of 'reinforced PR' (giving additional seats to the leading party or parties). The majority system was adopted once, in 1952; and the 1956 election was held under a mixture of this and PR. From 1958 onwards, some form of reinforced PR prevailed, and usually gave a majority of seats to the leading party, with some representation to minor parties.[16] Electoral manipulation was combined with continuous official pressure in rural areas, which prevented many left-wingers from voting for EDA. So the conduct of elections was far from fair, although it did allow a wide degree of public discussion and competition between parties.

Governmental authority was exercised at the local level by the 52 prefects, who were appointed by the national government, and were responsible for coordinating the work of most government departments, as well as directing public works such as road building, and issuing a range of government licences. They closely supervised the elected local authorities, giving special attention to their finances. These local authorities consisted of 169 municipalities and 5,642 communes and, although valued by the public, had been reduced over many years to a menial status, except for the largest such as that of Athens. In fact no local elections were held between 1934 and 1951; and in the latter year were preceded by careful precautions against the left. Even then about 500 left-wing councillors were arbitrarily dismissed by Papagos's government, an act for which there was precedent before 1936. In general, though, the elections succeeded to some extent in restoring public esteem for local authorities. Thereafter, local elections were held every four years, and their results were treated with increasing respect by national governments.

But local authorities had been stripped of major responsibilites by developments since the 1830s, and especially since the 1890s. As we saw in Chapter Two, some centralising innovations of the Metaxas dictatorship were maintained. The proportion of government revenue which local authorities received was even in the 1980s – by which time some decentralisation had occurred – only about 11 per cent, of which just over one-half was locally collected (by officials of the national government).[17] Only in Portugal, among countries of western Europe, was there by this time a similar degree of centralisation. The responsibility of local government was in the main restricted to a limited range of physical services such as maintenance of local roads and drainage systems, and management of parks and common pastures. About six of the municipalities ran hospitals, and some ran institutions for needy groups such as orphans or unmarried mothers. Although most municipal mayors and commune presidents were locally prominent, their importance derived largely from their position in a chain of centralised authority, and they had to spend much time soliciting funds from the government. Most other authority figures in rural areas were appointees of central authorities: besides the prefects, there were gendarmes, agrarian constabulary (responsible for keeping order and resolving disputes in villages), judges of the Courts of First Instance, officers of the Battalions of National Security, officials of agricultural cooperatives and schoolteachers. Priests were appointed and paid from above, and so in their way they too were official figures, although in their mentality and way of life they tended to be close to their parishioners. In towns the chambers of commerce and trades councils (representing trade unions) were likewise subject to strong government influence. National politicians formed another type of external force, and won support by patronage from a population fragmented by family loyalties. Many older people remembered with nostalgia the vigorous local politics before 1936, which had revived under the auspices of the National Liberation Front in thousands of villages and towns during the German occupation.[18] But politicians' need to retain patronage and suppress dissent were irresistible motives for centralisation of power. Thus national power centres thoroughly penetrated local communities, and prevented the development by their inhabitants of a sense of collective responsibility, and hence of civic consciousness.

Trade unions and agricultural cooperatives

The General Confederation of Greek Workers (GSEE) was from the early 1930s onwards the main union confederation, flanked by the much smaller civil servants' federation, known from 1954 as the Supreme Directorate of Civil Servants' Unions (ADEDY). The GSEE and its affiliated unions consisted of thousands of primary, or base-level bodies, dozens of secondary-level federations and dozens of municipal trades councils. Governments secured the loyalty of a virtual caste of union bosses (whom employees ironically nicknamed 'workers' fathers') by financing their pay, pensions and social security benefits. Elections to the executive of the GSEE, as well as elections of base-level trade unions, union federations and trades councils, were influenced by the police through its trade union branch, and – if they nevertheless went against the government – were invalidated by judges who likewise specialised in trade union matters. Successive governments perpetuated the extreme fragmentation of unions, because small localised unions were easier to control.

Government regulation of collective bargaining was systematised in Law 3239 of 1955, which confined the right of concluding legally binding agreements to the GSEE. While all employees had to pay a levy to unions (collected and dispensed by the government), they were not compelled to become members, which they were in Spain and Portugal. Wage levels were negotiated by the approved unions with employers; and then given legal force by the government. Disputes were settled by compulsory arbitration in tribunals in which the GSEE, certain employers' federations, judges and the Ministry of Labour were represented. Non-wage benefits (including holidays, working hours and even overtime rates) were determined not by collective bargaining but by government decrees. In practice the system worked so as to depress wage levels in accordance with the wishes of conservative governments and employers' interests. Not surprisingly, unions were discredited in the eyes of employees, who resorted increasingly to unofficial strikes in the 1960s.

Workers' power to resist this system was weakened by the fragmentation and paternalistic structure of businesses. Only about one-third of the labour force in the 1950s consisted of employees, the majority of whom worked in small enterprises, a situation which naturally did not lend itself to unionisation. Not more than one-quarter of employees were unionised, with union membership being concentrated in public utilities, the civil service, banks, transport and larger manufacturing enterprises.[19]

Because agricultural cooperatives remained as in the 1930s subject to state control, farmers viewed them as an arm of bureaucracy (see above, p. 51). The Panhellenic Confederation of Unions of Agricultural Cooperatives remained and still is a partner of the Ministry of Agriculture in the implementation of government policy. The partnership had some constructive outcomes, because it was through the cooperatives that the state created large new food-processing industries in the 1960s.[20]

Police measures

Police confidence in the effectiveness of repression and surveillance resulted in the steady decline of political prisoners after the civil war. Excluding an unknown number detained temporarily without charge, there were 17,089 in January 1952, 5,396 in November 1955, and 1,655 in November 1962. By 1967 there were hardly any left in prison, and perhaps a few hundred in detention camps.[21]

Measures against Communism, dating from the 1920s, were maintained with rigour in the 1950s, and relaxed in the mid-1960s, before being reinvigorated by the dictatorship in 1967. Throughout this period a strict apparatus of internal security was maintained. Thus 21,997 people were deprived of their citizenship and 1,722 people were deported to internal exile between 1952 and 1967, some on orders of Security Commissions.[22] In the same period many suspects were sentenced by courts martial; and there seem to have been 70 people in jail under such sentences in 1963, when Georgios Papandreou's government accelerated the process of liberalisation. As a result of police measures, the Communist Party almost ceased to exist as an organised force within the country, and maintained only a surrogate existence through EDA, which was in fact established on Communist initiative and in compliance with Stalin's recommendation. Right-wing governments, acting on shrewd police advice, let EDA exist, partly because it caused Communists to operate in the open where they were conspicuous, partly because it could take support away from the centrist parties.

In Greece, as in Portugal and Spain, police repression stood in inverse ratio to state provision for social welfare. A public prosecutor who participated in Security Commissions later observed that the process of deporting troublemakers without trial to islands served as a cheap substitute for a welfare state.[23]

The government kept in reserve various powers to censor the broadcast and print media. The sole civilian radio station was run by the government as a mouthpiece of the ruling party, with powers of preventive censorship in the hands of the prime minister. Governments favoured friendly newspapers with subsidies or advertisements, and discounts on paper tariffs and postage, while the police hindered left-wing or even centrist newspapers from circulating in rural areas. Journalists might be required by the police to obtain certificates of lawful opinions. Governments occasionally used powers in the penal code to prosecute newspapers of any political colour for allegedly insulting the authorities or causing public alarm. Thus the editor and the publisher of one prominent national newspaper received long jail sentences under Karamanlis's government in 1962 for publishing a scandal about the royal family.[24] On the other hand, the government felt secure enough, even in the 1950s, to allow some freedom of discussion about cultural matters on the radio, and to tolerate even the EDA press in the cities.

Economic interest groups developed little autonomy. Because all farmers, and most manufacturers, retailers and merchants worked in small businesses, they could not assert themselves against the state; and the few large-scale pressure groups could not claim to be representative. Partial exceptions were two business pressure groups: the Greek Shipowners' Union (founded in 1916), and the Federation of Greek Industrialists (founded in 1907 and re-labelled the Federation of Greek Industries in 1979). The former was influential because of its members' immense resources, their readiness to base their operations abroad and their personal contacts with leading politicians. The latter, because of its cohesion and the efficiency of its staff, had much influence in representing larger firms, and until 1962 provided the government with statistics on industrial production. National chambers of commerce were less influential because of divisions among them.

In general, the intellectual climate of the 1950s, and to a lesser extent the 1960s, was characterised by repression and sterility. As in Spain in the 1940s and 1950s, this was a consequence of civil war, because many of the country's intellectuals, having been attracted to the defeated side, were now silenced by exile, censorship or death. The prevalent paranoia about Communism, and the need of the right-wing establishment to defend 'Hellenic-Christian civilisation', discouraged critical discussion in the cultural, social or political spheres. As pointed out by Konstantinos Tsoucalas,[25] the only cultural activities to flourish were those that did not require critical reference to contemporary society: the visual arts, music and poetry. The cultural atmosphere was illustrated in the archaism and aridity of curricula in secondary schools and universities, though these features may not have been more marked than in, say, Portugal or Spain – or even than in Italy where civil liberties were more secure. In all these countries the ideological conservatism of teachers reinforced their professional conservatism, and they were protected by the authoritarianism of teaching institutions. In Greek as in Italian universities, the philosophy and political science curricula terminated in the eighteenth century; and among the social sciences preoccupied with contemporary society, economics alone attained an important status in universities. The history curriculum was devoted to a remote and idealised past – as perhaps in many other western European countries – with the consequence in Greece that the younger generation was denied knowledge of the resistance and civil war. There was no systematic social research until the establishment in 1959 of what became the National Centre of Social Research; and for a long time it was too poorly resourced to produce many reports.[26]

The Communist Party

The culturally oppressive atmosphere of this period can also be attributed to Communist influence. The exiled Communist leaders provided EDA with little inspiration, and instead hindered it by inappropriate orders from afar. They tried in particular to curb the realistic inclination of Communists within EDA to work through constitutional procedures and cooperate with other parties.[27] Isolated in exile, leading Communists suffered more than ever from sectarianism and dogmatism, and quarrelled savagely among themselves. Zachariadis was ousted during the destalinisation process in 1956. He was later exiled to a remote settlement in Siberia where he repeatedly petitioned to be allowed to return to Greece to face trial, and finally committed suicide in 1973. His successor as leader did not adopt any new strategies or ideas, and remained subservient to Soviet policies. Thus the leading Communists failed to adapt their ideas to changes in Greek society, and neglected the western European languages in which was published much of the new socialist thinking relevant to Greek conditions. Their cultural conservatism, which was characteristic of Soviet communism, was illustrated in their condemnation of long hair and casual dress among youth. At a more serious level, it was illustrated by the fact that a basic text of western feminism, Simone de Beauvoir's *The Second Sex*, was not translated into the language of any Soviet satellite country. Meanwhile the status of women in Soviet bloc countries suffered for lack of a feminist movement.[28] Perhaps the greatest damage which the Communist Party did to Greek political life was that it continued to prevent the growth of a social democratic movement suited to the political environment. The feeble attempts in this direction were either undermined by the Communists, or stifled by the anti-communist paranoia of the other parties.

The Church

As in Italy, Portugal and Spain, the Church cooperated with the state in maintaining political legitimacy and social discipline. The Church's official status was reaffirmed in the constitution of 1952, which stated that Orthodox Christianity was an essential part of Greek nationality. It was almost impossible in practice for other denominations legally to seek converts or even open new churches. The Church maintained a monopoly over legitimate marriages or burials; certificates of baptism were a prerequisite for children's admission to school; and Orthodox theology was an obligatory part of primary and secondary school curricula, except in schools catering for the officially recognised Muslim minority in Thrace. Thus there was no system of church-run schools providing general education, as there was in Catholic countries. The Archbishop of Athens and All Greece swore in ministers and officiated at the opening of parliaments. In these respects, the Church's traditional role was reaffirmed, although to it was now added an anti-communist mission, which was furthered by state intervention in the election of successive Archbishops in 1959, 1967 and 1974. The Church for its part had always advocated obedience to established authorities in politics and society as an essential part of its faith, while inculcating an attitude of fatalistic submission to them by its other-worldliness, its abstract discourse and discouragement of critical thought. The Communist Party, because of its loyalty to its Soviet mentors, was plausibly presented by governments and ecclesiastical authorities as a threat to Christian values. These conditions encouraged a passive attitude to contemporary society. What reliable American observers said in 1947 – 'one does not find ecclesiastics trying to grapple with the great social issues' – remained true for long after.[29] The result was that, in the more liberal climate of the 1960s, the Church was slower than its Roman Catholic counterparts in Italy and Spain to distance itself from conservative forces. Some bishops did so, however, in response to brutally provocative actions by the dictatorship of 1967–74.

The numbers of clergy varied with the number of positions which happened to be vacant. The number of bishops was 56 in 1963, and the number of parish priests was 7,150 in 1952. During this period there were perhaps about 2,000 monks and another 2,000 nuns. The Church was governed by a small Holy Synod of bishops elected each year by the general assembly of bishops. The Holy Synod's decisions had to be ratified by the government; and the Church's constitution was subject to the jurisdiction of the secular courts. The Church and the religious movements ran many charitable institutions, which were estimated in the 1990s at 700, with 20,000 staff and inmates combined. They included old people's homes, orphanages, hostels for children living away from home for educational purposes and charitable funds.[30] Thanks to the initiative of many individuals, priests and laymen, religious movements had expanded in the first half of the twentieth century, and now put immense effort into preaching, publication, religious instruction, devotional groups and charities. Although unofficial, the movements were supported by bishops, and from 1945 were coordinated by the Holy Synod. In 1959 the most extensive movement, *Zoï*, organised 2,355 Sunday Schools with 155,487 pupils, as well as 'Circles of Friendship' in which 80,000 adults participated, and issued a newspaper with over 165,000 subscribers, and a magazine for children which ran to 130,000 copies.[31]

Orthodox Christianity was integrally associated with Greek nationality in the minds of most of the population, even those who did not feel themselves to be religious. The familiarity of the public with Christian symbolism and language is to this day constantly evident in newspapers. Opinion polls in the 1970s and 1980s indicate that most people did indeed regard themselves as in some way members of the Church, and attended baptisms, marriages and funerals. Regular church attendance was not such an important manifestation of faith as in Roman Catholic or Protestant societies, and was conventionally seen rather as a woman's duty. As a result, those who attended church frequently (such as every month) seem to have been a small minority. A survey of church attendance on an ordinary Sunday (not a Feast Day) in various provincial regions in 1970–72 revealed percentages varying from 11.6 per cent to 33.5 per cent of adults.

The content and nature of most people's faith is another matter. It seems that tradition and convention rather than religiosity accounted for many people's attendance at church on Feast Days, especially Easter. As in all western countries, an extended revolution was taking place in beliefs and values, as people adopted an increasingly materialistic and scientific view of the world. The clergy was ill-equipped to meet this challenge. The parish priests' influence was weakened by their predominantly peasant background and low educational level: only 12 per cent of them in 1952 had completed secondary education or any kind of theological studies, and only 5 per cent in the 1960s had some sort of tertiary education. Relatively few, especially in rural areas, were qualified even to preach or hear confession. The large theology faculties at the universities of Athens and Salonika made little contribution to public debate about religious issues, or to the intellectual life of the Church.[32] Parish clergy were badly paid even by Greek standards and in a subservient relationship to bishops, who were relatively affluent. In the 1960s the opposition parties advocated an increase in priests' pay, which was accomplished by a reformist government in 1964–65.

Yet in some ways the Church was proving itself a resilient force. The clergy's educational level was rising; and ecclesiastical seminaries like religious movements had expanded greatly since the 1930s. Presumably stimulated by the challenge of Marxism, a general revival of religious activity had been in process for some time, directed towards all social strata, and based in towns but extending into rural areas.[33]

The revival of party politics

The party system

In 1950 the old tri-partite division of politicians between right, centre and left reappeared. Left and right opposed each other on their attitudes to Communism; the American alliance; inequalities of wealth and education; the monarch's power and participatory democracy. Although the centre parties (consisting chiefly of Liberals) took intermediate positions on these issues, the bulk of their members felt closer to the right than to the left. Politics in the 1950s was still overshadowed by the civil war, and so dominated by the division between 'national' and 'democratic' camps.

It took a long time for parties to revive after the damage inflicted since 1936 by dictatorship, invasion and civil war. The political right had united behind the campaign to restore the monarchy in 1946, but then crumbled, mainly through lack of effective leadership. Between the 1950 election and that of September 1951, both right and centre were disunited. Then Papagos pulled the right together so that it formed the basis of stable government from the election of November 1952 to that of November 1963.

In the parliamentary parties of right and centre, by far the largest occupational group consisted of lawyers, followed in order of magnitude by doctors, army officers, public officials and businessmen. Ability to dispense favours so as to win clienteles was an important asset for an MP; and in this respect lawyers and doctors tended to be well qualified.[34] The main right-wing party from 1951 consisted largely of experienced politicians from diverse backgrounds – including some centrists, Metaxists and adherents of the old People's Party – who assembled around Papagos and his successor Karamanlis.

The major parties were handicapped by dependence for survival and cohesion on the influence of individuals with their friends and families. Thus politicians could hold leading positions on the basis of personal connections rather than administrative ability. In fact it needed an outstanding personality to hold together a parliamentary party and to make the normally unwieldy and inert state machine work effectively; and there was a hiatus of such personalities as head of government between the death of Metaxas in 1941 and the accession of Papagos of 1952. Since 1945, the two major parties had been in decay, each relics of the National Schism and led by undistinguished relatives of prewar leaders, the People's Party by Konstantinos Tsaldaris, nephew of the prewar leader, and the Liberal Party since 1949 by Sophocles Venizelos, son of the legendary Elevtherios. Both parties were short of new ideas or young talent, with the conspicuous exception of Karamanlis in the People's Party.

The right

After winning the 1952 election, Papagos maintained iron discipline in his party. After his death in October 1955, Karamanlis, helped by royal and American backing, acquired comparable authority over the party, which became cohesive enough to survive his long-term withdrawal from politics in 1963.

Karamanlis (1907–98) became the most influential and revered political leader of the second half of the century. He was born in a Macedonian village under Ottoman rule, the son of a schoolteacher who became a prosperous tobacco farmer. His birthplace became part of Greece only after the Balkan wars of 1912–13, and then was repeatedly threatened by Bulgarian claims until 1944. After qualifying as a lawyer, Karamanlis entered parliament on behalf of the right during a particularly tumultuous phase of the National Schism in 1935; then, after living for much of the occupation under the shadow of EAM's bid for power, was re-elected to parliament in 1946. He seems to have been one of the few members of the People's Party to show more interest in economic reconstruction than in vendettas against Liberals or Communists. From 1946 to 1955, he successively held ministries responsible for labour, transport, social welfare, defence and public works, and won general acclaim by his ability to get publicly beneficial things done. Seeing that government in Greece required forceful leadership and supervision to work efficiently, he dominated his cabinet, and followed through in detail the implementation of policies. Handsome and dignified in appearance, and austere in speech and manner, he won the devotion of many colleagues and parliamentary followers.[35]

The centre and left

The main competitors for government were the centre groups, which for a long time lacked a leader of comparable authority. The Liberal Party, thanks partly to its power base in Crete and partly to the Venizelos legend, survived under the opportunistic and unstable leadership of Sophocles Venizelos. During the years 1950–61, therefore, the centre was divided between Venizelos and other party chiefs, notably Nikolaos Plastiras and Georgios Papandreou. These divisions, the effects of which were exacerbated by the electoral system, allowed EDA to win a sensationally high vote of 24 per cent in the 1958 general election, and so become for a time the main opposition party.[36] This result alarmed centre and right politicians, who feared renewed polarisation of the electorate on civil war lines. To avoid that prospect and their own destruction, centre politicians managed finally to unite as the Centre Union (EK) under Papandreou one month before the general election of October 1961. Thereafter the EK began its ascent to power.

Papandreou (1886–1968) thus became chief antagonist of the right, although his authority in the EK never approached that of Karamanlis in his party. He was perhaps the most seasoned of politicians. After obtaining a postgraduate degree abroad, like several other prime ministers in the twentieth century, he started his career in 1915 as a provincial governor appointed by Elevtherios Venizelos. Then, as Venizelos's lieutenant, he took a prominent part in the tumultuous early phase of the National Schism in 1916–22, at one time being imprisoned. He distinguished himself as a reforming Minister of Education in Venizelos's government of 1928–32. Appointed by the British as head of the government-in-exile in April 1944, he provided inspiring and decisive leadership to the national camp during the following eight months when the country seemed likely to be taken over by EAM. While strongly opposing Communism for the rest of his life, he also grasped the need for radical social reform. However he lacked significant organised support among politicians, and so was forced by his violent break with EAM in December 1944 to resign as prime minister. In the 1960s, his gift for inspirational and demagogic oratory found ample scope; but, because of his egoistic and reserved character, he did not have Karamanlis's capacity to inspire personal devotion from politicians, so that his circle of confidants remained restricted.

Of the two major parties, only the EK began to evolve towards a modern party structure, in the sense of a mass organisation with formal provisions for membership, professional cadres, national conventions and formal procedures for the succession of leaders. Only in the larger cities, and mainly on the side of the EK, were there stable organisations at constituency level, and only there did most election candidates have to rely heavily on the appeal of the national leader and his programme. In the rural and small-town environment in which the majority of voters still lived, candidates relied primarily on their personal influence and individual resources of patronage. So they had much independence in relations with the leader.

In the 1960s, Papandreou saw the need to appeal to a growing urban electorate, and so tried to organise the EK both on vertical lines (central to local) and on horizontal lines (in occupational, women's and youth groups). All that he really succeeded in doing was create youth organisations. However the parliamentary party's cohesion was reinforced increasingly by pressure on MPs from partisan voters as the political temperature rose. The views of the major parties were propagated by newspapers, most of which were partisan and dependent on politicians for information.

By contrast with parties of the centre and the right, EDA had from the start the features of a modern organisation with a distinct ideology. By the 1960s it had about 70,000 members, nearly 250 local branches, a flourishing youth organisation, and two national daily newspapers. So little did it depend on personal influence that its leading members were not particularly well known. This feature had been shared by EAM, and could be attributed to the fact that both bodies were directed from behind the scenes – EDA more indirectly and loosely than EAM – by the Communist Party. Its control of EDA was no secret, and made obvious for example in the attitude towards it of the Communist 'Radio Free Greece'.

During the 1950s, the right and centre parties were vague about their ideological and programmatic disagreements. Nor did they differ clearly from each other in their electoral support and social composition. As the political scientist Jean Meynaud observed, the centre and right parties really represented different versions of conservatism, liberal and traditional. The place of the centre had in northern Europe been taken long before by social democratic parties with distinct ideologies and social bases; but such a party had not appeared in Greece, partly because the potential trade union base was too weak, and partly because of Communist competition.[37] So the real ideological division lay between the bourgeois parties and EDA, and it was essentially the same confrontation that had existed since 1945, with adaptations to the later Cold War scene. EDA had prominent aims which differentiated it from the other parties: disarmament, détente in the Cold War and withdrawal from NATO.

The establishment under attack

Changing social environment

The establishment was vulnerable for various reasons, once anti-communist paranoia began to decline. Opposition to it was facilitated by population movements and economic growth. The poorer farming population, which could be controlled by patronage or intimidation, was declining; while the city population, which formed a basis for radical movements and new forms of political action, was growing. As in the rest of western Europe, improved communications and rising educational levels, combined with a rise in living standards, enabled those hitherto repressed to assert themselves politically and economically.[38] Economic development required expansion of the education system, and so caused an increase in professionals and students, who were especially ready to criticise the authorities. Economic development also concentrated employees geographically, and increased their bargaining power as labour shortages began to be felt in some sectors. The proportion of literates in the adult population was as we saw rising. The proportion of the population exposed to broadcasting (on the assumption of four listeners per radio) rose from 15.7 per cent in 1953 to 45.2 per cent in 1967. In Greece, as in Italy, the development of mass communications enabled the political parties to extend their influence through modern forms of organisation.

Economic want and social inequality remained prominent in the minds of a majority of voters. Opinion polls asked voters in the metropolitan area, in 1958 and again in early 1967, what was for them the main political issue. The percentage which named a combination of economic growth, improvement in the standard of living, and price stability, was 47 in 1958 and – after ten years of rapid economic growth and price stability – still as high as 42 in 1967. The percentage that named unemployment and jobs was 20 in 1958 and 17 in 1967.[39] The mounting attacks that were made in the 1960s on various aspects of the power structure were largely driven, therefore, by economic needs and anxieties. Given the Greek tradition of vigorous party politics, it was understandable that the attacks and the response to them should be made through political parties. As Nicos Mouzelis pointed out, there appeared in Greece an explosive combination: the extreme social inequality that normally accompanies rapid industrialisation fuelled by foreign investment, combined with long traditions of vigorous party politics and also of revolutionary communism.[40]

A turning point was the fraudulent parliamentary election of 1961. The directors of the fraud were a group of army officers, appointed by the general staff and cooperating with the police, in what was code-named the 'Pericles Plan'. Their aim was to reverse EDA's gains in 1958. The conspirators acted on behalf of the ruling party, the ERE, and they worked partly through vigilante groups and the village militia. Since the civil war, the establishment, in order to achieve international acceptance and internal stability, had avoided flagrant intimidation, relying rather on silent pressure to influence election results. Now the fraud was more open, as it had been in the election and referendum of 1946.[41] According to the psephologist Ilias Nikolakopoulos, 5 per cent of rural voters were forced to switch their support from left to right. It seems that over 100,000 right-wing voters were illegally enrolled in the metropolitan area (in one case 218 police giving the same small house as their residence). Organised intimidation by vigilantes led to the killing of two left supporters.

The unrelenting struggle

The fatal miscalculation of the Pericles Plan was that it provoked what was about to become the main opposition party, the EK, given that many voters were ready to transfer support between it and the left, and given that vigilantes were not selective. Thus the election victory of the right was pyrrhic, because after it the centre and left campaigned furiously to reverse it; and, despite their mutual distrust, attacked the same targets. They demanded a new and fair election, and an end to the establishment's least defensible practices: favouritism to big capitalists, especially foreign investors; deference to American wishes in foreign policy and other matters; appointment of former wartime collaborators to prominent positions; repression of the left through harsh security measures; and maintenance of glaring social inequalities.

Best known now by Papandreou's name 'unrelenting struggle', the campaign was waged on various fronts until the general election of November 1963: public assemblies across the country aroused by Papandreou's fiery oratory; student demonstrations; industrial action which included political demands; constant attacks through parliament and the press. On occasion, tens of thousands of demonstrators in the capital surrounded police cordons protecting central districts. The police sometimes reacted violently, so causing several deaths over time. The best known fatality (featuring in the internationally famous film Z of 1969 directed by Costa Gavras) was the murder of an EDA deputy, Grigoris Lambrakis, at a rally in Salonika in May 1963. This murder was perpetrated by vigilantes in a counter-demonstration covertly organised by the police. The funeral was attended by over half a million people, and the incident inspired the organisation by the left of a national youth movement, named after Lambrakis, with the famous Communist composer Mikis Theodorakis as its leader. The Lambrakis movement achieved a membership of over 40,000, and took a prominent part in popular politics in the following three years.

By these means the opposition parties discredited Karamanlis's government, and with it monarchical influence, in the eyes of much of the electorate. As the confrontation between the two major parties intensified, their cohesion and influence increased; so that in the elections of 1963 and 1964 they secured the great majority of votes. Meanwhile the participation in voting by the registered electorate rose by 6 per cent between the general election of 1958 and that of 1964; and the circulation of newspapers rose to record heights. While the EK gained strength as an alternative party of government with a charismatic leader, EDA declined because it had neither of these assets, and was hampered by Communist direction.

Opposition to the right-wing establishment also came from militant employees. After resting at a low level in the 1950s, strike activity rose until in 1966 the number of strikers was eight times that of 1959, and the number of hours lost in strikes was twelve times higher.[42] The reasons for this dramatic change were the increased bargaining power of labour, and the growing public repudiation of police repression, which caused a reaction against the low wages that had hitherto prevailed. The same process occurred at much the same time in Italy, Portugal and Spain.[43] An illustration of the process in February 1967 was the National General Collective Agreement of Labour which secured a 20 per cent wage increase for unskilled workers.

Moreover employees rebelled increasingly against legal restraints on industrial action. The proportion of strikes which included demands for greater trade union rights and political liberalisation tended to increase, and action by various categories of workers led to bloody clashes with police. Industrial action spread to broader categories of the workforce, starting with construction workers, spreading to other industrial workers, then to employees in major public utilities (where strikes were illegal), and farmers. Action by the last was not included in strike figures, and included mass demonstrations in country towns and the withholding of produce. All these demands formed in effect tributaries of the 'unrelenting struggle', and were partially satisfied by Papandreou's governments of 1964–65.

One stimulus to challenges against the right-wing establishment was the Cyprus issue, and another was the students' movement, which became more organised and militant from the late 1950s. The close relationship between educational qualifications and the political spoils system made government educational policies intensely controversial. Therefore movements for greater equality of opportunity focused on the educational system, especially on access to its higher levels. There was intense competition among secondary school students to qualify for university entrance; and, to enable them to do so, cramming schools flourished. But students showed less interest in the quality of the education offered than in its accessibility, this irresponsibility being due to prolonged authoritarian control by governments and teachers. Accordingly, from 1956, there was a continual student campaign for fee reduction at the tertiary level. This campaign later focused also on the demand that 15 per cent of the budget be spent on education. The students' associations were dominated by the opposition parties; and the mass demonstrations which they organised led periodically to clashes with the police.

Georgios Papandreou in power

The 'unrelenting struggle' deterred the king and right-wing politicians from repeating the electoral fraud of 1961. Thus the centre and left entered the election of November 1963 under relatively fair conditions, and with the impetus generated by two years of mass mobilisation. Papandreou boosted his party's appeal with promises to alleviate a range of social and political injustices. Meanwhile the king and queen had forced the resignation of Karamanlis in June 1963, in effect treating him as a scapegoat for the 1961 election. Karamanlis's successor as prime minister, and as leader of the ERE, Panagiotis Kanellopoulos, was widely respected for decency of character and showed strong concern for the stability of democratic institutions, but did not have Karamanlis's authority over voters or his party.

Perhaps for all these reasons, the election produced a dramatic swing towards the EK of 12 per cent or more, which gave Papandreou, with EDA's help, a parliamentary majority just large enough to enable him to form a government and lay his vote-catching programme before parliament, before going to the polls again in February 1964. This time he had authority over the police and the state administration. The EK achieved a further swing of nearly 12 per cent, giving it 171 seats out of 300. Its gains were especially large in more prosperous agricultural regions, where police control was much weakened, and it encroached also on left-wing votes, especially in lower middle-class areas. The ERE was reduced to greater reliance on prosperous middle-class urban districts and the poorest rural areas. Much of its electoral base had been destroyed.[44]

While in power, in 1964–65, Papandreou's government consolidated its electoral support by overdue reforms. It catered for lower socio-economic strata by increasing farmers' pensions and prices of agricultural produce; increased wages of large categories of workers; and made the system of election in the General Confederation of Greek Workers fairer. It abolished fees for universities and secondary schools; increased the intake into universities; and appointed many additional university teachers. The period of compulsory education was extended from six to nine years; primary education was to be conducted completely in demotic, which was also to be equal in status to the official *katharevousa* in secondary schools; and a free meal service was provided at primary level. At secondary level, new subjects were to be introduced, including sociology and economics, while modern languages were given more emphasis. Educational expenditure increased by over one-third in one year, and by 1967 accounted for 11.6 per cent of the budget.

The government relaxed police measures in various ways including the release of most remaining political prisoners, except those sentenced by courts martial. It also dissolved many anti-communist vigilante groups.

The breakdown of parliamentary government

The July events

What brought down the government was conflict with the king over control of the armed forces. Papandreou was regarded by the king's followers, the army and the ERE as a threat to the whole political system. So they all conspired against him. Papandreou initially appointed a Minister of National Defence who enjoyed the king's confidence and who in turn appointed senior officers loyal to the king. But relations with the king worsened as Papandreou fell out with politically active officers, who used their contacts with right-wing politicians and the king's entourage to accuse him of politicising the officer corps and the Central Intelligence Service (KYP). They also accused the government of encouraging a political association among officers known as *Aspida* (Shield), and claimed that Papandreou's son Andreas, a junior minister in his government, was involved in it. Georgios Papandreou retaliated against several politically active officers by transferring them to distant posts, or retiring them or blocking their promotions.

American representatives initially restrained Papandreou's changes in military appointments. But they lost their moderating influence after becoming estranged from him over the Cyprus issue, and so could not avert the clash which broke out between Papandreou and the king, when Papandreou asked that he himself be appointed Minister of National Defence as a preliminary to removing the Chief of General Staff. The king demurred on the grounds that Andreas was under investigation for alleged involvement in *Aspida*, and sacked the prime minister on 15 July 1965.

The stormy consequences are known as the *Ioulianá* (the July events). For several weeks there were hundreds of demonstrations, some on a massive scale, as well as a general strike, and many other strikes with political overtones. Over the following twenty months or so the demonstrations subsided, but tension remained high, so that many hundreds of people were injured and several killed in clashes with police. Coinciding with increasing economic militance by workers and farmers, these events gave conservatives the impression of a general breakdown of order. The survival of the monarchy was inevitably at issue, even though Papandreou and EDA were prudent enough to avoid raising it.

Meanwhile the king struggled – apparently using his own funds – to seduce MPs from Papandreou's party to support a government loyal to himself. MPs were under such strong pressure from their own voters that they needed large bribes, such as ministerial office, to succumb; but eventually 45 'apostates' did so. The king failed, however, to end the sense of crisis which was discrediting the whole political system. Another cause of tension was that a senior and openly right-wing public prosecutor, in 1967, sentenced fifteen officers for participation in *Aspida*, which it now appears was harmless. He then sought to investigate the role in it of Andreas Papandreou, who had parliamentary immunity.

To restore stable parliamentary government, Georgios Papandreou and Kanellopoulos agreed with the king in December 1966 that a general election be held not later than May 1967. Papandreou promised not to seek EDA support for his government; and the two politicians presumably promised to keep the king's powers out of debate. The electoral result that was generally expected was a large majority for Papandreou, which would humiliate the king and threaten the military conspirators' jobs. The conspirators prevented this outcome by a coup on 21 April 1967.

The military coup

Since 1961, it seems that the great majority of officers had become restive as they lost confidence in the crown and saw the establishment crumble. Andreas Papandreou contributed much to the tension after July 1965 by inflammatory attacks on the whole establishment, so undermining his father's promises of moderation. Andreas attracted to his support 41 MPs of the EK, and acted with increasing independence of his ageing father, whom he seemed likely to succeed soon as party leader. Even so, most right-wing politicians believed that they could deal with the Papandreou family's challenge by constitutional means.

By 1967 many in the establishment knew of plans for a military coup. The Chief of the General Staff, Grigorios Spandidakis, and his colleagues eventually decided to ask the king to activate the old NATO-approved plan to seize power and, in response, the king vacillated until it was too late. On learning of their superiors' move, a group of middle-ranking officers (mainly colonels), had decided to activate the plan themselves.

They were determined and seasoned conspirators. Possibly all belonged to IDEA, and at least some belonged to its offshoot of 1958 the Union of Young Greek Officers (EENA). The key figure was Colonel Georgios Papadopoulos (1919–99), and two other prominent conspirators were Nikos Makarezos and Sylianos Pattakos. Papadopoulos had graduated first in his year from Military Academy in 1940, just before participating with distinction as an artillery officer in the war against Italy in 1940–41. He opposed the left during the German occupation, and participated in the later stage of the civil war. He then held successive posts vital to his main preoccupation: conspiracy designed to ensure that control of the state remained securely in anti-communist hands. Joining the Central Intelligence Service (KYP) in the 1950s, he became chief of national security and counter-intelligence, and subsequently the commander of an artillery unit. Officers of the KYP worked continuously with the Central Intelligence Agency (CIA). The CIA, like the American diplomatic service, knew about the conspiracies, and warned their participants to desist.[45] Having been entrusted by the general staff with a key role in the Pericles Plan of 1961, Papadopoulos was prominent in conspiring against Papandreou's government. He, Makarezos and Pattakos were late in 1965 appointed to key posts in or near the capital by Spandidakis. Papadopoulos himself was appointed in 1966 deputy chief of operations in the Army General Staff, a position from which he could launch a coup. So he and his colleagues made their preparations with thoroughness born of long experience.

Notes

1 Nicos C. Alivizatos, *The Institutions of Greece during Crises, 1922–74* (in French, Paris 1979), 146–7, 197–201; Jean Meynaud, *Political Forces in Greece* (Greek translation, n.d.), 70–1, 263, 270–1, 352.

2 Alexis Papachelas, *The Rape of Greek Democracy. The American Factor, 1947–67* (in Greek, 1998), 35, 39.

3 Stavros B. Thomadakis, 'Notes on Greek–American economic relations', in Theodore A. Couloumbis and John O. Iatrides (eds), *Greek American Relations. A Critical Review* (New York 1980), 77–8.

4 John O. Iatrides, 'Greece and the United States: the strained partnership', in Richard Clogg (ed.), *Greece in the 1980s* (1983), 152.

5 Papachelas, *Rape*, 87, 93, 115, 239.

6 Ibid., 239.

7 W.H. McNeill, *Greece: American Aid in Action, 1947–56* (New York 1957), 152–4; Martin Clark, *Italy, 1871–1982* (1984), 338; Hubert R. Gallagher, 'Administrative reorganization in the Greek crisis', *Public Administration Review* 8 (1948), 253.

8 *Vima*, 21 November 1999, A50–1, Ioanna Mandrou.

9 (New York 1992).

10 Gallagher, 'Administrative reorganisation', 253–6; Kalliope Spanou, 'Elections and public administration. The electoral activation of clientelist mechanisms within the administration', in Christos Lyrintzis and Ilias Nikolakopoulos (eds), *Elections and Parties in the 1980s. Developments and Prospects of the Political System* (in Greek, 1990), 193.

11 Nancy Bermeo, 'Greek public enterprise: some historical and comparative perspectives', *Modern Greek Studies Yearbook* 6 (1990), 3.

12 *State, Society, Work in Postwar Greece* (in Greek, 1987), 88–91.

13 *Kathimerini*, 22 October 2000, 19, Georgiou Velli.

14 Nicos C. Alivizatos, 'The presidency, parliament, and the courts in the 1980s', in Richard Clogg (ed.), *Greece, 1981–9. The Populist Decade* (New York 1993), 68–9, 70–2; Rousos Koundouros, *The Security of the State* (in Greek, 1978), 154–60; Pavlos Delaporta, *Notebook of a Pilate* (in Greek, 1977), 246–7.

15   Nicos C. Alivizatos, 'The difficulties of "rationalization" in a polarized political system: the Greek Chamber of Deputies', in Ulrika Liebert and Maurizio Cotta (eds), *Parliament and Democratic Consolidation in Southern Europe. Greece, Italy, Portugal, Spain, and Turkey* (1990), 131–3; P. Nikiforos Diamandouros, 'Politics and constitutionalism in Greece: the 1975 constitution in historical perspective', in Houchang E. Chehabi, Juan J. Linz and Alfred Stepan, *Politics, Society and Democracy* (1995), 283–6.

16   Richard Clogg, *Parties and Elections in Greece. The search for legitimacy* (1987), 193–4.

17   *Vima*, 21 October 1990, D1; Rallis Gekas, 'The new relationship of central and local government', *Greek Review of Political Science* 15 (in Greek, 2000), 76; Ernestine Friedl, *Vasilika. A Village in Modern Greece* (New York 1962), 95–6.

18   Frank Smothers, William H. and Elizabeth McNeill, *Report on the Greeks* (New York 1948), 148; Alkis Rigos, *The Second Greek Republic, 1924–35* (in Greek, 1988), 298–9; Anna Collard, 'Researching "social memory" in the Greek case', in Evthymios Papataxiarchis and Theodoros Paradellis (eds), *Anthropology and the Past. Contributions to the Social History of Modern Greece* (in Greek, 1993), 365–72.

19   Theodore K. Katsanevas, *Trade Unions in Greece. An Analysis of Factors Determining their Growth and Present Structure* (Athens 1984), 87–246; Stella Zabarloukou, *State and Labour Unionism in Greece, 1936–90. A Comparative Approach* (in Greek, 1997), 58–96; Kostas A. Lavdas, *The Europeanization of Greece. Interest Politics and the Crises of Integration* (1997), 82–3, 91–2.

20   Adamantia Pollis, 'US intervention in Greek trade unions, 1949–50', in John O. Iatrides (ed.), *Greece in the 1940s. A Nation in Crisis* (1981), 264–73; John Campbell and Philip Sherrard, *Modern Greece* (1968), 353–5; Neil Collins and Leonidas Louloudis, 'Protecting the protected: the Greek agricultural policy network', *Journal of European Public Policy* 2 (1995), 100–2.

21   David H. Close, 'The legacy' in David H. Close (ed.), *The Greek Civil War, 1943–50. Studies of Polarization* (1993), 218–9.

22   Koundouros, *Security*, 41.

23   Delaporta, *Notebook*, 246–7.

24   Thimios Zaharopoulos and Manny Paraschos, *The Mass Media in Greece: power, politics, and privatization* (Westport, CT 1993), 23–32.

25   *The Greek Tragedy* (1969), 114–20.

26   Jane Lambiri-Dimaki, 'Sociology in Greece: trends and prospects', *South European Society and Politics* 1 (1996), 123–4; Maria Petmesidou, 'Higher education and the social sciences in Greece', *International Sociology* 13 (1998), 369–70; Koula Kassimati, 'Development of social research in Greece', *International Sociology* 13 (1998), 346–7.

27 E. Demertzis, 'Factionalism in the Greek Communist Party' (PhD dissertation, New York University 1979), 150–1.

28 Sylvie de Chaperon, 'De Beauvoir in Retrospect', *Le Monde Diplomatique*, January 1999, 13.

29 Smothers, McNeill and McNeill, *Report*, 144; Vasiliki Georgiadou, 'Secular State and Orthodox Church', in Christos Lyrintzis, Ilias Nikolakopoulos and Dimitris Sotiropoulos (eds), *Society and Politics: Aspects of the Third Greek Republic, 1974–94* (in Greek, 1996), 270.

30 *Vima*, 13 July 1997, A42, Bishop Nektarios; *Kathimerini*, 18 May 1997, 30, Spyros Alexiou; Haris Symeonidou, 'Social protection in contemporary Greece', *South European Society and Politics* 1 (1996), 82–3.

31 Jean Meynaud, *Political Forces*, 358–9; Christoforos Vernadakis and Giannis Mavris, *Parties and Social Alliances in Pre-Dictatorship Greece* (in Greek, 1991), 170; Kallistos Ware, 'The Church: a time of transition', in Clogg (ed.), *Greece*, 222–3; Theofanis G. Stavrou, 'The Orthodox Church and political culture in modern Greece', in Dimitri Constas and Theofanis G. Stavrou (eds), *Greece Prepares for the Twenty-first Century* (Baltimore, MD 1995), 50; Peter Hammond, *The Waters of Marah. The Present State of the Greek Church* (1956), 123–38.

32 Ware, 'The Church', in Clogg (ed.), *Greece*, 218–19; Nikiforos Diamandouros, 'Greek political culture in transition: historical origins, evolution, current trends', in Clogg (ed.), *Greece*, 57; Charles A. Frazee, 'Church and State in Greece', in John T.A. Koumoulides (ed.), *Greece in Transition. Essays in the History of Modern Greece, 1821–1974* (1977), 146.

33 Renée Hirschon, *Heirs of the Greek Catastrophe. The Social Life of Asia Minor Refugees in Piraeus* (Oxford 1998), chapter 9; Hammond, *Waters*, 132, 144.

34 Meynaud, *Political Forces*, 314–15.

35 C.M. Woodhouse, *Karamanlis. The Restorer of Greek Democracy* (Oxford 1982), 32–3, 53–6, 101.

36 Ilias Nikolakopoulos, *Parties and Parliamentary Elections in Greece, 1946–64* (in Greek, 1985), 242, 249.

37 Meynaud, *Political Forces*, 318–29.

38 Nicholas A. Michas, 'Economic development, social mobilisation, and the growth of public expenditures in Greece', *American Journal of Economics and Sociology* 39 (1980), 31–48.

39 Vernadakis and Mavris, *Parties*, 135.

40 *Politics in the Semi-Periphery. Early Parliamentarism and Late Industrialisation in the Balkans and Latin America* (1986), 121.

41 Nikolakopoulos, *Parties*, 255–81.

42 Vernadakis and Mavris, *Parties*, 146–58.

43 Giovanni Arrighi, 'Fascism to democratic socialism', in Giovanni Arrighi (ed.), *Semiperipheral Development: the Politics of Southern Europe in the Twentieth Century* (1985), 272–3.

44 Vernadakis and Mavris, *Parties*, 223–30; Nikolakopoulos, *Parties*, 305.

45 Thanos Veremis, 'Greece: veto and impasse, 1967–74', in Christopher Clapham and George Philip (eds), *The Political Dilemmas of Military Regimes* (1985), 32; Papachelas, *Rape*, 82, 90, 104, 237, 278, 296.

CHAPTER SIX

Military Dictatorship, 1967–1974

The nature of the regime

Establishing power

In the early hours of 21 April 1967 the conspirators won over their patron Spandidakis who gave orders to activate the NATO plan. Then, confronting the king with a *fait accompli*, they prevailed on him to appoint a puppet government, while real power lay thenceforth with Papadopoulos. During the day, prominent politicians were arrested and several senior military figures were deprived of their commands. In the following weeks, several thousand people were put under house arrest, or jailed or deported to prison islands.

The speed with which the political ferment of the previous few years was silenced, and the duration of the dictatorship, must be explained largely by the authoritarian and centralised nature of the political system before the coup. The strength of support for anti-communist institutions and authoritarian methods among a range of elite groups – officers, judges, civil servants, professors and bishops – provided dictators with many potential collaborators.

Under the dictatorship (known usually in Greece as the Junta), the powers which the police already used against communists were turned against other dissidents; and the police were flanked by the National Military Security (ESA) under one of the military conspirators, Colonel Dimitrios Ioannidis. Budgetary allocations to all branches of security were much increased. Those to the Ministry of Public Security alone, which was responsible for the civil police, rose by 40 per cent in two years, while much of the greatly increased budget of the armed forces was evidently allocated to police work.

The Junta ousted and replaced many leading figures in each of the institutions under direct or indirect state control: the armed forces, police, civil service, judiciary, universities, schools, the Church, as well as those institutions previously subject to popular election: local authorities, the trade unions and agricultural cooperatives. Over 2,700 army officers (more than one-third of those on the active list) were retired for political reasons by April 1972. The king, after an ill-prepared attempt at a military coup in December 1967, fled the country.

Some of the purged institutions deserve more attention. Universities were subject to direct police control, which included the regular auditing of lectures.[1] In the end, nearly one-third of teaching staff were dismissed, and most of the rest avoided any suggestion of political criticism. They were directed to keep to a minimum the number of foreign books in reading lists; and ensure that classes were conducted entirely in *katharevousa*. The proportion of secondary school leavers proceeding to higher education fell sharply.

The Church's constitution was arbitrarily changed, and the Archbishop of Athens was replaced by the militantly anti-communist Ieronimos, who was chaplain to the king and head of the religious brotherhood *Zoï*. Under Ieronimos, 33 bishops were replaced. But in December 1973, Ieronimos himself retired after losing political favour, being replaced by another militant anti-communist, who took the title Serapheim. He was a former participant in the main anti-communist resistance group during the German occupation, led by Napoleon Zervas (see above, p. 28); and his decisive asset was friendship with another ex-member of the same group, Ioannidis, who dominated the dictatorship from November 1973. Under Serapheim, twelve more bishops were forced into retirement. These events created lasting divisions in the Church, and damaged its reputation for long after the dictatorship.

Among trade unions, the limited trend towards emancipation during the 1960s was thrown into reverse. The property of those bodies dominated by left-wing executives, which as a rule were outside the GSEE, was confiscated. It seems that grass-roots (or first-tier) bodies, and bodies at the level above them, were dissolved. Those that remained were largely subservient to the regime, and rendered incapable of strikes or other resistance.[2]

The presence of the police was felt everywhere. Political surveillance of the population had declined markedly during the 1960s, but was suddenly extended again. The keeping of files on suspects was massively increased, as was the pressure on a wide range of government agencies and employers to ensure that political suspects could not earn a livelihood. Informers were active in government departments, trade union cells and even among emigrant communities. Political discussions in public – or for that matter over the phone or by mail – were generally regarded as risky. So were organised discussion groups of any sort unless they had police permission.

The torture of political prisoners was evidently widespread, and in some cases resulted in death. Rumours of brutalities were welcomed by the regime, as a means of discouraging dissent, and so contributed to the general atmosphere of fear.

The Junta's severity was, however, restrained by deference to western opinion, and especially by its desire to keep American support. Thus Andreas Papandreou was eventually allowed to leave the country; while the irrepressible plotter Alekos Panagoulis, who was caught after trying single-handedly to blow up Papadopoulos, and then caught again after escaping from jail, was spared execution. The number of political prisoners, detainees and exiles declined after a few years, as the regime felt more secure, but still seems to have been over one thousand in 1971.[3]

Values and supporters

The nature of the dictatorship invites comparison with that of Metaxas in 1936–41, which it resembled, because at least twelve out of fifteen leading members of the Junta had been through officers' training academy under that regime. Metaxas, however, possessed qualifications which the colonels sorely lacked: assured social status, a king's confidence, broad intellectual interests, refined cultural tastes, experience in leading roles as a staff officer and politician, and a sense of political vision. The values which Papadopoulos and his fellow-conspirators tried during seven years to impose – summed up in hackneyed slogans about country, religion, family and communist iniquities – had hardly changed since the conspirators' formative years in the 1930s and 1940s. Their training in military academy, like that in other countries, had been brutal, and the political ideas which they imbibed there were crude and dogmatic.

The anti-communism which they inherited from that period was still obsessive: 'the blood [of the civil war] is still fresh', said an officer to one interviewer. Even centrist politicians with a strong anti-communist record, like Georgios Papandreou, were suspect because they had done electoral deals with EDA. The officers supporting the Junta still believed vividly in the reality of a slav communist peril from the north, even while the government improved diplomatic relations with Balkan countries.[4] Anti-communism was indeed a fixed mentality – impervious to the facts – among the whole right-wing establishment before the coup: the king for example had referred in a speech in January 1967 to the virus of communism, when he should have been thinking about the virus of military conspiracy. So it was natural that the Junta should refer to a communist plot as a pretext for the coup, though they never found a trace of one.

The puritanical and provincial values of the regime were imposed in absurd ways. Among the most ridiculed was a ban on miniskirts for women and long hair for men, the latter made sillier by the fact that long hair had always been required of men in religious orders. The censorship of publications resulted in many strange decisions: any reference to Russia or to historical revolutions was likely to be vetoed.[5] Imaginative writers and artists responded to the new regime by going collectively on strike: literary periodicals and the literature columns of newspapers, for example, ceased to appear for about three years. When they began to reappear, after the relaxation of censorship, the numerous works containing veiled criticisms of the regime were enthusiastically received.

In schools, the regime promoted its values by for example ordering church parades on Sundays, and flag-raising ceremonies each morning; while forbidding mixed-sex social events. The effects of these measures on children were of course the opposite of those intended. More seriously, the regime annulled most of Papandreou's educational reforms. About 2,500 primary schools in remote villages were closed; the pay and conditions of teachers declined; and the share of the budget devoted to education cut from 11.3 per cent in 1967 to 9.2 per cent in 1972.[6] These measures typified the regime's anachronistic character. Its policies were opposed in every sphere to the requirements of modernisation: in political organisation, economic policy, education, industrial relations and gender relations.

The officers' values are partly explicable by their social origins. Looking at the fathers of the leading fifteen plotters, we find that five were farmers (only one of these relatively well off), eight were petty bourgeois (including one priest and two primary schoolteachers), one a labourer and one unknown. The four most powerful conspirators were brought up in villages and scorned the old political and administrative elites. In their modest and provincial backgrounds the conspirators were fairly typical of the whole officer corps.[7]

The people whom the dictatorship appointed to ministries and to leading administrative posts were derived mainly from the upper and middling ranks of the traditional establishment, consisting of civil servants, judges, lawyers, professors, economists and officers. The mass promotion of middle-ranking people in the armed forces and the civil service provided the Junta with grateful supporters. To some extent it served a useful purpose. For example, there had been a serious promotion blockage in the officer corps: an after-effect of its expansion in the late 1940s, followed by a decline in military expenditure during the 1960s. The deficiency of the new elites was lack of aptitude for and experience in leading positions, a weakness shared by members of the Junta. Constantine Danopoulos, in his interviews with civil servants during the regime,[8] perceived a breakdown of relations between them and their masters. The civil servants saw the ministers' objectives as unrealistic and ill-defined, and withheld information from them; while the ministers tried to secure their compliance by intimidation and spying.

Another deficiency of the senior administrators was that they were unrepresentative. They included very few politicians of any ability, or businessmen, or members of agricultural cooperatives or trade unions. In these respects again, the Junta differed from the Metaxas regime. These deficiencies reflected another basic weakness of the regime, which was its shortage of talent, because many people with necessary qualifications and experience were unwilling to work for it.

A different source of power was American support, which became obvious soon after the coup. After initially suspending arms supplies, the American government soon resumed them, despite continued Congressional criticism of the regime. America's economic dominance was so much weaker than in the early 1950s that its government could no longer insist that its satellites be democratic. Meanwhile, various developments in the late 1960s increased the value of the Greek alliance. The Soviet Union, now a naval power in the Mediterranean, took advantage of the tension in Cyprus and the Arab–Israeli war (which broke out in June 1967), to increase its influence in the region. In September 1969, a coup in Libya led to the loss of the American bases there. The United States now needed naval facilities in Greece, which were granted by the Junta in 1972, so that the metropolitan coastline provided a 'home port' to the American navy. The Junta also showed itself to be an enthusiastic ally in NATO by permitting more frequent military exercises on Greek soil.[9]

Awareness of American backing made much of the public temporarily resigned to the coup. What also contributed to this mood was the political turmoil before April 1967, which for a time made it difficult for many to feel enthusiastic about a return to parliamentary politics.

The fall of the dictatorship

Underlying weaknesses

The regime could not, however, remedy its lack of legitimacy. It showed deference to parliamentary tradition by promising repeatedly, throughout its life, to restore democratic rule, and so fed public expectations. Moreover it was too dependent on foreign investment and US backing to try creating an ultra-nationalist movement as fascist parties had done. In these two respects, as Mouzelis has shown, it resembled the contemporary military dictatorships in two other countries that could be described as economically semi-peripheral to the advanced industrialised countries: Chile and Argentina. Where it differed from them is that it could not claim to be protecting capitalist or landowning classes against radical social reform.[10]

Thus its support base was fragile. It is significant that the overwhelming majority of politicians and their supporters, on all points of the spectrum except the extreme right, opposed the regime. Consequently it arrested many right-wing politicians among others, so differing again from contemporary Latin American dictatorships.[11] The extent of opposition was due to the complete lack of justification for the coup. Still less than before Metaxas's coup in 1936 was there any sense of economic or social crisis. The buoyancy of the economy before the coup was indicated by a high rate of investment, and by the proliferation of new businesses. The extent of opposition to the regime was manifested by the attendance of several hundred thousand people at Georgios Papandreou's funeral in November 1968, which became in effect a mass demonstration for return to democracy. The Junta's reliance on repression was bound to cause increasing resentment in a country accustomed to vigorous debate. Also relevant was the traditional importance in politics of favours, or *rousfetia*. Dictatorships in Greece in the twentieth century have provoked much resentment by confining spoils to a relatively limited set of people, which the Junta did, despite its promise to clean up the political system.

The Junta strove to win popularity in various ways. One was a large increase in expenditure on promoting sport, and another was state assistance to the proliferation of television sets following the introduction of television broadcasting in 1966. There was a large increase in state expenditure on construction projects most likely to be appreciated, such as public squares and gardens. The colonels were hampered, however, by their personal inability to charm or inspire the public.

The regime's economic policies appeared highly successful until 1973, in that the average annual rate of growth of GDP for over six years was 7.6 per cent, with a gradual fall in unemployment. Also significant however was the decline of 1.8 per cent in 1974, with a rise in unemployment, and a leap of inflation to 15.5 per cent in 1973 and 26.9 per cent in 1974. Although in large part a result of international recession and the sudden increase in international oil prices, this downturn was also due to policy weaknesses which had lasting consequences.

Some of the weaknesses resulted from lack of legitimacy.[12] The regime greatly increased expenditure on the construction sector, in which public and private investment were already so large as to make it a bottleneck in the economy. As a result, this sector caused inflationary pressures. Such pressures also came from a large increase in the budget deficit, resulting partly from expenditure on internal security. By 1974 the public debt, much of it owed to foreigners, was nearly three times the level of 1967. This fault was more serious because it coincided with an increase in the expense of imports caused by inflation in developed, western economies. The public debt and inflation slowed down the growth of investment in agriculture and manufacturing, so reducing the long-term capacity of those sectors to generate their own profits for reinvestment.

The rate of increase in the inflow of foreign capital also declined, partly because the EEC, in reaction to the dictatorship, froze long-term development loans and suspended lending facilities from the European Investment Bank. Moreover there was a big fall in income from foreign tourism, which was also due to western hostility. Thus the balance of payments, which had been in surplus for many years before 1967, went into large deficit from 1967 onwards. This change put pressure on the drachma and consequently depleted reserves of gold and foreign exchange, so necessitating an increase in interest rates. The regime was forced to rely on undesirable forms of investment, such as loans from foreign contractors for projects which the contractors themselves undertook, which tended to prevent the regime from benefiting by competition between them, and were risky because they were short-term loans for long-term expenditure. The regime tried without success to meet these difficulties by encouraging foreign investment, to which end it added still further to the legal privileges of foreign capitalists and Greek shipowners. Foreign investment declined however during the year 1973, the decline being worsened by the sudden rise in international oil prices in the second half of the year.

The regime claimed to represent the interests of workers and farmers, and accordingly made some populist gestures. In practice, however, it put development policy in the hands of neo-liberal economists and civil servants, and favoured wealthier businessmen. To the Greek Shipowners' Union, Papadopoulos said in 1968, 'tell us what you want us to do. I can assure you that the government will grant your wish', and in reward was later elected Honorary President.[13] Among the regime's populist gestures were the cancellation of farmers' debts to the Agricultural Bank; a generous-sounding scheme of housing loans for workers; and a loan scheme and free textbooks for university students. It founded the Organisation for the Employment of the Labour Force (OAED) which still exists, and greatly increased expenditure on occupational training.

But these moves were not systematically related; and the main trends of social policy were regressive. Wages as a proportion of GNP declined by about 10 per cent during the life of the regime, a trend accelerating after 1969. Partly or mainly because of a reduction in price support for farm produce, the rate of growth of farmers' incomes also fell until 1973, when the puppet administration in that year decreed a massive increase in prices of agricultural produce, in the hope of winning farmers' favour to compensate for the regime's growing unpopularity in cities. Expenditure on social benefits, health and education also declined as a proportion of GDP, at a time when such expenditure was increasing in much or all of western Europe.[14] Meanwhile the tax system was made still more regressive, through various reductions in income tax and taxation of businesses.

At the outset, the regime suppressed the means whereby workers and farmers might defend their standard of living. The elected councils of trade unions and agricultural cooperatives were replaced by appointees, and the rights to strike or demonstrate were abolished. While farmers' producer cooperatives were suppressed, certain businessmen were granted monopoly rights to buy agricultural produce.

Resistance

There were many resistance movements and protests, several of them heroic; but until 1973 none that was threatening. Their effect, intangible and indirect, was to undermine the regime's legitimacy, partly by broadcasts from major capitals of Europe. By contrast with the resistance to the Metaxas dictatorship, the resistance to the Junta owed relatively little to Communists, a fact symptomatic of their increasing irrelevance in western Europe. The official Communist Party failed even to see the coup coming, and was by its own admission in no position to respond to one.[15] The party finally provoked a revolt from its long-suffering followers within Greece by habitually giving orders irrelevant to local circumstances. The rebels formed a schismatic party in 1968, which for many years would name itself simply the Communist Party of the Interior. It embarked on a moderate Eurocommunist course, while the official body enjoyed the vital advantage of Soviet approval and therefore much greater resources. The Soviet invasion of Czechoslovakia in August 1968 exposed the divergence between the two, being supported by the official party and opposed by the dissidents. This split reduced still further the Communists' ability to play any role in resistance.

The Communists' weakness allowed greater scope for socialists of various kinds, such as the Panhellenic Liberation Movement in exile led by Andreas Papandreou. This was the genesis of a social democratic movement independent of the Communist Party. Even so it was more significant for its impact on the future evolution of the left than on current events.

The movement which had the greatest impact was largely spontaneous and led by students. This was a period of mass student protest throughout the western world, for reasons which Greece shared in part with other countries: the sudden growth in numbers of students, whose values and expectations conflicted with traditional university environments and with most other social authorities. As in other countries, a wide generation gap was caused by the contrast between the experiences of students brought up in the 1960s and those of their parents: this led students, in particular, to a more sympathetic view of the left and a more hostile view of American hegemony. In Greece, the Junta's control of universities affronted the great majority of students continually and directly. In September 1969 one student, Costa Yorgakis, committed suicide in public in Genoa by setting fire to himself. As students' resentment grew, it focused particularly on the Junta's denial of the right to elect their unions.

The regime reacted in the most provocative way possible. Under international pressure, it relaxed censorship considerably in 1970, so permitting a big increase in subversive discussions and publications. But it also harassed student activists by, for example, hauling them in frequently for police interrogation. From early in 1973, student protest was continual, in the capital and the provinces, and supported even by conservative politicians and bishops. Meanwhile, intellectual discussion was dominated by people of left-wing or liberal views.[16]

The student movement culminated in the occupation of the university institution commonly known as the Athens Polytechnic in November 1973.[17] Through a radio transmitter the occupiers appealed over two days for public support. Their occupation became the focus of protest against the regime by several thousand people drawn from various social groups, particularly workers. Perhaps under the workers' influence, there was a socialist tinge to some of the slogans; but essentially the protestors' demands were limited to social justice and the restoration of political liberties. The protestors were addressed sympathetically by Panagiotis Kanellopoulos, the leading right-wing politician before the coup; while the exiled Communist Party – characteristically out of touch – denounced the whole affair as a *provokatsia*.

Armed police and army units suppressed the demonstrations savagely; and the occupation of the Polytechnic ended in the small hours of 17 November with a tank crashing through the main gate. Possibly about seven thousand people were arrested; hundreds of people wounded; and scores killed by troops and armed police during about five days in the capital. The death toll was never ascertained, because friends and relatives of those killed avoided reporting their deaths. The names of 43 dead were published after the dictatorship, but the real total was probably closer to 80. The sympathy of the great majority of the urban population was with the demonstrators; and it was clear that the regime held power solely by force.

Self-destruction

Immediately afterwards, though in a coup long premeditated, Ioannidis ousted Papadopoulos as effective leader of the regime. His motives were jealousy of Papadopoulos's concentration of power, and alarm at his recent attempts to restore some appearance of constitutional government. Ioannidis soon destroyed the regime by bringing the country to the brink of a potentially catastrophic war with Turkey over Cyprus. The leaders of the armed forces reacted, on 20 July 1974, by moving towards a decision to restore full power to civilian politicians. On 23 July, after a ceasefire in Cyprus had been arranged by US intervention, they summoned Ioannidis and told him in effect that he was fired. The plotters immediately convened several veteran right-wing politicians, who decided to invite Karamanlis – the most prestigious of politicians – to become prime minister. On being phoned, Karamanlis arrived instantly from Paris, in an aircraft lent by the French President, to a hero's welcome at Athens airport at 2 a.m. on the 24th.[18]

The fall of the Junta is a turning point, the consequences of which are still unfolding. A survey more than twenty years later found that the great majority of the public could name resisters to the dictatorship, and agreed in blaming it on some group in the old establishment, especially the Americans.[19] In opposing it, intellectuals and political activists of the right and left found common cause and worked together for the first time since the civil war. They now appreciated as never before the value of fair and free elections. They also saw clearly the unacceptable features of the post-civil war system which the Junta embodied in extreme form. Two which stood out were the politicization of the army and the enforcement by police measures of ideological conformity. These and other faults were confronted by successive governments from 1974 onwards.

Notes

1 Kostas Kribas, 'Higher education in the time of the Junta', in Gianna Athanasatou, Alkis Rigos and Serapheim Seferiadis (eds), *The Dictatorship. 1967– 74. Political Actions, Ideological Discourse, Resistance* (in Greek, 1999), 139.

2 Stella Zabarloukou, 'Trade union movement and state intervention in Greece since 1974: a comparative approach', in Christos Lyrintzis, Ilias Nikolakopoulos and Dimitris Sotiropoulos (eds), *Society and Politics. Aspects of the Third Greek Republic* (in Greek, 1996), 98.

3 Oriana Fallacci, *A Man* (New York 1982); 'Athenian', *Inside the Colonels' Greece* (1972), 129–53; Maurice Goldbloom, 'United States policy in post-war Greece', in Richard Clogg and George Yannopoulos (eds), *Greece Under Military Rule* (1972), 250.

4 George A. Kourvetaris, 'The contemporary army officer corps in Greece: an enquiry into its professionalism and interventionism' (PhD thesis, Northwestern University, Evanston, IL 1969), 80–1, 141–2.

5 Rodis Roufos, 'Culture and the military', in Clogg and Yannopoulos (eds), *Greece*, 151.

6 'N.N.', 'Traditionalism and reaction in Greek education', in Clogg and Yannopoulos (eds), *Greece*, 134–8.

7 Meletis Meletopoulos, *The Dictatorship of the Colonels* (in Greek, 1996), 51–2, 61.

8 'Military professionalism and regime legitimacy in Greece, 1967–74', *Political Science Quarterly* 98 (1983), 485–506.

9 C.M. Woodhouse, *The Rise and Fall of the Greek Colonels* (1985), 112; Giannis G. Valinakis, *Introduction to Greek Foreign Policy, 1949–88* (in Greek, Salonika 1989), 114.

10 Nicos P. Mouzelis, *Politics in the Semi-Periphery. Early Parliamentarism and Late Industrialisation in the Balkans and Latin America* (1986), 181.

11 Nancy Bermeo, 'Classification and consolidation: some lessons from the Greek dictatorship', *Political Science Quarterly* 110 (1995), 444.

12 Meletopoulos, *Dictatorship*, 408–12, 435–8; John Pesmazoglou, 'The Greek economy since 1967', in Clogg and Yannopoulos (eds), *Greece*, 75–108; Susannah Verney and Panos Tsakaloyannis, 'Linkage politics: the role of the European Community in Greek politics in 1973', *Byzantine and Modern Greek Studies* 10 (1983), 179–94.

13 Meletopoulos, *Dictatorship*, 415–30; Pesmazoglou in Clogg and Yannopoulos (eds), *Greece*, 89, 123; Gelina Harlaftis, *Greek Shipowners and Greece. 1945–74* (1993), 164–5.

14 Maria Petmesidou-Tsoulouvi, *Social Inequalities and Social Policy* (in Greek, 1992), 137; Dimitrios A. Sotiropoulos, 'Social policy of the dictatorship', in Athanasatou *et al.* (eds), *The Dictatorship*, 117–30.

15 Antonio Solaro, *History of the Communist Party of Greece* (in Greek, 1975), 219.

16 Kribas, 'Higher education in the period of the Junta', in Athanasatou *et al.* (eds), *Dictatorship*, 239–43; Alkis Rigos, 'The student movement and the dictatorship', in *idem*, 225–32.

17 Woodhouse, *Greek Colonels*, 126–41.

18 Woodhouse, *Greek Colonels*, 157–66.

19 Panagiotis Kafetzis, 'The regime of the 21st April in the collective memory of Greek society', in Instiouto V–Project Research Consulting, *Public Opinion in Greece, 1999–2000* (in Greek, 1999), 290–305.

CHAPTER SEVEN

Foreign Relations, 1950–1974

The Cold War

The American alliance

After the civil war, the alliance with the United States continued to be welcomed by the right and centre parties as a guarantee both of economic recovery and military security. Thus entry into the NATO in 1952 was seen as important for defence. It was American pressure that persuaded NATO partners to drop their initial objections to acceptance of Greece and Turkey, so extending the alliance to the eastern Mediterranean. Thereafter, it was through NATO that Greek operational planning integral to the American alliance was implemented. The United States continued to supply a large part of the Greek armed forces' equipment and funding (over two billion dollars' worth in the years 1948 to 1964). Under its Military Assistance Program from 1950 to 1969, the United States provided training, on US soil, to 11,229 officers and 1,965 students.[1] Thus American representatives exercised direct influence over the armed forces, which encouraged officers to seek their favour. Papagos willingly agreed in 1953 to a treaty hosting US military bases, and granting virtually extraterritorial rights to American servicemen. From 1955 to 1976, the Ellenikon air base formed an American enclave on the outskirts of the metropolis. In 1959–60, a Greek government signed secret agreements to allow the installation in American bases of nuclear missiles, as well as the location in them of aircraft and artillery with nuclear capacity.

Frozen peace with the Balkans

Although 'the threat from the north' stayed in the minds of leading politicians and officers for many years after the civil war, it soon ceased to be active.[2] Relations with Albania remained stormy for a brief period because Britain and America used Greek soil as a base for attempts to undermine Enver Hoxha's regime. But peace was formally restored in 1952, when the Greek government renounced the use of force to resolve its traditional claim on southern Albania. The following year, the Greek government signed a treaty recognising the Bulgarian frontier. Relations with the northern neighbours then developed at a glacial pace. Full diplomatic relations were restored with Bulgaria in 1964, and at the same time various technical agreements were signed with that country. Diplomatic relations were restored with Albania in 1971, with the implication that Greek territorial claims would be shelved indefinitely, and that the Albanian government would respect the rights of ethnic Greek inhabitants of Albania. But attempts by Greek and Albanian governments to cooperate on a wide front did not follow until the mid-1980s. It was not until 1987 that the two governments ended the state of war which had technically existed between them since 1940.

Meanwhile, Yugoslavia, as we have seen, restored peaceful relations with Greece in 1949. The two countries exchanged ambassadors in 1950, and even concluded a defensive alliance in 1953. This promptly ceased to be effective when Yugoslavia restored friendly relations with the Soviet Union in 1955. But the two countries retained an interest in possible military cooperation against any threat from the Soviet bloc. They also retained common trade interests. For Greece, Yugoslavia was a land route to the rest of Europe; for Yugoslavia, Salonika was an outlet to the Aegean.

The United States and Soviet Union never, from 1945 onwards, showed any inclination to risk a confrontation over the Balkans, or to let their client states provoke one. The latent fear in Greece that conflict between the superpowers might set the northern frontiers aflame disappeared altogether in the 1970s.

Nevertheless, the important point is the limited scope of relations between Greece and the rest of the Balkans until the 1990s, contrasting with the ever-strengthening contacts between Greece and western Europe.[3] For forty years after the civil war, less than 5 per cent on average of Greek trade lay with Balkan countries. There was little contact between the populations residing on opposite sides of the northern frontiers. Tension with Bulgaria was worsened by the fact that it, alone among Balkan states, continued throughout these years to maintain a close and friendly political and military relationship with the Soviet Union. The Albanian regime sealed its country off from the rest of the Balkans, and in the 1950s provided the Soviet Union with naval bases. Between Greece and both Albania and Yugoslavia there were disputes over minority populations. Greek governments tried with little success to safeguard the interests of compatriots in southern Albania, whom they believed to be persecuted and estimated at 400,000; while the Albanian regime estimated them at 60,000. The government of the contiguous part of the Yugoslav Federation, the Socialist Republic of Macedonia – increasingly assertive of its ethnic identity and spurred on by civil war refugees from Greece – continued to complain that numerous compatriots were mistreated within Greece. Traffic across the Bulgarian frontier remained restricted; while there was none at all across the Albanian frontier until 1984. The Greek army restricted movement, and economic development, in a broad zone along the Greek side of the northern frontiers until 1995.

Thus the Cold War strengthened the psychological barriers between Greece and other Balkan nations. These barriers need some explanation. As the national identities of the Balkan peoples had been largely constructed in recent times, claims of cultural uniqueness and venerable origins were psychologically vital to each of them. Almost inevitably these claims were irreconcilable in their territorial implications, and caused intolerant attitudes towards their neighbours. Thus the school textbooks of Greece, Albania, Bulgaria and Turkey emphasized past periods of their peoples' greatest territorial power. So did those of Serbia and Yugoslav Macedonia before the 1940s and after the 1980s, though between those decades they were constrained by the line imposed by the federal regime.[4] The democratic traditions of these states other than Greece were weak or non-existent; and, until the 1990s, their regimes, except for Yugoslavia, allowed little scope for defence of their ethnic minorities.

But in Greece also, the prevailing emphasis on the organic unity and timeless character of the nation discouraged respect for ethnic minorities. The schools and the media emphasised that the Orthodox religion and Greek language were essential elements in Greek ethnicity, and kept most of the population virtually ignorant about the existence of fellow citizens who were not fully assimilated, with some exception for the recognised Muslim population. This lived mainly in Thrace, with religious and cultural rights guaranteed by the Treaty of Lausanne of 1923, and numbered about 120,000 in the 1990s, of whom 49 per cent spoke Turkish, 33 per cent spoke Pomak (a form of Bulgarian) and 18 per cent the gypsy language Romany. Apart from them, the general emphasis on cultural homogeneity was illustrated by a survey of primary school children in various places in 1993 which found over 70 per cent saying that they would be unwilling to sit at the same desk as a Jehovah's Witness, an atheist or a Muslim, with many tending to identify religion with ethnicity.[5] Until the 1990s, ethnic discrimination was enshrined in law, notably in the liability of emigrants who were not ethnically Greek to lose citizenship.

Balkan peoples showed little interest in each other's cultural achievements and ethnic sensitivities. In Greece, for example, a minister about to become Minister of Foreign Affairs, Michalis Papakonstantinou, complained publicly in 1992 that the languages of neighbouring countries were not being taught at all.[6] No Greek–Albanian dictionary existed at this time. By contrast, knowledge of western European languages (chiefly English) was extensive and growing. Admittedly there were many Greek students – 4,750 in 1990 – enrolled in eastern European including Balkan universities; but their motive seems to have been not cultural interest but inability to gain places in Greek institutions to study technical subjects like engineering and veterinary science.[7]

A point about which the Greek government remained especially sensitive was the presence in its province of Macedonia of an uncertain number – apparently many thousands even in the 1990s – of people whose mother tongue was slav Macedonian, although nearly all spoke Greek as well. They continued after the civil war to provide a pretext for irredentist claims by the Socialist Republic of Macedonia. Their numbers steadily declined as a result of assimilation and emigration, which is perhaps why they never asserted a desire for autonomy even in the increasingly liberal conditions of the 1980s onwards. Official Greek sensitivity was shown until the early 1990s in the discouragement of the slav Macedonian language and culture, and the prevention of visits by slav Macedonian exiles to their relatives in Greece.[8]

Cyprus and Turkey

The issues at stake

From 1954 onwards, official and public interest shifted from the Balkan neighbours to Cyprus. Although the island was British-controlled, it soon appeared that Turkey was the main obstacle to Greek aspirations for union with it. The result was a dramatic reorientation of public attitudes. Turkey replaced the Soviet bloc as the main target of official and public hostility. Eventually, from 1963, the threat of war with Turkey became the main focus of military planning as well. Because the United States, Britain and other NATO powers tended to support the Turkish position, they became targets of public resentment. For this reason the NATO alliance was increasingly seen by the public as a distasteful necessity, partly for protection against any potential threat from the Soviet bloc, and partly as a precondition of American military aid, which might otherwise be diverted entirely to Turkey.

It was in 1954 that the government, no longer needing to defer to Britain, openly took up the Greek Cypriots' cause by submitting it to the United Nations General Assembly: the first of several such moves in the next few years – all unsuccessful, mainly because of opposition by other NATO powers. Ever since 1878, when Britain took over the administration of Cyprus from the Ottoman empire, the Greek Cypriots had looked forward to eventual *enosis*, or union, with Greece. As they were ethnically Greek and formed 80 per cent of the Cypriot population of 600,000, whereas the Turkish Cypriots formed only 18 per cent, *enosis* was a natural expectation, by the criteria of national self-determination increasingly accepted in Europe since the early nineteenth century. As international opposition to colonialism intensified after 1945, the Greek Cypriots' wishes became insistent. They became more effective with the appearance of an able and charismatic leader, in the person of the American-educated, 37-year-old shepherd's son who became Archbishop of Cyprus in 1950 under the title Makarios. He cooperated with a Greek colonel, and recently a guerrilla fighter against the left in the civil war, Georgios Grivas, in establishing the National Organisation of Cypriot Fighters (EOKA). Thus began in April 1955 a campaign of terrorism against British rule, which led to some fighting between the Greek and Turkish communities, and within a few years wore down British opposition to independence.

Turkish opposition remained. Turkey had to accept passively the transfer of the Dodecanese Islands (also close to its mainland) from Italy to Greece in 1947, because its diplomatic position was still weak, on account of its neutrality in the Second World War and its need at that time for western support against Soviet pressure. But Turkish military leaders and the public were thereafter determined that Greece should not acquire yet another offshore base, especially not one inhabited partly by ethnic Turks. Turkey's military superiority over Greece was overwhelming and destined to increase. Its population was four times that of Greece in the 1950s, growing to six times in the 1990s. Its armed forces were three times in personnel those of Greece in the 1950s, also growing to six times in the 1990s. Because of the legacy of Kemal Atatürk, the army enjoyed extraordinary respect in Turkey, and since 1960 has asserted its right to intervene in politics to safeguard alleged Kemalist principles. Military leaders have in the process declared startling and sometimes aggressive views on foreign policy. Defence policy and expenditure were quarantined from control by democratically elected governments, whereas from 1974 onwards they were subjected fully to such control in Greece.

From the 1950s the Turkish armed forces were modernised with NATO equipment, which was designed to give Turkey greater offensive capacity than Greece, because Turkey was regarded by the United States as a more valuable ally. In response to possible attack by the Soviet bloc, Turkey might realistically be expected to guard the Straits of Constantinople and the oil supplies of the Middle East; whereas Greece could not even be counted on to defend its northern frontiers. Turkey was, moreover, recognised as being more independent of US patronage because of its greater power and economic self-reliance. Mainly for these reasons, the United States usually inclined towards the Turkish view over Cyprus.

Turkey had additional advantages. One was proximity to Cyprus, which was 40 miles from Turkey's mainland, but 500 miles from that of Greece. Another was the attitude of the British government which, as a way of blocking *enosis*, treated the Turkish Cypriots' case with respect.

Greek–Turkish hostility

The eruption of the Cyprus issue suddenly wrecked Greek relations with Turkey, which had been friendly since 1930 at the government level, even though popular antipathy continued. Expressed in school textbooks, this antipathy was mutual, and was based on the formative historical experiences of both nations, which consisted of fierce conflicts, cultural and military. Since 1930, however, Greek and Turkish governments had been drawn together by common enemies: fascist Italy before 1941, and the Soviet Union since 1944. The latter threat made them both keen to join the American-dominated sphere of Europe from 1948 onwards. Greece and Turkey sent contingents to the Korean war in 1950, and entered NATO together in 1952, whereupon their military cooperation increased. But, from 1954, the Greek support for *enosis* brought the two governments into opposition; and military cooperation within NATO broke down. Support for *enosis* was passionate and universal in Greece, while opposition to it was passionate and universal in Turkey. Greek hostility intensified when, as a way of putting pressure on Greece, the Turkish government in September 1955 covertly instigated riots which destroyed Greek shops, schools, churches and houses in Istanbul and Izmir. Also at risk were ethnic Greeks on the Turkish islands of Imbros and Tenedos in the approaches to the Dardanelles. This pogrom was the beginning of the end of the community of 100,000 Greeks in Istanbul which, like the Muslim population of about the same size in Greek Thrace, had guaranteed status under the Treaty of Lausanne of 1923. This and later bouts of persecution, including the closure in 1972 of the main training college of the Ecumenical Patriarchate, caused that community to decline to about 2,500 mainly elderly people today.

By 1956, the Cyprus issue overshadowed all others in Greece. Intense anger prevailed, especially among the young, over the American and British attitudes, and the anger turned against the whole western alliance. Eventually, in the mid-1960s, this resentment eclipsed fading fears of the Soviet bloc. From 1954 the anger was expressed in mass demonstrations which were tolerated by the police because they supported the Greek government's desire for *enosis*, even though they turned immediately against the United States. Thus they stimulated the reawakening of radical politics after the civil war, and strengthened the left and centre parties against the right. In the early 1960s the opposition parties' target was the settlement in effect imposed on Cyprus by NATO, and embodied in the Zurich and London agreements of 1959 between Britain, Turkey, Greece and the two communities of Cyprus. Karamanlis's government had, in reluctant deference to American pressure, joined Turkey and Britain in guaranteeing this settlement. Under the agreements, Cyprus became independent in 1960 with Makarios as president. But *enosis* was explicitly precluded, while the Turkish Cypriots were guaranteed the power to block unfavourable changes, and were also guaranteed far greater representation in the legislature and public service than their population warranted. Britain retained (until the present) sovereign rights over two military bases; while Greece and Turkey were entitled to maintain limited numbers of troops in Cyprus, and to take military action in Cyprus to counter threats to the settlement. Karamanlis justified this settlement by a gradualist strategy, according to which the Greek Cypriots would peacefully dominate the island by weight of numbers, by their greater economic skills and hence their disproportionately greater wealth.[9]

Sadly, all that the 1959 settlement achieved was to end British rule over Cypriot territory except for the bases. But it left the country with a constitution which was unworkable because it affronted the great majority of the population. In consequence relations between the two communities remained unresolved. Perhaps encouraged by the accession to power of Georgios Papandreou, who unlike Karamanlis pursued *enosis* impetuously, Makarios proposed in November 1963 to rescind the Turkish Cypriots' rights. This move provoked the worst bout yet of intercommunal fighting, with Greece and Turkey supplying the two sides. The Turkish government, in retaliation, expelled thousands more ethnic Greeks from Istanbul. Turkey also supported the Turkish Cypriots with bombing raids over Cyprus, and made preparations for invasion. The latter were checked by an ultimatum to the Turkish prime minister in June 1964 from the American President Lyndon Johnson, who – among other arguments – pointed out the danger of Soviet intervention, referring to the arrival in the Mediterranean two months earlier of a Soviet naval force. This, rather than sympathy for the Greek position, was clearly the motive for the unusual American intervention against Turkey.[10]

The Greek prime minister Papandreou meanwhile infuriated the Americans by deferring to Makarios's opposition to the proposed American solution. This had been submitted to the Greek and Turkish governments in June 1964 by the former Secretary of State Dean Acheson, and proposed that a base on Cyprus would be granted to Turkey, and one or two cantons carved out for Turkish Cypriots to live in with guaranteed rights, while the rest of the island would join Greece. Papandreou covertly authorised the dispatch to Cyprus of a heavily armed Greek division (far greater than allowed under the Zurich–London agreements), which was put under Grivas's command. An outcome of the inter-communal conflict was the flight, in the months up to March 1964, of 25,000 persecuted Turkish Cypriots to enclaves which were thenceforth supplied by Turkey, so that they could survive the economic blockade to which they were subjected by Greek Cypriots. After Grivas's forces attacked one of these enclaves, in November 1967, Turkey once again prepared to invade Cyprus, and had to be dissuaded by an American mediator. Thus Turkey condemned itself to witness the continuing decline in the status and welfare of Turkish Cypriots in their enclaves; but at least secured the withdrawal from Cyprus of Grivas and the Greek division.[11]

Thus disappeared the only deterrent to a future Turkish invasion. The text of President Johnson's ultimatum of 1964, when published in the Turkish press in 1966, provoked an uproar, which evidently strengthened the Turkish government's determination to take tough action if the Turkish Cypriots were again threatened. No longer could Turkey be influenced by fear of Soviet intervention, because it had improved relations with the Soviet Union, which in 1965 accepted a Turkish proposal of federation for Cyprus.

Commitments to NATO, added to tension with Turkey, led to heavy Greek expenditure on land, sea and air forces. Thus, military expenditure relative to economic resources remained high by the standards of Italy and Spain, and high also by those general in northern Europe. It averaged 7.4 per cent of GDP and 44 per cent of public expenditure in the 1950s; and the corresponding figures for the years 1960–66 were 5.1 per cent and 33.2 per cent. This expenditure (which was supplemented by American grants, though these were very small after 1962), was open to political criticism as excessive in a country with extensive poverty and low expenditure on social welfare. Because all armaments and much equipment had to be obtained from abroad, the expenditure drained scarce foreign exchange reserves and investment capital.[12] Among the aims of the left-wing opposition was disarmament, to be made feasible by a foreign policy of detente and non-alignment.

Turkish invasion

An opportunity for invasion was provided to Turkey by the Greek Junta. From 1967 onwards, this pursued the Acheson solution of 'dual *enosis*', which had been accepted, after Papandreou's fall, by the government of Stefanos Stefanopoulos in 1966. The goal seemed attractive because it fulfilled the traditional ideal of Greece as the national centre – which the Junta fervently advocated – according to which the rightful destiny of Greek Cypriots was inclusion in the Greek state. It followed that the Greek government should determine policy, not Makarios. Dual *enosis* would also comply with US wishes and bring Cyprus into NATO. These incentives blinded Greek governments to the realism of the policy of Cypriot independence now preferred by Makarios.[13] The obstacles to dual *enosis* were insuperable, and appeared immediately that negotiations started with Turkey in 1966. Turkish conditions were beyond what the Greek or Greek Cypriot public could accept; and Turkey was poised to invade the island to protect its compatriots. While remaining publicly committed to simple *enosis* as the ideal solution, Makarios recognised now that it was unattainable, and besides had no wish to see democratic Cyprus absorbed in the Junta's Greece. This attitude, combined with his popularity in Cyprus and his support for democratic critics of the Junta, provoked the Junta into an obsessive campaign against him, to the extent of encouraging at least four assassination attempts. The Junta worked through a paramilitary force EOKA-B, led by Grivas after his secret return to Cyprus in 1972, and after his death in 1974 by another EOKA veteran, Nikos Sampson, whom the US Secretary of State Henry Kissinger characterised as a 'mafioso'. Makarios meanwhile relied for defence on the Reserve Corps, which fought at length with EOKA-B.

The Junta's policy was taken to extremes by Ioannidis. A retiring and ascetic character (who had shown a recklessly bloodthirsty attitude to Turkish Cypriots while an intelligence officer in the Cypriot armed forces in the early 1960s), Ioannidis conducted a foreign policy of his own for which he had no qualifications. He was in regular contact with CIA representatives, who – like American diplomats and journalists in Cyprus – gave ample warning to Washington of his intentions to accomplish *enosis* by toppling Makarios. This raises the question – especially in Greece where it has been asked constantly – of US culpability for the ensuing debacle. The facts are that the American ambassador and CIA officials in Greece did warn Ioannidis not to provoke Turkey by instigating a coup against Makarios, but they did not warn him with nearly enough urgency or emphasis. The reasons for this omission seem to have been, in part, the chronic neglect of Greek domestic affairs by the Department of State, and in part the seriously oversimplified view of Kissinger that Makarios was an obstacle to a deal on dual *enosis* between Greece and Turkey. Kissinger later admitted Cyprus to have been one of his greatest failures.[14]

The coup occurred on 15 July 1974, when members of the Cypriot National Guard under Greek officers overthrew Makarios by a bloody coup and installed Sampson as President. The act was plainly instigated by the Junta and naturally seen by Turkey as a threat, because Sampson boasted of his prowess as a Turk-killer and campaigner for *enosis*. Ioannidis then failed to realise the seriousness of the obvious preparations by Turkey for invasion, which were concealed from the Greek public by the censored media. Although the US administration knew of these preparations, it differed from all other governments in hesitating to condemn Sampson's coup, and made little effort to restrain Turkey – if indeed restraint was possible.[15] Turkish forces invaded Cyprus in overwhelming strength on 20 July. The same day, Ioannidis responded by ordering a general mobilisation of reservists with a view to declaring war on various fronts against Turkey. It immediately became clear that defence was yet another area of policy which the dictatorship had grossly mishandled. The general mobilisation was a shambles. Morale, equipment, fortifications and organisation were all inadequate; and leading figures in the armed forces rejected the necessity and feasibility of a war. Sampson was overthrown by Greek Cypriots after eight days, and a democratic regime restored in Cyprus.

From 1973, the Cyprus dispute was accompanied by various others over rights in the Aegean. These disputes can be interpreted as a natural result of Turkey's growing political and military superiority. It was perhaps inevitable that Turkey should in time challenge the territorial settlements of the early twentieth century, which left Greece in possession of almost the entire Aegean archipelago, comprising about 2,200 islands – with their air space and territorial waters – extending right up to the Turkish coast.[16] In 1973 the obvious disarray of Greek defences, and the Junta's unpopularity inside Greece and internationally, provided Turkey with an opportunity, while the rise of international oil prices provided the incentive, for the first challenge. This was the granting by the Turkish government to a survey vessel, in November 1973, of exploration licences for oil in areas of sea bed which Greece had hitherto claimed as part of the continental shelf of some northern and eastern Aegean islands.[17] Unfortunately for peace, oil was discovered at this time near the northern Aegean island of Thasos. During the following year, the Junta made known that it was considering a partial solution to this dispute by exercising Greece's right under international law to extend its territorial waters from six to twelve nautical miles from its coasts, a move which would increase the total extent of those territorial waters from one-third to two-thirds of the Aegean sea. Greek governments maintained this right thenceforth, even though Turkey let it be known in June 1974 that such extension would be a *casus belli*. Then, in August 1974, the Turkish government began to dispute the Greek right (according to a decision by the International Civil Aviation Organisation in 1952) to be notified of air traffic in the Aegean, and in addition soon asserted that Greek air space did not extend four nautical miles further than the six-mile territorial waters of the mainland and islands (according to a Greek claim in 1931), but coincided with this limit. The dispute over air traffic notification led for some years (1974–80) to a cessation of direct air traffic between Greece and Turkey. Violations by Turkish military aircraft of Greek air space continued thenceforth; and, because they were routinely countered by Greek intercepting flights, caused a constant danger of crisis. All the Turkish challenges seemed designed to implement the principle proclaimed by a Turkish prime minister in January 1975: 'half of the Aegean belongs to us'.[18]

Reaching towards western Europe

The western orientation of all Greek governments from 1944 led to prompt participation in various postwar movements for unification of western Europe, movements which were strongly encouraged by the United States in the hope of enabling the region to recover from the war and become self-reliant. Thus Greece and Turkey were among 16 countries to participate in the Organisation for European Economic Cooperation (later the OECD), founded at American instigation in April 1948. The other members, apart from Austria, were all western European. This organisation would do much to remove obstacles to trade among its members.

Greece also participated in the Congress of Europe held in The Hague the following month in May 1948. The latter led to the establishment in 1949 of the Council of Europe, which Greece and Turkey joined in August of that year. The Council of Europe was inspired by western liberal ideals of democracy, and by the long-term goal of European unity. Presumably the Greek and Turkish governments were motivated in joining by desire to become associated with the American-dominated sphere of Europe, rather than by concern with human rights. The Council of Europe formulated the

European Convention on Human Rights and Fundamental Freedoms in 1950, expressing ideals which some Council members especially Turkey are still struggling to realise. The European Commission of Human Rights was simultaneously established to supervise implementation of the Convention; and, in 1956, Greece complained to the Commission about British activities in Cyprus.[19] The European Court of Human Rights was established in 1959 to hear appeals against violation of the Convention, although Greece did not allow its citizens to make such appeals until much later.

Thus Karamanlis acted in accordance with established policy by applying in 1959 for associate membership of the two-year old EEC, which then included as members Belgium, France, West Germany, Italy, Luxembourg and the Netherlands. Countries which joined in 1973 were Britain, Denmark and Ireland. The EEC was initially seen in Greece as the economic counterpart of NATO, and for a long time thereafter was disliked by the left for that reason.[20] Karamanlis saw association as a way of ensuring that Greece became integrated with a western system of trade and investment, and valued it as a means of stimulating the modernisation of the economy by capitalist rather than socialist methods. The treaty of association came into effect in November 1962, and envisaged that Greece would eventually become a full member. It provided for the rapid reduction of EEC tariffs against Greece (so that in fact they disappeared in 1968); the disappearance over 22 years of Greek tariffs against the EEC; and large development loans to Greece.

After the military coup in 1967, associate membership acquired a value which Karamanlis had presumably not foreseen, which was to expose Greece to pressure for a return to democracy. The EEC promptly precluded further negotiations or agreements with Greece under the treaty of association until democracy was restored. Influenced by the many prominent Greek exiles in European capitals, the EEC was becoming by 1972 an increasingly prominent channel of criticism of the Junta. Yet at this time the Community was granting improved access to its own markets to some of Greece's Mediterranean competitors including Turkey. Meanwhile, the importance of the EEC to Greece was shown in the continued increase in trade, despite the formal freeze on relations. By 1972 the EEC provided 55 per cent of Greek imports and took 61 per cent of Greek exports, whereas the corresponding figures for Greek trade with the US were only 6 per cent and 10 per cent; and for Greek trade with eastern Europe in 1970–74 they were 6.6 and 17.2 respectively. Since then well over half of Greek trade has been with the EEC, much more than with any other region. In 1972, it was becoming evident to most Greek observers – politicians, businessmen and the Junta itself – that Greece's economic and even political future lay with the EEC, and that Greece was in danger of exclusion from the further process of integration. It seems that only left-wing politicians disagreed with these views. Events were moving towards solution of a dilemma facing the Greek state since its foundation: its external orientation.

Notes

1 Thanos Veremis, 'The Military', in Kevin Featherstone and Dimitrios Katsoudas (eds), *Political Change in Greece. Before and After the Colonels* (1987), 221; Nicos C. Alivizatos, *The Political Institutions of Greece during Crises, 1922–74* (in French, Paris 1979), 198.

2 Giannis G. Valinakis, *Introduction to Greek Foreign Policy, 1949–88* (in Greek, Salonika 1989), 56, 192.

3 Axel S. Wallden, 'Greece and the Balkans: economic relations', in Van Coufoudakis, Harry J. Psomiades and Andre Gerolymmatos (eds), *Greece and the New Balkans. Challenges and Opportunities* (New York 1999), 74–6, 114–15.

4 *Kathimerini*, 28 January 1998, 12; Sofia Vouri, *Slavic Textbooks of Balkan History (1991–3). Nations in Conflict* (in Greek, 1997), *passim*.

5 Eleni Sella-Mazi, 'Language contact today: the case of the Muslim minority in northeastern Greece', *International Journal of Social Linguistics* 126 (1997), 83; *Vima*, 12 April 1998, A48, Panagioti Bitsika; Efi Avdela, 'The teaching of history in Greece', *Journal of Modern Greek Studies* 18 (2000), 239–53.

6 *Vima*, 7 June 1992, A22.

7 Vima, 29 April 1990, 30, Bank of Greece statistics; Paschalis M. Kitromilidis, 'The Greek cultural presence in the Balkans', in Coufoudakis, Psomiades and Gerolymatos (eds), *Greece*, 194.

8 Loring Danforth, *The Macedonian Conflict. Ethnic Nationalism in a Transnational World* (Princeton, NJ 1995), 116–26; Anastasia N. Karakasidou, 'Politicizing culture: negating ethnic identity in Greek Macedonia', *Journal of Modern Greek Studies* 11 (1993), 1–28; *idem*, 'National ideologies, histories and popular consciousness; a response to three critics', *Balkan Studies* 35 (1994), 113–46; Victor Roudometof, 'Nationalism and identity politics in the Balkans: Greece and the Macedonian question', *Journal of Modern Greek Studies* 14 (1996) 270.

9 Tozun Bahcheli, *Greek–Turkish Relations since 1955* (1990), 51.

10 Van Coufoudakis, 'Greek–Turkish relations in the post-Cold War era: implications of the American response', *Cyprus Review* 9 (1997), 9.

11 Bahcheli, *Greek–Turkish Relations*, 77–8, 83.

12 Maria Petmesidou-Tsoulouvi, *Social Inequalities and Social Policy* (1992), 35, 133; Jean Meynaud, *Political Forces in Greece* (Greek translation, n.d.), 422; Nicos Pantelakis, 'The Army in Contemporary Greek Society' (in French,

PhD dissertation, Université René Descartes, Paris V (1980), 154; Nikos Antonakis, *The Political Economy of Defence in Postwar Greece* (in Greek, n.d.), 103; Nicholas (Nikos) Antonakis, 'Guns versus butter: a multisectoral approach to military expenditure and growth with evidence from Greece, 1960–93', *Journal of Conflict Resolution* 43 (1999), 511.

13 Paschalis Kitromilides, 'The Greek state as national centre', *Contemporary Themes* 13 (in Greek, 1981), 61–80.

14 Helen Laipson, 'US policy towards Greece and Turkey since 1974', in Dimitri Constas (ed.), *The Greek–Turkish Conflict in the 1990s* (1991), 166.

15 Theodore Couloumbis, *The United States, Greece, and Turkey. The Troubled Triangle* (New York 1983), 88–9.

16 Athanasios Platias, 'Greece's strategic doctrine: in search of autonomy and deterrence', in Constas (ed.), *Greek–Turkish Conflict*, 93.

17 Richard Clogg, 'Troubled alliance: Greece and Turkey', in Richard Clogg (ed.), *Greece in the 1980s* (1983), 133–5; Thanos Veremis, *History of Greek–Turkish Relations, 1453–1998* (in Greek, 1999), 121.

18 Platias, 'Greece's strategic doctrine', in Constas (ed.), *Greek–Turkish Conflict*, 93.

19 A.H. Robertson, *The Council of Europe. Its Structure, Functions, and Achievements* (1956), 3–7, 12–23, 154–67.

20 Susannah Verney, 'Greece and the European Community', in Kevin Featherstone and Dimitrios K. Katsoudos (eds), *Political Change in Greece. Before and After the Colonels* (1987), 253–70.

CHAPTER EIGHT

Democratic Transformation, 1974–1989

Collapse of the south European dictatorships

The collapse of authoritarianism in Greece coincided closely with the same process in Portugal and Spain. In Portugal, a coup launched by junior army officers in April 1974 destroyed the dictatorial regime initially established by Salazar in 1932–33, and led in 1976 to the first fully democratic elections that the country had known (democratic in that all adults voted in free and fair conditions). In Spain the death of Franco in November 1975 doomed the dictatorship which he had established in 1939, and was followed likewise by fully democratic elections twelve months later. In all three countries parliamentary democracy stabilised thereafter, being consolidated in the 1980s by their accession to the EEC.

The form of transition differed in each country. While in Portugal the break with dictatorship soon turned into a popular uprising, in Spain and Greece it was arranged by conservative elites, which relegated the public to the role of spectators. While in Portugal and Greece, army officers took the decisive role, exasperated by their regimes' foreign adventures, the army in Franco's Spain had no such motive, and tolerated the transition to democracy with a dislike restrained only by its loyalty to the king who was the choice of General Franco, as the new head of state. But in all three countries the armed forces had by the mid-1980s become loyal to democratic governments, after abandoning a tradition of political intervention.[1] Even in Italy, where the transition from dictatorship to democracy was basically accomplished in 1943–46, there were important moves towards liberalisation in the 1970s: devolution from the national government to elected regional governments, the break between state and church symbolised by the legalisation of divorce, and the ending of the government's monopoly over broadcasting.

Evidently there were common forces of liberalisation at work, despite the fact that Greece differed so profoundly from the countries further west in political traditions and social structure. Although parliamentary government had a longer history in Greece than in Portugal and Spain, its democratic character was as we have seen restricted. Greece was like Spain in having suffered a civil war within the previous forty years. Greece, Spain, Portugal and southern Italy could all be described as economically semi-peripheral to the developed regions and countries of Europe.

Their peoples were therefore influenced by the success of the developed countries since the late 1940s in combining economic prosperity with parliamentary democracy. It was the northern democracies, rather than the dictatorships of southern Europe, which could claim since the Second World War to be the best guarantors for the security of property and investments. Why then should the peoples of southern Europe, who were increasingly educated and well informed, tolerate any longer the fear and indignity of military rule and police states? The societies of the semi-peripheral countries had also been transformed by economic growth, which had been especially rapid in the 1960s. This had greatly reduced old causes of revolutionary feeling, by raising the general standard of living and, in particular, by making possible the emigration of surplus rural populations to the cities or to wealthier countries. Economic growth had increased the size of the professional and business classes and the industrial working class. An increasingly large and well-organised working class needed free trade unions through which to assert its claims. Urban society needed better social services, which could be provided only by governments democratic enough to respond to its needs. Throughout southern Europe, increasingly educated and prosperous peoples found collective bargaining and parliamentary democracy more attractive than dictatorship.

Meanwhile, old forms of authority were declining. Traditional concepts of patriotism, identified with military and religious values, were appearing anachronistic to increasingly cosmopolitan peoples for whom the prospect of war between European states was becoming unthinkable. In Portugal, Spain and Greece, the dominant church found itself discredited by association with wealth and political oppression. In schools and universities, the authority of the teacher was weakened by the increasing restiveness of pupils, and the need to teach children to think for themselves rather than learn by rote. In the family, the father's authority was undermined by women's increasing participation in paid work outside the household, and the declining likelihood that children would follow their father's profession.

In all three countries, public discontent with authoritarianism was further strengthened in the early 1970s by inflation and then in 1974 by international recession.

The process of democratisation

Stabilisation of multi-party democracy

The transition occurred especially fast in Greece, being described as the *metapolitevsi*, the sense of which can best be conveyed as 'democratic transformation'. Even by the early 1980s, Greece ranked among the more stable democracies, by such criteria as the consensus on maintaining its essential features, the fair conduct of elections, the low level of civil disorder, the durability of governments and the apparently high level of voters' trust in parliament and satisfaction with the political system.[2] The main threat to political stability was the vehemence of party controversy, which reached its peak in the first half of the 1980s, but never led to violations of the constitution. The democratic aspirations of the majority were quite effectively embodied in the new constitution enacted in 1975. Admittedly it took many years for these aspirations to be realised in full; and in some respects the process is still continuing.

The relative success of democracy can be explained by the therapeutic effect of dictatorship on a people which already had long experience of parliamentary politics. The importance of this experience was shown even twenty-five years after 1974 by the large proportion of prominent politicians in all parties, especially those of the left, who claimed to have resisted the Junta.[3] Anyone tainted by collaboration with it was excluded from his party by Karamanlis.

In steering the transition to democracy, Karamanlis displayed vision and authority. For nearly six years after his return – the first three marked by extraordinary legislative activity – he directed nearly all the major work of government. His overriding aim, and that of all parties, could be summed up as modernisation on a broad front (in the sense defined in Chapter One), a goal which seemed especially urgent after the Junta's comprehensive attempt to put the clock back. It was generally agreed now that, as a prerequisite, the worst relicts of the civil war must be buried. But the government and opposition parties disagreed profoundly about the methods by which that and other goals of modernisation should be attained. Alternative methods were adopted by Andreas Papandreou, as head of a left-wing government in 1981–89.

Within a few months of becoming prime minister, Karamanlis took several key decisions, his authority being reinforced by the real danger of war with Turkey. Although the decisions were largely dictated by circumstances, Karamanlis can take credit for the fact that they were taken so fast and with so little question. Within a few weeks he took steps to distance his government from NATO and the United States. No longer did the political right boast of its special relationship with the Americans, whom most people held guilty of implication in the coup of 1967, and then of acquiescence in, or encouragement of, the Turkish invasion of Cyprus.

The next month, September, Karamanlis legalised the Communist Party. This decision was a natural outcome of the cooperation between right and left in opposing the Junta, and of the fact that right-wing politicians had become victims of the anti-communist measures which they had once supported. The proven ineffectiveness of the Communist Party during the Junta must also have made the decision easier. But the implications of the change were far-reaching, and included the disappearance, in the following years, of a range of institutions which the persecution of Communism had necessitated since the 1920s: the police tyranny based on decrees which threatened everyone's civil rights, and the apartheid imposed against the left by measures such as certificates of lawful opinions. Gone was the excuse which the army and police had for stigmatising all those suspected of subversion. Gone too was the pretext of the army and police, and the vigilante groups and spies whom they had employed, for undermining democratic procedures.

Prominent Communists promptly started to return from exile in order to reconstruct the party's organisation. This was to be helped by Soviet bloc countries with lavish subsidies, which the Greek party invested shrewdly. Communists and left-wingers were still subjected to discrimination by many officials who could not easily abandon their old ways: for example the military authorities continued to record the political views of conscripts; some public prosecutors harassed those connected with left-wing publications; and police on occasion obstructed commemorations of the wartime resistance. Until 1981, when a left-wing party came to power, it remained extremely difficult for alleged Communists to obtain public employment. However the intensity of persecution immediately started to diminish so that left wingers began losing their fear of the police.

A further stage in the reincorporation of the left was the honourable recognition of all resistance groups, left-wing and right-wing, by a law of 1982, which was proposed with inspirational oratory by Andreas Papandreou and vehemently opposed by the party of Karamanlis (who had retired from its leadership). This was a measure of great psychological significance. Among its practical consequences were pensions for resistance veterans with disabilities, and the removal of remaining legal obstacles to the return of ethnically Greek political exiles, who were also given some financial help for their economic rehabilitation. Eventually about 280,000 resistance veterans received pensions; while about 45,000 political exiles or their offspring returned permanently, the majority of them after 1981. The final move towards political reconciliation was made by a coalition government in August–September 1989, by a law which outlawed all forms of discrimination against the defeated side in the civil war, and promised pensions to disabled veterans of the Democratic Army. Nearly 6,000 such pensions would be granted. Thenceforth, politicians habitually referred to the civil war in conciliatory terms. When we compare Greece with other countries of continental Europe – nearly all of which underwent savage divisions in the 1930s and 1940s – what seems remarkable is the generosity with which the wrongs of the past were eventually treated.

An immediate result of the legalisation of the Communist Party in 1974 was that the state abandoned much of its mission to impose ideological conformity on all institutions under its direct or indirect influence. At varying rates, the Church, universities, judiciary, local government and much of the media became more independent of the government, and the army became politically neutral.

An early step towards democratisation was the insistence of Karamanlis's government on fair elections. The new spirit was shown in the parliamentary election held in November 1974. Its democratic conduct was probably unprecedented, taking into account the relaxation of police and army pressure in rural areas. Irregularities were often complained of thereafter, but were not systematically directed against any one party; and complaints declined as party conflict became more restrained in the 1990s.

The same respect for democratic procedure was shown in the referendum of December 1974 on the future of the monarchy, in which Karamanlis's government was scrupulously neutral: a contrast with the role of governments in flagrantly rigging the two previous referenda on the monarchy, in 1935 and 1946. The vote of 69 per cent against restoration was the public verdict on King Constantine's identification with the old system of repression and his destabilisation of democracy in 1965–67. Thus ended a controversy which was over fifty years old. Under the new constitution of 1975, the king's successor was to be a president elected by at least 180 MPs out of the 300. Although at first the president was given extensive and controversial powers, they were never used before being abolished in 1986. Thus the president's role was to be essentially ceremonial, leaving a parliamentary government, which after 1974 was normally formed by one party, as the unchallenged source of authority. The resulting concentration of power in the executive was greater than in any western

European country, because other checks on it were weak, as will be explained later.

The conclusion drawn by most participants in the events of 1974 was that the army must devote itself exclusively to defence and submit to a civilian government. The lesson was not immediately clear to all officers; so that for over six months after Karamanlis's return, a military coup seemed possible. But the officer corps was kept obedient by its sobering experience of near-catastrophe in July 1974, and by its agreement thereafter with successive governments in seeing Turkey as a serious threat, which required a stronger defence system. For their part, successive governments consulted the leaders of the armed forces on important issues such as participation in NATO.

The termination of military conspiracies was ensured by the purge of prominent participants in the Junta. Karamanlis, because of his strong position and public anger, was more severe than the governments of Spain or Portugal, though not as severe as many people wanted. After highly publicised trials, quite large numbers of people, mostly soldiers, were sentenced to prison terms: eighteen people for plotting the coup of April 1967, 22 for involvement in the Polytechnic massacre of 1973 and 49 for torturing dissidents. (Some were sentenced for more than one of these offences; but the total sentenced for these or other offences was 104.) The death sentence passed on the leading plotters of the coup was commuted to life imprisonment.[4] Papadopoulos was still a prisoner when he died in hospital in 1999, and Ioannidis is still in jail. In 1974–75, many pro-Junta officers were retired – over 100 within a year of Karamanlis's return. In addition many civilian appointees of the Junta were dismissed, so that the total number purged was about 100,000.[5] In the electorate, devotees of the Junta rapidly declined, like their counterparts in Spain and Portugal. When represented by their own party in the general election of 1977, they numbered 7 per cent of the vote. Thereafter they were absorbed into New Democracy.

Thus by the end of 1975, Karamanlis's partners in the old establishment had been deprived of political power: the Americans, monarchy and army. Henceforth power was concentrated in political parties, which could no longer use the police to intimidate voters.

The over-mighty executive: its relations with parliament, media and trade unions

Democracy remained deficient partly in the weakness of parliament, the role of which was further curtailed by new standing orders in October 1975. Reflecting Karamanlis's belief in a decisive executive, this change was generally accepted at the time. After the 1977 election, in which the present party system took shape, the power of the government over parliament was strengthened much further – in a way that could not have been planned – by party discipline. Most seats were thenceforth held by the two major parties; and nearly all their MPs were either ministers, or aspirants to become minister, or ex-ministers. Thus parliament became primarily a forum for gladiatorial combat between party representatives, whose vague and repetitive monologues tended to dominate debates. In any case, major debates were rare and senior ministers disinclined to attend. Parliament remained unable to provide for the accountability of the executive, or adequate scrutiny of legislation, or satisfactory monitoring of expenditure or searching debate on major issues of the day. How far Greece diverged in these respects from western practice is indicated by the percentage of all legislation initiated by opposition parties and passed by parliament in the period December 1974 to June 1987: 30.2 in Italy, 60.2 in Portugal, 10.5 in Spain, and less than 0.1 in Greece. In June 1987, standing orders were adopted which reaffirmed the supremacy of the executive. By this time there was a growing tendency for parliament to delegate legislative responsibility to ministers through decrees. On occasion, ministers even announced decisions subject to ratification by laws which were not passed until some years later.[6]

The status of parliament was further reduced by the explosive growth of non-government radio and television broadcasting from the late 1980s; so that the media became the chief arena for politicians. Of delegates to a congress of the ruling party in 1996, only 11.5 per cent rated parliament as a powerful force.[7] Parliament's weakness had dire consequences for political life: ill-considered legislation, poorly respected laws and habitually obstructive and irresponsible opposition. It was also reflected in what was generally considered the low average calibre of MPs. An informed newspaper in 1998 reported that the leadership of one of the two major parties, New Democracy, tended to select candidates for parliament for many reasons other than merit, and that the majority of these candidates were 'mediocre, irrelevant, or unsuitable', with the result that party leaders had to find some ministers outside parliament. There is no reason to think that the other major party was better.[8]

The great majority of MPs were professionals of some kind. Lawyers and doctors continued to be especially prominent, and comprised for example nearly half the MPs elected in April 2000. Other important groups consisted of engineers, economists and academics. A sizeable minority of MPs combined their occupation with their parliamentary duties.[9]

Only in time did the broadcasting media become noticeably more independent of the government than before 1967. It was apparent even in 1975, when parliament regulated the status and role of broadcasting, that the public wanted it to be freed from the government, and that a majority of MPs wanted the media to cover current affairs in an objective and balanced way. But Karamanlis was evidently uninterested in such innovations; and few people if any foresaw the political importance of television, and the need therefore to ensure its independence. To this day, governments use the state television channels and radio stations to publicise tediously their own activities, although to an increasing extent allowing a voice to other parties, especially at election time. The staff of the broadcasting authority tended to be appointed on political criteria rather than merit:[10] a practice reflected in the often low quality of programmes and presentation. For some years after 1974, governments muffled debate about controversial current issues, such as discussion of recent history, or of the new social movements such as those led by women's, environmental and student associations. We shall see later how the public responded as soon as private broadcasting became established in 1987.

Governments in the later 1970s still had some influence over newspapers which, remaining in the hands of small or middling enterprises, continued to rely on direct or indirect state subsidies. In general, newspapers stayed closely tied to parties. However, at least controversy flourished again, ensured in part by the revival of a strong left-wing press, as well as the appearance in 1975 of a lively mass-circulation daily, *Elevtherotypia*, which publicised the new social movements.[11]

The institutional relationship between the government and organised labour was for some time an authoritarian survival, absent in Portugal and Spain. Governments used the legislation, with much of the practices, of the 1940s and 1950s to maintain their influence over the official trade union movement and collective bargaining. The major difference from the past was that successive governments relied much less on the police and much more on material concessions and on party organisation of union supporters. The opposition parties also organised their union supporters. By a law of 1982, a left-wing government strengthened collective bargaining, by guaranteeing employees' right to join and participate in unions; protecting the right to strike (subsequently curtailed in 1985 in public corporations); and making the system of elections in the General Confederation of Greek Workers (GSEE) truly democratic. The law of 1982 certainly strengthened the bargaining power of labour, and gave legal protection to the more independent type of unionism, based on the workplace, which had emerged and expanded since 1974. During the 1980s union membership increased to about one-third of wage and salary earners, who had increased so that they formed in 1981 just under half the labour force. However a left-wing government ensured its dominance of trade unions in the 1980s through its party's trade union branch, and continued the old practice of using subservient law courts to change the executive of the GSEE. The government has continued until now to collect levies on all employees and distribute the proceeds to unions. Moreover, automatic wage indexation in 1982–91 gave the government considerable control over workers' pay. In general, government influence continued to exacerbate industrial conflict by provoking an adversarial approach to industrial relations, and obstructing the development of conciliatory and cooperative processes of collective bargaining.[12]

Foundations of democracy: local government, the Church, education, women's status, civil liberties and the general revolt against authority

The 1975 constitution emphasised the importance of elected local government as a basis of democracy, and foreshadowed a long-overdue restoration of its powers. However national governments moved slowly, being reluctant to lose their patronage. The government doubled central grants to local government in 1979–81. In that year, a left-wing government increased the pace because it was confident that its party organisation would break its opponents' hold on local authorities, and it tripled central grants in 1982–84. Municipal councils were encouraged to form developmental syndicates with private enterprise or with agricultural cooperatives so as to encourage local economic activity. They were also given responsibility for establishing open care centres for the elderly and day nurseries. Within municipalities, elected neighbourhood councils were established in an effort to encourage grassroots democracy.

Advisory councils to prefects were restored in 1982, and given responsibility for decisions on local investment and local amenities. They were no longer appointed from above, but instead based on election by local authorities and professional associations. These measures were followed by increased expenditure on a wide range of local developments (including roads and schemes for drainage or irrigation), on public housing and child-minding centres, as well as factories and animal farms.[13] It is open to question how far decisions on development were actually devolved from national bureaucrats and party leaders to local authorities at the prefectural or municipal level. What is sure is that the historic decline of the provinces was being reversed through the renewal of their economic and political life.

The new constitution of the Church, enacted in 1977, stipulated that it should be self-governing, and terminated the traditional practice of governmental intervention in the choice of the Archbishop.[14] The Church showed increasing readiness to defend its influence against government policies. An early indication was its protest against Karamanlis's move to cultivate good relations with the Vatican. Its relationship with the left-wing government from 1981 onwards was sometimes stormy and included mass demonstrations. Thus the Church forced this government to abandon attempts to make civil marriage obligatory, appropriate monastic property and enable laity to participate in elections of parish and episcopal advisory councils.

Another prerequisite of democracy which was implemented by Karamanlis's government in the late 1970s was educational reform, which reinstated the changes introduced by Georgios Papandreou's government. The intake into universities resumed its upward trend. The minimum period of compulsory education was restored to nine years, meaning a minimum school-leaving age of fifteen, which became effective again in 1979. In 1977, *katharevousa* ceased to be the language of education or of the state – a momentous and controversial break with the past, going further than Georgios Papandreou had dared. Government expenditure on education as a proportion of GNP rose from 1.9 per cent in 1960; to 2.8 per cent in 1975; 2.9 per cent in 1980; and 3.7 per cent in 1989. The percentage of the 20–24 age group enrolled in all forms of tertiary institutions in Greece was 13.4 in 1971–72, 18.4 in 1975–76, and 24.5 in 1988–89. Adding the persistently high number studying in foreign universities (about 19 per cent of all tertiary students in 1990), the participation rate in tertiary education was again above average for southern Europe. Especially great was the almost sixfold increase in enrolments in higher technical education between 1974 and 1989.[15]

The trend towards greater freedom of academics to criticise the government could only be gradual, because control over curricula and appointments remained in government hands. The key reform was a law of 1982, which transferred power from professors to representatives of the entire department (including undergraduate students) who elected academic administrators from departmental heads upwards. This reform also gave junior staff more opportunity to teach their own courses and conduct research. In time, more departments were established, and staff appointed, in fields relevant to contemporary issues, such as sociology, politics and psychology. The National Centre of Social Research had its funding greatly increased – so that its publications proliferated – and additional centres of social research were established by universities.[16] So increasing numbers of academics were appointed who were qualified to be independent critics of society.

Further progress towards legal equality of the sexes occurred in the 1980s. The left-wing parties in the early 1980s dominated the women's movement that developed strongly from 1974, with a leading role being played by

Margaret Papandreou, American wife of Andreas. The Greek movement drew its inspiration to some extent from its north American counterpart (like the women's movements in many western countries), but still more from the wartime National Liberation Front, which had been a potent liberating experience for many women still alive. Andreas Papandreou's government appointed an influential advisory body which became the General Secretariat for the Equality of the Sexes in 1985.[17] The landmark family law of 1983 gave women legal equality in the family, decriminalised adultery and abolished the legal claim to the dowry, while providing civil marriage for those wanting it and giving equal status to children born outside wedlock. The family law also made permanent provision for divorce by consent, introduced on a trial basis in 1979. After 1979 the divorce rate rose to one for every ten marriages, over twice the rate of 1970, although still low by the standards of northern Europe. (It is likely that a high proportion of divorces until the 1970s were between childless couples.) Most divorces after 1979 were by consent, and an increasing proportion were initiated by women. The facilitation of divorce was a liberating measure for women, as it was in Italy, Portugal and Spain, where it also occurred in this period. For example one half of all divorce proceedings in the 1980s were on grounds of cruelty, of which women were the more common victims.[18] Abortion was decriminalised by a law of 1986, as also occurred in this period in Spain and Italy. Until then abortion was virtually prohibited in all circumstances, but was nevertheless practised on a massive scale. The new law introduced what amounted to abortion on demand, financed by health insurance, in the first twelve weeks of pregnancy.[19]

In tertiary education, progress was steady, with the proportion of women students rising from a third to a half between 1971 and 1989. A series of laws in the 1980s raised women's status in other ways. Gender discrimination in employment, and in pay, was banned. Farmers' wives became eligible to join cooperatives in their own right, and entitled to their own pensions. The obvious limitation of some measures was that they were merely decreed from above. What really mattered is whether the necessary changes of public attitude were occurring. Survey evidence shows that to some extent they were:[20] the question remains how far and how fast.

Remnants of authoritarian tradition survived in various restrictions on individual liberties, restrictions which did not get much attention in the first ten years or so of the *metapolitevsi*. The constitution reaffirmed the obligation of all citizens without exception to do military service, with the result that at any time until 1997, hundreds of conscientious objectors were in military jails. The police (until 1994) and newspapers continued to refer to people on trial as guilty before the verdict was pronounced.[21] Although the constitution stipulated for the first time that religious expression was free, it qualified that freedom in ways which were frequently abused by the police and the courts. The restrictions on proselytisation by, and new places of worship for, minority religions remained for a long time prohibitive; and the inclusion of religious denomination on state identity cards continued in practice to be required.[22] In 1985, however, the Greek government took a step of great importance in the future by allowing appeals by citizens to the European Court of Human Rights. In international context, Greece did not rate badly on civil liberties, as it was conventionally ranked at about the same level as Portugal and Spain, although all three came behind Italy.[23]

The collapse of the Junta led to an assault on traditional values and personal authority in every sphere, wherever in fact it was not grounded on force as in the army or on affection as in the family. This trend occurred primarily among youth. A generation gap which was opening up in the mid-1960s widened. An example of the new self-assertiveness of youth was the annual commemoration on 17 November of the fall of the Polytechnic in 1973, a ceremony founded and led by youth. In time it was celebrated with solemnity by the political establishment as well. So revered thereafter was the sanctuary of university precincts that, rather than admit the police, academic authorities let the Polytechnic and other tertiary educational institutions be vandalised on 20 occasions in 1974–91, by people who over the years were less and less likely to have any evident political motivation.[24] Nevertheless, the commemoration of the Polytechnic became the Bastille Day of democracy.

The widespread hostility to western influence and to big business since 1974 has been expressed until the present day in attacks against property and individuals by terrorist groups, attacks which were for a long time frequent. At first the terrorists' slogans called for class struggle and armed revolution; and later they were characterised rather by vague populism. The groups included 'The 1st May', the 'Anti-State Struggle', 'Revolutionary Solidarity' and the 'Revolutionary Popular Struggle', the last of which for a time issued a periodical and up to September 1994 detonated 250 bombs. Pre-eminent for its professional deadliness was the '17th November', which from December 1975 to June 2000 assassinated 23 people and has still evaded the police.[25] Favoured victims of the terrorists were western diplomats with military or intelligence roles, prominent businessmen, right-wing politicians and representatives of the repressive arms of the state such as judges, police officers and prison officials. The police had scant success in retaliation – their score of convicted terrorists in the 1990s being just two. This failure contrasts with the success of their predecessors in crushing Communism before 1974, and with the Italian police victory over left-wing terrorism in the early 1980s. The Greek police after 1974 were crippled by lack of resources or training, by a weak sense of professional mission and a low level of competence. In the anti-authoritarian atmosphere which now prevailed, they suffered also from lack of the public support which they needed for sweeping powers to recruit informers, protect witnesses and wrest information from suspects. The lack of public respect for the police was illustrated by a survey of 614 people in 2000–1, which found that of those who learnt of illegal practices *and disclosed them to others*, only 14 per cent went to the police or another appropriate authority.[26]

The new party system

PASOK and New Democracy

Both Karamanlis and his rival Andreas Papandreou recognised that democracy required parties organised on modern lines, with ideologies, programmes and mass organisations. With this end in mind, they both produced manifestoes in September 1974, and proceeded to create what became the two dominant parties. Since the parliamentary election of 1977, no other party has received more than 13 per cent of the vote; and none other than the two Communist parties has lasted more than a few years. Both major parties retained for some time a traditional feature: dependence on the leader's personality. Karamanlis and Papandreou created their respective parties by formulating their ideologies and key policies and, with the help of friends, selecting their parliamentary candidates.[27]

Karamanlis named his party New Democracy (ND). Although its leadership came from his old party the National Radical Union (ERE), the latter's ideas were adapted to the new environment. Moreover, 64 per cent of ND's MPs entered parliament for the first time in November 1974, whereas in the elections of 1950–64 the highest proportion of new MPs elected to a right-wing party had been 26 per cent for ND's ancestor the Greek Rally in 1951. Admittedly, many new MPs in 1974 were related to politicians before 1967. Because of Karamanlis's prestige, and the general feeling 'either Karamanlis or the tanks', the party won an overwhelming majority in the November election. The slump of the Centre Union's vote is explicable by Karamanlis's capture of the middle ground with his liberalising decisions, and by many opposition voters' move leftwards in reaction against the Junta, so as to support Andreas Papandreou's newly founded Panhellenic Socialist Movement (PASOK), which won 13.6 per cent of the vote, or the Communist parties allied with the old United Democratic Left (EDA), an alliance which won 9.5 per cent. As subsequently became apparent, the Centre Union and United Democratic Left were losing their *raison d'être*, and were to be absorbed by PASOK or the Communist parties.

Voters late in 1974 were especially preoccupied by three interlinked issues: establishing democracy, terminating dependence on America and greater social justice. In consequence, left-wing, and especially Marxist, ideas prevailed among students and intellectuals. They were eagerly discussed in periodicals, treatises, theoretical books and particularly in works about a hitherto suppressed subject, the left-wing movements of the 1940s. This was the intellectual environment of 'the generation of the Polytechnic', which later rose to prominence in politics, the media, public service and the professions.

To become effectual, the left needed a leader who could counter Karamanlis, and a party which could use the opportunities for mass organisation created by 25 years of economic growth and social development. The Communist Party could not expand beyond a core of traditional devotees and a fringe of ideologues, basically because it remained attached to the forbidding Soviet model of dictatorship.[28] For many years it saw no need to adjust its ideas and policies to parliamentary democracy and the western alliance; while its leaders never expressed a formal apology for the party's atrocities in the 1940s and its savage treatment of dissidents thereafter. The support which it received came mainly from the working class of Athens, Piraeus and Salonika, and the traditionally left-wing farmers and workers of Thessaly. In the 1977 election it received 9.4 per cent of the vote, compared with 2.7 per cent for various left-wing groups including the Communist Party of the Interior. The last moved increasingly towards reformism – for example supporting the application to join the EEC in 1975 – but could not extend its appeal far beyond radical intellectuals.

Thus the role of a progressive party of government was filled by Andreas Papandreou's PASOK. Its percentage of the vote rose fast to 25.3 in the 1977 election, making it the main opposition party, and then to 48.1 in the general election of October 1981, giving it a large parliamentary majority.

Andreas Papandreou (1919–96) had highly educated parents, and had become prominent in radical politics and academic economics.[29] As a student in the late 1930s, he was twice arrested by Metaxas's police – the second time for participation in a Trotskyist group – and was beaten up in jail, but allowed to leave for the United States in 1939, where he gained a PhD at Harvard in 1943, and during the next eighteen years held a series of academic posts in economics including chairs at Minnesota and Berkeley. He returned at Karamanlis's invitation to become in 1961 adviser to the Bank of Greece, and head of an economic think-tank funded by American institutions and sponsored by the Academy of Athens. Being elected to parliament in 1964 as a member of his father's Centre Union, he embarked on a stormy political career. In exile from the dictatorship, he held academic chairs successively in Sweden and Canada, and campaigned actively against the Junta. In the process he formulated a body of left-wing rhetoric and ideas which appealed to youth after 1974. He presented himself to voters as an economic wizard with a record of resistance to right-wing authority.

Although his ministerial experience was limited, his campaigning experience was not, and he was gifted with a magnetic personality and splendid oratorical powers, while he enforced his authority ruthlessly. Thus he bound together people with diverse origins and skills: experienced politicians from the old Centre Union, socialist intellectuals, students and professionals such as economists.[30] The great majority – 80 per cent – of PASOK MPs elected in 1977 were first-timers, while a remarkably high proportion – 67 per cent – were relatively young, being aged 30 to 49. Nearly all of PASOK's Central Committee in 1977 were, likewise, newcomers to party politics. Several who were prominent in the party in the late 1970s held key ministries in the PASOK government twenty years later. But a majority of ministries in Papandreou's first government in 1981 were held by veterans of the Centre Union.

Andreas brought together in one movement the growing number of people who wanted a decisive break with the past. The 'Declaration of the 3rd September [1974]' propounded an original and nationalistic form of socialism based on the expectation that national independence, economic and military, would lead to the realisation of popular sovereignty, which in turn would be the prerequisite for social liberation and political democracy. It referred also to the new social movements, women's and environmental. Dilution of these principles started well before the 1981 election, so that the emphasis shifted from socialism to 'change', and from 'classes' to the 'privileged' and 'non-privileged'. So charged was the word 'change' with expectations of social justice, participatory democracy and modernisation on a broad front that it aroused great enthusiasm among all social strata. PASOK persuaded voters that it was a left-wing party, in the same camp as the Communist parties, and sharply opposed to the traditional right, allegedly represented by New Democracy. It maintained this stance during subsequent years in government, while betraying wholesale its supporters' expectations, the betrayal being camouflaged by Papandreou's personality and rhetoric.

This programme appealed especially to young people, as indicated by a survey of November 1985 in the greater metropolitan area, the voters of which were some percentage points further to the left than the rest of the country.

Table 8.1 *Comparison of opinions of two age cohorts in 1985*[31]

	Under 35 %	Over 49 %
Voted New Democracy in 1985 general election	19	51
Voted PASOK in 1985 general election	54	3
Had a good opinion of the United States	24	48
Blamed exclusively or mainly the Communists for the civil war	11	60
Blamed exclusively or mainly the government forces for the civil war	65	26
Trusted the Federation of Greek Industries	26	62
Trusted the General Confederation of Greek Workers	60	40
Opposed premarital sex	7	56
Trusted the Greek Orthodox Church	38	86
Went to church every Sunday or often	1	42

Papandreou's outstanding achievement was to create a party of government, based on a mass organisation, which was formidably successful in winning power.[32] In this respect he achieved what his father had attempted in the 1960s. PASOK in the late 1970s formed branches, and devised policies, adapted to diverse sectors of society. In rural areas, mass political participation consequently became possible for the first time since the National Liberation Front of the 1940s. By the 1981 election, PASOK had over 110,000 members organised in hundreds of rural branches, and hundreds more branches among trade unions, student unions, agricultural cooperatives, women's groups and a range of professional associations. It had also moved far towards dominance of local government.[33]

The combination of mass participation with Andreas's charisma was powerful; although from the start the contradiction between the party's promise of democratic procedures and its authoritarian leadership led to large-scale expulsions and resignations. The strength of its grass-roots organisation gave PASOK an advantage over New Democracy during most of the 1980s. The PASOK government broadened the scope for challenge to traditional authorities by establishing election by PR for the executives of professional associations, agricultural cooperatives, civil servants' associations, the chambers of small businessmen and university faculties. All were thus opened to party competition, at the expense however of their ability to represent their members and promote their interests effectively.[34] Significantly, PR was not introduced to local government elections, where it might have weakened PASOK's dominance.

New Democracy had been slower to define its ideology and construct an organisation, primarily because of Karamanlis's lack of interest in party work and conservative MPs' desire to preserve their local influence (a preference rationalised by principle). Thus the extra-parliamentary organisation was still rudimentary when Karamanlis quit the leadership in May 1980. Bereft of his charisma, and wanting to win the support of Junta sympathisers, the party drifted rightwards. Thus it played into the hands of Papandreou, who in preparing for power was trying to appear more moderate.[35]

New Democracy learnt from its defeat of 1981 that mass organisation was vital, and so it followed PASOK's example. Konstantinos Mitsotakis became leader in 1984, and continued the construction of the party machine as the basis of his authority at the expense of the party 'barons'. Starting his professional career as a lawyer, Mitsotakis (born 1918) had first been elected to parliament in 1946 and had held various ministerial portfolios since 1951. He was obnoxious to the left as one of the 'apostate' MPs of 1965 (see p. 108). Spurred by the party's second defeat in 1985, Mitsotakis followed PASOK's example in organising branches for interest groups, such as professional bodies, women's organisations and even schoolchildren.

Parties in the 1980s

By 1986 the two major parties had about 600,000 members between them, not counting their youth sections.[36] The centre of every little market town acquired its PASOK and New Democracy offices. The importance of parties was illustrated between June 1989 and April 1990 when no party had a parliamentary majority: commercial activity was seriously affected, and the public service and trade unions were partly paralysed.

The power of parties was, as Richard Gillespie showed, paralleled in Italy, Portugal and Spain in these years. The explanation lay in their traditionally centralised political systems, which weakened the autonomy of the public service and of social institutions such as chambers of commerce or trade unions. In all these states, the power of the state had checked the growth of civil society.[37] Thus the passing of dictatorship left a vacuum which was filled by leader-centred parties. Consequently, there was tension between party power and the desire of an increasingly educated and self-assertive public for freedom of association. In Greece, Portugal and Spain, in the 1980s, the party state appeared to threaten civil liberties and civil society.

In Greece the power of parties was based partly on a spoils system which seems to have been still more deep-rooted than in the other southern

European countries. For most rank-and-file members, the main motive to join was the desire for official appointments or favours. European surveys showed for example that the proportion of young people favouring state employment as a career option was extraordinarily high in Greece in the 1980s (over two-thirds).[38] The resulting expansion of public employment was especially sudden after 1981, when PASOK had to satisfy its supporters. The new phenomenon of mass party membership made it possible for PASOK bosses to confine the spoils of office systematically to their supporters or to left-wing allies. Political criteria were applied, for example, to many leading positions in the armed forces, to all principals of secondary schools, and to all managers of state banks, public hospitals and nationalised industries.

The cohesion of each party was guaranteed increasingly by the mass organisation, over which the leader's authority was overwhelming. MPs lost much of their old power as independent sources of patronage.[39] Their role was increasingly to act as intermediaries between voters and either the party or the government.

Campaigns between parties were conducted in a rowdy way which was considered remarkable by observers of elections in other southern European countries.[40] The intensity of party competition increased expenditure on organisation and publicity. Then the advent of private broadcasting increased electoral expenditure by far more from the late 1980s. It seems for example that well over $10 million was spent by the major parties and their candidates at the parliamentary election of 2000. The PASOK government passed a law in 1984 providing public subsidies to the parties, which in one non-election year (1991) amounted to the equivalent of $12 million; but this source covered only a small part of the parties' expenditure. The newspaper *Kathimerini* estimated in 1994 that each major party derived one-fifth of its resources from its members.[41] The rest of expenditure, by candidates and party organisations, seems to have been funded from donations by businesses – especially those which wanted or received public contracts – and before the 1990s in loans to the ruling party from state banks.

In the first half of the 1980s, 70 per cent of voters identified themselves with a political party, a proportion high by southern European standards.[42] Both the extent of political discussion among voters, and the degree of polarisation perceived by voters between the major parties, were found by surveys during these years to be greater in Greece than elsewhere in western Europe.

Some of the explanation for this polarisation was social. PASOK claimed to defend the underprivileged masses against privileged oligarchies, while New Democracy increasingly represented the wealthy and socially conservative, as PASOK lost support in the higher socio-economic groups after 1981. New Democracy was stronger among businessmen, and relatively weak among industrial workers. PASOK appealed to the less prestigious professions, but also to senior executives and the generally wealthy self-employed professionals. Both drew strong support from farmers and self-employed business people such as shopkeepers. Thus the social divergence between the camps was not clear-cut.[43]

There was however a clear distinction in ideological tone in the 1980s. PASOK emphasised state ownership and redistribution of wealth; while New Democracy increasingly spoke the language of economic liberalism. PASOK appealed more to the secular-minded, and New Democracy to religious conservatives. PASOK convinced its supporters that it was more devoted to national independence, while accusing New Democracy of subservience to the United States.[44]

But what more than anything else made the polarisation vehement were the memories invoked by PASOK, which claimed to represent the dispossessed and persecuted left of the past fifty years, and accused New Democracy of representing the police state of the post-civil war era. New Democracy for some time let the myth flourish by claiming to represent traditional social and moral values, including the old hierarchies of wealth and education. The importance of the past was reflected, during the election campaign of May–June 1985, in constant recriminations between parties and partisan newspapers over events since the 1930s.

Disillusionment with PASOK

Relations between parties changed a few months afterwards, when the PASOK government was forced by economic realities to abandon its anti-western and anti-capitalist stance. To escape from the problems caused especially by a mounting public debt and plummeting reserves of foreign exchange, the government accepted a massive loan from the EEC, as a condition of which it imposed a harsh austerity programme, raising interest rates, cutting social expenditure, curbing wage increases and limiting even the right to strike. The effect was to reduce real wages by about 12 per cent in 1986–87, and cut the annual rate of real growth in social expenditure from 10 per cent in 1980–85 to 1 per cent in 1985–90. PASOK thus moved to full support for integration in the EEC, a policy which was becoming popular as loans and subsidies flowed in. PASOK soon ceased to see itself as ideologically orientated towards developing and non-aligned countries, and looked instead towards western Europe. PASOK leaders began to associate prominently with western European social democratic politicians, whom they increasingly resembled in ethos.[45]

In trying to revive investment, the government provided various incentives to private business, and improved its relations with the Federation of Greek Industries. Thus it moved to something like the traditional strategy of development: wage restraint so as to retain the economy's competitive advantage, and generous incentives to private including foreign investment, with the legal guarantees of the 1950s and 1960s being effectively superseded in time by EEC safeguards for the free movement of capital.

This about-turn provoked uproar among the government's supporters and allies, which was expressed in the resignation of one minister, the expulsion of another from the party, a serious split in the party's trade union wing, increasing opposition by the Communist Party and a long-running series of strikes and demonstrations, including blockades of roads by farmers and a wave of strikes by many major unions in early 1987. The government eventually resorted to civilian mobilisation to break several strikes, and to tough police measures against demonstrations. Not surprisingly, the slogan of 'change' and socialist ideology lost much of their appeal. Disillusionment was especially noticeable among young people, many of whom lapsed into apathy or turned to New Democracy.

Disillusionment was also caused by major financial scandals inculpating the government. That which dominated attention was probably the worst to have occurred since 1945. It centred on Georgios Koskotas, owner of the Bank of Crete and media magnate, who in November 1988 was arrested while being investigated on suspicion of embezzling a sum proved later to be over $200 million from his bank, with the help of some ministers, to whom in return he offered the support of his powerful magazines and newspapers. The Deputy Prime Minister Agamemnon Koutsogiorgas was shown to have received a bribe of $2 million to facilitate the fraud and so was forced to resign in March 1989. In the first half of 1989, the government was also under suspicion of robbing the public by paying hundreds of millions of dollars too much for imported military aircraft, and of robbing the EEC by the re-export of Yugoslav maize fraudulently labelled as Greek (the Deputy Finance Minister being involved in the latter). Within several months following Koskotas's arrest six ministers resigned in disgust with their government.[46]

Meanwhile the government was shaken also by periodic breakdowns in Andreas's health, and by his unedifying private life. Much of the public was also worried by the government's assertions of arbitrary power. Andreas continued to use the national broadcasting organisation as a public relations agency, while his ministers openly threatened unfriendly newspapers.[47] It emerged in 1989 that the National Information Service (successor to the Central Intelligence Service), through the state telecommunications organisation OTE, had been bugging over 46,000 phones of politicians, journalists, businessmen and lawyers; and that the information thus obtained was apparently used by the prime minister for party purposes.[48]

The financial burden imposed on taxpayers by the PASOK spoils system became mountainous before the general election of June 1989. The austerity programme promised to the European Commission was disregarded; and the increase in real wages in 1988–89 more than made up for the decline in the previous two years. In the six months before the election, public appointments were bestowed on about 90,000 people, few of whom, it seems, were either needed or qualified. This was at a time when the proportion of public revenue devoted to debt service was rising to one-quarter. 'A boundless lunatic asylum' was how the retired Karamanlis publicly described the situation in January.[49]

The opposition parties had since 1985 reorientated themselves so as to exploit the government's vulnerability. New Democracy emphasised the neo-liberal ideology now influential in the western world and preached the virtues of small government and private enterprise. It dropped Cold War themes, and in the parliamentary election of June 1989 called for reconciliation between historically opposed forces. The Communist Party reciprocated and, at the prompting of Mikhail Gorbachev, the reforming leader of the Soviet Union, moved in 1988 towards acceptance both of parliamentary democracy and of EEC membership. It formed an alliance in December 1988 with the former Communist Party of the Interior in an alliance calling itself the Coalition of the Left and Progress (abbreviated to Coalition), which hoped to displace PASOK as the major party of the left. In the same month, representatives of the Communist Party, the Communist Party of the Interior and New Democracy met to concert policies, prominent in which was *katharsis* (cleansing, meaning investigation and trial of corrupt members of the PASOK regime).[50] This agreement between the ideological extremes to strengthen democratic institutions can be seen as the ultimate proof of those institutions' stability.

The public mood at the time of the election of June 1989 was completely different from that of four years earlier. The disillusionment of PASOK voters coincided with the visible crumbling of Communist dictatorships in the Soviet Union and throughout eastern Europe. The result in Greece as in other countries was a collapse both of faith in and fear of socialism, and hence a drop in the ideological temperature. In this atmosphere, in August, leading politicians of all parties supported a grand ceremony of reconciliation between opposed forces in the civil war, and saw this as the close of an era.

What is nevertheless noteworthy about the election results of June 1989 was the stability of voter alignments (see Appendix 2). PASOK suffered a predictable decline, compared with its 1985 result, of 6.7 percentage points, but remained a major party. The Coalition secured only a marginal increase over the combined vote of its constituent parties in 1985, and so failed decisively to displace PASOK. New Democracy fell just short of an absolute majority of seats, thanks to the relatively pure version of PR which the PASOK government had just introduced for precisely this purpose. The main reason for the stability of voters' allegiance was revealed by a survey of their ideological identification. In particular the majority of PASOK voters still saw themselves as opposed both to the right and the far left, while feeling an affinity with other left voters. The loyalty of PASOK voters had evidently been cemented by their party's achievements in redistributing income in favour of lower income groups and farmers.[51]

Thus the party system which emerged in the late 1970s had become embedded in voters' minds. This stability explains why there was no lasting change in the party system during the following ten months of uncertainty, when there were two coalition governments and two more elections. The eventual outcome was that New Democracy formed a single-party government based on a slim parliamentary majority in April 1990, with PASOK as the main opposition party.

A new deal

Policies favouring wage-earners

In the liberated atmosphere after July 1974, a ferment of organisational and strike activity spread through industry, made possible by employers' unprecedented demand for labour. In many enterprises, workers bypassed the official trade unions and the Communist Party by forming workplace cells to press their claims. The number of hours lost by strike activity in 1976–81 was twelve times the figure for 1961–66. Among farmers, there were widespread demonstrations and other forms of collective action to defend their recent income gains.

Karamanlis's government responded to the prevalent mood by taking reprisals against those sections of big business which had collaborated with the Junta, especially a large section of shipowners led by Stratis Andreadis, head of an empire which included the giant Commercial Bank. Thus the government facilitated the takeover of the Greek Shipowners' Union by a favoured group of shipowners and nationalised the Commercial Bank. As in Portugal and Spain, many ailing business enterprises were nationalised in order to save jobs in conditions of slower growth and declining foreign investment. This process was started by Karamanlis in the mid-1970s and continued by PASOK in the 1980s.

The government also decreed substantial increases in wages to make up for ground lost under the dictatorship. Thus Karamanlis earned the accusation of 'socialmania' from businessmen. In the five years after the fall of the dictatorship, real earnings of blue-collar workers in manufacturing rose by 11 per cent. The New Democracy government of 1980–81 reduced maximum working hours from 48 to 40 hours a week, and introduced legislation compelling employers to grant paid holidays, and to improve safety conditions in places of work. Table 8.2 shows how sudden was the increase in the share of national income received by employees.

Meanwhile, from 1974 to 1983, rents, profits and other middle-class incomes in Greece fell from 29.8 per cent of national income to 16.8 per cent. Also illustrative of the new climate was the greater regard for occupational safety. Between 1970 and 1990 the number of occupational accidents recorded by the main employees' insurance organisation, IKA, fell by 28 per cent, while the employees insured with IKA doubled.[53]

PASOK's social reforms

Total expenditure on social welfare (including health but excluding education) as a percentage of GNP was 9.7 per cent in 1965 and 10.9 per cent in 1975; but then leapt to 14 per cent in 1980 and 20.9 per cent in 1985. So the increase occurred disproportionately in the initial years of PASOK rule.[54] In Italy by contrast, the rise was gradual during this period. Greek expenditure on old age and disability pensions (which as in Italy were particularly favoured by politicians for electoral patronage), was 4.8 per cent of GNP in 1975 (compared with an OECD average of 7.1 per cent) and 5.8 per cent in 1980, then leaping to 10.7 per cent in 1985 (the OECD average by then being only 8.9 per cent).

The PASOK government took to new lengths the use of public appointments as a form of social policy, providing secure jobs to masses of people from lower income groups, with preference later given also to people with special needs like parents of large families or disabled veterans of the wartime resistance. In its hostility to hierarchy, PASOK populism was

Table 8.2 *Share of wages/salaries in national income*[52]

	1959–60	*1974–75*	*1981–82*
Greece	45.3	48.8	62.2
Spain	51.8	61.8	62.3
Italy	52.1	66.2	67.8

anti-meritocratic. The standard tests of merit for appointment to permanent posts in the civil service – competitive exams – were abolished; while merit was used much less as a criterion for promotion. Trade union officials – who were usually members of PASOK – played a key role in appointments, promotions and personnel management in public sector enterprises. The performance of state departments and enterprises deteriorated visibly, while their wage and salary bills mounted.[55] Thus the PASOK regime undermined the competence of the public service, while demanding that it perform increasingly ambitious roles.

Government employees numbered 320,000 in 1971 (including the regular army and state-owned industries), which relative to the labour force was little higher than the 250,000 in 1950. This rose to 500,000 in 1981 and then to 700,000 in 1991: 18 per cent of the labour force at the last date. This proportion was no longer high by western European standards, but it was grossly disproportionate to what the public sector achieved.[56]

While greatly increasing educational expenditure, PASOK showed more interest in promoting social equality than economic modernisation. PASOK aimed in particular to satisfy the popular demand for a broad ladder through tertiary education to secure government jobs. As before 1974, the majority of university graduates proceeded to some sort of public employment; and, as we have seen, access to university education expanded rapidly. On the other hand, after the university law of 1982, the selection of teaching and research staff became generally more meritocratic. The disadvantage, typical of PASOK reforms, was the creation of a new party arena in the electoral procedures which determined departmental policy and staff appointments.[57]

Like left-wing parties in Italy, Portugal and Spain in this period, PASOK aspired to make good health care accessible to all, regardless of income. This was the aim of law 1397 of 1983, establishing a National Health Service, a measure which alas achieved few of its objectives, mainly for lack of expenditure, and also because training of medical staff was ill coordinated.[58] As a percentage of GDP, government expenditure on health was 3.8 in 1981 (compared with an average of 4.8 in Italy, Portugal and Spain), and 4 in 1989 (compared by then with 5 in Italy, Portugal and Spain, but more by other estimates). Total expenditure on health (public and private) rose from 4.5 per cent of GNP in 1975 to 7.2 in 1987. The percentage of hospital beds provided by the public sector or charities increased from 59 in 1981 to 70 in 1989, because the government banned both new private hospitals and private-sector practice by doctors employed in the public sector. The latter ban was widely evaded; and it was estimated that black market expenditure on health, as a percentage of total health expenditure, increased from 13 in 1982 to 23 in 1987. The quality of care in public hospitals, and the efficiency of their administration, did not noticeably improve.

The establishment of health centres to provide primary care in rural areas, however, was popular and partially successful. By 1989, 160 of them, located in nearly all prefectures, catered for over 40 per cent of the population. But they remained seriously under-resourced and short of general practitioners, nurses, dentists and other staff, even though the number of nurses relative to population increased greatly in the 1980s. In 1992, the health centres still had only two-thirds of the physicians that they needed. The inequalities between the health care provided by different insurance funds remained wide. It seems significant however that, in successive surveys of health care among OECD countries, Greece rose from 29th place in 1982 to 13th in 1992.[59]

The fate of PASOK's health reforms illustrates a constraint on all its social policy: lack of government expenditure, because revenue was limited by the sluggish growth of the economy. Much expenditure, in any case, was devoted instead to increasing numbers of public employees and pensioners. Despite these constraints, the PASOK government did manage to reduce social inequalities by raising minimum wages and pensions and extending social services. According to one authority, Ioannis Stournaras, the numbers in relative poverty fell from 2.1 million in 1980 to 1.8 million in 1986, despite a rise in unemployment.[60] Unfortunately, much of this progress towards greater equity was precarious because it was financed by unsustainable means.

Notes

1   Richard Gillespie, 'The consolidation of new democracies', in Derek W. Urwin and W.E. Paterson (eds), *Politics in Western Europe Today* (1990), 234–48.

2   Theodore A. Couloumbis and Prodromos Yannas, 'The stability quotient in Greece's post-1974 democratic institutions', *Journal of Modern Greek Studies* 1 (1983), 359–72.

3   *Vima*, 25 April 1999, A54, Petros Evthymiou. They comprised seven out of nine members of the Communist Politburo, and ten out of thirteen members of the PASOK Executive Committee, as well as two former leaders of New Democracy.

4   The last death sentence carried out in Greece was in 1972 (*Vima*, 5 December 1993, A61).

5   C.M. Woodhouse, *Karamanlis. The Restorer of Greek Democracy* (Oxford 1982), 231.

6   Nicos Alivizatos, 'The difficulties of "rationalization" in a polarized political system: the Greek Chamber of Deputies', in Ulrike Liebert and Maurizio Cotta (eds), *Parliament and Democratic Consolidation in Southern Europe* (1990), 134–45; *Ta Nea*, 15 June 1989, 10, Phaidon Vegleris; P. Nikiforos Diamandouros, 'Politics and constitutionalism in Greece: the 1975 constitution in historical perspective', in Houchang E. Chehabi, Alfred Stepan and Juan J. Linz, *Politics, Society and Democracy* (1995), 293–4; *Vima*, 17 December 2000, 18, Richardou Someritis.

7   Institouto V–Project Research Consulting, *Public Opinion in Greece* (in Greek, 1999), 119; Stavros Lygeros, *The Game of Power* (in Greek, 1997), 254, 367.

8   *Kathimerini*, 19 July 1998, 4.

9   *Vima*, 28 January 2001, A27, B. Chioti, Gr. Tzovara.

10   Thimios Zaharopoulos and Manny E. Paraschos, *Mass Media in Greece: Power, Politics and Privatization* (Westport, CT 1993), 174.

11   Maria Komninou, 'The role of the mass media in the Third Republic, 1974–94', in Christos Lyrintzis, Ilias Nikolakopoulos and Dimitris Sotiropoulos (eds), *Society and Politics. Aspects of the Third Republic, 1974–94* (in Greek, 1996), 225–9.

12   Thomas W. Gallant, 'Collective action and atomistic actors : labor unions, strikes, and crime in Greece in the postwar era', in Dimitri Constas and Theofanis G. Stavrou (eds), *Greece Prepares for the Twenty-first Century* (Baltimore, MD 1995), 156; Stella Zabarloukou, 'Trade union movement and state intervention in Greece after 1974: a comparative approach', in Lyrintzis *et al.* (eds), *Society and Politics*, 91–115; Calliope Golomazou-Papas, 'The General Confederation of Workers of Greece: a case of an intermediary within an authoritarian licensed corporatist practice', in Speros Vryonis Jr, (ed.), *Greece on the Road to Democracy. From the Junta to PASOK, 1984–86* (New York 1991), 252.

13   Paraskevi D. Christofilopoulou, 'Decentralization policy in post-dictatorial Greece', *Local Government Studies* 13 (1987), 6–13; *Ta Nea*, 14 May 1985, 15, Kosta Chardavella.

14   Vasiliki Georgiadou, 'Secular state and Orthodox Church: the relationship between religion, society, and politics since 1974', in Lyrintzis *et al.*, *Society and Politics*, 252–62; *Vima*, 17 May 1998, A8, Aristovoulos Manesis.

15   Ioanna Lambiri-Dimaki, 'Educational trends in Greece', in Ioanna Lambiri-Dimaki and Nota Kyriazis (eds), *Greek Society at the End of the Twentieth Century* (in Greek, 1995), 208–11; Maria Petmesidou, 'Mass higher education and the social sciences in Greece', *International Sociology* 13 (1998), 362.

16   Koula Kassimati, 'Development of social research in Greece', *International Sociology* 33 (1998), 350–1, 357.

17   Adamantia Pollis, 'Gender and social change in Greece: the role of women', in Theodore C. Kariotis (ed.), *The Greek Socialist Experiment. Papandreou's Greece, 1981–9* (New York 1992), 295–300.

18 Peter Loizos and Evthymios Papataxiarchis, 'Gender and kinship in marriage and alternative contexts', in Peter Loizos (ed.), *Contested Identities. Gender and Kinship in Modern Greece* (Princeton, NJ 1991), 7; *Vima*, 13 October 1991, A52, Ioanna Mandrou; *Vima*, 7 March 1993, A36–7, Ioanna Mandrou; *Vima*, 17 April 1994, A51, Ioanna Mandrou.

19 Stephanie Ginger, 'Abortion in Greece', *Contemporary Review* 243 (1983), 253–5; *Vima*, 20 June 1993, A52, Ioanna Mandrou.

20 Panayoti E. Dimitras, 'Changes in public attitudes', in Kevin Featherstone and Dimitrios K. Katsoudas (eds), *Political Change in Greece. Before and After the Colonels* (1987), 73.

21 *Vima*, 3 January 1993, A34, Ioanna Mandrou; *Vima*, 20 March 1994, A48, Ioanna Mandrou.

22 Nicos C. Alivizatos, 'A new role for the Greek Church?' *Journal of Modern Greek Studies* 17 (1999), 23–40.

23 Michael Sullivan, *Measuring Global Values. The Ranking of 162 Countries* (New York 1991), 285.

24 *Vima*, 27 October 1991, A36.

25 *Vima*, 25 September 1994, A44; George Kassimeris, *Europe's Last Red Terrorists. The Revolutionary Organisation 17 November* (2000), *passim*.

26 *Vima*, 1 April 2001, A50, Panagioti Bitsika.

27 *Vima*, 3 October 1999, A16, Sofia Giannakas; Michael Spourdalakis, 'Securing democracy in post-authoritarian Greece: the role of political parties', in Geoffrey Pridham and Paul G. Lewis (eds), *Stabilizing Fragile Democracies. Comparing New Party Systems in Southern and Eastern Europe* (1996), 174; Christoforos Vernadakis and Giannis Mavris, *Parties and Social Alliances in Pre-dictatorship Greece* (in Greek, 1991), 178; Christos Lyrintzis, 'Political parties in post-junta Greece: a case of "bureaucratic clientelism"?', *West European Politics* 7 (1984), 106; Takis S. Pappas, *Making Party Democracy in Greece* (1999), 74, 86–9.

28 Richard Clogg, *Parties and Election in Greece. The Search for Legitimacy* (1987), 177–8.

29 Alexander Kitroeff, 'Andreas G. Papandreou: a brief political biography', *Journal of the Hellenic Diaspora* 23 (1997), 7–32.

30 Lyrintzis, 'Political parties', p. 110; Michael Spourdalakis, 'From protest party to New PASOK', in Michael Spourdalakis, (ed.), *PASOK. Party, State, Society* (in Greek, 1998), 20–2.

31 Dimitras, 'Changes', in Featherstone and Katsoudas (eds), *Political Change*, 81–3.

32 Michael Spourdalakis, *The Rise of the Greek Socialist Party* (1988), 69, 193–9.

33 Spourdalakis, 'From protest party', in Spourdalakis (ed.), *PASOK*, 59; Paraskevi Christofilopoulou, 'PASOK and elected local government', in *ibid.*, 196–200.

34 George T. Mavrogordatos, 'Civil society under populism', in Richard Clogg (ed.), *Greece 1981–9. The Populist Decade* (New York 1993), 47–64.

35 Pappas, *Party Democracy*, 154–5, 177.

36 Spourdalakis, *Rise*, 249.

37 See also Kostas A. Lavdas, *The Europeanization of Greece. Interest Politics and the Crises of Integration* (1997), 187–8; Dimitris A. Sotiropoulos, 'The ventriloquial authority: civil society and central state in the Third Greek Republic', in Lyrintzis *et al.* (eds), *Society and Politics*, 119–20.

38 *Kathimerini*, 11 June 1989, 5, interview with Papandreou by Akis Kosonas.

39 George T. Mavrogordatos, 'From traditional clientelism to machine politics; the impact of PASOK populism in Greece', *South European Society and Politics* 2 (1997), 15–17.

40 E.g. *Ta Nea*, Manolis Mavromati, 6 June 1989, 4; Kevin Featherstone, 'The party state in Greece and the fall of Papandreou', *West European Politics* 13 (1990), 110.

41 *Vima*, 7 February 1993, A3, Nikou Nikolaou; *Kathimerini*, 10 February 2000.

42 Leonardo Morlino, 'Political parties and democratic consolidation in southern Europe', in Richard Gunther, P. Nikiforos Diamandouros and Hans-Jurgen Puhle (eds), *The Politics of Democratic Consolidation. Southern Europe in Comparative Perspective* (Baltimore, MD 1995), 331; Stathis N. Kalyvas, 'Polarization in Greek politics: PASOK's first four years, 1981–5', *Journal of the Hellenic Diaspora* 23 (1997), 83–104; Spourdalakis, 'From protest movement', in Spourdalakis (ed.), *PASOK*, 68.

43 Spourdalakis, *Rise*, 212; Yannis Papadopoulos, 'Parties, the state and society in Greece: continuity within change', *West European Politics* 12 (1989), 62.

44 George Kourvetaris and Betty Dobratz, 'Electoral voting preferences and political orientations of Athenians in Greece: a three-perspective model', *European Journal of Political Research* 9 (1981), 287–307.

45 Susannah Verney, 'The Greek Socialists', in John Gaffney (ed.), *Political Parties and the European Union* (1996), 178.

46 Theodore C. Kariotis, 'The rise and fall of the green sun', in Theodore C. Kariotis (ed.), *The Greek Socialist Experiment. Papandreou's Greece, 1981–9* (New York 1992), 26.

47 *Kathimerini*, 18 May 1985, 7, editorial; Michalis Spourdalakis, 'PASOK in the 1990s: structure, ideology, political strategy', in José Maravall (ed.), *Socialist Parties in Europe* (Barcelona 1992), 172.

48 *Vima*, 30 July 1989, 22.

49 Antonis Makridimitris, 'Karamanlis–Papandreou: parallel lives', *Kathimerini*, Special Issue, 1–2 January 2000, 28.

50 Susannah Verney, '"Compromesso storico": reunion and renewal on the Greek left', *Journal of Communist Studies* 5 (1989), 202.

51 Ilias Nikolakopoulos, 'The electoral influence of the political forces' and Dimitrios K. Katsoudas, 'Voting and ideology', in Lyrintzis and Nikolakopoulos (eds), *Elections and Parties*, 203–48.

52 Giorgos Karabelias, *State and Society in the Democratic Transition* (in Greek, 1989), 273.

53 *Vima*, 24 February 1991, A7.

54 Karabelias, *State and Society*, 118–20; Maria Petmesidou-Tsoulouvi, *Social Inequalities and Social Policy* (in Greek, 1992), 133.

55 Mavrogordatos, 'Traditional clientelism to machine politics', 17–19; *Kathimerini*, 27 September 1998, 4, Antoni Karakousi.

56 Karabelias, *State and Society*, 249.

57 Constantine Tsoucalas and Roy Panagiotopoulou, 'Education in socialist Greece: between modernization and democratization', in Kariotis (ed.), *Greek Socialist Experiment*, 325–6.

58 Yiannis Tountas, Helga Stefannson and Spyros Frissiras, 'Health reform in Greece: planning and implementation of a national health system', *International Journal of Health Planning and Management* 10 (1995), 283–304; Maria Petmesidou, 'Social protection in Greece: a brief glimpse of a welfare state', *Social Policy and Administration* 30 (1996), 331–2.

59 *Vima*, 7 October 1990, A28, L. Pipili; *Vima*, 29 June 1997, A17, Petrou Evthymiou.

60 *Vima*, 29 March 1992, D3, Nikou Nikolaou.

CHAPTER NINE

Restructuring the Economy, 1974–2000

Decline and recovery: an outline

The first fact to be explained about the economy between 1974 and 1993 is the worsening performance of most sectors for much or all of the period. From 1973 to 1979, annual growth rates of GDP were, at 3.6 per cent, lower than before 1973, but still above the average for western Europe, which was suffering from the aftermath of the international recession of 1974. But from the second recession in the western world in 1980–82 until the end of the third in 1993, the average rate of growth was among the lowest in capitalist Europe: only 1.3 per cent, and 0.5 per cent in 1990–93.

It is generally accepted that, for a time at least, real growth rates were somewhat higher than nominal growth rates, owing to growth in the black or untaxed economy, from what is commonly taken as about 20 per cent of official GDP in the 1970s to about 30 per cent in 1988 (when GDP was officially recalculated in an attempt to take account of it) and 37 per cent in the late 1990s. Contrary to general opinion in Greece, the black economy may not have been much larger than those of some other European countries, such as Italy and Hungary.[1] The most likely reasons for its size seem to be the importance of small family businesses and self-employment, the complexity of the tax system, and the inefficiency of the tax department. The long-term growth seems to be due to increases in taxation and social insurance contributions, and the intensification of EEC competition in the formal economy. But the size of the black economy does not alter the fact that Greek performance was poor by western European standards even before 1988.

By the late 1980s it was apparent that Greece had fallen behind the other developing countries of the EEC, and was being overtaken by what had until recently been the poorest, Portugal and Ireland, in the movement towards the official goal of convergence between the GDP per capita of the poorest member countries (at purchasing power parity, or PPP) and the EEC average. By 1995, the Greek percentage of the EU average was 66 – still about what it had been in 1988 – and behind Portugal's 68, Spain's 75, Ireland's 75 and Italy's 101.[2] Although these figures were not a very accurate measure of comparative human welfare, they made a strong impression in Greece. They did indicate that Greece had somehow failed to benefit from a massive influx of EEC subsidies and loans, for which its governments had bargained forcefully, and had become the Community's seemingly incurable invalid – a despised one at that, given the flagrant way in which Community aid had been wasted in corruption and vote buying. Greece's backwardness was further exhibited in its exclusion from the launch of the Economic and Monetary Union in 1999, alone among the twelve EU countries which wanted to join, which included Italy, Portugal and Spain.

The low regard for Greece was expressed publicly by leading politicians and bureaucrats of the EEC, and spilt over into foreign policy and defence, being reflected in lack of sympathy for Greece's complaints about territorial threats from neighbouring countries. From at least as early as 1985 until at least as late as 1998, international agencies such as the International Monetary Fund (IMF), the OECD and the European Commission, besides various research institutes, periodically reported serious faults in the economy, and put Greece bottom of the capitalist European league in economic competitiveness (of which labour productivity was the key component). During most of the 1990s Greece was under humiliating supervision by the European Commission and IMF, which both tried to ensure reduction of the budget deficit. Not surprisingly, Greek commentators tended to be pessimistic for many years from the late 1980s. The economy seemed stuck in a vicious cycle of low investment, sluggish growth, dependence on state subsidies, deficit financing by governments, high inflation and tight credit. The traditional sense of backwardness deepened.[3]

So habitual was pessimism that observers were slow to appreciate the significance of the recovery which occurred from 1994 onwards. Rates of growth in GDP averaged 3.1 per cent a year in the six years 1995–2000, making Greece one of the better performers in the EU. Still more impressively, this growth was combined with falling inflation, which in 2000 was 3 per cent, just above the EU average.[4] This good performance is therefore the main fact to be explained about the period between 1994 and 2000.

Falling investment

The process of decline

The economy's poor performance from 1974 can be explained in part by the disappearance of the earlier conditions for growth: regimes friendly to big business, extremely low wages and farmers' incomes, tariff protection and an increasingly frenetic growth of the international economy, which generated capital that investors directed towards developing economies of southern and eastern Europe.

What needs special attention is the decline of investment, foreign and domestic, after 1974. From 1974, foreign *private* investment declined, and the trend continued until 1994, after which it rose only a little. This trend coincided until the late 1980s with a decline in investment from other sources. Consequently, whereas gross fixed asset formation had multiplied six times over in the previous period (1951–73), it declined by about one-sixth during the years 1973–85.[5] Total investment from all sources had increased by an average of 7.9 per cent a year in the years 1950–73, but declined at an increasing rate – averaging 1.6 per cent a year – in 1973–85. In the longer period 1973–90, the decline in investment from the peak years, 1968–73, was greater than in any of the other 23 OECD countries.[6] Private investment as a percentage of GDP fell from 18.9 in 1971–75 to 12.5 in 1986–90, the fall being especially large among non-residents. Public investment as a percentage of GDP fell from 8 to 4.9 in the same periods. There was still no recovery in either by 1992.

The withdrawal of foreign investment after 1973 were not confined to Greece. As Kostas Vergopoulos pointed out, the flow of capital from the developed economies turned away from the developing economies of southern and eastern Europe between the mid-1970s and the early 1990s, and inwards towards the developed economies.[7]

A long period of low investment had predictable effects in much of the economy: a high propensity to import, backward technology, low productivity, poor profitability and in consequence a low rate of growth in consumption and wages. Growth rates in productivity in various branches of the economy fell after 1973, and from 1985 to 1996 were by far the lowest in the EEC. Greece came bottom of the EEC table by 1990–91 in rates of return on fixed capital. Real average wages between 1982 and 1990 rose only by 7.5 per cent, compared with 11.5 per cent in the EEC as a whole.[8]

Industry

The decline of foreign investment hurt manufacturing particularly, because this is where it had been concentrated before 1974. The opposition to this argument by Stavros Thomadakis[9] does not seem valid. His grounds are that there was a compensating increase in EEC subsidies for infrastructure in the 1980s. (Actually it was in the latter half of the 1980s that these subsidies rose sharply.) But this is to assume that EEC investment replaced the earlier private foreign investment, and was devoted to the same sectors of the economy for similarly productive purposes. In fact, much of it seems instead to have been wasted in corruption or else spent on purposes of electoral benefit to the government.

One obvious reason for the decline of investment was the decline in the profitability of industry in the years 1974–82, as a result of the diminution of markets in western economies, the decline of tariffs against other EEC countries and the rising prices of imported inputs such as energy and technology. Greek industry, like that of Portugal and other developing countries, was heavily dependent on imported materials, and therefore sensitive to foreign price increases; and these were exceptionally large because of the high international inflation of the 1970s and early 1980s. There occurred, however, a revival in Greece of traditional light industries such as textiles, leather goods and clothing which required relatively little capital and benefited especially from low labour costs.[10] The second leap upwards in international oil prices in 1979, followed by international recession in 1980–82, repeated the effects of the first oil price shock and subsequent recession of 1974: a shrinkage of foreign markets for Greek industrial products and a big increase in prices of imported materials. Then during the 1980s, Greece shared in the de-industrialisation widespread in western developed countries, as manufacturing moved increasingly to countries outside Europe where labour costs were even lower than those of Greece.

The relative contribution of manufacturing to GDP hardly changed during the 1970s, and then declined to the level of the 1960s, so that it fell from 21 per cent in 1971 to 16.9 per cent in 1993. From 1977 to 1994 the total assets of industrial companies declined by 18.3 per cent, while employment in them declined by 19.3 per cent. The contribution of construction to GDP fell from 9.7 per cent in 1971 to 5 per cent in 1993; while that of agriculture fell from 15.5 per cent to 11.9 per cent. Meanwhile, the contribution of the service sector rose from 41.4 per cent to 53 per cent, mainly because of the growth of the state administration and the state-owned banks. The importance of construction increased again in the later 1990s, in response to the stimulus of EU subsidies.[11]

The underperformance of the economy was especially serious because of the traditionally large deficit on visible trade, which tended to narrow from the 1950s until the 1970s, but widened again from the 1980s. Exports were worth 58 per cent of imports in 1985 and 42 per cent in 1995 (the two combined being worth 31 per cent of GNP at the latter date).[12] Thus any attempt to increase consumer demand and investment resulted in a disproportionate increase in imports. Invisible earnings failed as before 1974 to cover the adverse trade balance, but swelled from the late 1980s with EEC subsidies. Thus the current account deficit persisted, being about 5 per cent of GNP in 1997–99 and widening to 7 per cent in 2000. The balance of payments was strained by foreign borrowing, to which governments had to resort increasingly in the 1990s, because the European Commission forbade the old expedient of making the Bank of Greece lend to governments at artificially low interest rates. EEC subsidies and credits were helping the balance of payments for the time being. But, given that they were destined to taper out, and that foreign debts have to be repaid, the future is obviously somewhat precarious.[13]

The trade deficit in the 1980s was increased by the penetration of EEC imports as the last tariffs against EEC countries were removed. As had long been anticipated, much of Greek industry and agriculture proved ill-equipped at first to face this competition. Most sectors of manufacturing suffered; so that manufacturers as a whole lost about 5 per cent of Greek market share to foreign competitors in the years 1980–87. In agriculture, wheat, meat and dairy production suffered especially; so that the former trade surplus in agricultural products turned into a deficit from 1986 onwards.[14]

De-industrialisation was accompanied in developed western economies by an expansion of employment in a high-technology service sector which provided jobs of good pay and status. Such expansion was slow in Greece, which remained technologically backward, with the lowest proportion in the EU of employment in technological services in 1999.[15] The public appetite for jobs in the public sector, and the keenness to participate in an antiquated educational system which led to those jobs, formed what one might call a culture of underdevelopment. This produced an extraordinary growth – relative to the size of the economy – in the public administration, which could not contribute satisfactorily to economic growth or public welfare, but was characterised by inefficiency. The social benefits of employment in the public sector were inequitably distributed and – given the traditional inefficiencies and structure of the tax system – financed in a regressive way. At the same time – thanks largely to EEC subsidies to agriculture – there was a decline in the transfer of workers from low-productivity agriculture to higher-productivity activities.

Agriculture

Despite EEC subsidies, investment declined also in agriculture; so that by 1987 it was 40 per cent of the 1973 level. It continued thereafter to decline steadily as a proportion of total investment. As a result agriculture contributed little to economic growth in the 1980s and 1990s.

There occurred some changes, as in other Mediterranean countries, in the direction of greater capitalisation and adjustment to EEC competition. For example, wheat and meat production declined; while there was increasing production of fresh vegetables and fruit, which were exported in refrigerated containers to northern Europe. Production was more organised, with a growing proportion of crops being produced under contract, and an increasing proportion through cooperatives.

Other much-needed structural reforms were however discouraged by farmers' increasing dependence on the state. Increases in state pensions greatly boosted farmers' incomes in the 1980s, as did EEC price support through the Common Agricultural Policy (CAP), which provided subsidies dispensed by the party in power. So were EEC subsidies for infrastructure. By the late 1990s the EEC accounted for about 45 per cent of farmers' incomes and government pensions for about 16 per cent. EEC subsidies benefited certain producers disproportionately, such as cotton growers.[16] Because the income originating in the EEC was not accompanied by incentives to improve productivity, it was spent instead by farmers on consumption and urban real estate.

However EEC subsidies for price support could not continue on this scale because they led notoriously to overproduction. To take one example, 265,000 tonnes of subsidised peaches were buried in landfills in 1989. So price support declined from the late 1980s; and the decline continued after the reform of CAP in 1992. The PASOK governments, having benefited from the patronage provided by EEC subsidies in the 1980s, failed to warn farmers of the decline in the quotas of produce that the EEC would cover by price support. Worse still for farmers – more exactly, for a wealthy minority of them – their traditional immunity from income tax ended in 1994, whenceforth they were subjected to increasingly effective inquisitions by tax inspectors. As farmers had now been converted by their new dependence on subsidies and pensions into yet another pressure group orientated towards the national government and organised by political parties, they expressed their plight in militant ways which seem to have been unprecedented in scale. In successive winters in the latter half of the 1990s, producers of various crops, including cotton, olive oil and citrus fruits, repeatedly blocked arterial roads with thousands of tractors for weeks on end.[17]

The real solution to their problems, as all observers recognised, lay in restructuring through schemes which would assist, among other reforms, the amalgamation and consolidation of holdings so as to facilitate investment in new technology; more effective marketing; and diversification of production. In these reforms, the Ministry of Agriculture and the agricultural cooperatives should have played a central role. But such tasks were beyond the capacity of politicians and bureaucrats; while cooperatives were debilitated by their old weaknesses: on the one side the control over them of governments and parties, and on the other the individualism of farmers. Also important politically was the sentiment of the majority of the public in favour of the small family farm. In practice, then, restructuring of agriculture was neglected by successive governments until it was taken up in a small way in the late 1990s. In 1997, Greece was the only EU country where no farmers had vocational training (although Portugal was only a little better). Comparatively little of Greek agricultural produce was marketed abroad under Greek labels. Much good-quality olive oil, for example, was sold to Spanish or Italian producers to be sold under their brand names. Greece also came last among EU countries in the negligible proportion of its land devoted to organic or environmentally sustainable farming, and therefore failed to utilise EU subsidies available to promote it. The main culprits here were allegedly the inert and ill-informed staff of the Ministry of Agriculture. The process of consolidating holdings (the agricultural area owned by someone) continued slowly but at an increasing rate; so that their average size increased by 23 per cent in 1970–90.[18] The size of *farms* (land cultivated or grazed by each farmer) increased by more, because by 1993, one-quarter of all agricultural land was leased by better-off farmers from absentee neighbours. However, fragmentation of holdings into scattered plots remained as great as ever. Meanwhile, inequalities were increasing between the poor farmers of the mountains and small islands, who produced mainly for subsistence, and the wealthy plains farmers who produced for the market and did relatively well, in fertile regions like eastern Crete, the northern Peloponnese, Thessaly and western Macedonia. But because the scope for investment in agriculture remained limited, there were still very few large-scale farmers able to invest much capital or employ many people.[19]

Thus farmers in the late 1990s were paying for their own and governmental sins of neglect. But as one militant and unusually frank olive grower admitted in January 1998, 'it's easier to protest than blame ourselves'.[20] It is apparent, too, that EEC subsidies had done harm by masking farmers' real problems. In the meantime, farmers continued to decline steeply, from 30.9 per cent of the labour force in 1981 to 17.8 per cent by 1997, of whom 36 per cent were aged 55 or more, compared with an EU average of 30 per cent. Half the farming households now included members with non-agricultural sources of income; a proportion typical of the poorer EU countries. Average real incomes from farming had grown strongly in the late 1970s and early 1980s, but then declined for about ten years before apparently stagnating in the latter half of the 1990s.[21] Given the poverty of a large sector of farmers and the problems of social isolation which they experienced, it is clear that the numerical decline will continue.

Deficit financing and credit policy

Another cause of decline in economic performance was the electorally motivated deficit financing of successive governments, especially PASOK in 1981-89. Before each of the eight general elections in the years 1974-93, the budget deficit and the current account deficit increased, in the 1980s by an average of over 50 per cent. The cumulative outcome of these practices was that the budget deficit reached crazy levels – peaking in 1990 at 19 per cent of GDP – leading to a public sector borrowing requirement over six times the EEC average. PASOK governments – and to some extent their predecessor and successors – spent money on buying votes (particularly with pensions, wage increases for public sector workers, and an increase in public-sector employment), rather than on investment in areas which could stimulate long-term growth, such as physical infrastructure and occupational training. Furthermore, each election was followed by increases in the prices set by the nationalised industries, in order to help pay for the big increase in their payroll before the election.[22] Only after the election year 1993 was this cycle broken by budgetary discipline.

An inevitable effect of such profligacy was inflation. In the 1970s this could be partly accounted for by inflation among Greece's trading partners. But in the 1980s, foreign inflationary forces diminished while domestic forces surged, so that inflation in Greece continued almost undiminished, and fluctuated in accordance with the public sector borrowing requirements of governments. In the 22 years from 1973 to 1994 inclusive, inflation averaged nearly 18 per cent – an extraordinarily high level by OECD standards. Only in 1995 did it fall below double digits. It continued to fall thereafter, in response to strenuous efforts by governments to reduce budget deficits and restrain wage increases.

Inflation, combined with a worsening current account deficit, weakened confidence in the drachma, so making it necessary for the government to take the step – unprecedented since 1953 – of devaluing the drachma, not just once in 1983 but again in 1985. In order to combat inflation throughout the 1980s, and to maintain the value of the drachma after 1985, the government restricted credit and the money supply. Governments also needed high interest rates in order to induce people to lend to them. Thereafter the government had to try after 1985 to keep the drachma at an artificially high level in order to contain the cost of foreign borrowing, and to reassure foreign investors worried by the size of the public debt and the current account deficit. The overvalued drachma encouraged imports by making them cheaper and discouraged exports by making them dearer, and so imposed a burden on producers and worsened the trade deficit. For much of the 1980s, interest rates were more than offset by still higher inflation; but from the early 1990s onwards, as inflation declined, they turned positive.

The availability of credit and the money supply (M1, that is the money in circulation plus that held in current accounts) declined throughout the 1980s. In the 1990s, high interest rates diverted investment to state bonds and discouraged domestic investment in improved productivity, especially for smaller businesses which had always had difficulty in obtaining credit from banks.[23]

The restriction on borrowing for economic development was due not just to government policy, but also to the high costs of banks and the lack of competition between them (noted in Chapter Three). The banking system remained extraordinarily concentrated by international standards, both in the sense that there were few credit institutions per head of population, and in that (in 1999) five banks owned three-quarters of banking capital. They were still dominated as we will see by state institutions, and like all public-sector enterprises were seriously overstaffed and suffered from a public-service mentality opposed to a spirit of service to customers. Because of these factors, the banks kept interest rates much higher than was necessitated even by the government's borrowing requirements. One example was a court ruling in 2000 that a bank's seizure of a debtor's property was illegal, on the grounds that the interest which the debtor had been paying was at least three times what would have been demanded anywhere else in the EU.[24]

Union power

The country's attractiveness to foreign and domestic investors was also reduced after 1974 by the increased likelihood of industrial disputes. During the decade 1984–93, for example, Greece had by far the worst record – in terms of days lost in strikes – in the OECD. The strikes occurred especially in state-controlled public utilities and industries, in which the workforce was almost completely unionised, and fought against government attempts after

1985 to reduce its incomes so as to curb budget deficits. Partly because of the increased power of organised labour after 1974, hourly wages increased sharply: by 65 per cent in 1974–82. Yet so low had they been before 1974 that they remained low by comparison with wages and labour costs in other countries both of the EEC and even of southern Europe. In 1980 the average cost of labour was 12.9 per cent of gross national industrial production, compared with 19.1 per cent in Spain, 18.4 per cent in Portugal, and 14.7 per cent in Italy.[25] It is clear then that labour costs in Greece were not in themselves an obstacle to industrial development, as conservatives claimed. There was a problem rather in the low productivity of labour, for reasons which we shall examine. According to a scale calculated by the OECD for about 2000, labour cost per unit of GDP was 3.7, thrice the EU average, compared with 1.2 in Italy, 4.2 in Portugal and 2.9 in Spain.[26]

Something else that seriously reduced profitability in strongly unionised branches of the economy were the non-wage rights won by unionists, rights to limitation of working hours and redundancy payments. The first made it difficult for employers to make hours more flexible, and the second made it difficult to redeploy workers. Little progress was made towards overcoming these obstacles in the 1990s, except indirectly, in the growing employment of non-unionised and usually illegal immigrants in many private trades.[27]

Economic democracy

It appears that the decline in private investment, from the mid-1970s to the mid-1980s, was due partly to the redistribution of national income in favour of the lower-paid which, as we have seen, was an overdue outcome of the advent of democracy in the economic and political spheres.

The redistribution was partly financed at first by a steep increase in taxation from 1974 onwards: a particularly striking example was the almost thirty-fold increase in taxation paid by hitherto privileged shipowners in 1975.[28] As the lower-paid had little or no surplus cash, they tended to spend their increased income on consumption rather than saving. The socialist and anti-business rhetoric of PASOK, in its radical phase until 1985, also discouraged investment, and continued to do so even after that date when the PASOK government began trying to conciliate business. All the deterrents to foreign investment which have been described so far were noted by a prestigious research institute, Business International.[29] PASOK attitudes were part of the prevalent climate of anti-American and anti-capitalist sentiment, which still continues to some extent, and was for a long time expressed in frequent terrorist attacks on business premises. Economic security was also weakened by the constant possibility of war with Turkey.

There were, in addition, traditional obstacles to economic growth which, after 1974, became more serious in their effects, because the international environment was more uncertain and competitive.

The parasitical state

Dimensions and composition

As an obstacle to economic development, the political spoils system attracted special interest from informed commentators. It is widely believed, with much plausibility, that in no other OECD country was it so economically disruptive.[30] State domination of the economy had, as we have seen, tended to grow since 1945, and it grew especially fast after 1974. The growth occurred also, for similar reasons, in Portugal and Spain after 1974; while public expenditure in Italy in the 1980s ran almost at the Greek level relative to GDP. But, because of the strength of anti-capitalist sentiment in Greece, the public support for the process was overwhelming, and remained much stronger than in other EEC countries.[31]

These examples show that the scale of public expenditure in Greece was high but not in itself extraordinary in the 1990s. Cause for concern lay still more in the way it was financed, administered and spent. Little of it, by EEC standards, was devoted to education, training, health, social assistance, or research and development, and one-third of it in 1995 was devoted to debt service, compared with an average of one-tenth in the EEC-12. Other relatively large components of public expenditure continued to be public administration and defence. Taxation was, as we shall see below, corrupt and inequitable. The inefficiency and corruption of public administration made the case for privatisation of state enterprises stronger than in politically developed countries.

Table 9.1 *Public expenditure as a percentage of GNP in Greece, Portugal, Spain and the EEC-12, 1980 and 1995*[32]

Country	1980	1995
Greece	30.4	46.7
Portugal	23.8	43.1
Spain	32.2	44.8
EEC-12	44.7	50.1

Let us, firstly, ascertain the extent of the public sector. By the mid-1990s, state-owned banks (four especially), accounted for about three-quarters of deposits, bank bonds and outstanding loans. Furthermore, the private banks were still strictly regulated, as before 1973, with government quotas for commercial investments and loans. The state possessed a near or complete monopoly in air and rail transport, urban public transport, the major harbour authorities, the postal service, telecommunications, electricity production, gas and water supply, and higher education, while dominating the field of hospital care. The state also owned most of the shipyards, dominated the petroleum industry, played a prominent role in the chemicals industries, and in car and life insurance, as well as a wide and diverse range of other industries, many of them unprofitable. By 1989, 30,900 people were employed in state enterprises aptly named problematic industries, accounting for 4.5 per cent of employment in manufacturing: all burdens on the taxpayer. Other large industrial firms in difficulties were propped up by state banks. The assumption of this burden by successive governments can be explained by the long-established state policy of maintaining employment, to the extent of forbidding private employers, even those in economic difficulties, to retrench more than a few people.[33]

Inefficiency

Most public enterprises, because they were protected both from commercial competition and from any sort of economic discipline, were not just grossly overstaffed but also overpaid and inefficient. Burdened by masses of unqualified staff, they could not afford to employ enough technically qualified people. The pay of employees in the fifty public utilities long under state ownership was in the late 1990s on average 50 per cent higher than in the private sector, while they required more labour and capital, in relation to the value of their products, than comparable private enterprises. Nearly half the public utilities were running at a loss, and most were burdened with large debts, partly because their accounting procedures were lax. Their debts amounted to 2 per cent of GNP in 1997; so that they contributed substantially to inflation. The cost to the state of subsidising them threw the burden of deflationary policy onto the restraint of private-sector wages and the restriction of social expenditure. So citizens who suffered daily from the poor service and discourtesy of state employees were obliged to subsidise them.

Because the privileges of their employees were protected both by law and by trade unions, the public enterprises were difficult to run efficiently. For example, a manager of a state bank, referring to union power, complained in 1998: 'I do not have the right to tell my staff to make special efforts to satisfy a good customer. So we lose the good customers, who go to the private banks. If I persist in my request, I risk losing my job.' An OECD report of August 1999 condemned the public utilities for faults which included backward technology, and considered that their staff could be halved. It pointed out that their managers needed to be appointed on merit not party preference, and to be free to make decisions on commercial grounds. It estimated that privatisation of the utilities would add 10 per cent to GDP over five years and reduce inflation by one percentage point.[34] The need to subsidise public utilities helps explain why the government budget was still in deficit in 1999, and why the public debt was still 105 per cent of GNP (one-third of it in foreign currencies).

The poor quality of state-owned utilities was another factor driving foreign investors and businesses to other countries. An outstanding example during the 1980s and early 1990s was the telephone service, which was characterised by dilatoriness and unreliability. In 1990 a customer had to wait on average seven years to get a new telephone connection; and the rate of breakdowns and faults was high. All these features of public utilities made them difficult to privatise, even partially. The government's current difficulties in finding buyers for Olympic Airways are a notorious example.

When the OECD referred, around 2000, to state intervention as the major obstacle to growth, it was not referring merely to state ownership, but to something wider: the general restriction of enterprise and competition by state regulation. A major obstacle to businesses – both Greek and still more foreign – was the demand for licences by bureaucrats, who had the worst reputation in the EEC for obstructionism, inefficiency and corruption. An American research institute reported around the start of 1989 that 'favouritism, red tape and dilatoriness remain serious problems. Bureaucratic procedures add 20 per cent to the cost of business enterprises'. Reports by the European Commission and the European Central Bank in 2000 concluded that these obstacles had prevented Greece from benefiting from increased foreign investment on the eve of its entry into the Economic and Monetary Union to the same extent as Spain and Portugal had recently done.[35]

State-subsidised industries competed against more efficient private firms and reduced their profitability. Together with the state-owned utilities and services, they employed 8.3 per cent of the labour force in 1991. They distorted the labour market, by reducing competition for jobs and keeping up the level of wages. Partly because of the opposition of public-sector unions, the government has recently failed to win the necessary agreement from the General Confederation of Greek Workers to give employers sufficient freedom to lay off workers or vary their working hours – reforms which economists consider essential to the reduction of unemployment.[36]

The restriction of competition by monopolies and unofficial cartels is supposed to be curbed by the Competition Commission, established in 1977. This body has proved largely ineffectual; and the government has just decided to give it greater powers. The Commission's weakness is typical of the general inefficiency of the state, and also of politicians' clientelistic tendency to favour particular interest groups. The Centre for Planning and Economic Research estimated in October 2000 that the ending of restrictive practices in fifty occupations, comprising 6 per cent of the labour force, would add at least 0.8 per cent to annual growth in GNP. There were effective monopolies or cartels in many private industries and services, including the manufacture of dairy products, oil refining, the marketing of fruit and vegetables, and ferries to islands. Analysts considered that in 1999–2000, prices were in consequence unnecessarily high in a wide range of goods and services.[37]

In the interrelated fields of privatisation, deregulation and competition policy, progress was much slower than in other southern European countries. By mid-2000, after ten years of bold intentions by successive governments, the balance sheet was unimpressive, a failure repeatedly criticised by the European Commission and the OECD.

There were however some achievements. Under EEC pressure, governments cut subsidies to what seem to have been quite sizeable sectors of industry, forcing them to become more competitive or close down. The 'problematic industries' were all sold off by 1998, as were some smaller state banks (notably the Ionic Bank) by 1999. The remaining state banks, Olympic Airways and the telecommunications company OTE were exposed to some private competition; while some large utilities including OTE were partially privatised as well. After Olympic Airways lost its monopoly of domestic flights in 1998, it lost half its share of them to competitors in two years. In all, 31 public companies were sold in the three years 1998–2000; and the proceeds in 1998–99 alone were $6 billion – twice as much as had been obtained in the previous ten years. The public has started to benefit from increased competition in some areas, such as air tickets, petrol prices and ferry tickets on at least one route.[38]

Governments have also reduced their interference in state-owned companies. Directors of public utilities are being selected increasingly for their managerial ability rather than party affiliations, and allowed to make decisions on their commercial merits. The government is now relinquishing control over appointments of directors of the state banks, leaving them to be elected by shareholders. Especially important was the liberation during the 1990s of state banks from burdensome obligations: for example to earmark a certain proportion of funds for financing state enterprises; to deposit part of their assets in the Bank of Greece; and to extend credit at rates dictated by the government to organisations which the government favoured.[39] The Agricultural Bank became a public liability company in 1991 as a first step towards independence. The Bank of Greece had since 1944 enjoyed considerable independence; and was made completely independent by law in 1997. As a result of increasing competition from private Greek banks and foreign banks, competition which is intensifying with entry into the Economic and Monetary Union, the state banks have reduced their costs to customers; improved their service; and proved readier to finance innovative enterprises. They have also managed to make bigger profits, and extended their activities to other countries. At least some public utilities have been compelled to subject their finances and the utilisation of their assets to professional accounting procedures.

Earlier, in 1991, the government had liberalised capital movements, including movement of foreign exchange to other EU countries.

Utilities which worked with noticeably greater efficiency by 2000 were the postal and telephone services, the metropolitan water corporation, the national railways and the national electricity corporation. Indeed, a Eurobarometer poll in 2000 found that Greeks were much more satisfied than other EU peoples with their public transport, water, postal and fixed-telephone services. Perhaps their expectations were low; but it seems that something had been achieved.[40]

Technological and managerial backwardness

Prominent among the weaknesses of the economy was a generally low level of technology, which was attributable to meagre investment, especially in research and development. The amount spent on it, as a proportion of GNP, was much the lowest in any EU country. Most of it was spent by government, with a comparatively low proportion of it devoted to industrial technology. Although it is now increasing fast, the ownership of computers by businesses and individuals is still the lowest in the EU, and is significantly lower than in Italy, Portugal or Spain. Exports of high-technology products are now increasing strongly, albeit from a low base.[41]

A shortage of managerial and technological expertise was another weakness. It could be attributed partly to deficiencies of the system of education and vocational training. Although technical colleges expanded greatly from the mid-1970s, they remained in all respects badly resourced by comparison with universities, and are still seriously short of staff, books, laboratories and buildings. Meanwhile they and universities continue to neglect skills needed by the economy, notably information technology, business management and applied economics. The labour market was too poorly organised and the government too inefficient to utilise effectively the funds made available by the EU during the 1990s for further education and training; so that the proportion of employees participating in training programmes in 1999 was the lowest in the EU. Throughout the 1990s, businesses complained that the educational system was not producing nearly enough people with the technical and professional qualifications which they needed. A survey of 607 businesses by the Federation of Greek Industries, early in 2001, found 60 per cent of them complaining of serious shortages of staff with specialised skills.[42] It is not surprising then that a series of international comparisons, from at least as early as 1985 until the present, have placed Greece at or near the bottom of the OECD league in managerial efficiency.

But it is also true that many businesses failed to utilise the services of available people with technical qualifications. The reason seems to have been the survival of the predominantly family basis of ownership and management, which led business firms to employ people on the basis of kinship or friendship rather than merit, and led to the survival of small family firms. In the 1980s the overwhelming majority of industrial firms still employed fewer than ten people. This is not simply to equate size with efficiency, because some small or medium-sized enterprises were outstandingly successful. But minuscule enterprises usually lacked capital and credit facilities, and suffered from excessive concentration of decisions in their owner–managers, who tended to lack professional qualifications in management, marketing and industrial relations.[43] The low rate of computer and Internet usage must also limit seriously the efficiency of small businesses.

We must therefore conclude that, although in the pre-1973 period family loyalty was often a valuable incentive to economic effort, after that date it became, at least in certain sectors, an increasing barrier to efficiency. It was indeed recognised as such, because impersonally managed and relatively large firms accounted for an increasing share of assets and business in diverse fields, including manufacturing, construction and retailing. An increasing proportion of businesses took the path trod long before by large businesses in northern Europe: separating ownership from management, publishing more information about themselves and seeking capital from stock markets, Greek and foreign. Even public companies tended to be seriously deficient in their procedures for disclosing information about themselves to potential foreign investors.[44] It seems, however, that productivity and profitability benefited in at least some sectors from these changes in business structure.

Reasons for recovery

EEC subsidies

Prominent among the factors causing economic recovery were EEC/EU subsidies for improvements in infrastructure and training. After Greece became a full member of the EEC in 1981, these subsidies, with agricultural subsidies, became the largest single source of invisible earnings, rising from about 2 per cent of them in 1981 to an average of about 25 per cent in the 1990s, a larger proportion than any of those old staples, tourism, shipping and emigrants' remittances. Net invisible earnings were themselves 13 per cent of GDP in 1980, rising to about 20 per cent in the mid-1990s.[45]

Agricultural subsidies continued in the 1990s to account for the majority of EEC transfers; but subsidies for infrastructure rose steeply from the mid-1980s, that is from the time when Andreas Papandreou secured them by threatening, if denied, to veto accession to the EEC by Portugal and Spain. From 1989 onwards, subsidies for infrastructure in poor regions of the EEC doubled again, being considered a necessary accompaniment to the accelerated programme of European integration; and they were administered through long-term programmes – known as Community Support Frameworks – in which the relevant departments (known as directorates) of the European Commission cooperated with national, regional and local governments. The programmes were known – after successive Presidents of the Commission – as the first and second Delors Packages (1989–93 and 1994–99) and the Santer Package (2000–6). In Greece, in the latter half of the 1990s, subsidies for infrastructure were generally hailed as the prime mover of economic development. In October 1995 the government spoke of 5,500 separate construction projects co-funded by the EU, the biggest of which were under way or near completion in 2000: conversion of most of the arterial roads in the country into multi-lane highways, a new highway from the Turkish border to the Adriatic, underground railway systems for Athens and Salonika, a giant new airport and a motorway bypass for Athens, bridges including one of three kilometres over the Gulf of Corinth, a road tunnel under the ocean mouth of the Ambracian Gulf, irrigation works, sewage treatment works and natural gas pipelines. There was besides a multitude of minor projects like hotels and office blocks.

The task of managing this torrent of money would probably have strained the administrative capacity of any country, and was far beyond that of the Greek civil service. National and local governments did not in the 1980s possess the planning mechanisms and the administrative experience to channel these funds to socially beneficial ends which were coordinated with each other. There were no processes to draw up regional development plans; nor to evaluate and monitor programmes of development.[46] Especially difficult to utilise were those funds earmarked for projects which required new expertise, or initiative of unaccustomed kinds, on the part of civil servants: for example vocational training centres, retraining programmes for bureaucrats, environmental surveys, or the installation of computers in school classrooms and the establishment of postgraduate programmes in universities. What happened was that public authorities treated the 'absorption' of EEC funds as an end in itself, and found it easiest to achieve this end through major construction works.

The common and predictable result of this attitude, in the earlier stages, was squandering of money on public works that were overpriced and sometimes unnecessary, or on research projects and training schemes that were bogus. Another serious difficulty was rivalry between contractors and between political parties, leading to time-wasting recriminations about, and enquiries into, alleged malpractices in the assignment of contracts. After a series of damning reports by the government and the European Commission, the authoritative daily *Kathimerini* concluded concerning the Delors Packages that 'Greek society enjoyed them only as a spectator. The squandering of the first on political cronies, and the mismanagement of the second, meant that they failed to achieve their intended benefit'.[47] The Santer Package is being devoted largely to projects that should have been completed by the first two. As late as February 1996, an investigation by a government committee found 'complete lack of coordination and planning in the management of the Community funds'.[48] Although some of the more obvious abuses were in time checked by tighter supervision and improved procedures, there remained others, such as serious faults in construction, revealed by regular monitoring procedures in over half of 515 selected projects in 1998–99. In some cases, such as university programmes, monitoring of implementation was neglected and in any case difficult.[49] Currently the government is emphasising its determination to utilise effectively the Santer Package, which is expected to total over $29 billion in EU subsidies.

Inevitably the dispensation of money on this scale contributed much to economic growth: it would have done if spent on building pyramids. However, many of the mega-projects stimulated by EU subsidies may indeed contribute greatly to welfare and capacity for future growth. Outstanding examples were the modernisation of the nation's telecommunications system in the mid-1990s, the opening of the Athens underground railway in 2000 and the construction of a sewage treatment plant for the metropolis. The allocation of subsidies to industry benefited from the advice of the Federation of Greek Industries. In the years 1989–93, structural subsidies were estimated to have reduced unemployment by two percentage points, and to have increased economic growth by half a percentage point, rising now to about one percentage point.[50]

There is however a grim price to be paid for some projects in damage to the natural environment, historic buildings and archaeological sites. Much of the damage seems avoidable. There were similar problems in other southern EU countries, which also had weak legal and administrative mechanisms for environmental protection. But Greece was the scene of two environmental scandals that – according to environmental lobbyists of the European Commission – did more than any others to stimulate reforms by the Commission in its rules and procedures for administering the subsidies for infrastructure. The first was the attempted establishment of a fish farm in Prespa Lakes National Park in 1986. The second was the long-running case, from 1987 to the present, of the projected damming and part-diversion of the river Achelöos, which threatened vast environmental and cultural damage for dubious economic or social benefit.[51] The European Commission – strongly criticised by Euro-MPs allied with Greek and European NGOs – eventually refused further funds for the latter – an unusually drastic step for a project of such political importance to a member government. But this move was too late to stop the government from proceeding with the destruction of much of the Achelöos valley. Thus some of the major public works are defeating the ultimate purpose which they are supposed to be fulfilling, which is an improved quality of life for all in the long term. The EU has admittedly provided large subsidies for environmental protection; but the Greek government has been slow and half-hearted in utilising them.

Increasing competitiveness of industry

The recovery of 1994 onwards was even greater than can be explained by EEC subsidies. Important general reasons for it, ascertained by the Institute of Economic and Industrial Research and others, was that large sectors of industry had during the long years of apparent stagnation responded successfully to EEC competition, by shedding surplus employees, investing in new technology and developing the sectors in which Greece had comparative advantage which included low labour costs.[52] Proof of the early success of industry in readjusting to the new international conditions lay in improvements in labour productivity, in capital assets per person employed, and in profitability. These improvements were especially marked in the early 1990s but were in some cases visible several years earlier. By 1992 the profitability of most industrial firms had been growing for some time. In

1993–98 the average profitability of 3,470 larger industrial firms was 20.5 per cent, and much higher in the largest firms, which were investing heavily in new technology. In the table of competitiveness compiled by the World Economic Forum, Greece climbed from 44th place in 1998 to 34th in 2000, still leaving it below all other EU countries, but evidently above the rest of south-eastern Europe.[53]

By the early 1990s, much of Greek industry was well placed to benefit from the opening up of new opportunities for investment and exports in the rest of the Balkans after the fall of the closed communist systems. By at least as early as 1996, exports to this region accounted for a major part of Greek industrial production. The economic development of the border regions in particular benefited from the progressive expansion of cross-border traffic with the three northern neighbours during the 1990s.[54] By the late 1990s, Greek enterprises were winning contracts and establishing branches in several ex-communist countries: food- or beverage-processing companies, banks, producers of computer software, a retail chain, and various consultancies. Because of their export orientation and high profitability, the leading manufacturing enterprises were in 1999 poised to make fresh inroads into Balkan markets. In 2000, Balkan markets seemed likely to grow, with the restoration of peace in most of former Yugoslavia, and a general economic recovery under way from the collapse of communism. Greek businesses also took advantage of the improvement in relations with Turkey late in 1999 (see below, p. 274) and, according to a British director of a bank in Istanbul, proved more adept than western counterparts at operating in the peculiar and risky Turkish environment. Nearly 100 Greek businesses participated in the first exhibition of Greek products to be held in Istanbul, in November 2000. Meanwhile, Greek industrial firms have even been buying partial or controlling interests in major companies in northern Europe, which would have been unthinkable until recently.[55]

Entry into EMU

A general stimulus to many sectors was the determination of successive governments to enter the Economic and Monetary Union (EMU) of the EU that was agreed to by the Treaty of Maastricht of 1992. To governments, businessmen and nearly all voters in Greece, EMU membership promised the following benefits: access to cheap credit from elsewhere in the EU, and therefore a decline in domestic interest rates; foreign investment which would otherwise be deterred by fear of inflation or currency depreciation; the removal of disadvantages for Greek businesses in foreign markets; the general facilitation of trade with the EU; and the availability to citizens of a currency internationally more respected than the drachma. For the government, EMU membership also offered protection against pressure from voters to spend too much.

Entry into the EMU was plainly imminent from March 1998, when Greece entered the Exchange Rate Mechanism (ERM) of the EU, limiting the fluctuation of the drachma in relation to other currencies. Foreign and domestic investment in Greek business was at once stimulated, assisted by a decline in interest rates which became precipitous in 2000. From January 2000 to February 2001, the real rate of interest on bank loans to business for short terms has fallen from 11 to 5 per cent, and on housing loans from 9 to 3 per cent. The natural result is a boom in consumer and housing credit.[56] Also stimulated were mergers of large businesses so as to equip them to meet stiffer competition within the EMU. The decision by the European Commission in June 2000 that Greece satisfied the requirements for EMU membership will result in the pegging of the drachma to the new currency, the euro, from 1 January 2001, and the replacement of the drachma by the euro in 2002.

Flawed prosperity

In other ways, too, the economic environment became more conducive to investors' confidence in the latter half of the 1990s. The scope for change in the parity of the drachma was restricted in March 1998 by entry into the ERM, as a precondition of which the drachma was devalued by 15 per cent, so boosting exports. Thereafter governments' determination to conquer inflation enabled interest rates to be reduced without imperilling the drachma. In July 1997, for the first time since 1945, the government issued eighteen-year bonds at fixed interest rates; and now it optimistically predicts for 2001 the first budget surplus since 1966, to be devoted to debt reduction.[57] The economy was also helped by a greater spirit of social peace in the latter half of the 1990s, albeit marred by periodic protests by farmers and by employees of public utilities. A long-term improvement in industrial relations was assisted especially by the landmark reform of the law governing collective bargaining in 1990 (see p. 255). PASOK brought to industrial relations, when it returned to power in 1993, the advantage of its prevalence in the trade unions, and the acceptance by its union branch of sacrifices to satisfy EU requirements. Industrial militance was also dampened by the rising rate of unemployment. PASOK governments brought about agreement on wage and price restraint, as well as some increase in flexibility of working hours. These agreements helped make possible the fall of inflation and an improvement of business competitiveness. Unfortunately, prolonged wage restraint and high unemployment have contributed to an increase in social inequality; so that the ratio of wages to profits in industry declined markedly during the years 1993–99.[58]

In these conditions, gross investments (as a percentage of GDP) increased markedly in the latter half of the 1990s, and returned to the level of the early 1980s. But if lower income groups were to be compensated for the years of austerity, and if unemployment was to be reduced, the rate of economic growth and therefore the level of investment needed to be higher still. What therefore caused increasing concern by 2000 was the failure of private foreign investment to rise as a percentage of GDP, despite the assistance to foreign investors given by the Greek Investment Centre that was established in March 1996, and the encouragement given by Greece's expected and then actual acceptance into EMU. As in the past, the most dynamic sectors of industry depended especially on external investment, and included the processing of food and beverages; petroleum products; pharmaceuticals, cosmetics and detergents; electrical goods; rubbers and plastics; and extensive branches of mining.[59] The level of domestic investment was also limited by the continuance of a low rate of private savings which, although increasing in the late 1990s, was still less than half the average rate in the years 1960–80.[60]

Much of the increased investment of the late 1990s was channelled into the Athens Stock Exchange. This until the late 1980s had little significance as a locus for investors or a source of finance for business. From 1977 to 1989 there was little increase in the number of listed companies and value of assets traded. But in the latter half of the 1990s there was a remarkable boom in the stock market, which was boosted by falling real interest rates. From 1990 to 1999, the number of companies listed on the Athens Stock Exchange nearly doubled, and the value of traded assets rose many times over. The result of the growth in the stock market was to liberate many companies from the expensive credit of banks.[61] In 1999, the stock market attracted 30 per cent of all private investment. Share ownership had spread rapidly, so that over one-fifth of households owned shares. By that time, however, the boom had become unhealthily speculative, being driven by rash investments and fraudulent dealings. In that month began a slump which has deepened until June 2001. But it is widely believed that the stock market will in time recover its importance. The disaster spurred the Capital Markets Commission, which began effective operations in 1998, to introduce stricter regulation of the stock exchange, as well as several provisions to facilitate trading.[62] The stock market has been upgraded by international investors to the status of a developed market in May 2001 (four years after the main stock exchange of Portugal), a change which is expected in time to attract foreign investment.

Another disappointment was the rising rate of unemployment (see below p. 200). A popular explanation for it was that illegal immigrants were taking the jobs. This was disputed by labour economists, partly on the grounds that the immigrants tended to take jobs spurned by Greeks, and partly because the immigrants' cheap and versatile labour was boosting economic growth. A more likely explanation for unemployment is that growth was occurring chiefly among large-scale industries which invested in technology rather than in labour; while small family businesses which were labour-intensive were declining. The government, and the European Commission, recognise the seriousness of this decline and are taking measures to check it.[63]

During this period, restructuring occurred with varying success in several sectors: chiefly in manufacturing, and also to a lesser extent in banking, the capital market, public utilities and agriculture. There was vast investment in infrastructure such as roads and telecommunications. Entrepreneurs in diverse sectors weathered profound changes: the redistribution of national income and the changes in labour relations which followed the onset of democracy from 1974, and the disappearance of remaining tariff protection against the EEC. From about 1993, thousands of businessmen, bankers and consultants showed remarkable initiative in penetrating the economies of south-eastern Europe and recently Turkey. Now the economy faces further challenges: the intensification of competition from other countries in the EMU, and the compensation of lower income groups for their sacrifices to make entry into the EMU possible.

Notes

1 *Economist*, 28 August 1999, 63; *Kathimerini* (English Internet edition), 7 June 2001, citing a report by the Institute of Economic and Industrial Research.

2 The Economist, *Pocket Europe in Figures* (4th edn, 2000), 47–9.

3 *Vima*, 11 May 1997, D4, Nikou Nikolaou; Kostas Vergopoulos, 'Economic crisis and modernization in Greece', *International Journal of Political Economy* 17 (1987), 114.

4 *Vima*, 9 May 1999, D35, Christou Pachta; *Vima*, 23 July 2000, D11, Vasiliki Nikoloudia.

5 Persefoni Tsaliki, *The Greek Economy. Sources of Growth in the Postwar Era* (1991), 4–5; Stavros B. Thomadakis, 'The Greek economy and European integration: prospects for development and threats of underdevelopment', in Dimitri Constas and Theofanis G. Stavrou (eds), *Greece Prepares for the Twenty-first Century* (Baltimore, MD 1995), 103.

6   Nicholas G. Pirounakis, *The Greek Economy. Past, Present and Future* (1997), 45, 172; Theodore Pelagidis, 'Economic policies in Greece during 1990–3: an assessment', *Journal of Modern Greek Studies* 15 (1997), 76–9.

7   'The political economy of Greece in the 1980s', in Theodore C. Kariotis (ed.), *The Greek Socialist Experiment. Papandreou's Greece, 1981–9* (New York 1992), 195–200.

8   Vergopoulos in Kariotis (ed.), *Socialist Experiment*, 186.

9   Thomadakis, 'Greek economy', in Constas and Stavrou (eds), *Greece*, 103.

10 Vergopoulos, 'Economic crisis', 117.

11 Tsaliki, *Greek Economy*, 6; *OECD Economic Surveys, 1994–5. Greece* (Paris 1995), 100; *Vima*, 29 April 2000, B2, Zoï Tsoli.

12 Tsaliki, *Greek Economy*, 158; National Statistical Service of Greece, *Concise Statistical Yearbook. 1998* (Athens 1999), 167, 267.

13 *Kathimerini*, 6 May 2001, citing Bank of Greece annual report; *Economist*, 24 February 2001, 122; Pirounakis, *Greek Economy*, 24–7.

14 Pirounakis, *Greek Economy*, 25; Thomadakis, 'Greek economy', in Constas and Stavrou (eds), *Greece*, 111–13; Tassos Giannitsis, 'World market integration, trade effects, and implications for industrial and technological change in the case of Greece', in Harry J. Psomiades and Stavros B. Thomadakis (eds), *Greece, the New Europe, and the Changing International Order* (New York 1993), 223–7, 249.

15 *Vima*, 9 May 1999, D34.

16 Giorgos Karabelias, *State and Society in the Democratic Transition, 1974–88* (in Greek, 1989), 347–53; *Vima*, 8 February 1998, A14, Michali Demouzi; Neil Collins and Leonidas Louloudis, 'Protecting the protected: the Greek agricultural policy network', *Journal of European Public Policy* 2 (1995), 98, 103.

17 L. Louloudis and N. Maravegias, 'Farmers, the state, and authority in Greece (1981–96)', in Ch. Kasimis and L. Louloudis (eds), *The Countryside. Greek Agrarian Society at the End of the Twentieth Century* (in Greek, 1999), 230–4.

18 Ch. Kasimis and A.G. Papadopoulos, 'The maintenance of family agriculture and the capitalist development of agriculture in Greece: a critical review of the literature', in *ibid.*, 99; *Kathimerini*, 18 February 2001, Tania Georgiopoulou; *Kathimerini* (English Internet edition), 8 May 2001, Constantine Kallergis.

19 Stathis Damianakos, 'The elusive model of Greek agriculture', in ibid., 55–84.

20 *Vima*, 22 October 1995, D6; *Kathimerini*, 31 January 1998, 6.

21 *Kathimerini*, 2 April 1995, 51; EU website, 'Agriculture in the EU. Statistical and economic information, 2000'.

22   Thomadakis, 'Greek economy', in Constas and Stavrou (eds), *Greece*, 107–8; Kenneth Matziorinis, 'Greek economy at a turning point: recent performance, current challenges, future prospects', *Journal of the Hellenic Diaspora* 19 (1993), 58.

23   Antigone Liberaki, 'Greece–EC comparative economic performance: convergence or divergence?' in Psomiades and Thomadakis (eds), *Greece*, 185; Pelagidis, 'Economic policies', 78–9.

24   *Vima*, 2 February 1992, A2, editorial; *Vima*, 7 February 1999, A59; *Vima*, 9 January 2000, D6; *Economist*, 1 May 1999, 105; *Kathimerini* (English Internet edition), 18 December 2000.

25   Vergopoulos, 'Economic crisis', 123–4.

26   *Vima*, 20 May 2001, B2, Zoï Tsoli.

27   *Vima*, 4 July 1999, D17, Th. P. Lianou.

28   Gelina Harlaftis, *Greek Shipowners and Greece, 1945–75* (1993), 176.

29   Paolo Mauro, 'Corruption and growth', *Quarterly Journal of Economics* 110 (1995), 684.

30   Stavros Thomadakis and Dimitris B. Seremitis, 'The destabilizing force of the electoral cycle in the Greek public economy', *Greek Review of Political Science* 3 (in Greek, 1993), 51–2.

31   Nancy Bermeo, 'Greek public enterprise: some historical and comparative perspectives', *Modern Greek Studies Yearbook* 6 (1990), 12, 16–17.

32   *Vima*, 4 May 1997, D2; Michael Sullivan, *Measuring Global Values. The Ranking of 16 Countries* (New York 1991), 117–22.

33   Pirounakis, *Greek Economy*, 56; Yannis Caloghirou, Yannis Voulgaris and Stella Zambarloukos, 'The political economy of industrial restructuring: comparing Greece and Spain', *South European Society and Politics* 5 (2000), 77; *Kathimerini*, 19 July 1998, 46, editorial. The ban on retrenchments was ruled illegal by the Supreme Court in 1998.

34   *Vima*, 10 May 1998, D2, Nikou Nikolaou; *Vima*, 12 December 1999, D4.

35   *Vima*, 29 January 1989, 11, Strati Evstathiadi; *Vima*, 18 March 1990, 2; *Vima*, 13 February 2000, D8, Nikou Nikolaou; *Kathimerini* (English Internet), 10 January 2001.

36   *Kathimerini*, 12 July 2000.

37   *Vima*, 25 July 1999, A19, Nikou Nikolaou; *Vima*, 13 February 2000, D8, Nikou Nikolaou; *Vima*, 15 October 2000, D3, Georgiou Bitrou; *Kathimerini*, 29 October 2000, Kleopatra Kontonika; *Vima*, 4 February 2001, A10, Nikou Nikolaou.

38 Caloghirou *et al.*, 'Political economy', 83; *Vima*, 15 April 2001, B2, Zoï Tsoli; The Economist, *Pocket Europe in Figures* (2000), 128; *Vima*, 10 June 2001, B8, Nikou Nikolaou.

39 George Pagoulatos, 'Governing in a constrained environment: policy making in the Greek banking deregulation and privatisation reform', *West European Politics* 19 (1996), 745–8.

40 *Vima*, 14 March 1999, D3, N.G. Charitaki; *Vima*, 18 July 1999, D8–9; *Kathimerini*, 26 October 2000.

41 Liberaki, 'Greece–EC comparative economic performance', in Psomiadis and Thomadakis (eds), *Greece*, 207; *Vima*, 9 May 1999, D35, Christou Pachta; *Kathimerini*, 27 August 2000, 45, Foti Kollia, citing OECD reports; *Vima*, 3 June 2001, B18, Zoï Tsoli, citing international surveys.

42 *Vima*, 8 September 1991, A30–1, St. Chaïkali; *Vima*, 24 September 2000, A54, Nota Tringa; *Kathimerini*, 1 July 2000, citing Iannis Papantoniou; *Kathimerini*, 4 March 2001 (Internet edition), Christina Kopsini; European Commission, *Living Conditions in Europe. Statistical Pocketbook* (2000), 36.

43 Vergopoulos, 'Economic crisis', 133; Lavdas, *Europeanization of Greece*, 61; Alec P. Alexander, *Greek Industrialists. An Economic and Social Analysis* (Athens 1964), 112–15.

44 Karabelias, *State and Society*, 164–5; Richard Clogg, *Parties and Elections in Greece. The Search for Legitimacy* (1987), 241; Lefteris Tsoulouvis, 'Urban planning, social policy and new forms of urban inequality and social exclusion in Greek cities', *International Journal of Urban and Regional Research* 20 (1996), 722; *Vima*, 8 July 1990, D2, Nikou Nikolaou; *Kathimerini* (English Internet edition), 26 March 2001.

45 Pirounakis, *Greek Economy*, 25, 27.

46 Fouli Papageorgiou and Susannah Verney, 'Regional planning and the Integrated Mediterranean Programmes in Greece', *Regional Politics and Policy* 2 (1992), 145; N.-K. Chlepas, 'Self-government and decentralization: towards the reordering of "competitive dealings"', *Greek Review of Political Science* 15 (June 2000), 46–7.

47 11 May 1997, 49; Desmond Dinan, *Ever Closer Union. An Introduction to European Integration* (2nd edn, 1999), 433–4, 438.

48 *Vima*, 25 February 1996, A14.

49 *Vima*, 29 August 1999, D18, Dionisou Stambogli.

50 *Vima*, 28 March 1993, D2; *Vima*, 3 June 2001, A8, Nikou Nikolaou.

51 David H. Close, 'Environmental NGOs in Greece: the campaign against the Acheloös diversion as a case-study of their influence', *Environmental Politics* 7 (1998), 55–77.

52 *Vima*, 22 November 1992, D2; *Vima*, 15 November 1998, D1; *Vima*, 22 November 1998, D4.

53 *Vima*, 24 September 2000, D13.

54 Kostas Vergopoulos, 'Regionalism and stabilization: the case of Greece in the EEC', in Dimitri Constas and Theofanis G. Stavrou (eds), *Greece Prepares for the Twenty-first Century* (Baltimore, MD 1992), 127; Dimitri Constas and Charalambos Papasotiriou, 'Greek policy responses to the post-Cold War Balkan environment', and Axell S. Wallden, 'Greece and the Balkans: economic relations', in Van Coufoudakis, Harry J. Psomiadis and Andre Gerolymatos (eds), *Greece and the New Balkans. Challenges and Opportunities* (New York 1999), 115–16, 231; *Vima*, 11 July 1999, D11, Ch. Korfiatis; *Vima*, 3 October 1999, D8, Trifon Kollintzas; *Vima*, 11 June 2000, D19, G.S. Skordilis.

55 Pirounakis, *Greek Economy*, 190; Lavdas, *Europeanization of Greece*, 65; *Vima*, 27 June 1999, D18, A.G. Christodoulaki; *Vima*, 18 July 1999, D6, Ch. Korfiati; *Vima*, 1 April 2001, B12, A. Kourkoula; *Kathimerini*, 12 November, 2000, 73, Athinas Kalaïtzoglou.

56 *Vima*, 29 April 2001, B14, G. Papaïoannou.

57 *Vima*, 6 July 1997, D4, Nikou Nikolaou.

58 *Vima*, 28 February 1999, D2, Nikou Nikolaou.

59 Pirounakis, *Greek Economy*, 185–6; *Kathimerini*, 6 June 1999, 70, D.G. Papakostopoulou; *Vima*, 5 March 2000, D8, Nikou Nikolaou.

60 *Vima*, 17 December 2000, D8, study by Institute of Economic and Industrial Research; *Kathimerini*, 29 October 2000, 63, Athinas Kalaïtzoglou.

61 *Vima*, 12 September 1999, D16–17, T. Mantikidis; *Vima*, 28 November 1999, A76, Vasili Moulopoulou; *Vima*, 5 December 1999, D4, Nikou Nikolaou; *Kathimerini*, 1 August 2000.

62 *Kathimerini*, 26 November 2000, 87–8, anon., citing the Chairman of the Capital Markets Commission.

63 *Vima*, 21 November 1999, A75, Nikou Nikolaou.

CHAPTER TEN

Old Values and New Tensions: Society, 1974–2000

Population growth and immigration

The falling birth rate

While population growth continued after 1974, its causes changed. As in the other poorest countries of western Europe – Ireland, Portugal and Spain – the fertility rate fell steeply from the 1970s, and from being comparatively high became comparatively low. The Greek rate fell from 2.2 in 1980 to 1.3 in 1998. The result was a continued fall in the rate of growth of the *officially recorded* population, which numbered 8,768,641 in 1971, 9,740,417 in 1981, 10,269,074 in 1991, and 10,498,836 in 1997. These figures failed however to capture the recent effects of mass immigration. The census of March 2001 has been more successful in this respect, and has consequently recorded a figure of 10,939,771.[1] Meanwhile, the surplus of births over deaths declined until it became a deficit from 1998. The percentage of those aged 14 or under fell from 29 in 1951 to 19 in 1991. The percentage of the population aged 65+ rose from 7 in 1951 to 14 in 1991, partly because of the declining proportion of children, partly because of increased life expectancy. Nearly everyone agreed that the low birth rate was a national problem because it threatened to weaken the country militarily, and to increase the burden of providing for the elderly.

The miniature baby boom of the 1960s among 15–29-year-old women continued through the 1970s. Then after 1980 fertility rates fell in this as in older age groups. As in the other developing countries of Europe, the fall in fertility was probably due to rising material expectations and cramped urban accommodation, as well as the meagreness of public welfare provisions such as family benefits, maternity leave, child care facilities, medical services and schools. A survey of 1983 found that the size of family which the average couple desired (2.5 children) was above the actual number of 2.2. Expectations became more realistic; and a survey of women in the metropolitan region in 1997 found that the majority did not want more than two children, while 17 per cent wanted only one, and 10 per cent did not want any.[2]

Increasing immigration

Net immigration from 1975 onwards was at first due to the cessation of large-scale emigration and the return of migrants from western Europe and to a lesser degree from elsewhere. Returned migrants accounted for the bulk of the *net* immigration of a third of a million in the six years after 1974. The *total* return movement in the ten years from 1976 was 420,862. In the same period, however, began an influx into Greece, as into Italy, Portugal and Spain, of immigrants from poorer countries in the Middle East, Africa and Asia. Then in the 1980s began a flow of immigrants from economically declining countries of eastern Europe.

The number of resident aliens remained small in the 1980s but increased gradually. Those officially recorded numbered 130,000 in 1981, including 4,000 political refugees. Those working without a permit were estimated by the authorities at an additional 70,000 in 1982. The numbers of unofficial immigrants grew from the mid-1980s, consisting predominantly thenceforth of economic refugees. Ethnic Greeks arrived from the Soviet Union between 1987 and 1995, and were readily granted official status although most could not speak Greek. They eventually totalled 163,000, most of them living in wretched conditions. Tens of thousands of ethnic Greeks arrived from Albania from 1990 onwards.

The flow of immigrants became a flood in 1991, with the mass arrival of Albanian citizens across a 170 km border which was too mountainous to police. Thenceforth, vast numbers of Albanians were regularly deported, promptly to return with increasing numbers of compatriots. They were supplemented by people from other countries and continents, who arrived by boat or on foot, many of them guided or transported by traffickers, of whom 2,500 were arrested in Greece in 1996 alone. About 4,000 people were caught while trying to cross the Aegean into Greece in 2000, and were reported to have paid on average $2,000–2,500 a head in Turkey for their passage.[3] The immigrants' purpose was to scrape a living or move on to western countries. They were estimated in 1992 by various analysts as including 100,000 Poles, 30,000 Romanians, 30,000 Bulgarians, 30,000 from former Yugoslavia, 110,000 Albanians (including at least 30,000 ethnic Greeks), 20,000 Filipinos, 20,000 Egyptians and 17,000 Pakistanis. There was also a growing flood of Kurds, Bangladeshis, Ethiopians and west Africans. Many of those from eastern Europe were gypsies.

Various authorities, including the National Centre of Social Research (EKKE), put the total number of immigrants of all types at around 800,000 in 1999 – the great majority of them unofficial and nearly two-thirds Albanian. By then, one-third of the babies born in the public hospitals of the metropolis had immigrant parents. By 2000, 9.7 per cent of primary schoolchildren and 3.7 per cent of secondary schoolchildren were aliens, about one-third being ethnic Greeks from Albania.[4]

The response to immigrants

Greece had suddenly become a multi-cultural society, and was acknowledged as such by the prime minister in 1996. But the legalisation of such vast numbers was too difficult for the cumbersome bureaucracy, and anyway beyond the tolerance of public opinion. The asylum procedure was so slow that few immigrants even tried using it: for example in 1999 only 1,528 asylum seekers were registered and only 146 applications were approved: the lowest rate in the EU (although Portugal and Spain did little better). Under a decree of November 1997, the government struggled to legalise immigrants by inviting applications for green cards (temporary residence permits); but only 215,000 had managed to secure one by December 2000.[5]

Many immigrants lived in densely packed apartments (often basements), or in makeshift shelters, or slept rough in railway stations or derelict buildings. It is generally accepted that in the late 1990s they formed as much as one-sixth or more of the total labour force, being found especially in menial jobs in agriculture, construction, transport, industry, catering, tourist services and domestic work, as well as drug trafficking and prostitution. Many were cruelly exploited, especially if their fate rested with particular employers. Many charities, church organisations and human rights groups battled to alleviate the immigrants' conditions.

Public resentment of aliens was, not surprisingly, widespread – in fact more than in any other EU country, being caused especially by the general belief that they were responsible for a wave of crime. The puzzling thing is that aliens did not form a disproportionately high number of those arrested and jailed. Albanians and gypsies were especially resented as being supposedly Muslims or lawless. Racially motivated violence and discrimination were increasingly common; and from mid-1999 police regularly rounded up hundreds of immigrants without residence permits, imprisoning many in grim conditions until they could be deported. In March 2001, the European Court of Human Rights awarded a Syrian refugee an immense sum in damages against the Greek government for inhuman and degrading treatment incurred in such a process.[6]

But there appeared no organised racist movement, partly because there was no disagreement on the essential point: all would control the illegal immigration if only they could. On the treatment of immigrants, however, human rights and charitable organisations disagreed with the majority of the public. Public resentment was mitigated moreover by the cheap labour which immigrants supplied, especially to small-scale businessmen, farmers and householders. The government admitted in 2000 that this labour was vital to the economy. These conflicting considerations explain why, in 1998, as many as 47 per cent of the public said that they were not irritated by the presence of foreigners, while 49 per cent said more predictably that they were. There was, moreover, survey evidence that by 2000 people were getting used to living close to immigrants, and that the young were becoming more tolerant of them than their parents.[7]

The immigrants' capacity for organisation, and for enriching the country's cultural life, was shown each year from 1996 in multicultural festivals featuring the cuisine, dancing, drama and music of the immigrant groups, with conferences about their problems. This activity could be explained partly by the fact that many immigrants were highly educated. Participants in the festival of 2000 included 80 human rights groups and representatives of 30 immigrant communities.[8]

Distribution of the national population

The generalisations which follow about standards of living and social stratification are largely confined to the officially recorded population, and would need much qualification were they to include unofficial immigrants.

The population of the country became geographically somewhat more dispersed. Whereas the metropolis *strictly defined* grew far faster than any other region in the four decades up to the 1981 census, it grew more slowly than any other except Thrace in 1981–91; and there was no sign that this trend changed in the 1990s. But what was really happening was that the metropolitan population was becoming more dispersed through the wider metropolitan region; so that in 1996 this contained about 39 per cent of the country's officially recorded population.

The metropolitan population remained more prosperous than any other. It and the Salonika region contained in 1991 a higher proportion of the economically active age group 15–64, and a lower proportion of the elderly, than any other region. The metropolitan region alone contained 45 per cent of the industry and 55 per cent of the cars in Greece.[9] Meanwhile the main provincial cities continued to grow quite strongly in the years 1981–91. Thus, whereas the metropolis (by the restricted, official definition) grew by 1.5 per cent in 1981–91, the next five cities in size (all with populations over 100,000) grew by an average of 9.9 per cent. Nevertheless the pace of urbanisation slowed down in the country as a whole, partly perhaps because of the greater prosperity of the provinces and countryside. The percentage of the population in towns with 10,000+ people became 4.9 points higher in 1971–81, but only 0.8 per cent higher in the next decade. The percentage of the population in villages with fewer than 2,000 people became 4.8 points lower in 1971–81, but only 2.1 points lower in the next decade.

One reason for the reversal of the trend towards demographic centralisation was the general recognition after 1974 that it had gone too far. In consequence, PASOK governments spent heavily on the development of the economy, social services and cultural life of the provinces. By a decree of 1984, designed to curb pollution, some industries were compelled to move out of the metropolis. Limited as it was, the strategy of decentralisation was enthusiastically supported by various social groups including youth organisations, farmers' organisations and local authorities. EEC subsidies did much to encourage regional development, firstly by supporting farmers' incomes and later by increasing expenditure on roads, communications and other infrastructure. Increasing numbers of professional people felt attracted to life in the provinces, partly because they felt an obligation to rejuvenate the social life of their ancestral regions, and partly to escape the dirt and bustle of the metropolis. The latter motive was increasingly powerful in the 1980s, especially among those who had the means or time to escape. A poll of 1998 found that 73 per cent of the inhabitants of the metropolis considered conditions of life 'insufferable' and 37 per cent wanted to leave. Commuting distance to the metropolis was increasing as motorways were developed.[10]

The standard of living

GDP per capita grew slowly from the early 1980s to the present, the trend being interrupted by four years of stagnation in 1990–93. In the census period 1981–90 the annual increase averaged 1.5 per cent, but in the following decade the figure is likely to prove higher, given the moderately strong growth of 1994 onwards. For example during the five years 1994–98 private consumption was higher in each successive year, the annual increase averaging 2 per cent. The big question is: who was benefiting from this growth?

Until the late 1980s there was a real improvement in the living standards of most of the population, as a result of increases in social benefits, social services, wages and EEC support for agricultural prices. The improvement in the living standards of many farmers was especially noticeable, and shown for example in a big increase in car ownership. For most of the 1990s however there seemed to be no improvement in the living standards of much of the population, as a result of rising unemployment, a decline in support for agricultural prices, prolonged restraint of wages and social benefits, and increasing taxation, the last needed to pay for the liabilities which governments had incurred in the 1980s.

Unemployment rose over most of this period, from about 2 per cent in 1979 to 12.4 per cent at the end of 1999, with the real rate at the latter date (that is, allowing for involuntary underemployment, and withdrawal from the official labour force of discouraged job seekers) about 3 per cent higher.[11] A disproportionately high number of unemployed lived in cities, and not many of them could resort to the unofficial economy, which catered chiefly for those who already had jobs (especially in the public sector) requiring some education or capital.[12] There were areas of industrial decay, for example in Piraeus, Elevsis, Patras and Salonika, where there were many long-term unemployed in serious poverty. The unemployment rate in 1999 was the second highest in the EU after Spain, and had continued to rise later than in other EU countries. In 2000 it was thought to be declining again, as in much of the EU.

The labour force as a proportion of the adult population aged 15–64 (i.e. the participation rate) was comparatively low, as in other poorer EU countries. It was, however, being increased by illegal immigrants (consisting disproportionately of men in economically active age groups), and by educated younger women who were entering it in ever larger numbers. Thus the participation rate was catching up with the EU average. In the 1980s, by contrast, it had declined because younger people remained longer in education and older people retired earlier. Thus the participation rate was estimated to be 60 per cent in 1983, 57 per cent in 1991 and 62 per cent in 1998.[13]

Unemployment was recognised by the later 1990s as an outstanding social problem. What worsened it was that unemployment benefits were the most restricted in the EU. Only one-quarter of the unemployed received the dole, because those seeking their first job (about one-quarter of the total in the mid-1990s) and those unemployed for more than twelve months (about one-half) did not qualify for it. The dole itself was only 28 per cent of the average wage in 1995; and the long-term unemployed suffered doubly because they could not acquire through work the insurance stamps needed for a retirement pension. But what mitigated the impact of unemployment was its incidence. As in other southern European countries, unemployment was concentrated among those who were not traditionally regarded as household bread-winners, that is the young and women. Only about 10 per cent of the unemployed were male heads of households, and just under one-third of them lived in households where no one else was employed.[14]

As in perhaps all developed economies, inequalities increased from the 1980s; and in Greece this trend reversed that of the years 1974–85. Figures by Eurostat (the statistical service of the EU) appeared early in 2000 showing a fairly close correlation between the level of an EU country's development and its degree of inequality. The ratio of the top 20 per cent of incomes to the bottom 20 per cent was highest in Portugal at 7.1, followed by Greece with 6.7, Spain with 6.0, Ireland with 5.8 and Italy with 5.2.[15] The prevalent view of economic analysts in 1998 was that during the previous fifteen years average real wage levels had stagnated or declined, whereas profits and dividends had increased enormously. This view is reflected in the survey of 'life satisfaction' periodically conducted by the EU in the 1980s and 1990s, which of course took into account people's expectations. By this test, Greece consistently came near or at the bottom of the EU table. In 1997 for example Greece had the highest percentage in the fifteen EU countries (37) reporting themselves not satisfied with life, and the highest (28) believing that life had deteriorated in the previous five years. Portugal, however, was almost as high on both scores. Both countries also had relatively high percentages of people (40 in Greece's case) who felt in 1997 that life had improved over the previous five years. This polarisation between satisfied and dissatisfied indicated an increase in inequality. The dissatisfied probably consisted in large part of wage earners who felt hard hit by wage restraint and rising taxation, and the satisfied of businessmen who benefited from booming profits.[16] So there was a widening gap between winners and losers. The winners included senior executives and professionals in the more advanced industries, in banking, the mass media, information technology, stockbroking and tourism. The losers included many farmers, industrial workers, service workers like waiters, and pensioners dependent on the main social insurance funds.

Since the 1970s, nevertheless, living standards had improved for most people. Ownership of consumer durables was one indicator. In 1998, 52 per cent of households (the average size of which was 3.3 people) owned a car, 86 per cent a colour television (and nearly all the rest a black and white television), 38 per cent a video-cassette recorder and 18 per cent an Automatic dishwasher. In 1989 there were 38 telephones per hundred inhabitants (amounting to nearly three-quarters of households), and reportedly a higher proportion in 1999. Six in ten of the population subscribed to mobile phones by 2001. These figures represent a big advance over those for 1976–77. Furthermore, by 1991 nearly all households in the country had electricity and 95 per cent had running water. More evidence of improvement is the percentage of household expenditure devoted to food. The National Statistical Service found from a national survey that it was 32.9 per cent in 1974 and 17.4 per cent in 2000. The percentage devoted to 'recreation and culture' increased from 3.4 per cent to 4.9 per cent, and the percentage devoted to 'hotels, restaurants and cafés' from 4.8 per cent to 9.4 per cent. The proportion spent on some form of entertainment was high by EU standards.[17]

As in Italy and Spain, most people lived in owner-occupied dwellings – 76 per cent in 1996 compared with an EU average of 60 per cent. Looked at another way, the picture was gloomier, with 42 per cent of the population living more than one to a room in 1996: the highest figure in the EU.[18]

Most other western European countries had admittedly done still better in these tangible indices of welfare. The rate of fixed telephone ownership was a little below the EU average; and the rate of car ownership remained the lowest, although in 1999 it was increasing rapidly. This was a mixed blessing in view of the appalling level of traffic accidents and air pollution. In ownership of consumer durables and cars, the growth of prosperity was especially marked in rural areas, although they still lagged far behind the cities.[19] The varied attempts that were made to measure human welfare, taking into account especially income per capita at purchasing power parity, educational levels and health, consistently placed Greece ahead of the rest of the Balkans in the 1980s, just ahead of Portugal, but below Spain and Italy.[20]

Most commentators in the 1990s took little satisfaction, however, in such evidence of material progress. Surveys asking people what they considered to be the leading problems facing the country consistently placed economic problems first, with inflation featuring prominently in the early 1990s and unemployment in the latter half.

The surveys that were made of household income and expenditure in the 1990s suggest a standard of living for a sizeable minority that was deprived, even leaving out of account the multitude of immigrants. Eurostat surveys found that in 1999, per capita purchasing power, taking into account differences in the cost of basic necessities, was still only 68.2 per cent of the EU average. Greece in 1996 had the highest percentage of households in the EU reporting that they had difficulty in making ends meet: 56 compared with 38 in Portugal. Surveys by Eurostat and by the Institute of Labour of the General Confederation of Greek Workers found that Greeks worked in

1997 the longest, and in 2000 almost the longest, hours in the EU, with many reporting that they had to work long hours to pay their bills, and 20 per cent of the labour force having a second job. As elsewhere, expenses conventionally defined as necessary were rising. Thus the national survey cited above found that the percentage of average household expenditure devoted to health rose from 4.7 in 1974 to 6.8 in 2000; while the percentage devoted to education rose from 1.3 to 2.8 in the same period. The conditions in which many people lived and worked were poor: Greeks along with the Italians had the highest percentage in the EU who were displeased with their jobs; while one-fifth were worried about noise and pollution; and the majority had little access to open space. But at least they were much less afflicted than any other peoples in the EU by fear of vandalism and crime in their neighbourhood.[21]

Social commentators and opposition politicians were increasingly concerned with social exclusion, a term adopted by the EU in preference to poverty because it included lack of access to social and civil rights. It was increasingly intrusive – for example in the form of beggars in central Athens, and shanty towns in parts of the metropolis and Salonika. Social surveys were increasingly effective in revealing it. An EU survey of 1996 found that 21 per cent of the population (the second highest percentage in the EU after Portugal) had an income, taking into account the cost of living, below the poverty line, defined as 60 per cent of the median income in their country. There were estimated in 1997 to be over 10,000 homeless people, consisting mainly of immigrants.[22]

Health

It may come as a surprise, then, that health was in general a success story. The Healthcare Europe index published by the Economist Intelligence Unit in 1998 covered 35 countries and included as indicators life expectancy, infant mortality, immunisation coverage, tobacco use, and rates of AIDS and cancer, and heart, respiratory and infectious diseases.[23] Greece ranked eighth, equal with four other countries. On an inverted scale (so that few points were better) Greece scored 11, compared with 10 for Italy, 11 for Slovenia, 12 for Spain, 15 for Portugal, 17 for Croatia, 19 for Bulgaria and 23 for Romania. On a subjective measure Greeks did still better: 76 per cent of them in 1997 saying that they felt well, compared with 59 per cent of Italians, 53 per cent of Portuguese, 64 per cent of Spaniards and 69 per cent of Germans.[24] Life expectancy at birth was 78 in 1998, the same as the average for Italy, Portugal and Spain, and six years higher than the average for the rest of the Balkans.[25] Greek life expectancy in 1998 was just higher than the provisionally estimated average of 78 in the EU-15, whereas in the 1960s it scored lower than the average for the EEC-6. Comparing the figures for the 1990s with those for earlier periods, we see evidence of major progress, lying mainly, as in most countries, in a continued fall in infant mortality, but also in a marked increase in life expectancy of the elderly.[26]

What happened to account for continued improvements in life expectancy? In part, the victories in the campaign against contagious diseases and infections through immunisation programmes and better hygiene. The percentage of deaths attributed by the National Statistical Service to these causes was 3.0 in 1972 and 2.5 in 1995. The advent of AIDS in the 1980s had little effect on these figures, and in 2000 its incidence was just over half the EU average. However, in the absence of public educational campaigns, it had been spreading rapidly.[27] What also increased life expectancy was an improvement in obstetric care that reduced the rate of infant, perinatal and maternal mortality. For example, maternal mortality at childbirth declined from 28.3 per 100,000 inhabitants in 1970 to 0.98 in 1990. These types of mortality were worse than the EU average in the early 1990s, but much better than in the rest of the Balkans; and they seem to have been caused mainly by the lack of obstetric and primary health care in remoter rural regions.[28] The fall in deaths from industrial accidents, referred to earlier, was presumably helped by government legislation of 1985 requiring employers to make provisions for occupational health and safety.[29] Reported suicide rates were the lowest in the EU in 1986 and 2000: 3.1 per cent of deaths in the latter year.[30] Under-reporting in a religious country may have reduced the figure; but, if accurate, it could be attributed to the strength of family and community ties. A different index of improved health was a report by the army's clothing department that the average height of conscripts increased by 3.7 per cent in the 1990s.[31]

Traditional features of Mediterranean diet were considered by medical specialists to be the most important reason for the country's relatively high life expectancy: it was comparatively high in fruit, vegetables, vegetable oil, bread and pasta, and comparatively low in meat and dairy products. In the early 1990s, the consumption of vegetables in Greece – 225 kilos per person each year – was far higher than anywhere else in the EEC, in which the average was 92. Consumption of alcohol was below the EEC average, even though wine was cheap. Also conducive to the health of older people was the physical activity required of village life before many people moved to cities, or acquired cars or motor bicycles.

Unhealthy features of modern life were however spreading, and accounted for a lower life expectancy among younger adults. The consumption of meat and dairy products was increasing, and was blamed by specialists for a marked increase in heart disease, bowel and breast cancer. Smoking had increased to the highest level in the EU in 2000, and was considered responsible for a large proportion of premature deaths.[32] Also the worst in the EU was mortality from traffic accidents, despite the low per capita ownership of motor vehicles. Elsewhere, mortality from traffic accidents declined markedly in the late twentieth century; but in Greece it rose sharply so that in 2000 it was twice the EU average.[33] City life was unhealthy not only in air pollution, but also in its lack of incentives or opportunities to take exercise. Thus obesity rates among children and young adults were high, and among men they were the highest in the EU. Recent surveys found that only 15 per cent of men and 12 per cent of women took exercise for health reasons, most of them having secondary or tertiary education.[34]

Occupational structure

Table 10.1 indicates changes in size of the main occupational groups, although according to current estimates it overestimates by three or four points the percentage of farmers in 2000.

Those in occupations of high income and status were continuing to increase (e.g. professionals), and those in occupations of low income and status were continuing to decline (e.g. farmers and unskilled industrial workers). These trends in themselves ensured much upward mobility between generations, which continued to be achieved largely through the educational system, for all its defects. Evidence of such social ascent was a survey in the

Table 10.1 *Occupational composition of the population, 1981–2000 (in percentages, the figures for 2000 being projections, based on trends in 1981–89)*[35]

Occupational groups	1981	2000
Professional workers	9.7	14.1
Managerial and senior executive staff	2.1	2.5
Clerical workers	9.0	12.2
Merchants and retailers	9.8	10.5
Employed in the provision of services	7.8	11.2
Farmers	30.9	21.5*
Skilled workers, artisans and labourers	30.7	28.0
Total	100.0	100.0

* See comment above.

early 1990s which found that 29 per cent of university staff in Greece, and 10 per cent of teaching staff in the prestigious Faculty of Medicine in the University of Athens, had parents with only primary education.[36]

Even in the 1990s it was estimated that nearly 10 per cent of children (mainly from poor backgrounds) failed to complete the nine years of compulsory education. In the late 1990s, 44 per cent of 17-year-olds (by far the highest proportion in the EU) were not participating in education or training. These facts help to explain why about half the population were estimated in the early 1990s to be functionally illiterate (compared with 19 per cent in Italy), with 9 per cent being totally illiterate. Surveys in the late 1990s of book-reading habits, computer ownership and Internet access showed the population as educationally at about the same level as the Spanish and Portuguese, although as we have noted, usage of computers and the Internet was comparatively slow to spread in Greece. Thus, in 1998, 19.5 per cent of youth aged 15–24 used a computer at least once weekly, compared with an EU average of 43.4 per cent.[37] The poorly educated were found disproportionately among the elderly, among women and in rural areas. Those adults who had not completed nine years of primary education included an overwhelming majority of farmers and a large majority of those employed in industry.

The young tended to be much better educated, as we have seen in an earlier chapter. The labour force in 1995 included 12 per cent who were graduates of universities and 5 per cent who were graduates of technical colleges, with much higher percentages in younger groups. As in developed countries of the west, professionals providing services – such as those relating to medicine, accountancy, advertising, environmental and information technology – were among the fastest-growing occupation groups. But some large professions – for example lawyers, schoolteachers and several categories of engineer – were congested because of the customary tendency of students to enrol in these fields. At a lower level of status, those providing skilled or semi-skilled services were also increasing: such as childminding, computer repairs, travel agencies and catering.

There were some lower-status jobs which expanded or remained numerous, and were filled largely by immigrants. They included casual wage labour in agriculture, catering, construction and domestic work. A higher-status category, clerical workers, also grew, largely because of the size of the public administration. As in other developed countries of the west, workers in industry were declining, because of de-industrialisation and investment in technology. Farmers, as in other EU countries, mobilised in an attempt to slow down their inevitable decline, which continued to go further than official figures indicate because of the growing dependence of farmers on non-agricultural incomes. Even so, the 17.8 per cent of the labour force who were farmers in 1997 was high by the standards of the EU (being 5.4 per cent in Italy, 12.6 per cent in Portugal and 7.4 per cent in Spain) although low by the standards of most Balkan countries. The proportion of the total labour force employed in family businesses was declining gradually, while the proportion dependent on wages and salaries continued to increase, from 48.4 per cent of the labour force in 1983 to 53.1 per cent in 1991. The latter figure was still very low by EU standards. Over two-thirds of the labour force consisted of wage or salary earners in Italy, Portugal and Spain, and still more in northern Europe.[38]

Social services in crisis

Social policy

The type of welfare system came to resemble in important ways those of Italy, Portugal and Spain.[39] Greece might in fact be taken as an extreme example of a southern European model of welfare. In all four countries, social policy was shaped by party manipulation, so that welfare benefits were distributed according to the political influence, rather than the need, of the recipients. This practice discouraged the development both by the state of a universal safety net and by citizens of a general sense of minimum entitlement. In Greece, governments still lack the basic data needed to identify all those in need, or estimate the requirements of a minimum standard of living. To satisfy their patronage needs, the dominant parties in the four southern countries relied heavily on creating jobs in the public sector, and on dispensing cash benefits like pensions for retirement or disability. In Greece, both types of expenditure were exceptionally heavy.

In all the southern countries, the major role in the welfare system of insurance schemes designed for certain occupation groups, and created or regulated by the government, resulted in a contrast between those belonging to relatively generous insurance schemes, such as public sector workers, and a wide range of groups, including casual workers or farmers, which were covered by poor schemes or by none. In Greece, nearly three-quarters of the working population belonged to the state schemes: IKA for private employees, and OGA for farmers, the members of which received relatively low benefits; while 10 per cent belonged to privileged schemes for public and bank employees. Not only pensions but even health treatment was administered through the insurance schemes.

The privileged groups had such a strong sense of entitlement that they defeated attempts by governments of either party to prevent or reduce inequalities between insurance funds. Thus some public-sector workers managed to defy the wage freeze imposed by the PASOK government in the late 1980s; while a broad alliance of public sector workers defeated, by a prolonged strike in 1990, an attempt by the New Democracy government to reduce differences between their insurance benefits.[40] Provision for those who fell outside the social insurance net – such as the long-term unemployed, or elderly people who had not paid the required number of insurance contributions – was meagre even by the standards of Italy, Portugal and Spain. The fact that the rate of poverty among these groups was not comparatively high in Greece indicates the continuing efficacy of the family as a welfare agency.[41]

As in the other southern European countries, the educational and health services provided by the state, which might have promoted social equality, continued to be poor in quality by northern European standards. In Greece, expenditure on education and health remained especially low. Meanwhile, the high proportion of social protection spent on retirement and disability pensions (69 per cent in 1991) – which were distributed largely by political criteria – left little to be spent on benefits targeted towards the destitute, large families and the unemployed. In 1997 the benefit that was provided to single mothers or to the elderly without actuarial entitlement to a pension was about $60 a month: effectively the welfare safety net. In Greece the proportion of GDP spent on social benefits, education and health was until the early 1990s just above the Portuguese level, but had been rising relative to the EEC average. By the mid-1990s it had slipped below the Portuguese level to become the lowest in the EU-12. Meanwhile the proportion of public expenditure devoted to superfluous public employees must have been among the highest in Europe.

In the 1990s it was becoming obvious that social services were breaking down, for several reasons. Firstly the traditionally inefficient state administration had been made more so by partisan abuse, and therefore could not meet public demands, which were growing in various ways, as the traditional relief agencies – the family and church charities – were less able to cope. The numbers of elderly were increasing, as well as the proportion of them who were separated from their children. There were also the long-term unemployed in decayed industrial centres, immigrants, homeless children, disabled people and drug addicts. Governments could not cater for growing needs because of their commitment to economic austerity.

There was overwhelming dissatisfaction with health and educational services, and with the system of social protection. The response of better-off citizens was to resort to private services. Some of the destitute benefited from the increasing role of voluntary charities, at least some of which found ways to cooperate with agencies of local and national government – a trend which was belated by the standards of Italy and Spain, but evidently increasing. Growing numbers of welfare recipients struggled with the cumbersome bureaucracy of the insurance schemes. An investigation in 1998 found that average claimants for a retirement pension from IKA had to spend 266 days in queues for three years while their files shuttled between departments. IKA's records are still not fully computerised. Applicants with inadequate documentation faced still worse delays, and many of them resorted to corrupt intermediaries – typically former employees of the department or insurance scheme in question – who in return for a slice of the benefit would expedite matters through friends inside the system.[42] The deficits of the major social insurance funds were reaching such an alarming level (15 per cent of GNP by 1995) that many people were frightened into withdrawing their pensions prematurely or transferring to private schemes. By EU standards Greek insurance schemes were distinguished by low benefits and high contributions, according to an authoritative report in 2000 commissioned by the General Confederation of Greek Workers.[43]

The mounting deficits of the main insurance funds are now, arguably, the government's worst financial headache. The causes of the deficits are complex: maladministration of the funds, including failure to ensure that everyone paid their dues; poorly controlled health costs; the actuarial time bomb of an ageing population; past government profligacy, in appointing too many public employees under generous insurance schemes; and chaotic financial relations over several decades between the funds and the state, so that there were ample grounds for dispute between the government and trade unions about culpability for the whole mess. For example, for over 30 years from 1955 the funds had been required to place their assets in the Bank of Greece at little or no interest; then from the late 1980s they had been increasingly subsidised by the government.[44]

Education

The ills of the educational system, especially at secondary and tertiary level, were constantly discussed throughout the 1990s, and were characterised in March 1999 by a leaked report from within the Ministry of Education, which spoke of a low standard of teaching at all levels, and curricula 'ill-adapted to contemporary social needs'.[45] The latter point was proved by growing unemployment among graduates (11.1 per cent in 2000), a problem which also existed in Italy, Portugal and Spain.[46]

Public funding of education declined slightly to 7.9 per cent of the budget in 1990, and 3.5 per cent of GNP in 1998. In 2000, these levels were the lowest, not merely in the EU, but in the 29 countries of the OECD.

One notorious consequence was the need of many schools – 40 per cent in 1998 – to cater for pupils in two shifts: one in the morning and another in the afternoon. Another was the delay in incorporating computers and the Internet into teaching, a process which was still in its early stages in secondary schools in 2000. The nominal ratio of pupils to teachers seems quite good: in the academic year 1997/98 it was 14.4 in primary schools and 12 in junior secondary schools. The first figure was a little higher, and the second distinctly lower, than the OECD average; and the Greek figures were under half those for 30 years previously (see above, p. 75). But actual class sizes were determined by teachers' availability; and there were complaints that teachers with appropriate qualifications were often unavailable.[47]

Private expenditure on education, at an estimated 2.1 per cent of household income in the 1990s, roughly equalled public expenditure. The majority of parents made heroic sacrifices for their children's education, and spent especially on cramming schools, which were attended by a growing proportion of schoolchildren, including by now three-quarters of those at the *lykeio* (senior secondary) level. A survey of provincial middle-class parents found that higher education had replaced goods as a daughter's dowry. A *lykeio* pupil cost parents on average $2,670 a year by 1999 in educational expenses alone.[48] Tertiary students were also a heavy expense: in the 1990s, 40 per cent of 20–24-year-olds depended solely on their parents. The numbers enrolled in private Greek tertiary institutions were increasing again, and are now more than officially indicated: about 30,000 or roughly 5 per cent of students. The high valuation of education were shown in a growing proportion of younger adults with tertiary qualifications, some from the Open University (which started teaching in 1998). The proportion of 18–24-year-olds undergoing tertiary education by 2000 was actually the highest in the EU: 32 per cent. The percentage of 30–39-year-olds with tertiary qualifications in 1999 was 24 (compared with 11 in Italy, 10 in Portugal and 27 in Spain), a percentage twice that for those aged 55+.[49] The quality of the education is another matter.

The secondary system was however plagued by problems, which were dramatised – every winter in the 1990s – by prolonged pupils' occupations of scores, sometimes many hundreds, of *lykeia* and often *gymnasia* (junior secondary schools) as well. Schoolchildren's demonstrations in the winter of 1990–91 led to violent incidents causing the deaths of five people. Those of 1998–99 caused chaos by barricading several highways between cities and many thoroughfares within cities. The proclaimed grievances varied over time, but consistently reflected exasperation with relentless cramming for exams by rote learning; lack of opportunity for self-expression or recreation; shortage of teachers and poorly prepared textbooks; shabby buildings and equipment; and lack of consultation over educational reforms, which were frequent and often ill-considered. Accustomed as they were to an authoritarian system, schoolchildren showed little aptitude for negotiation and little sense of responsibility. Governments belatedly learnt the need for consultation with teachers and pupils: thus the government in 1998 announced at last the convening of the National Education Council established in 1985 – but without subsequently giving it any clear purpose. A Minister of Education, late in 1999, conceded the schoolchildren's main point by slashing drastically the workload of *lykeio* pupils.[50]

An indication of underlying problems was a survey of 1992 which found that 49 per cent of parents and pupils were 'very dissatisfied' with their secondary school; 37 per cent of pupils complained of 'lack of dialogue' with teachers; and only 28 per cent of them considered their relations with teachers to be good. A survey of the educational attainments of 13-year-olds in 41 countries in 1997 found Greece rating poorly: 29th in natural sciences and 33rd in mathematics.[51] The majority of parents believed the teaching in private schools to be superior. These were attended in the mid-1990s by 7 per cent of the country's pupils, a proportion which, not surprisingly, has increased in recent years. There is stiff competition to enter certain elite institutions such as the College of Athens and the Moraïtis School.[52]

The system for appointing and promoting secondary teachers for a long time emphasised applicants' entitlements, without sufficient regard for their ability to teach. Under provisions introduced in 1970, appointments to teaching positions were available to all university graduates who applied, in chronological order of preference from the date of application, with some further preference to those who got outstanding grades. Their university course put a premium on rote learning, and those appointed were assured by PASOK reforms in the 1980s of automatic promotion with no provision for evaluation of performance. The majority of school principals, as well as temporary teachers (8 per cent of the total) were appointed on political criteria. Eventually, in 1998, an examination was introduced for those seeking appointment as teachers, with a view to progressively replacing the old appointments system by a more meritocratic one. The fact that three-quarters of applicants failed (a result repeated in 2001) was attributed by informed commentators to the serious inadequacies of their university degrees. Private schools achieved their superiority by selecting teachers and assigning them to teach only the subjects for which they were qualified.

The importance which everyone attached to education would lead one to expect some improvement in its quality. There is some evidence that this occurred. A survey of primary schools in 1988 and 1999 concluded that teachers were making more effort to help pupils, and resorting less to sarcasm and corporal punishment.[53]

The gateway from school to university remained too narrow for applicants, the ratio of university places to candidates being 1:7 in the 1980s. National examinations for entrance to tertiary education were a stressful experience for increasing numbers of candidates: some 170,000 in 1997. Governments responded to this pressure by fixing the intake at a level beyond the capacity of universities, a bad practice started by Georgios Papandreou in 1964.

Once they entered university, however, students embarked on an all-too-easy road to graduation. Largely as a result of the PASOK reform of 1982, students had acquired a sense of entitlement to a degree attained with free tuition and textbooks, and periodically fought for their demands with mass protests and occupations. Staff who cared for their profession were dismayed by the prevalence among students of rote learning at the expense of critical thinking, and the continued expenditure of ministerial funds on free textbooks rather than on libraries, which remained very inadequate. The staff/student ratio in 2000 was 1:26.3 (the OECD average being 1:14.6).[54]

The basic problems remained in the late 1990s, including hasty and poorly financed expansion to deal with rocketing numbers of students (whose numbers increased by 66 per cent in 1993–99). Universities scrambled in the latter half of the 1990s to qualify for EU funds to finance postgraduate programmes, for which there had been little provision anywhere in the 1980s. The number of postgraduate students in Greece more than trebled between 1994 and 2001 (but were there libraries, laboratories and scholarships to provide for them?). Enrolment at foreign institutions remained high: it was 27 per cent of all university students in 1994, of whom one-fifth were postgraduates. As before 1967, the private expenditure on these students exceeded public expenditure on tertiary education.[55]

One crude measure of research performance was a comparison, made by the University of Patras, of the number of publications by academics, relative to size of population, in EU countries in 1996–2000. Greece came eleventh in the EU. This was creditable, because Greece came fifteenth in funding for research; and this funding was only 24 per cent of the EU average. There were evidently some excellent scientists, because a comparison – based on the *Science Citation Index* – of the number of much-cited articles published in 1987, in relation to population, showed Greece as performing well by southern and eastern European standards.[56]

Health

Health care suffered not from insufficiency of expenditure (if private expenditure is included) but from irrational allocation of resources, and inefficient administration of hospitals and of insurance systems. Greeks spent 7.9 per cent of GNP on health in 1991, rising to 9.1 per cent in 2000, which was comparatively high. The figure for Spain in 2000 was 7.5 per cent and for Italy 7.6 per cent.[57] As all Greeks could see, they were getting poor value, and the burden of financing this expenditure was inequitable. By the late 1990s the level of public dissatisfaction with the health services was, with the Portuguese, the highest in the EU. A poll in 1995 found that, although 83 per cent of the public believed doctors to be highly trained, only 50 per cent believed that they 'fulfilled their social and humanitarian mission'.

State hospitals were under-resourced and, with one or two exceptions, poorly administered. As with other public corporations, their managers were for a long time appointed on partisan criteria at the expense of merit, and their excessive staffing levels were dictated by public-sector trade unions. Among examples of maladministration of hospitals were their generally squalid physical conditions, and the rigid allocation of beds to specialities, so that there were long queues for some beds while others were empty. The great majority of hospital buildings dated from before 1940. In response to public exasperation, the government announced in August 2000 the emergency appointment of 5,350 more medical staff, largely for hospital work, and a campaign to make hospital administrators more efficient.[58]

The distribution of doctors continued to be skewed by the interests of the influential medical profession (in 1992, 48 MPs were doctors). Greece continued to compare badly with other south European countries in numbers of general practitioners and nurses. According to the National College of Public Health in 2001, the total number of physicians of all types was one-third greater than necessary, but the number of general practitioners was only one-seventh of what were needed to provide an adequate system of primary care.[59] Many nurses left the profession in despair with their working conditions. These imbalances perpetuated the lack of primary and preventive care. Many people had to go to the casualty ward of a hospital instead of a general practitioner; and most patients in public hospitals had to be cared for by their families. There was in addition a serious neglect of dental health, expenditure on which was almost the lowest in the EU, with the result, for example, that there was a comparatively high rate of gum disease and tooth decay in all age groups. For example, 60–65 per cent of 13-year-olds in 1998 suffered from serious tooth decay.[60] Governments had done little since 1974 to remedy the maldistribution of medical staff. In 1989, 54 per cent of the 6,648 doctors in the state National Health System worked in the metropolis and 20 per cent in Salonika. Only 622 worked in the rural Health Centres (see also above, p. 163).

Greek surgeons managed, during the 1990s, to provide an increasingly diverse range of operations, as shown by a steep decline in the number of patients insured with IKA (which covered 55 per cent of the population) who had to go abroad for operations: from 2,581 in 1990 to 748 in 1999. But the total number of people (including private patients) who sought treatment abroad was still 35,000 in 1997, at a cost in foreign exchange of $17 million.[61]

A sizeable number of doctors was actually corrupt. Most patients in public hospitals reported that they gave unofficial payments to doctors, and many to nurses also; while 46 per cent of those interviewed in 1995 used their personal acquaintance with a doctor, or other contacts, to jump the queues for attention in hospital.[62] A foreign committee of investigation, under the chairmanship of Brian Abel Smith, found in 1994 the scale of under-the-counter and untaxed payments in medicine to be extraordinarily high by OECD standards. Another survey found that doctors practising in the public sector supplemented their inadequate salaries by taking commissions for over-prescribing medication and for unnecessary references to specialists, so adding greatly to the deficit of the social insurance funds. Many doctors who drew salaries from the public system also worked, illegally, in the private sector. Eminent surgeons declared in 2000–1 what most people suspected anyway: that many of their colleagues performed unnecessary operations, among the examples being heart-bypass and open-heart surgery, and caesarian sections.[63] The administration of the insurance organisations was not efficient enough to monitor doctors' activities.

Naturally, those with the means avoided the public system. During the 1980s and 1990s, the proportion of expenditure on private care rose, contrary to the intention of the health law of 1983. In permitting again, in 1992, the establishment of new private hospitals, the New Democracy government recognised reality. By the late 1990s, 42 per cent of all health expenditure was private – an extraordinarily high proportion by European standards.[64]

The family

Any description of the family in Greece must emphasise its continuing cohesion, which was demonstrated in the 1990s by various cross-national surveys. The percentage of people over 15 who were married was 67, the highest in the EU, compared with 62 in Portugal and 59 in Spain. Women married at the relatively early average age of 23.5, as a rule to men several years older. Of married women aged 25–9, 40 per cent devoted themselves entirely to housework and children, the same as in Spain and Italy, but well above the average for the whole of the EU of one-third. The overwhelming majority of women still chose to make the family their top priority in life. A survey in 2000 of married women's sexual experience (taking 1,500 school-teachers as the sample) found about one-quarter to be generally dissatisfied; but the author concluded that this proportion was low by comparison with other countries.[65] The divorce rate remained comparatively low, although increasing. Divorces numbered 17 per cent of marriages in 1998, compared with 4 per cent in 1970–74. In addition, though, legal separations without divorce numbered one for every ten marriages in 1995, compared with one in twenty in 1970.[66] Two per cent of couples cohabited without marrying, about the same as in Italy, Portugal and Spain, but far lower than in northern Europe. The percentage of births outside marriage was rising gradually but in the early 1990s was only three, the lowest in the EU, by contrast with five in Italy, six in Spain, eighteen in Portugal and over 25 in several northern European countries. Unmarried mothers in Greece still tended to be stigmatised, to the extent that most pretended that they were divorced. They were still at risk of being denied support by their own families, and as we have seen they got very little financial support from the state.[67]

Family loyalty remained generally strong. More young people than in any other EU country (54.6 per cent) said that they would not leave their parents in an old people's home (compared with 47.9 per cent of Italians, 40.7 per cent of Portuguese and 41.7 of Spaniards); and 82 per cent of the elderly lived near enough to their children to be in frequent contact. A survey in 1993 found 78 per cent of the rural population and 47 per cent of the Athens population agreeing that 'the most significant priority in my life is providing for my children'.[68] Greek parents were still more likely than those in Italy, Portugal and Spain to emphasise the importance of a stable family background and comprehensive family care for children. Young people still felt protective of their families' reputation and honour. Most school leavers claimed to be influenced in their choice of studies after school by parents or relatives, rather than by other people; while the majority of university graduates studied the same subjects, in the same universities, as their fathers. Those aged 25+ who still lived with their parents increased as a result of rising unemployment, and in 1997 comprised two-thirds of men and over one-third of women. Though weaker than formerly, extended family ties were stronger than in northern Europe. A survey of young people in the 1990s found that, whereas Dutch, British and German respondents contacted aunts, uncles and cousins only on special occasions, Greek respondents claimed to contact them at least every fortnight.[69]

Nevertheless, family relationships continued to change as a result of economic development and rising educational levels. A survey of students in the late 1980s found them strongly rejecting the views that the father should be the sole bread-winner; that the woman's only destiny was to be a mother; that pre-marital chastity was necessary for women; and that marriages must be celebrated in church. Another survey of 1980 found that only 25 per cent of those aged under 35 agreed that divorce should be confined to exceptional circumstances, compared with 70 per cent of those aged over 49. The model of married relationship shown by various surveys to prevail among young people was companionate and equal, with most young people agreeing that wives should have their own career, and over three-quarters of the total population agreeing wholly or substantially that the father should have an equal role in bringing up children, though the last view was more strongly supported by women.[70] In such matters as in others, people tended to give the responses which they felt were expected of them; but the change in values was real. Thus a survey in 1996 by the National Centre of Social Research discovered that the traditional division of roles between sexes still prevailed in 57 per cent of metropolitan households, but that this was a much smaller proportion than in the past, and that roles were equally divided among 55 per cent of young and highly educated couples.[71]

Relationships between generations were changing as well. As in other developed countries, young people living in cities were increasingly likely to be influenced by their peers, and less likely to be influenced by their parents, still less by their grandparents. Meanwhile television, and increasingly the Internet too, reduced conversation between family members.[72]

As perhaps in any society where patriarchal authority was strong, cases of abuse between family members, sexual or violent, tended to be concealed; and, when they did become known, rarely resulted in punishment for the perpetrator. In Greece in the 1990s, women who were victims of psychological or physical abuse were evidently numerous, but deterred from escape by an unsympathetic social climate and lack of institutional support.[73] Abuse of children was also found on investigation to be disturbingly common. For example one survey of students found that 7 per cent of males and 17 per cent of females reported having been sexually abused as children, one-third by members of their own families. A survey of 1989, extrapolating from the number of reported cases, estimated that 35,000 children ran away from home each year.[74] Cases of rape were officially very few, but were found by surveys to be seriously under-reported, because of the stigma for the victim and the improbability that the perpetrator would be prosecuted.[75] As in other southern European countries where women's independent participation in the labour force was recent, sexual harassment in the workplace afflicted the majority of women at some time.

Attitudes were changing. For example, the media were giving more publicity to domestic violence; and there were organisations – official and voluntary – offering help to women victims. The first government refuge for battered women was opened in 1988 and the second in 1999; and the first was contacted by 818 women in 1999 alone. Doctors of the Red Cross Hospital reported in July 1994 that the numbers of battered women whom they treated had doubled in the previous five years, many of them victims of extreme violence.[76]

Women's status

As in other southern European countries, later stages of economic development led to increasing participation by women in the labour force. The proportion of women aged 15+ in work or seeking work reached a low point in 1982 of 27.9 per cent, and rose to 37.3 per cent in 1997. Expressed as a percentage of the labour force aged 15+, women increased from 30.7 to 39.2 per cent in those years. In this respect, the Greek figure in the late 1990s was higher than those for Italy and Spain, but lower than that for Ireland, and much lower than those for Portugal or the richer countries of the EU.[77] One reason for the rise in Greece was the continuing expansion of free public education, from which women benefited proportionately more than men. The numbers of women graduating from tertiary educational institutions continued to rise, until by the early 1990s they exceeded those of men, and by the late 1990s they formed a large majority. Their numbers were especially high in social sciences (including law), languages, humanities and also in medicine, and relatively low in engineering, mathematics and natural sciences.

Another reason for women's increasing participation was economic. As elsewhere, many occupations considered suited to women were growing: teaching and nursing, clerical work, sales work and various services like banking, insurance, domestic work, child care and the restaurant and hotel trades. Many of the labouring and industrial jobs traditionally taken by men were declining. Farm labouring and unskilled production line work, which had employed many women, were also declining; but their decline was outweighed by the growing occupations referred to.[78] Especially important for its effect on women's status was the steadily increasing entry by many women into university teaching, medical and legal practice. In the public examinations in about 1997 for entry into the public service, women formed a majority of successful applicants. The small family businesses, in which women tended to have subordinate roles, were declining.

To judge by the condemnations uttered by the General Secretariat for the Equality of the Sexes, discrimination against women in job applications remained widespread. Evidence of it continued in the relatively high unemployment rate of women – 16.3 per cent in 1999. Pay differentials between the sexes narrowed somewhat in the 1980s, because of the centralised bargaining process establishing minimum wage rates, and pressure by the EEC. But they widened again in the 1990s because the relative value of minimum wages fell. Thus in the late 1990s, a Eurostat survey found that women's pay was on average 68 per cent of men's, the lowest percentage in the EU.[79] Furthermore, women's working week – combining unpaid housework with paid work outside the home – was on average one-fifth longer than men's, with the differential being greater among uneducated women.[80]

Greece diverged even from the rest of southern Europe in the extent of men's grip on authority. Admittedly, there are now a few prominent female politicians, distributed among several parties. But men continued to dominate the leading positions in political parties and in every major occupation group, professional organisation or political institution: for example trade unions, businesses, universities, journalism, the judiciary, civil service and police. Women formed only 18 per cent of employers and 19 per cent of the self-employed in 1999. As a result of recent increase, women are now about 10 per cent of the personnel of the armed forces, including some officers up to the rank of brigadier. The officers had graduated through training colleges for nurses, and women are still excluded from the other training colleges. In the Orthodox Church, of course, women hold no responsible position at all. In other professions, the chief problem seemed to be the familiar one of tacit cooperation by men in authority to exclude women. This is indicated for example by the variance in the proportion of women between medical specialities: relatively high among anaesthetists, dermatologists and pathologists, and low among many others. The new constitution enacted in 2001 has abolished limits to the proportion of women who can serve in any occupation, such as the police and fire brigade.

Female politicians cannot induce the party machines to adopt significantly more women candidates for parliament, even though they have made increasingly organised efforts to this end, in cooperation with the General Secretariat for the Equality of the Sexes, women's groups and trade unionists.[81] In parliaments elected from 1981, the percentage of women MPs edged up from four in 1981 to ten in 2000; by which year the corresponding figure in municipal and prefectural councils was just seven. Time will tell whether the PASOK government can fulfil its promise, on International Women's Day on 8 March 2001, to require a one-third gender quota for each party's candidates at the next local elections in 2002. Prominent among the obstacles to women in politics were their reluctance to stand for election, and – according to party organisers – the reluctance of voters to support them.

It is not surprising then that the Gender Empowerment Measure, devised by the United Nations Human Development Programme, rated Greece in 1998 the lowest in Europe and 51st on its scale, while Spain came 16th, Portugal 22nd, Italy 26th, Bulgaria 43rd and Turkey 85th. It seems that Orthodox Christianity is still more opposed than Roman Catholicism to women's rise in status outside the household. On broader criteria – including comparative health, educational levels, marital status and social discrimination – Greece ranked somewhat higher, but still below Portugal, Yugoslavia, Italy and Spain. Two factors make it seem especially likely that women's status in Greece will continue to improve, albeit slowly. One is women's rising educational level and in consequence their increasing participation in highly regarded professions. Another is that – largely because of western influence – discrimination against them lacks legitimacy. For example, a survey in 1988 found that only 15 per cent of women and 10 per cent of men thought that politics should be chiefly a man's affair; while a reliable poll of 1995 found that 51 per cent of women would accept compulsory military service including combat duty.[82]

Values

Religion and moral values

In moral values also, the outstanding characteristic of Greece – even by comparison with Italy, Portugal and Spain – was conservatism. For example, a Eurobarometer poll of the late 1990s found Greek youth to be more opposed than any others in Europe to euthanasia (68.5 per cent) and to gay marriages (47.7 per cent). But youth themselves regarded their elders as conservative. Forty-eight per cent of youth said that their elders did not understand how much had changed in society: about the same percentage as in Portugal and Spain, but more than in Italy, which was close to the EU average of 39 per cent. Another survey in 1997 found, as did interviews with urban families by Mariella Christea-Doumanis in around 1970, that teenage girls were especially likely to resent parental supervision as too strict.[83]

Despite the inroads of secularisation, Greeks ranked as the most religious people in western Europe on various indices. A survey of the mid-1990s found that 75 per cent (presumably of adults) considered God to be very significant in their lives. A survey in 1999 by the National Centre of Social Research found 47 per cent of 16–17-year-olds claiming that they often felt the need to pray, and 30 per cent claiming to attend church several times a year or more. A survey of 1985, asking people which institution they considered to be the most powerful in their society, found that the Church was named by a higher proportion in Greece (33 per cent) than in Italy (29 per cent), Portugal (14 per cent) or Spain (12 per cent). Greece was apparently the only country in capitalist Europe in which the proportion of the population claiming that God was important in their lives increased: from 58 per cent in 1985 to 77 per cent in 1994, according to a Eurobarometer survey. This is probably because the Church was recovering from its past association with the right-wing establishment, and possibly, too, because of a reaction against Marxist socialism.[84] A survey of 1985 found that only 16 per cent of the Greek population claimed that they never attended church, compared with 23 per cent in Italy, 29 per cent in Portugal and 37 per cent in Spain. The small minority who were frequent churchgoers were found by a survey in 1996 to be uncharacteristically conservative on moral issues: being for example more biased against the physically disabled; more in favour of the death penalty and cultural censorship; and more xenophobic.

The Church continued to be regarded by most people as essential to national identity; so that for example religious ties with Serbia and other Balkan states were invoked by governments in the 1990s to justify their policies towards them. Although periodically discussed from 1974 onwards as a logical step towards modernisation, the separation of Church and state remained politically out of the question. The growth in the numbers and the rise in the educational level of monks in the monasteries of the autonomous monastic republic of Mount Athos in the northern Aegean ('The Holy Mountain' to Greeks) indicated the attraction exerted by the Church's devotion to tradition and by its mystical, as distinct from intellectual, approach to religious worship.[85]

The influence of the clergy might have been still greater had they responded more to the laity's needs. The bishops were regarded as excessively autocratic in their relationship with the parish clergy, and their conservatism in other respects was strengthened by their average age: in 1996, 30 out of 80 were over 70 years old. For some time after 1974, the majority of bishops consisted of people who had attained their positions thanks to the Junta, a fact of which the Holy Synod reminded the public by appealing in August 1989 for the release from jail of the former military dictators. One Junta appointee was Archbishop Serapheim, under whose uninspiring leadership (1974–98) bishops were discredited by squalid legal disputes among themselves and by financial scandals. A legacy of the latter was that a bishop, who was former director of the Church's finance department, was

charged by a public prosecutor in June 1999 with repeated fraud, embezzle-
ment and forgery. The influence of the 9,334 parish priests and deacons
(in about 1990) was still limited by their rather low educational level and
their mainly rural background; and recruitment was declining, though not
yet to a critical extent.[86]

The Church's influence was also limited by the fact that its priorities
were out of tune with social needs. The evidence, direct and indirect, is that
most people wanted the clergy to act more as social workers, and take a
greater interest in pressing social problems. Two-thirds of the population in
1996, including over one-quarter even of active churchgoers, considered
that the Church did not meet the needs of society.[87] To most educated
people, the clergy and devout laity seemed somewhat obscurantist. This is
not surprising seeing that the clergy strongly opposed contraception, abortion even when the mother's health was endangered, the use of corpses for
medical purposes, organ transplants, cremation, the theory of evolution, the
removal of religious affiliation from state identity cards, or civilian alterna-
tives to military service. Many advocated a militant brand of nationalism
which could not benefit their spiritual mission, for example by taking a conspicuous role in nationalistic demonstrations against the Former Yugoslav
Republic of Macedonia in the early 1990s.[88]

Christodoulos – elected Archbishop in April–May 1998 – was a new type
of leader. He began to reform various aspects of Church organisation, and
launched some widely acclaimed programmes, for example to cure drug
addicts and help AIDS sufferers. Controversially outspoken on many issues,
Christodoulos is also skilful in communication and genial in manner, and
has won great popularity, so revealing the Church's latent strength.[89]

The increase in drug-taking, especially by youth, was a subject of general
anxiety. It was agreed that in 1992 at least 25,000 young people were
addicted to heroin; and that the total number of recorded drug addicts
of all ages was 80,000, compared with 4,000 twenty years earlier. Police
reported 265 drug-related deaths in 1999 compared with 28 in 1986. The
National Centre for Documentation and Information on Narcotics and
Addiction reported that, in 1998, 28 per cent of boys and 15 per cent of
girls aged 17–18 admitted to having tried marijuana, double the figure for
1993. There was reportedly a big increase also in consumption by youth of
amphetamines, ecstasy, LSD and alcoholic drinks. But various surveys found
that the rate of drug addiction among Greek youth is still quite low by
western European standards.[90]

A different form of indulgence, sex, had also increased among young
people. A survey of female students at the University of Athens found
that in 1991, 33 per cent of them had sexual intercourse by the age of 18
(compared with 17 per cent in 1978), and that there was now no difference

in this respect between students of urban and rural background, as there had been formerly. The use of contraceptives had become more common, largely because of the fear of AIDS; and so the rate of abortions had declined, although according to a professor of Gynaecology in 2000 the number performed each year was still about 200,000.[91] However, society has conformed with religious precepts on a different issue, euthanasia, which is not even discussed very much.

A professor of Criminology at the University of Athens, Nestor Kourakis, argued plausibly that many young people were alienated by the prevalent materialism and economic competitiveness of society, and by a weakening sense of community in cities. The last trend was revealed by a national survey of 1998 which found that only 37 per cent of people claimed to have close relations with neighbours, and only 30 per cent agreed with the general assertion that people helped each other. These problems were not helped by schools which concentrated on cramming for exams, and parents who were preoccupied with earning money. 'Traditional values are gradually becoming obsolete but have not been replaced yet by new values', Kourakis concluded. This view was supported by a survey of teachers in 1999, which found that a majority adhered to traditional values – for example in condemning homosexuality – but found it difficult to justify them. Thus they were unsure whether they should teach young people about contraception.[92]

Crime

An obvious result of changing values was an increase in crime. Among crimes recorded by police in 1980 and 1997, robberies multiplied by twenty-three times, thefts by five, forgeries by seven, murders by three, drug offences by fifteen and rapes by two.[93] Such trends seem to be general in societies with rapidly growing cities, in which social ties weaken and material expectations outpace their attainment. In Greece the rise in many types of crime accelerated after 1974, apparently because of the sudden relaxation of police powers, and the return from abroad of hundreds of thousands of men in their 20s and 30s, demographic groups especially likely to commit crimes. However, in the 1980s and 1990s, the proportion of crimes committed by women and juveniles was also increasing rapidly, perhaps because of the tendency of those groups to be concentrated in low-paid and insecure jobs, which failed to satisfy their material expectations. The dramatic increase in crime by women in the 1990s could also be attributed to their increasingly independent status. Petty crime by young people could be attributed in large part to a weakening of parental discipline. A survey of the early 1990s found that the majority of teenagers admitted to having at some time committed minor offences, such as painting graffiti, shoplifting, taking illegal drugs or acting violently in a demonstration.[94]

Increased crime led to generally increased feelings of insecurity, which were attested by opinion polls. 'In the capital and large provincial towns – even in small market towns and villages', wrote a journalist specialising in legal matters, 'the days are gone when one could leave doors unlocked and take a carefree stroll at night.'[95] The alarm was in part a reflection of commentators' conservative values. It was also due in part to sensational treatment by television, and understandable lack of faith in the police and courts (see below, p. 232). In fact seven out of twelve common crimes recorded by the police in 1980–97 (forgery, fraud, resisting police, bodily harm, revenge, rape and abuse) declined after 1991. Moreover the general crime rate was much lower than in northern EU countries, and lower also than in other southern EU and Balkan countries.

It was just as well in a way that the police and courts were ineffective, because the jails were seriously overcrowded and were themselves centres of organised crime. They currently hold 8,190 prisoners, 74 per cent more than they were designed for. Not surprisingly, their conditions are wretched: they have recently been condemned by a committee of the Council of Europe, and led to a series of very destructive riots in the 1990s.

The strength of family ties still served to limit crime, because to commit a crime was to dishonour the family; and there was little or no tradition of criminal families such as exists in southern Italy. Rates of most crimes in western Europe roughly correlated with the degree of modernisation; so that northern European countries tended to have higher rates; and it was accepted by key surveys that the variations between countries were not a product of differential reporting rates. Nevertheless, it was generally agreed that Greek police were sadly unprepared for the increasingly well organised and equipped criminals who confronted them (using firearms, stolen cars and mobile phones), or for the increase in organised prostitution (the prostitutes being mainly from eastern Europe), sophisticated white-collar crime and trafficking in immigrants, drugs and antiquities. Criminals in Greece were not highly organised by European standards: the problem was that the police and judiciary were too inefficient and ill-resourced to deal with them. With their immense profits, the new type of criminals could bribe poorly paid police and officials of jails and law courts. Much of the organised crime was said by the police to be based in other Balkan countries or in southern Italy: yet here too the role of foreigners seemed to be exaggerated, because the majority of people arrested were Greeks.[96]

Notes

1 Official website www.greece.gr.

2 Michail Papadakis and Georgios Siambos, 'Demographic developments and prospects of the Greek population, 1951–2041', in Ioanna Lambiri-Dimaki and Nota Kyriazis, *Greek Society at the End of the Twentieth Century* (in Greek, 1995), 36; *Vima*, 11 May 1997, A50, Dimitra Kroustalli; Heather Paxson, 'Demographics and diaspora, gender and genealogy: anthropological notes on Greek population policy', *South European Society and Politics* 2 (1997), 35, 48–50.

3 *Athens News*, 6 January 2001.

4 *Athens News*, 24 September 2000; *Vima*, 5 November 2000, A48–9, Marny Papamathaiou.

5 Martin Baldwin-Edwards and Rossetos Fakiolas, 'Greece: the contours of a fragmented policy response', *South European Society and Politics* 3 (1998), 192; *Athens News*, 11 July 2000; *Athens News*, 11 March 2001.

6 *Athens News*, 23 March 2001.

7 *Ta Nea*, 28 January 1998, 1; *Vima*, 22 March 1998, A35; *Vima*, 15 March 1998, A35, D. Nikolakopoulou; *Kathimerini*, 21 March 2001, English Internet edition; Theodoros Iosifides and Russell King, 'Socio-spatial dynamics and exclusion of three immigrant groups in the Athens conurbation', *South European Society and Politics* 3 (1998), 212, 223–5.

8 *Athens News*, 9 July 2000.

9 Kostas Rondos, 'The development of the regional and urban population of Greece, 1951–2001', in Ioanna Lambiri-Dimaki and Nota Kyriazis (eds), *Greek Society at the End of the 20th Century* (in Greek, 1995), 64–107; *Vima*, 2 May 1999, A50–1; *Kathimerini*, 4 October 1998, 7, Fotini Kalliri.

10 *Ta Nea*, 28 January 1998, 17; N.-K. Chlepas, 'Self-government and decentralisation; towards restructuring of an "antagonistic interchange"', *Greek Review of Political Science* 15 (in Greek, 2000), 59–60.

11 *Vima*, 16 May 1999, D16, Kosta Papadi; *Vima*, 30 May 1999, D4, Nikou Nikolaou; *Kathimerini*, 14 January 2001.

12 Nikolaos P. Glytsos, 'Prospects of the Greek labour market', in Lambiri-Dimaki and Nota Kyriazis (eds), *Greek Society*, 122; *Vima*, 16 May 1999, D16, Kosta Papadi.

13 *Kyriakatiki Avgi*, 7 September 1997, 8, Ilia Ioakeimoglou; *Vima*, 17 December 2000, Nikou Nikolaou.

14 Duncan Gallie and Helen Russell, 'Unemployment and life satisfaction: a cross-cultural comparison', *European Journal of Sociology* 39 (1998), 254, 275.

15 *Vima*, 14 May 2000, D2. Luxembourg and Sweden were omitted from the comparison.

16 *Vima*, 27 December 1998, D4, Nikou Nikolaou; *Vima*, 3 December 2000, A14, Nikou Nikolaou; European Commission, *Eurobarometer*, no. 47, Spring 1997, 3.

17 *Kathimerini*, 19 November 2000, 70, Evgenia Tsortzi; *Ta Nea*, 20 January 2001, citing Eurostat figures; *Vima*, 29 July 2001, B8, P. Bouloukou.

18 Nicholas G. Pirounakis, *The Greek Economy. Past, Present, and Future* (1997), 214; European Commission, *Living Conditions in Europe. Statistical Pocketbook* (Luxembourg 2000), 92, 95–7.

19 Roi Panayotopoulou, '"Rational" individualistic practices in the context of an "irrational" political system', in Christos Lyrintzis, Ilias Nikolakopoulos and Dimitris Sotiropoulos (eds), *Society and Politics. Aspects of the Third Greek Republic, 1974–94* (in Greek, 1996), 144.

20 Michael Sullivan, *Measuring Global Values. The Ranking of 162 Countries* (New York 1991), 147, 198, 219.

21 *Vima*, 18 June 2000, A10, Zoï Tsoli; *Kathimerini*, 12 October 1997, 29, Dora Antoniou; *Vima*, 27 April 1997, A33, Panayota Bitsika; Kostas Vergopoulos, 'Regionalism and stabilization: the case of Greece in the EEC', in Dimitri Constas and Theofanis G. Stavrou (eds), *Greece Prepares for the Twenty-first Century* (Baltimore, MD 1995), 129; *Athens News*, 23 January 2000; European Commission, *Living Conditions*, 70–1, 94.

22 Antonis Mousidis, 'Social transformation and aspects of social exclusion in rural areas: the problem of the elderly', in Koula Kasimati (ed.), *Social Exclusion: the Greek Experience* (in Greek, 1998), 149; *Kyriakatiki Avgi*, 5 October 1997, 17; *Vima*, 16 July 1995, A44; *Vima*, 5 November 1995, A6; *Vima*, 16 November 1997, A44–5; European Commission, *Living Conditions*, 74–5.

23 *Economist*, 12 December 1998, 118.

24 *Vima*, 14 September 1997, D15.

25 European Commission, *Living Conditions*, 100–1; *Economist*, 6 November 1999, 21, citing World Bank. Balkan figures are for 1997 and exclude Slovenia.

26 *Vima*, 1 October 1995, A52, citing World Health Organisation figures for 1993.

27 *Kathimerini*, 2 December 2000 (English Internet edition).

28 *Vima*, 15 December 1991, A52; *Vima*, 1 October 1995, A52.

29 *Ta Nea*, 7 June 1989, 4, editorial; *Vima*, 24 February 1991, A37.

30 *Vima*, 21 May 1989, 30; *Vima*, 18 June 2000, A11.

31 *Kathimerini*, 5 March 2001 (English Internet edition).

32 *Vima*, 2 April 2000, A54–55, Elenas Fyntanidou.

33 *Vima*, 21 May 1995, A49; *Vima*, 11 June 2000, A11.

34 *Vima*, 7 February 1999, A61; *Kathimerini*, 16 July 2000, 2, Galini Fourna; T. Panayotopoulos and N. Sideris, 'Health and health services: present and future', in Lambiri-Dimakis and Nota Kyriazis (eds), *Greek Society*, 154–5.

35 Cited in Glytsos, 'Prospects of the Greek labour market', 137; European Commission, *Living Conditions*, 44.

36 *Vima*, 25 October 1992, A41, Sylvana Raptis; *Vima*, 31 October 1993, A44, Christou Katsika.

37 *Vima*, 26 April 1998, A8–9; *Kathimerini*, 8 October 2000, 35, Apostolou Lakasa; *Kathimerini*, 16 January 1998, 3, 7.

38 Dionisis Gravaris, 'The building of the welfare state: from party discourse to state policies', in Michalis Spourdalakis (ed.), *PASOK. Party, State, Society* (in Greek, 1998), 109; *Kathimerini*, 8 November 1998, 22, Apostolou Lakasa.

39 Maurizio Ferrara, 'The "southern model" of welfare in social Europe', *Journal of European Social Policy* 6 (1996), 17–37; Maria Petmesidou, 'Social protection in Greece: a brief glimpse of a welfare state', *Social Policy and Administration* 30 (1996), 324–47.

40 Maria Petmesidou, 'Statism, social policy and the middle classes in Greece', *Journal of European Social Policy* 1 (1991), 42.

41 Ian Gough, 'Social assistance in southern Europe', *South European Society and Politics* 1 (1996), 9–10.

42 *Vima*, 8 February 1998, A52, B.G. Lambropoulou; *Vima*, 3 May 1998, A50, D. Nikolakopoulou.

43 Savvas G. Robolis, 'Demographic changes and social insurance', in Lambiri-Dimaki and Kyriazis (eds), *Greek Society*, 172; *Vima*, 22 July 1990, A22; *Vima*, 21 February 1999, A24, Nikou Nikolaou; *Kathimerini*, 4 October 2000, editorial.

44 *Vima*, 29 April 2001, B4, D4.

45 *Vima*, 4 October 1992, A43, Silvana Raptis; *Vima*, 11 April 1999, A30, Natasa Roungeri.

46 *Vima*, 27 February 2000, A10; *Kathimerini*, 4 June 2000, 1, 30–1, Apostolou Lakasa; *Kathimerini*, 19 November 2000, 35, Apostolou Lakasa.

47 *Vima*, 17 September 2000, A60, Marny Papamathaiou; National Statistical Service of Greece, *Statistical Yearbooks* for 1973 and 1998.

48 *Vima*, 21 March 1999, A59, Natasa Roungeri; *Vima*, 19 September 1999, A6, Marny Papamathaiou.

49 Constantine Tsoucalas and Roy Panagiotopoulou, 'Education in Socialist Greece: between modernization and democratization', in Theodore C. Kariotis (ed.), *The Greek Socialist Experiment. Papandreou's Greece, 1981–9* (New York 1992), 316–17; Harry A. Patrinos, 'The private origins of public higher education', *Journal of Modern Greek Studies* 13 (1995), 184; George Psaharopoulos, *Journal of Modern Greek Studies* 13 (1995), 170–5; European Commission, *Living Conditions*, 28; *Kathimerini*, 23 September 2000 (English Internet edition), Apostolou Lakasa.

50 Georgia Kontogiannopoulou-Polydorides *et al.*, 'Citizen education: silencing crucial issues', *Journal of Modern Greek Studies* 18 (2000), 295; *Vima*, 27 May 2001, A63, Alexi Dimara.

51 *Kathimerini*, 13 April 1997, 25.

52 *Kathimerini*, 12 March 1995, 20; *Vima*, 29 November 1992, A46; *Vima*, 6 May 2001, A45, Nota Tringa.

53 George Th. Mavrogordatos, 'From traditional clientelism to machine politics: the impact of PASOK populism in Greece', *South European Society and Politics* 2 (1997), 5–7; *Vima*, 23 August 1998, 1–2, Stavrou Psychari; *Vima*, 29 August 1999, B10–11, Giorgou Babinioti; *Kathimerini*, 22 July 2000.

54 *Kathimerini*, 8 October 2000, 35, Viki Flessa.

55 *Ta Nea*, 17 March 2001, Internet edition; Gregory M. Sifakis, 'The impasse of Greek higher education', in Spyros Vryonis Jr (ed.), *Greece on the Road to Democracy. From the Junta to PASOK, 1974–86* (New York 1991), 293; Haris Symeonidou, 'Social protection in contemporary Greece', *South European Politics and Society* 1 (1996), 80–1; *Vima*, 19 July 1998, B7, G.B. Dertilis; *Vima*, 27 February 2000, A6–8, Natasa Roungeri.

56 *Vima*, 21 January 2001, A55, Marny Papamathaiou; Stephen Cole and Thomas J. Phelan, 'The scientific productivity of nations', *Minerva* 37 (1999), 4–11.

57 *Kathimerini*, 29 May 2000, editorial; *Vima*, 4 February 2001, A52, Elenas Fyntanidou.

58 *Kathimerini*, 29 August 2000.

59 *Vima*, 25 February 2001, A41, Elenas Fyntanidou.

60 *Ta Nea*, 16 May 1985, 24; *Vima*, 1 October 1995, A52; *Kathimerini*, 5 Februry 1998, 7.

61 *Vima*, 7 January 2001 (Internet, in Greek), Marina Petropoulou.

62 *Vima*, 1 October 1995, A52, Dora Pipilis; *Vima*, 20 April 1997, A35; *Economist*, 4 July 1998; *Kathimerini*, 1 June 1997, 1, 62; *Kathimerini*, 11 June 1995, 8.

63 Yannis Tountas, Helga Stefannson and Spyros Frissiras, 'Health reform in Greece: planning and implementation of a national health system', *International*

Journal of Health Planning and Management 10 (1995), 283–304; *Vima*, 11 June 2000, A1, 53.

64 *Kathimerini* (English Internet edition), 7 June 2001, citing a report on conditions in 2000 by the Institute of Economic and Industrial Research.

65 *Athens News*, 19 February 2000.

66 *Vima*, 11 May 1997, A50, Dimitra Kroustallis; National Statistical Service of Greece, *Concise Statistical Yearbook 1998* (1999).

67 *Vima*, 15 June 1997, A42, Natasa Roungeri; *Kyriakatiki Avgi*, 11 May 1997, 31, Dimitras Kokkotakis, citing EKKE research; *Economist*, 26 September 1998, 60; European Commission, *Living Conditions*, 24.

68 *Kathimerini*, 25 January 1998, 26; *Vima*, 13 June 1993, A46, G. Papaïoannou; *Vima*, 12 December 1999, A52–3, Elenas Fyntanidou.

69 James Georgas *et al.*, 'The relationship of family bonds to family structure and functions across cultures', *Journal of Cross-Cultural Psychology* 28 (1997), 303–20; *Kathimerini*, 8 October 2000, 35, Apostolou Lakasa.

70 James Georgas, 'Changing family values in Greece: from collectivist to individualist', *Journal of Cross-Cultural Psychology* 20 (1989), 80–91; Panayote E. Dimitras, 'Changes in public attitudes', in Kevin Featherstone and Dimitrios Katsoudas (eds), *Political Change in Greece. Before and After the Colonels* (1987), 82–3.

71 *Kathimerini*, 21 January 1996, 18.

72 *Vima*, 13 June 1993, A46, G. Papaïoannou; *Vima*, 16 July 1995, A42–3, K. Chalvatzakis.

73 *Athens News*, 14 April 2000.

74 *Vima*, 20 April 1997, A42; *Ta Nea*, 21 October 1989, 14–15.

75 *Vima*, 9 August 1992, A28, Ioanna Mandrou; *Vima*, 1 March 2000, A21, Maria Tsoli; *Kathimerini*, 11 July 1999, 31, Athina Karali; *Kathimerini*, 22 October 2000, Dora Antoniou, summarizing a study by Angelos Tsingris; *Kathimerini*, 28 November 2000, Christina Damoulianou.

76 Calliope D. Spinellis, *Crime in Greece in Perspective* (Athens 1993), 234–47; *Vima*, 9 February 1997, E6, Natasa Roungeri, citing research by Maria Samartzis; *Athens News*, 6 February 2000.

77 *Vima*, 7 March 1998, A71, K. Chalvatzaki.

78 Trends illustrated in Nota Kyriazis, 'Feminism and the status of women', in Constas and Stavrou (eds), *Greece*, 287.

79 Kyriazis, 'Feminism', in Constas and Stavrou (eds.), *Greece*, 290; Betty Dobratz, 'Socio-political participation of women in Greece', in Gwen Moore and Glenn Spitze (eds), *Research in Politics and Society* 2 (1986), 119–46; *Athens News*, 23

January 2000; Christine Cousins, 'Women and employment in southern Europe: the implications of recent policy and labour market directions', *South European Society and Politics* 5 (Summer 2000), 101, 109–10.

80   *Kathimerini*, 16 July 2000, 21, Galini Fourna.

81   *Vima*, 5 July 1998, A26, Richardou Someriti.

82   *Vima*, 8 September 1999, 8–9, Natasa Roungeri, reviewing a book by Maro Pantelidou-Malouta; *The Athenian*, October 1995, 11.

83   Reported in *Kathimerini*, 15 November 1998, 37; *The Greek Mother. Formerly and Today* (in Greek, 1989), 149.

84   European Commission, *Eurobarometer* 42 (1995), 75; Vasiliki Georgiadou, 'Secular state and Orthodox Church: relations between religion, society, and politics in the democratic transition', in Christos Lyrintzis *et al.* (eds), *Society and Politics*, 266–7; *Vima*, 30 July 1995, E1, Richardou Someriti.

85   Kallistos Ware, 'The Church: a time of transition', in Richard Clogg (ed.), *Greece in the 1980s* (1983), 223–4.

86   *Athens News*, 9 June 1999; Theofanis G. Stavrou, 'The Orthodox Church and political culture in Greece', in Constas and Stavrou (eds), *Greece*, 50.

87   *Vima*, 9 May 1993, A14, I.M. Konidari; Dimosthenis Dodou, 'The people of the Church', in Institouto V-Project Research Consulting, *Public Opinion in Greece, 1999–2000* (in Greek, 1999), 229.

88   *Vima*, 25 January 1998, A20, Richardou Someriti; V-PRC, *Public Opinion*, 235, 241–3.

89   V-PRC, *Public Opinion*, 244; *Vima*, 17 October 1999, A50, Maria Antoniadou.

90   *Vima*, 21 June 1992, A42, Ioanna Mandrou; *Vima*, 13 December 1998, A68, Richardou Someriti; *Vima*, 2 April 2000, A55; *Kathimerini*, 2 July 2000, 30, Christina Damoulianou; *Kathimerini*, 23 August 2000, Dora Antoniou and Thanassi Tsingana.

91   *Vima*, 16 October 1994, A49, Dimitra Kroustalidi; *Athens News*, 10 November 2000.

92   *Kathimerini*, 4 January 1998, 16, Athena Karali, reporting view of Nestor Kourakis; *Vima*, 21 November 1993, A52, summarising findings by Calliope D. Spinellis; *Vima*, 20 April 1997, A42–3, Ioanna Mandrou; V-PRC, *Public Opinion*, 251; *Athens News*, 18 December 1999.

93   *Vima*, 25 October 1998, A28.

94   Thomas W. Gallant, 'Collective action and atomistic actors: labor unions, strikes and crime in Greece in the postwar era', in Constas and Stavrou (eds), *Greece*, 181–4; Spinellis, *Crime in Greece*, 291; *Vima*, 21 June 1992, A42, Ioanna Mandrou; *Vima*, 20 February 2000, A52, G. Antonopoulou.

95 *Vima*, 1 November 1998, A43, Ioanna Mandrou; V-PRC, *Public Opinion*, 250.

96 International Crime Victims Survey website; Spinellis, *Crime in Greece*, 318–19; *Vima*, 17 November 1991, A37; *Vima*, 27 October 1996, A24; *Vima*, 15 March 1998, A55, D. Nikolakopoulou; *Vima*, 21 November 1993, A51; *Vima*, 25 October 1998, A28, Ioanna Mandrou; *Vima*, 18 June 2000, A54, V.G. Lambropoulou; *Athens News*, 28 June 2000; *Kathimerini*, 9 March 1997, 18, Kosta Michailidi; *Kathimerini*, 24 February 2000, 3, Apostolou Lakasa; *Kathimerini* (English Internet edition), 5 October 2000; *Ta Nea*, 23 March 2001.

CHAPTER ELEVEN

Converging with Western Europe: Politics, 1989–2000

Reforming the government

The challenge of integration

A sign of a new era for Greece was the acceptance by EEC governments, in June 1989, of a report by the President of the European Commission, Jacques Delors, on means of progress towards economic and monetary union. The need for participation in this process was accepted by most Greek voters, and especially business elites, as a result of the vast inflow of EEC subsidies and loans, and continuing commercial integration with the EEC. Indeed, association with the developed countries of western Europe was coming to be seen as an aspect of national identity.[1]

But it was clear that the country was hopelessly ill-prepared for the challenge of integration, because of the continuing stagnation of the economy and the chaotic state of the public administration. The most urgent problem was the chronic budget deficit, resulting in high inflation and a huge public debt. Governments in the late 1980s and early 1990s lived close to the limit of their capacity to borrow in order to finance even day-to-day activities. Thus the tasks of increasing revenue and restraining expenditure dominated government policy during the 1990s. Governments in the early 1990s could only hope that they would thus create the conditions for a return to economic growth.

Crisis of confidence in the state

What was also becoming clearer at this time was the inability of the state to fulfil the changing and increasingly complex needs of a modern urban society.

These needs were sharpened by comparisons which the media frequently made with conditions in western Europe. The inadequacies of the whole gamut of state services were discussed from the late 1980s onwards, including hospitals, schools, police, law courts, jails and social insurance funds.

The capacity of the public administration had been weakened by PASOK's anti-meritocratic practices. During the 1990s only one-quarter of civil servants were university graduates, compared with a half in the 1960s. Most sectors of government were extremely wasteful because of the laxity of their accounting procedures, which led the Court of Auditors, to declare in 1999 that it could not do its job.[2] For ordinary citizens without strings to pull, the dilatoriness and arrogance of officials were a nightmare. The expansion of social services by PASOK governments in the 1980s had increased the scope for discontent by bringing people increasingly into contact with officialdom.

Examples of administrative inefficiency were regularly given headline treatment in the 1990s. Some higher law courts were still recording their proceedings in longhand, while stacks of files clogged their corridors and their backlog of cases grew, reducing their ability to punish crime. According to plausible allegations at least as recently as 1996, some judges were corrupt. Public hospitals around 1990 were years overdue in computerising their records, and so in imminent danger of failing to qualify for EEC subsidies; while many of their patients suffered in summer from lack of air conditioning. Most of the police had, in accordance with established practice, been appointed for partisan reasons, so that they were riven by factionalism. Most police received only a few months' training, and were not taught about hard drugs or explosives, which did not matter greatly because they had to spend most of their time in paper shuffling, delivering court orders or guarding politicians. Consequently they were until recently helpless to combat rising crime and persistent terrorism. The proportion of all criminal cases which they solved fell by almost half in the 1980s; and in 1997, only one-ninth of thefts and one-third of robberies were cleared up. Periodically the country was disgraced by some case of inefficiency or corruption. A recent example is the large number of illegal naturalisations of immigrants by officials, with the result that Greeks, alone among EU citizens, still need visas to enter the United States.[3]

By the late 1980s the public was also alarmed by the government's incapacity to respond to the diverse environmental problems which had moved to the forefront of attention. Nearly every summer in recent decades, vast areas of woodland were lost to fire, and the authorities failed to prevent illegal encroachment on the scorched remains by builders and graziers, who in many cases were the arsonists. The amount of topsoil lost to the sea by fires each year has been, according to a professor of Forestry, enough to

cover 35 square kilometres to a depth of 2.5 metres. The prerequisite for protection of public woodland – a national land register – is still nowhere near
completion, despite the availability of EU subsidies. Most of the hundreds
of thousands of tonnes of hazardous waste produced each year is still being
stored, or dumped, without regulation. Little of the country's wonderful
scenery and biodiversity is yet included in reserves, and little of these receive
effective protection from multiple threats.[4] The constantly discussed smog
over the metropolis declined a little during the 1990s, mainly because of
the availability of cleaner cars subsidised by the government. But it is now
increasing again, as the conurbation continues to grow and cars proliferate.

The need to overcome this complex of problems, administrative and
economic, was summed up in the term modernisation, an old preoccupation which had never perhaps been so intense. Although there were still in
1989 different schools of thought about the road to modernisation, the
differences between them were fading. In practice, most agreed that the
only way was convergence with norms set by the EEC, and that the major
task was rationalisation of the government machine. The attainment of this
goal obviously required the abandonment of old clientelist practices.

Corruption

A defect of government which attracted special attention was corruption.
Immediately after PASOK's fall from power in 1989, parliament initiated
the constitutional procedures for the investigation and trial of PASOK
ministers and officials. The process lasted nearly three years, causing extensive acrimony; and it tackled the major scandals of the PASOK regime
including its alleged tolerance of terrorism. The defendants were tried by
thirteen judges whom a coalition government selected by lot in 1989. Thus
the process suffered from the flaws, firstly, that it was run by political parties
(which meant New Democracy, because the Coalition Party soon lost enthusiasm for prosecuting its former ally), and secondly that it politicised the
judicial process, because several of the judges were believed with some
reason to be biased. Those eventually found guilty and sentenced to varying
jail terms (some expiated by fines) included four former ministers and seven
former managers of public utilities. Papandreou was himself charged with
accepting bribes and breach of trust, but acquitted by the vote of a majority
of judges in January 1992. So acute was tension between the major parties
that the acquittal came as a relief to most observers.[5]

It was soon PASOK's turn to take a hand at 'cleansing', after the New
Democracy prime minister was revealed in 1993 to have emulated Papandreou in extensive telephone bugging, which PASOK deputies subjected to

investigation after their party regained power. Eventually, in 1995, their government dropped the proceedings in order to end what had become a squalid vendetta. These scandals had some good effects in that the media became more alert, while politicians seem to have became more circumspect in avoiding flagrant peculation.

Meanwhile corruption elsewhere was of greater concern than ever. The media periodically revealed cases of it among most elites, including academics, doctors, judges and bishops, as well as civil servants including diplomats. In 1993, 40 per cent of a sample of 139 public officials – presumably reluctant to denigrate their own profession – admitted that corruption among them was serious. Another survey in 1996 found 65 per cent of the public taking this view, and 35 per cent admitting that they themselves had bribed officials. Unofficial payments are reportedly still normal for, among other things, driving licences and building permits. Much of the public is ambivalent about the practice. A survey in January 2001, by the Greek branch of Transparency International, found 85 per cent of respondents expressing the belief that society could progress only through transparency and meritocracy; but on the other hand, 40 per cent seeing nothing wrong with some unofficial payment to expedite business.[6]

There was special concern, from the time of the Koskotas scandal in 1988–89, with what were referred to as 'interwoven interests', referring particularly to an alleged network of big business groups which either controlled, or bought favours from, politicians, civil servants and party cadres. There are two reasons for believing that this problem had grown: the proliferation of public works contracts co-financed by the EEC, and the growing independence of the media from governments.[7] Public contracts – which had been immense also in the 1950s – grew again in the 1990s, so as to account for 5.5 per cent of GDP by 2000, and formed a rich source of undercover payments to public officials. In the latter half of the 1980s, newspaper proprietors invested considerably in modern technology, and consequently became more dependent on advertisers and circulation, and less beholden to political parties. Then the legalisation of private radio and television provided business and publishing magnates with a still wider field of influence, also largely independent of the parties.[8] Of special concern were those media tycoons who had interests in public contracts, several of whom were household names, and were occasionally criticised in parliament. There was in addition the new scope for corruption in the sale of state-owned industries in the 1990s. In making these sales, and putting out to tender contracts for vast construction projects, the New Democracy government of 1990–93 became mired in accusations of improper dealings. Later, more impartial procedures were devised and established for privatisation and for public tenders. But most observers believed that certain business interests had become so powerful that they could influence the competition for power within the parties.[9]

There are reasons, however, for thinking that it was publicity about bribery that was increasing rather than bribery itself. International comparisons of the estimated extent of bribery have shown a rough inverse correlation between it and economic development as indicated by income per capita, and a rough positive correlation, also, between economic development and media publicity about corruption. Various surveys indicate that Greece was not particularly corrupt by comparison with other European countries at a similar level of economic development. For example, successive comparisons in the late 1990s by the well known research institute Transparency International – based on diverse survey evidence – showed Greece as somewhat more corrupt than Portugal and Spain but less so than Italy, Turkey and the former communist countries of eastern Europe.[10] Corruption in Greece was probably limited by the centralisation of the political system and the customary concentration of power in a single party: both reduced the number of snouts at the trough. Contemporary comments on Greece in the nineteenth and early twentieth centuries indicate that corruption among officials and politicians used to be very extensive indeed when the country was poorer. The number of prosecutions for corruption tended to decline from the 1950s onwards; though they temporarily increased after the PASOK scandals of the late 1980s. Some reasons for supposing that the public was more critical were the increasing independence of the media, rising levels of education and citizens' higher expectations of diverse services by the state.

It does seem that certain branches of the public service were increasingly exposed to temptation. The police were increasingly likely to be offered bribes by illegal immigrants or drug dealers. Officials responsible for public works handled unprecedented sums of EU subsidies. The tax department had to extract ever greater sums from citizens. The areas which, in a survey of 2000, citizens found to be most corrupt – in this order – were public hospitals, town planning departments and the tax department. Talk about corruption certainly fuelled citizens' cynicism about politics. A survey of 1996 showed that 83 per cent of citizens trusted the army and 77 per cent trusted the Church, but only 42 per cent trusted the state and 23 per cent the political parties.[11]

Increasing revenue

In attempts to cut the budget deficit, the driving force was the European Commission as stern creditor. Its authority was reinforced by the need to fulfil the prerequisites for membership in the projected Economic and Monetary Union (EMU) of the EU, prerequisites laid down in the Treaty of Maastricht, which was ratified without question by both major parties in 1992. The European Commission's requirements extended to structural reform of the economy so as to reduce the state's role and broaden the scope for market forces. Thus the Commission dominated the main areas of domestic policy in the 1990s.

As increase in revenue was vital, it was unfortunate that the tax department epitomised the worst features of the bureaucracy. Respect for it had been weakened still further by the PASOK governments' practice in the 1980s of waiving collection before elections.[12] Tax collection was bound in any case to be more difficult than in other countries because so much of the labour force was self-employed or engaged in small businesses. But some problems of the tax department were internal. Because of its corruption, appointments to it were especially sought after. For a long time, it enjoyed relative immunity from investigation; and to this day few citizens trust its impartiality.[13] Neither the tax department nor the judiciary had the training, the resources or the clout, to tackle large businesses; nor for a long time did successive governments want them to, because they did not want to alienate friends or drive away foreign companies.[14]

Tax officials tried to make up for these failings by bullying smaller businesses and low wage earners. From 1990, they used the power to demand of taxpayers in relation to their assets 'where did you get the money?' From 1994 governments at last confronted several powerful groups which had enjoyed relative immunity from income tax, including self-employed lawyers and doctors, businessmen and farmers. In that year, governments were given the power and duty to apply what were euphemistically called 'objective criteria' to such people, or in other words to inspect their premises and assess their tax obligations from their visible assets. In 1996, the Simitis government established a unit to pursue tax evaders, the Corps for the Pursuit of Economic Crimes (SDOE); began regularly to publish lists of tax evaders so as to shame them into paying up; and began to implement the Integrated Programme of Tax Information (TAXIS), which included computerisation at last of the mechanism to collect Value-Added Tax (VAT, introduced in 1987 to replace other consumer taxes, in conformity with other EEC countries). The SDOE found in 1997 that 41 per cent of businesses were evading VAT. The Institute of Economic and Industrial Research has just published a study which concludes that the total scale of evasion has declined since 1997. From 1998, the government made more determined efforts to tax big companies.[15]

By these means, governments have in recent years achieved even greater increases in revenue than they expected. They did still better than the

Italian, Portuguese and Spanish governments, which engaged in the same struggle. As a proportion of GNP, government revenue in Greece (the majority consisting of taxation) rose by about 30 per cent from 1990 to 2000, by which time it accounted for 47.2 per cent of GNP, compared with 44.9 per cent in Italy, 42.5 per cent in Portugal and 36.9 per cent in Spain.[16]

As in those countries, the prolonged battle to balance the budget caused much hardship and some debate about whether it was worth the suffering and discontent which it caused. Greek taxation was weakened by its inherent inequity, as indicated by the low ratio of direct to indirect taxation. Facing down mass revolts by farmers and small businessmen, governments finally achieved an increase in this ratio from 3:7 in 1991 to 4:6 in 2000. The tax system may at last have become somewhat fairer; but the majority of income tax continued to be paid by pensioners and wage/salary earners, most of whom were on low incomes; while businessmen and farmers paid relatively less. By the late 1990s, the high level of taxation was a major cause of governmental unpopularity; and it was being criticised by the IMF as an obstacle to consumption and investment. What made it especially unpopular was that everyone knew of people who were managing to avoid paying their share. A survey in 1992 found that 72 per cent of the public considered tax evasion to be a necessity imposed on them, and another study in 2000 estimated that two-thirds of households participated in some way in the black economy.[17]

Administrative reform

Another government priority was to improve the competence and efficiency of public officials. After the fall of the PASOK government in June 1989, there was growing and general recognition of this need. In 1985 the government had tried to remedy the deficiency by establishing a training college on the model of the French École Nationale d'Administration. Although it received vast sums of EEC money, it has failed so far to serve much useful purpose; and most departments have declined to recognise the value of its training. The persisting lack of a civil service elite was illustrated in the government's negotiations with the European Commission in 1991 to enter the Economic and Monetary Union. Ministers relied on a few individuals who lacked support from an established bureaucratic structure. A government survey of civil servants in 1996 found a majority admitting that they lacked relevant qualifications and were drawn to their job by its security of income. Still more said that politicians interfered (presumably for partisan purposes) in substantial parts of their work.[18]

Because the state administration was so inefficient, estimation of its size, and cost relative to GDP, was difficult. According to what seems the most reliable source, the number of people in all types of public employment in 1991 reached 700,000 or 18 per cent of the labour force, apparently twice the proportion of the early 1960s. This figure included teachers, police, local government employees, the professional armed forces and employees of state-owned industries and utilities. Those pensioned off from public employment were estimated at 297,000 people at this time, half of them under the age of 55, and many of them presumably still in the labour force.[19] By western European standards, the percentage of the population on the public payroll was no longer high: the problem lay in its poor performance.

Governments during the 1990s curbed some of the worst abuses. The landmark reform was the Peponis Law of 1994, which stipulated that public, competitive examination, managed by an independent body, the Supreme Council for the Selection of Personnel (ASEP) should be the sole route to permanent places in the civil service. Over the next few years, ASEP, with growing cross-party support, extended the principle to local government, state banks and the teaching profession. Although in 2000 some short cuts had to be introduced to the slow ASEP procedures, most opportunities for partisan appointments were closed; and the patronage of MPs and party organisations was drastically reduced. A further refinement was the publication in 2000 of the technical requirements for appointment to different branches of the public service. The contribution by the judiciary to the new policy was shown by the landmark ruling of the High Court in 1999 that heads of government departments were free to promote people on merit rather than seniority or formal qualifications.[20]

The need to improve relations between officials and citizens was recognised by leaders of both major parties. The prime minister made an admission to his cabinet in September 1991 which received much publicity (although it might have been made at any time in modern history), that 'there are many government departments which merely harass citizens without doing anything for them'.[21] As one attempt to remedy this problem, a body nicknamed 'Evert's Commandos' (after the minister Miltiadis Evert) was established in 1991 to investigate complaints from citizens, and establish a case for compensating them or prosecuting officials. But it proved ineffective in both respects, because it lacked sufficient legal powers or support from other ministers.[22] From 1998 onwards, the Simitis government made more determined efforts, the most important of which was the establishment – after much opposition within the government – of the ombudsman's office. It was given the prime ministerial backing needed to rectify abuses, and get a respectful hearing from ministers for its recommendations of reform. In its first two full years of operation, 1999–2000, it received the remarkable total of 21,000 complaints, finding a majority to be justified. Although it encounters increasing resistance by the public administration and local authorities, it seems as if it will contribute in time to a change in official culture.[23]

Fresh efforts were made by ministers – before and after the election of April 2000 – to improve services to citizens, under the stimulus of opinion polls which showed that citizens were primarily concerned now with 'everyday problems' for which the inadequacies of public services seemed largely responsible.[24] One reform was the opening of a Citizens' Information Centre, easily accessible by telephone. An increase of police numbers, and their increased attention to crime prevention and traffic control, brought about a marked reduction of burglaries, robberies, murders and lethal driving during the two years 1999–2000. Within the police, an organisation to suppress corruption was established in 1998, and soon revealed some sensational cases. Publicly funded construction projects (the cause of so much recrimination in the early 1990s) were systematically monitored from 1997 by a unit which also revealed sensational cases of malpractice. Ministers paid somewhat more attention in 2000 to dialogue with interest groups affected by their reforms: something conspicuously lacking, for example, in the tempestuous relations between the Ministry of Education and schools throughout the 1990s.

Other features of the public administration showed little sign of change. Rationalisation of its ramshackle structure – composed of multitudinous and overlapping ministries, directorates and sections – evidently proved impossible. After the expansion of the state from 1974, it was difficult even to describe the monster; and this was not accomplished until 1994. There has been no effective progress with reorganisation, according to specialists in public administration.[25] Red tape also remained a serious and ubiquitous problem, as illustrated by one professor, who having requested authorisation for a routine visit to a provincial town, got it two months late with a file containing thirty documents, which had received the attention of the head of his university, the university senate, four government ministers, three departmental directors, three typists and four messengers.[26]

The much-publicised attempts by successive governments to prune the public sector did have some effect; but not enough to prevent the core public service (excluding public utilities and nationalised industries) from growing. The growth was admittedly confined to local government, education and the police – all areas where there existed a genuine need for more staff. Other sectors experienced a slight decline and some complained of serious shortages, which might of course have been remedied by more efficient structures and procedures. By 2000 or earlier, at least one major utility was progressively reducing its staff and wage bills with a voluntary redundancy scheme. Meanwhile the national labour force was growing. So as a result of these cuts, and the sale of some state-owned industries and banks, public employment declined as a proportion of the labour force during the 1990s by about 30 per cent. In 1997, it was down to 15.3 per cent.[27]

The state-owned sector of the economy

Reform also required drastic reduction in the state-owned sector of the economy. As the majority of, if not all, public utilities were strikingly inefficient in the early 1990s, the case for privatisation seemed clear and conformed with New Democracy's neo-liberal ideology. Furthermore, governments badly needed the money. But events proved that New Democracy was as subservient as PASOK to the clientelist system. The attempts at privatisation and de-regulation by the prime minister Mitsotakis were obstructed by his own colleagues and his party machine, both clinging to their patronage. Linked to the machine were the scores of 'chair-centaurs', the managers of public enterprises who had been appointed by New Democracy while it participated in the recent coalition governments of 1989–90. Behind these were the formidable public-sector trade unions which fought furiously to keep their members' legally guaranteed and privileged jobs, and were dominated by the left-wing parties. Private business interests joined the opposition, so as to protect their lucrative contracts with state industries. Because the state industries and utilities were so inefficient, it was difficult in any case to find purchasers for them, and none to pay for all their redundant staff. The electorate itself was divided over the need for privatisation in the early 1990s, with only ND voters showing a majority in support of it. Given the extent of popular aspirations for government appointments, and the high level of unemployment, many people sympathised with public employees whose jobs were threatened. After tough and prolonged battles, all that Mitsotakis's government achieved in over three years was to obtain 5.5 per cent of one year's revenue by selling companies employing in total 26,000 people.

PASOK also needed time to give up its attachment to state socialism.[28] Papandreou's government actually restored to state ownership three of the larger companies which Mitsotakis's government had privatised. So in the late 1990s Greece still seemed to possess – as one prominent politician remarked – 'the only communist economy in the EU', by contrast with Italy, Portugal and Spain, which had recently sold off much of their state-owned enterprises.[29] But EEC pressure and the need for revenue left PASOK governments with no choice. So in time they started selling industries or portions of them, and confronting the public-sector unions. With gradually strengthening political support, PASOK governments managed in 1998–2000 to secure substantial revenue from privatisation (see also above, p. 181).[30] Currently, the government claims to be on the brink of a further major round of total or partial sales of public utilities.

Efforts by governments during the 1990s to improve the efficiency of state services had some effect, although improvement was bound to be gradual. The implementation of the Peponis Law probably improved the competence and mentality of the public administration. Even experienced and cynical observers of the public services believed that they saw signs of improvement in 1999, for example in the response by firefighters to the annual spate of forest fires, and by various public utilities to the Athens earthquake. Relative public satisfaction with several utilities in 2000 has been referred to earlier, with evidence of improvement in the police and in primary school teaching (p. 182). Behind the European Commission, the long-term forces for reform are rising public expectations and the need to improve international economic competitiveness.

The politics of convergence

The New Democracy government

When Mitsotakis became prime minister in April 1990, he had just strengthened his case for a tough policy by arranging the publication of a warning from the President of the European Commission that the Greek government risked exclusion from the process of European unification unless it reformed its finances. But Mitsotakis lacked the authority for this task – inside or outside his party – and was unlucky in having to pursue a programme of austerity in a period of economic stagnation.

In broader economic reform, perhaps his greatest achievement was based on consensus between the parties. This was the landmark Law 1876 on industrial relations in 1990 (see below, p. 255). Another measure of economic liberalisation was the termination, in 1991, of the automatic indexation of wages to inflation which the PASOK government had introduced in 1982. Although maintaining real wages, this had hampered labour market mobility. Other reforms de-regulated shop trading hours, and freed shops and other businesses to use more part-time labour. State-owned banks were freed from the obligation to help finance government operations, and from the need for government approval in their recruitment of personnel and their procurement policies.[31]

What made this government memorable, however, was the strength of protest against its austerity policy. Apart from restraining public-sector and private-sector wages, the government increased both VAT and contributions to social insurance funds while reducing the funds' benefits and raising the pensionable age. Real wages and salaries fell by 13 per cent in the four years 1990–93, whereas in 1985–87 the decline caused by PASOK's austerity policy had been offset by a pre-election increase in 1998–99. Social expenditure per head, having peaked in 1986, declined until the mid-1990s, by which time it was by far the lowest in the EU. Austerity policies were still harsher, and opposition to them still stronger, in Greece than in Italy, Portugal or Spain, which were fighting a similar battle at this time.[32] The government failed to spread more equitably the burdens of austerity, particularly by trying to make the self-employed pay income tax. What made this reform especially necessary was the bonus given to the wealthy by the reduction of marginal tax rates. The government also failed to take measures to encourage economic revival. This and other omissions, combined with attempts at privatisation and reduction of public employees, led to a series of extraordinarily prolonged and extensive strikes. These must have inflicted great damage on the economy and certainly shook the nerve of government MPs, who had to be pulled into line by Mitsotakis's threat that the government's survival was at stake.

The government worsened its difficulties by ill-judged attempts to enforce old-fashioned authoritarian values. Thus at the end of 1990, it provoked the first of an annual series of school occupations by trying to restore discipline over pupils, particularly by making their parents responsible for their absenteeism. It also made martyrs of the editors of nine newspapers by jailing them for publishing a manifesto by the veteran terrorist group the '17th November': a move which the public saw as a poor substitute for catching the terrorists.[33]

The public resentment of austerity policies made possible PASOK's revival – which would have seemed inconceivable in 1989 – and Andreas Papandreou's return to power after winning the election of October 1993. New Democracy immediately responded by changing both its policies and its leader. Miltiadis Evert became leader in November, and soon announced the abandonment of dogmatic neo-liberalism – which much of the party had never liked – in favour of the more pragmatic 'radical liberalism' of Karamanlis. Like other proclamations of ideology by major parties in Greece, these labels were largely rhetorical. After PASOK saw the need to liberalise the economy, leaders of New Democracy promised to do so still faster – and neither party carried much conviction.[34]

The new PASOK

PASOK presented itself at the 1993 election as a convert to fiscal responsibility, while disagreeing from New Democracy in its commitment to social justice and to more extensive state ownership. Immediately after the election, however, it drew closer to the previous government's course. An important step was Papandreou's appointment in April 1994 of the junior minister Iannis Papantoniou as Minister of National Economy with the mandate of fulfilling the prerequisites for entry into EMU, which Papantoniou privately considered as 'rather like trying to square the circle'.[35] This left PASOK governments with little choice but to tread the same rocky path as New Democracy. Even before the 1993 election, Papandreou had begun to see the need for reducing the state sector.[36]

PASOK was better qualified than New Democracy for this task because of its strength in the trade unions. Perhaps for this reason, it was more successful in seeking consensus with trade unions and employers, for which end it established in 1994 the Economic and Social Committee to advise the Ministry of National Economy on measures which might provoke conflict. Moreover the process of social dialogue was institutionalised between the government, the General Confederation of Greek Workers and the Federation of Greek Industries. This was in effect an extension of the traditional National General Collective Agreement of Labour so as to cover all matters bearing on industrial relations, including the increase in productivity and employment, and improvements to the welfare system, especially in guaranteeing a minimumum standard of living.[37] Acceptance by trade unions of austerity was achieved partly by PASOK party authority, and partly by the arguable absence of any viable alternative. So closely was the government tied by EU supervision that it could not significantly relax the austerity programme until 1995; and after that the increase in real wages in 1995–99 just outweighed the decline in 1990–94. In addition, there were extensive increases in social expenditure in the later 1990s, as well as some shift in the relative tax burden from low to high income earners. These must have helped to secure unions' acquiescence.[38]

Nevertheless, PASOK encountered stiff opposition – much of it from former supporters who were hurt by the ending of its old policies of state protectionism and clientelism – and much also from activists of New Democracy and the Communist Party who naturally tried to make trouble for the government. Left-wing parties benefited from voters' widespread reaction against government austerity policies and cynicism towards the major parties. The Communist Party had a few years earlier seemed doomed to extinction, but now – although its supporters were comparatively elderly – found new relevance for its anti-capitalist and anti-western lines, which it was again free to pursue after the fall of Gorbachev in 1991. Calling Gorbachev 'Judas' for abandoning Marxism–Leninism, the Communist Party withdrew from the Coalition Party in 1991, leaving within it many dissidents. The party's survival may be partly explained by a comparative survey in 2000, showing public distrust of employers to be greater in Greece than in eleven other EU countries including Italy, Portugal and Spain.[39] Early in 1995, the government's attempt to extend income tax by the 'objective criteria' provoked mass demonstrations from small-scale businessmen as well as farmers, the latter supported by Communists. In April–May 1999, the Communist Party also participated prominently in protests against the NATO bombing of Serbia. The other left-wing party, the Coalition Party, increased its strength in the election of 1996 by gaining the votes of many who were disillusioned with both major parties; but in the longer term suffered from the incoherence of its social and organisational base. PASOK itself suffered in October 1995 from the secession of a prominent member, Dimitrios Tsovolas. Protesting against the government's policies of austerity and liberalisation, he established a splinter party, the Democratic Social Movement, which detached many PASOK votes in the parliamentary election of 1996.

The policy gap between the major parties largely disappeared; and surveys of public opinion showed the old division between left and right to have blurred. Indeed, by 1999 the parties appeared superficially to have exchanged their old positions. The PASOK government boasted about the growth of the stock market and enjoyed the confidence of businessmen; while New Democracy emphasised the need to improve social services and combat social exclusion. In the parliamentary elections of September 1996 and April 2000, PASOK progressively lost ground among lower income groups; so that, after the latter, it won much more support than New Democracy from those who considered that they were well off, and far more from those who felt that they had recently become so. New Democracy's attraction of lower-class protest votes nearly won it the election of 2000. Although PASOK ministers had become more affluent over the years in their acquaintances and consumption habits, New Democracy MPs were still, on average, wealthier.[40]

From late 1999, New Democracy also criticised the government's new policy of détente with Turkey, although this opposition seems to have been an expression not of ideology but of demagogic nationalism, such as voiced earlier by Andreas Papandreou. New Democracy did, however, remain more conservative in social values. It showed more sympathy with the Church in the latter's confrontation with the PASOK government over identity cards, and was more inclined to be tough on crime. The rank-and-file supporters of each party retained considerable loyalty to their traditions;

but it was a loyalty based increasingly on sentiment rather than agreement with their leaders' current policies.

An increasingly important distinction cut across party lines: that between European-orientated modernisers and nationally orientated traditionalists.[41] The distinction showed itself in conflict between those who tried to make the public administration more efficient and adherents to clientelist politics, and another type of conflict, between those emphasising civil liberties and those emphasising ethnic cohesion. Traditionalists were fragmented and usually on the losing side; but on some issues they could win strong support, for example in fighting job losses by sale of state-owned industries, or on the identity card issue (for which see p. 246).

The Simitis programme of modernisation

Given the ideological convergence between the major parties, each depended for its cohesion on strong leadership and on tenure of government or hope of capturing it. During 1995, when Papandreou's strength was failing, while Evert proved ineffectual as leader, both parties floundered. Evert's successor as leader from March 1997 was the younger Konstantinos Karamanlis. Nephew of his namesake, he illustrated the importance of dynasties in the major parties. Being without ministerial experience, he was overshadowed by veteran colleagues disinclined to accept his leadership, and for some years could not secure the cooperation of several of the most talented and influential people in the party. Institutional provisions for collective leadership were weaker in ND than in PASOK, so that for some time Karamanlis could keep several of the party 'barons' at arm's length or even expel them. These personal divisions have weakened the party's performance in opposition.

Another difficulty was Karamanlis's lack of room for manoeuvre in policy. Like the government he accepted the requirements of the European Commission, as well as the increasingly pressing need to improve social services. So in order to oppose the government he had to be destructively negative. Moreover his party suffered from a chronic problem of identity, because Evert's abandonment of neo-liberalism was the party's second change of persona since 1985. But at least Karamanlis kept the party together, and managed to put up some sort of opposition.

PASOK, meanwhile, regained effective leadership in January 1996 when Kostas Simitis (born 1936) succeeded Papandreou as prime minister. From a left-wing family, and an influential founding member of PASOK, Simitis subsequently won the confidence of business, as well as much respect from other parties, by his extensive ministerial experience and devotion to sound finance. He had been a professor of Commercial and Civil Law in Germany, and had then, since 1981, been successively Minister of Agriculture, National Economy, Trade and Industry, and Education. He was elected by the party as prime minister and then leader against strong opposition from Andreas Papandreou's devotee Akis Tsochatzopoulos, who appealed to those nostalgic for populist practices and for more generous social policies. Simitis, by contrast, agreed with the Minister of National Economy Papantoniou in regarding the 1981–89 era as 'eight lost years', referring presumably to the decline in the efficiency of the public administration and in the strength of the economy.[42]

The divergence between the Simitis and Tsochatzopoulos groups has continued. So Simitis could not at first dominate the government, and depended on allies in key ministries. Not until he had won two successive elections (in 1996 and 2000) did he gain enough authority in the party to allocate portfolios as he chose; and even now he has difficulty in controlling Tsochatzopoulos and appeasing his followers. The latter's motivation and strength are illustrated by a survey in 1996 of delegates to the party congress. A large minority felt that their party did not really represent such core constituents as workers, farmers and pensioners; while one-quarter thought an explosion of discontent from lower income groups likely in the near future.

Simitis was persistent and articulate in his advocacy of modernisation of the government and of the economy, for which goal he sought and won sympathy across party lines. Within PASOK he attracted a recognisable bloc of 'modernisers' among leading members. He believed strongly in convergence with the developed countries of the EU as a panacea for the country's problems, especially in organisational efficiency, civil liberties and living standards. When he first became prime minister, his chief allies in the government had, like him, acquired postgraduate degrees or pursued postgraduate studies in northern European universities. Simitis rejected the atavistic nationalism of Andreas Papandreou, and managed in time to improve relations both with Turkey and FYROM (Former Yugoslav Republic of Macedonia). In 2000, his confrontation with the Church (supported at first by a majority of the public) in removing religion from state identity cards proves his commitment to western liberal ideals. Like contemporary social democratic leaders in western Europe, he also rejected the old socialist goals of redistribution of income and state ownership of the economy.

One of Simitis's problems was that these ideas were alien to the old PASOK, and another was that he lacked Andreas Papandreou's forcefulness and charisma. This deficiency became painfully apparent in the daunting tasks of structural reform which his government has faced. Simitis has, however, earned popularity by his manifest and fairly effectual concern that

246

his government appear honest and serve citizens better. Thus he gave his government a distinct sense of purpose, and enjoyed a long-anticipated triumph in June 2000, when Greece was judged by the European Commission to have satisfied the requirements for membership of EMU. This was acclaimed across the political spectrum (except of course in the Communist Party) as proof that Greece had shed its former image of a poor relation and been accepted by the developed countries of Europe as one of themselves. Even Archbishop Christodoulos – who had been loudly criticising the general deference to western Europe – congratulated the government. The task which Simitis now faced was to maintain the momentum of reform.

Voters' disillusionment

The disappearance of ideological differences between the major parties during the 1990s, and their agreement in pursuing harsh policies, contributed to a marked change in public attitudes. Surveys from the mid-1980s onwards showed a decline both of ideological commitment and of trust in politicians. Admittedly, the political parties kept many active supporters, united by sentiment and material benefits. Thus PASOK supporters, contrary to the expectation of other parties, closed ranks in defence of their disgraced leaders in 1989, and they still numbered 220,000 card-carrying members in 1999.[43] But the major parties were becoming less like mass movements and more like professionally managed machines for running election campaigns, relying less on volunteers and more on paid workers. To fuel these machines, the parties agreed in 1995 to increase state subsidies by half, and in practice they did not enquire whether candidates overspent their legal limit.[44]

Public interest in the parties declined steadily. In May 1989, 45 per cent of the public saw politicians as remote and unsympathetic; while, in September 1996, 74 per cent did. The percentage of voters who engaged in two or three forms of party activity fell from about 30 in the late 1980s to under half that in September 1996. The proportion claiming to be very or moderately interested in politics declined from 58 per cent in 1985 to 39 per cent in 1995. The percentage of undecided voters shortly before the election of September 1996 was about twice the level at the corresponding stage before the election of June 1989, which was in turn about three times the level of 1985. The percentage of voters expressing confidence in the way that democracy worked was one of the highest in western Europe in the late 1980s, and one of the lowest in the late 1990s.[45] Detachment or cynicism were especially marked in younger age groups.

Similar trends have been evident in most developed countries, and are evidently due to long-term social changes. The trends have presumably been strengthened in Greece by the obvious way in which the main lines of government policy have been dictated by external bodies.

Disillusionment with parties and institutions did not represent disillusionment with democracy per se: on the contrary there was a widespread desire, reflected in the growth of voluntary associations, for more genuine self-management and consultation. It seems that a majority of MPs in the mid-1990s, both of New Democracy and PASOK, saw the need for more internal party debate, and wanted election campaigns to be built around discussion of issues rather than mindless rallies.[46] An experienced journalist, Petros Evthymiou, suggested in 1994 that, among other qualities, it was the regimentation common to PASOK, New Democracy and the Communist Party which put people off, as it did in other western democracies. Another poll in 1989 showed that the qualities formerly admired in a political leader (and associated with Andreas Papandreou and the senior Karamanlis) – strength, authority, charisma, oratory – were generally discounted in favour of concern for the country's problems and ability in solving them.[47]

Thus the change of voters' attitudes since the late 1980s has led to some alienation from the political system. But in other ways it revealed a healthy maturity.

Devolution of power

The devolution of power from the national government, which had started with the renaissance of democracy in 1974, proceeded on several fronts in the 1990s.

Local government

The long-promised strengthening of elected local authorities was made urgent in the 1990s, firstly by the need to qualify for EEC funds earmarked for them, and secondly by widespread recognition that over-centralisation was weakening public respect for government. There was indeed a common tendency by this time to see devolution as a remedy for governmental incapacity. To some extent devolution was already under way, as we noted earlier. The percentage of state employees working for elected local government had been increasing since the 1970s, and by the late 1990s may have reached a level two or three times that of twenty years earlier. Municipal resources were being increased in the 1990s by EEC grants.

Then, from 1994, PASOK governments boosted the process of devolution in a more determined although poorly planned way, which caused prolonged confusion of responsibilities between the four tiers of government: municipal and communal (the first tier), prefectural (the second), regional (the third) and national (the fourth). In 1994, the government provided that the 54 prefects and their advisory councils should be directly elected by voters, simultaneously with municipal and communal authorities. Thereafter legislation was passed nominally ceding to the prefectures many of the functions of central government, although in practice the devolution was much delayed by the central ministries. Meanwhile, the prefects lost their remaining powers of supervision over decisions by municipalities and communes. They had already lost much of their control over funds for public works, when the supervision of those financed by the EEC passed to new regional secretariats in the late 1980s. So they lost much of their old role, although gaining greatly in independence.[48]

The creation in 1987 of the thirteen regional secretariats was necessitated by the need to utilise EEC regional funds. The secretariats were advised by councils representing the lower tiers; but were not based on any kind of corporate regional identity. In practice they were mere instruments of central government, which retained the real responsibility for planning the expenditure of EEC regional funds. Provision for the reinvigoration of the regional secretariats was made by legislation in 1996; but does not promise to be very effective.[49]

The importance of municipalities was boosted by the 'Capodistria programme', which met a long-recognised need in 1997 by amalgamating several thousand minuscule communes in new municipalities. By this means, the number of municipalities was increased from 454 to 900, letting only 133 communes survive. Additional responsibilities were transferred piecemeal to municipalities and communes from 1994. Most of the new municipalities are still finding their feet, and suffer from shortage of funds and qualified staff. This is perhaps why a nationwide survey in September–October 2000 found that municipalities in general enjoy a rather low level of public confidence: although 91 per cent of respondents could name their mayor; 68 per cent considered their municipal finances to be mismanaged.[50]

Meanwhile, enterprising mayors of established municipalities were seizing the initiative, so as to benefit from their increased resources and from contact with counterparts in other EU countries. 'Anything that affects the citizen is our problem', declared the mayor of Kalamarias in 1998. 'Sleeping giants' was how the Mayor of Amarousi referred in 1996 to larger municipalities.[51] It is clear that the political climate in the late 1990s favoured devolution, and that some municipal governments were attracting capable and public-spirited people. To varying degrees, therefore, municipalities took responsibility for diverse new responsibilities, including economic development, town planning, tourist facilities, crime prevention, traffic control, environmental protection, and additional welfare functions like sports facilities and meeting-places for recreational and social clubs.

The new importance both of prefectures and municipalities was shown by the unprecedented interest in the local elections of October 1998. Ambitious national figures, including many present or former politicians, participated in them and competed to be adopted as candidates by their parties.[52]

The national parties discovered in 1998, however, that they had lost much of their former control over local elections. They now needed to attract as candidates personalities with strong local influence and could not rely on their loyalty once they were elected. Many successful candidates rebelled against their parties or emphasised their independence of them. Although the great majority of prefects and mayors adopted party labels in the local elections of 1994 and 1998, they built up their own power bases with resources which came from the local authorities' greatly increased funding, coming either from the EU, or from local levies, or – after a law of 1989 – from funds guaranteed by the central government. Moreover, party alignments were seen by many voters and mayors as irrelevant to most local problems: thus at a conference of the Central Association of Municipalities and Communes in 2000, there were marked disagreements on geographical not party lines.[53]

Judiciary

Another institution which became increasingly independent of the executive was the judiciary. This was in accordance with a European-wide trend, behind which the probable driving force was an increasingly assertive and educated public. PASOK championed the independence of judges against the New Democracy government in 1990–93, and when it returned to power immediately passed a law strengthening the independence of junior judges against their seniors and thus against the government, which appointed the leading judges. Thus in general governments have shown greater respect for adverse judgments; and are less willing or able to put pressure on judges to discipline the media or trade unions.[54] For their part judges and judicial prosecutors showed increasing readiness to defy governments, even though they did not, like contemporary counterparts in Italy and Spain, take the initiative in investigating senior politicians. But at lower levels the over-mighty executive, habitually careless of the law and weakly checked by parliament, provoked critical scrutiny. A strong stimulus was a series of judgments against the government by the European Court of

Human Rights, which strengthened citizens' protection against illegal actions by the state. It became common in the late 1990s for citizens to sue state agencies successfully for compensation, even for such sins of omission as failure to prevent vandalism or maintain roads.[55]

Judges and prosecuting magistrates were becoming better qualified for their more independent roles. By the early 1990s a great majority of the total of approximately 3,400 had been born since 1950 and appointed in the liberal conditions since 1974. Recruits were increasingly well educated and influenced by western European ideas. In 1994 the National College of the Judiciary was established, and a four-year course in it became the obligatory gateway to the profession. Its graduates (most of whom were women) were said to be far better qualified than those appointed before the college opened.[56] Thus judges were more prepared than before to resist arbitrary or illegal actions by government, and in doing so received public support.[57] In diverse ways they showed their independence and social conscience: by forming voluntary associations to promote civil liberties, or by investigating diverse abuses which had been tolerated too long, such as industrial pollution or administrative corruption.

A particularly striking example of this constructive spirit of initiative was the defence of the built and natural environment, from at least as early as 1987, by Section Five of the Council of State. It did particularly distinguished work in the 1990s under Michalis Dekleris, a professor with a PhD from Yale University. As a one-time adviser to the European Commission, he was well qualified to interpret environmental law because most of it was based on EU Directives. Section Five ruled illegal on environmental grounds numerous construction projects (many of them important to the government); provided authoritative interpretations of key issues, such as the necessary scope of environmental impact assessments; and framed codes of conduct on some controversial subjects, such as building on islands. The judiciary's constant obstruction of construction projects strained the tolerance of successive governments. In the process of constitutional revision in 2000–1, the major parties retaliated – defying massive protest by environmental organisations – by restricting the environmental powers of the judiciary, and in particular of the Council of State.

Media

There had always been newspapers associated with opposition parties, except of course under dictatorships. It is significant that the Union of Athens Daily Newspaper Editors was one of the few professional unions to resist PASOK dominance at its peak in the 1980s.[58] Then, in the latter half of the 1980s, party dominance of the press was, as we have noted, eroded by economic developments. Newspapers fell increasingly into the hands of large-scale business interests (especially those connected with construction, shipping, energy, sport and entertainment) which modernised their equipment, brightened up their appearance, and relied more on advertising revenue and less on party funds. Mass-circulation tabloids – some of which in Greece contain serious political news – could thus appeal to growing cynicism about politicians. This trend towards commercialisation also led in the 1990s to some revival of the provincial press, and enabled newspapers to recover a large share of advertising revenue from the broadcast media.[59]

Private radio became a force in 1987, when the mayor of Athens, belonging to the main opposition party, defied the government by establishing a municipal radio station which provided access on equal terms to all parties. So popular was this innovation that the government could not suppress it, and instead had to legalise private radio broadcasting. Non-government stations then proliferated, reaching a total of nearly 660 in 1990 and immediately capturing the bulk of listening time from the official radio stations. They showed their power by exposing PASOK's failings in the general election of June 1989. One-quarter of the population in 1996 claimed to listen to the radio news daily, and very few listened to government stations.

Private television was promptly legalised by the coalition government which followed PASOK's downfall in June 1989, and reacted against its hegemony. Private television stations started to broadcast in 1990, and proved still more popular than non-government radio stations. Within a year or two there were over 220 private and municipal television channels, which quickly captured most viewing time from the two government channels. In 1996 two-thirds of the population claimed to watch news daily on television; and in 1999 it was found that the government channels accounted for only 13 per cent of viewing time (about one-third the average for Italy, Portugal and Spain).[60] Even the 13 per cent can be attributed to the fact that a government channel had sole rights to show basketball.

Sadly a similar revolution did not occur in cinema. The Greek Centre of Cinematography, established by the Junta in 1970, became an introverted body dominated by trade union interests. It was not sustained by any institute of film studies, and was assured of state finance regardless of the public reception of its products. The predictable result was that, for a long time, it produced films many of which were dismally bad. There has been some revival of Greek cinema in recent years. But relatively few films made in Greek have provoked debate about social issues or been artistically original.[61]

The amount of time which the population as a whole devoted to newspapers, in which party influence remained comparatively extensive, was of course low, compared with that devoted to the broadcast media. In 1992, for example, 42 per cent of the population aged 15–64 (the proportion being twice as high among women as among men) had read no newspaper in the previous seven days. Sale of newspapers in 1996 was 83 per 1,000 inhabitants, compared with 61 in Portugal, 108 in Italy and 109 in Spain.[62] Newspapers were, as elsewhere, important in circulating information among people with political power and influence.

Parties, parliament and independent authorities

Within the major parties authority remained centralised but became more collective. The patriarchal and charismatic style of leadership represented by Andreas Papandreou now seems anachronistic, partly because of the decline in ideological conflict. Andreas had in the early 1990s lost the power to expel dissidents from the party on his own volition, and had to cede a formal role in candidate selection to the local party organisations. In both respects, New Democracy moved in the same direction. The leaders of both major parties kept the power to expel rebels from the parliamentary party (as distinct from the wider party), but found it difficult to refuse endorsement to MPs seeking re-election, especially those with high status.[63] The leaders worked with other senior party members – some based in parliament and some in the organisation – in selecting candidates for parliament, while retaining complete control over selection of candidates for the twelve 'deputies of state' in the national parliament, and for the 25 members of the European Parliament. Primary elections of candidates for parliament by local party organisations were treated by national headquarters merely as recommendations. An important criterion for success in these elections has become prior success in municipal or prefectural elections.[64]

Disagreements between prominent members of the major parties – and even on occasion between leading cabinet ministers – were frequently publicised in the media. Because PASOK governments from 1993 needed the cooperation of the mass party organisation in winning public support for their policies, they quite commonly discussed major policies in its highest tiers, the Executive Bureau and Central Committee. These debates were publicised in the media.

Meanwhile, the role of backbench MPs in policy formulation remained humble. In both parties many MPs were in the late 1990s showing dissatisfaction with lack of consultation over legislation or policy, to which the PASOK government responded in 1999 by promising to consult regularly. Both major parties at this time offered backbenchers the chance to specialise in some policy area.[65] In parliamentary debates in 2000–1 over revision of the constitution, the two parties acknowledged that the accountability of the government to parliament needed to be strengthened. The government proposed, accordingly, to require more matters to be referred to standing committees specialising in policy areas, and to give parliament more opportunity to criticise legislation. Debates and hearings of standing committees may have become increasingly important, because in recent years they have frequently been publicised in the press.

Independent administrative authorities seem to have first appeared in 1989, although some originated earlier, apparently with a different legal status. There are now at least eight of them.[66] Among the better known, the Bank of Greece and Competition Commission (responsible for preventing cartels, monopolies and other restrictive trade practices) originated before 1989. Then appeared the National Council of Radio and Television (responsible for allocating licences for television and radio stations, and monitoring their conduct); the Supreme Council for the Selection of Personnel (responsible for supervising public appointments); the Authority for the Protection of Personal Data (which instigated the deletion of religion from state identity cards); the ombudsman or Citizen's Advocate; and the Capital Markets Commission (responsible for regulating the Athens Stock Exchange). In recent years the government has given these authorities more backing; and their role has attracted growing public attention. The government has promised, in particular, that the potentially important Competition Commission and National Council of Radio and Television – which have been ineffective and meagrely staffed until recently – will at last exercise major responsibilities. Potentially these authorities represent an acquisition of power by parliament, which is supposed to vet appointments to them, as well as (since 1989) to directorships of public utilities. In practice, the parliamentary control has been wielded by the ruling party (the latter situation being much debated but not substantially changed during the current revision of the constitution).

Business and trade unions

Economic interest groups were also becoming more autonomous. The importance of the Federation of Greek Industries (SEV) increased markedly during the 1980s, both as a representative of large industrialists and as a negotiating partner with governments,[67] as we noticed earlier (p. 185). The recent development of the Athens Stock Exchange, and the growing independence of the state banks, were also described earlier (pp. 181, 189).

The trade union branches of parties also became more independent during the 1990s. From 1989 onwards, not even a PASOK government could count on having a majority of supporters in the Executive of the General Confederation of Greek Workers (GSEE). At the time of the GSEE congress in March 2001, the PASOK trade union branch was described by a journalist as acting like a separate party.[68] Trade unions in general also acquired greater independence of the government in collective bargaining, as a result of Law 1876 of 1990, which abolished compulsory arbitration by the government and institutionalised provision for voluntary mediation. This law proved effective in encouraging voluntary collective bargaining of a less adversarial kind than had earlier prevailed.[69] But the withdrawal of the state from collective bargaining did not maintain the membership level of trade unions, which is said to have declined, although they still comprise one-third of wage and salary earners. While the public sector remains highly unionised and contributes the majority of all union members, the decline in union membership occurred chiefly in the private sector.[70]

Interest groups and NGOs

Ministers were paying increasing attention to independent, or partially independent, bodies and interest groups outside parliament. Examples included non-government organisations (NGOs), the SEV, the GSEE, the Technical Chamber of Greece (representing civil engineers), municipalities and the groups represented in the Economic and Social Committee established by the Ministry of National Economy.

Among external sources of influence were non-government think tanks. In 1992 there appeared the Foundation for Economic and Industrial Research (IOVE), which filled a gap by providing authoritative economic analyses independent of those offered by the government-influenced Bank of Greece and the Ministry of National Economy.[71] Non-governmental commentators on foreign affairs, the Hellenic Foundation of Defence and Foreign Policy (ELIAMEP, founded in 1988) and the Institute of International Relations (IDIS, founded in 1989) became increasingly influential, and likewise satisfied a long-felt need.[72] In relation to big business there was the SEV. The GSEE became independent enough to shape government policy towards immigrants, and through its Institute of Labour commissioned expert and influential reports on, for example, the impact on the labour market of mass immigration and the financing of social insurance. Notably lacking, however, was a similarly effective advisory body on agriculture.[73] On environmental issues, both academic experts and voluntary organisations like the Society for the Protection of Nature and the Cultural Heritage, Greenpeace and the World Wide Fund for Nature, received increasing attention from the media and from the government.

The last were examples of NGOs, which won government recognition in the latter half of the 1990s as a new and valuable force. A government survey in 1999 tallied over 3,500 of them; and ministers were by now acknowledging their value in advising them and informing the public. For example, in December 2000, the Minister of Health, accompanied by many MPs, presented awards to 56 groups doing welfare work: the third successive year that such a ceremony had taken place.[74] National and local governments were increasingly prepared to utilise the labour and skills of NGOs for ends which included the rehabilitation of drug addicts, support for destitute immigrants, relief to earthquake victims or environmental education in schools. Local authorities tended to be sensitive to, and often appreciative of, locally based community groups. For example, in May 2000, the government announced a programme with a budget of $165 million for that year alone to equip and train, in cooperation with municipalities, a nationwide network of voluntary groups for preventing and fighting forest fires.[75] Governments were presumably impressed, not merely by the work performed by volunteers, but also by the close relations between many NGOs and supranational bodies like the European Commission and the European Court of Human Rights.

The growth of NGOs was occurring also in Italy, Portugal and Spain. It is generally agreed that, until the 1990s, voluntary associations devoted to issues of public interest were feeble in Greece. In the 1980s they multiplied, but were weakly organised and most – though not environmental associations – seem to have been vulnerable to penetration by political parties. In the 1990s, however, various types of association developed vigorous organisations, and attracted devotion and idealism of a type which the parties were notoriously losing. They took full advantage of the opportunities offered by the proliferation of non-government radio and television stations, the strengthening of local government, and the increasing independence of the judiciary.

This growth of voluntary activism is illustrated by a detailed government analysis in 1996 of environmental NGOs.[76] Of the 194 which replied to the government's survey, 79 per cent had been established since 1985; 81 per cent corresponded with a fairly wide range of print and broacast media (in most cases reporting satisfactory relations with them); and 41 per cent had contacted elected local authorities, or the local forestry officials. They, with the provincial branches of major national organisations, were found in all parts of the country. Although only 11 per cent had more than 500 paid-up members, 31 per cent occupied an office which they rented or owned; and 21 per cent employed paid staff. Four reported 10,000 or more regular supporters; and one of these, WWF, employed 48 people. Another type of organisation, the Greek Red Cross, employed about 600 people and 18,000 volunteers in 105 branches throughout the country. A voluntary drug rehabilitation programme, subsidised by the government, ran numerous centres for information, detoxification, social reintegration and assistance to families and prisoners.

Increasingly, NGOs received extensive and often favourable publicity in the media, because many of them were tackling neglected problems; and also because many were run by articulate professionals adept in communication skills and litigation. It seems, then, that they were shaping public opinion in important areas, although, in relation to the needs which they were trying to meet, they appear pitifully inadequate. One can conclude that the 1990s saw the rise of the key feature of civil society as conventionally defined.[77]

A reason for this development was the increasing proportion of citizens with skills of organisation, analysis and expression, as well as values, that were derived from advanced education, many of whom were prepared to associate with fellow-citizens in order to promote certain causes. Readiness to participate in some kind of organisation was found by a survey in Greece in 1997 to be thrice as high among citizens with tertiary education as it was among those with only primary education.

Towards a civic community?

On one necessary element of a civil society – respect for civil liberties – Greece still rated rather poorly by western standards, although improvement occurred during the 1990s. The chief force for progress seems to have been the pressure of western opinion (as expressed for example in rulings by the European Court of Human Rights) and the responsiveness to it of western-educated Greek politicians. Sadly, little pressure for improvement came from most of the Greek public. A Eurobarometer poll of 1993 found that only 21 per cent of Greeks considered tolerance a quality that parents should encourage in their children, compared with percentages ranging from 42 to 62 per cent in the other countries of the EEC-12.[78]

But there was vocal and growing support for civil liberties by many voluntary associations. In 1997, 52 such organisations established a centre, with an office, a library and hotline for reports of discrimination. Such groups were responsible for many of the over 700 appeals made by 1998 to the European Court of Human Rights, one of which resulted in payment by the government of the largest award in the court's history.[79] In 1998, an alternative to military service at last became available to conscientious objectors; and around this time restrictions on religious freedom were somewhat relaxed. But, even in 2000, New Democracy tried in parliament to prevent the construction of the first mosque for the estimated 60,000 Muslims of the metropolis. Meanwhile, the American body Freedom House rated Greece poorly, by western standards, on press freedom, although better than any other Balkan country or Turkey.[80] The treatment of un-documented immigrants was referred to earlier (p. 197).

The strengthening of voluntary associations and civil liberties might be interpreted as moves towards a civic community, interpreted as a political system based on general readiness by citizens to respect each other's rights and cooperate in promoting the public interest.[81] But in 2000 the attainment of this ideal still seemed remote, because essential prerequisites were lacking: habitual and general respect for the law; confidence in governments' ability to promote the public interest impartially; competent and innovative public administration; government accustomed to consult with interested parties before making changes which affected them, and citizens ready to negotiate in a constructive way with governments. Successive surveys from 1976 to 1996 showed that interpersonal trust among citizens was rather low in Greece by western European standards, although much higher than in Italy.[82]

One constantly discussed example of public disrespect for the law and for government, referred to earlier (p. 70) is continuing encroachment on public woodland by unlicensed property developers, which results from the failure of the national or local governments to plan urban growth. Another example of this failure is the chaotic way in which the metropolitan conurbation has spread, a process now continuing near the new airport east of Athens. There are powerful groups with an interest in the continuance of this disorder: for example politicians and public officials who value the patronage which it allows them, and individual citizens wanting to build wherever they like. Another notorious example of the shortage of social capital is the extraordinarily high rate of traffic accidents.

The chronic incapacity of the state has given rise to the widespread belief that Greeks are generally incapable of large-scale organisation. This impression is not supported by examples cited in the present book. There have appeared ideologically inspired movements which were very impressively organised, such as those of the Communist Party in the 1940s, and some NGOs in the 1990s. Vigorous organisations based on local communities were, as we saw earlier, suppressed in the 1930s and 1940s by the all-embracing tentacles of the state; but, with the partial retreat of the state in the 1990s, they seem to be reviving. Examples are some of the better-led municipalities, or the cooperative credit institutions.[83]

However, the increasing assertiveness of interest groups actually raised the problem of anarchy in new forms. Each tended to fight for its own interests, in the absence of effective institutional procedures for resolving such conflicts. A common example was the militant defence by munici-palities of their environmental resources, by for example excluding through traffic, preventing the appropriation of their natural water supplies, or denying the use of their land for waste disposal or power lines. There was no public administration capable of planning and implementing solutions; nor was there any apparent recognition among warring interest groups of a public good embodied in law.

Among many conflicts between municipalities and the national govern-ment was one over the location of a plant for processing toxic waste in western Crete. It was, typically, resolved by inaction: for at least thirteen years, those who produced the waste dumped it in a stream bed. For this neglect, the government became, in June 2000, the first in the EU to be fined by the European Court of Justice. The solution to such problems that was found in other countries was cooperation between the government, municipalities and private interests in establishing facilities for processing waste. In Greece, the proportion of waste to be recycled is the lowest in the EU, and litter is a ubiquitous eyesore, as well as a health and fire hazard.[84]

Notes

1 Thalia Dragonas and Dan Bar-on, 'National identity among a neighbouring quartet: the case of Greeks, Turks, Israelis and Palestinians', *Journal of Modern Greek Studies* 18 (October 2000), 341; Georgia Kontogiannopoulou-Polydoridis *et al.*, 'Citizen education: silencing crucial issues', ibid., 291; Susannah Verney, 'Greece: a new era', *Mediterranean Politics* 2 (1997), 194–5.

2 *Vima*, 21 March 1999, A1, 52, Ioanna Mandrou.

3 *Vima*, 29 November 1992, A53; *Vima*, 18 February 2001, A73, G.K. Bitrou; *Kathimerini*, 13 January 2001.

4 *Vima*, 31 December 2000, A40–1, Panayotis Bitsika and Machis Tratsa; *Kathimerini*, 28 March 2001 (English Internet edition).

5 Stavros Lygeros, *The Game of Power* (in Greek, 1996), 124–9, 156–67, 182–92, 216.

6 *Athens News*, 25 February 2001.

7 *Vima*, 7 February 1993, A3, Nikou Nikolaou.

8 Thimios Zaharopoulos and Manny E. Paraschos, *Mass Media in Greece: Power, Politics, and Privatization* (Westport, CT 1993), 144–5.

9 *Kathimerini*, 27 July 1997, 3; *Kathimerini*, 18 January 1998, 16.

10 *Economist*, 16 September 2000, 124.

11 Kostas Panagopoulos, 'Greeks confess', in Alexandra P. Nikolopoulou (ed.), *The State and Corruption* (in Greek, 1998), 72, 274, 292; Kleomenis S. Koutsoukis, 'Corruption as a phenomenon in the modern Greek state', in ibid., 150–4; idem, 'Sleaze in contemporary Greek politics', *Parliamentary Affairs* 48 (1995), 690; *Vima*, 21 September 1997, D16, survey by Transparency International; Paolo Mauro, 'Corruption and growth', *Quarterly Journal of Economics* 110 (1995), 385–7; Nikolopoulou, *State and Corruption*, Appendix, 274; *Kathimerini*, 4 February 2001.

12 Stavros B. Thomadakis and Dimitris B. Seremitis, 'Fiscal management, social agenda and structural deficits', in Theodore C. Kariotis (ed.), *The Greek Socialist Experiment. Papandreou's Greece, 1981–9* (New York 1996), 216–17; Kalliope Spanou, 'Elections and public administration. The electoral activation of clientelist mechanisms in the administration', in Lyrintzis and Nikolakopoulos (eds), *Elections and Parties*, 171–2; *Vima*, 12 April 1992, D2, Nikolaou; *Vima*, 10 April 1994, A4, Nikolaou.

13 *Vima*, 17 January 1999, A46, Ioanna Mandrou; *Kathimerini*, 4 February 2001, anon.

14 *Vima*, 11 January 1998, D2, G.K. Bitrou; *Vima*, 26 July 1998, A16, Nikolaou; *Vima*, 13 December 1998, A22, Nikolaou.

15 *Vima*, 10 June 2001, B6, I.K. Siomopoulou.

16 *Vima*, 3 March 1996, D2, Nikolaou; *Kathimerini*, 16 January 1998, 17; *Vima*, 26 November 2000, D8, Nikolaou, citing IMF statistics.

17 Theodore Pelagidis, 'Economic policies in Greece during 1990–93: an assessment', *Journal of Modern Greek Studies* 15 (1997), 74; *Vima*, 20 July 1997, D4, Nikolaou; *Vima*, 8 November 1998, A6, Nikolaou; *Vima*, 11 December 1994, A2; *Vima*, 25 October 1992, D4; *Vima*, 17 January 1999, D4, Nikolaou; *Vima*, 9 May 1999, G.P. Zania; *Vima*, 19 October 2000, D4, Nikolaou; *Kathimerini* (English Internet edition), 7 June 2001, citing a report by the Institute of Economic and Industrial Research.

18 Antonis Makridimitris, *Government and Society. Public Administration in Greece* (in Greek, 1999), 252, 279; Kevin Featherstone, Georgios Kazamias and Dimitris Papadimitriou, 'Greece and the negotiation of Economic and Monetary Union', *Journal of Modern Greek Studies* 18 (2000), 400–1; *Vima*, 30 March 1997, A49, D. Nikolakopoulou; *Kathimerini*, 18 June 2000, 32, Georgiou Malouchou.

19 National Statistical Service of Greece, *Concise Statistical Yearbook of Greece 1998* (1999); Dimitris Demekas and Zenon Kontolemis, 'Labour market performance and institutions in Greece', *South European Society and Politics* 2 (1997), 103; *Economist*, 15 January 2000, 55.

20 George Th. Mavrogordatos, 'From traditional clientelism to machine politics: the impact of PASOK clientelism in Greece', *South European Society and Politics* 2 (1997), 24–5; *Vima*, 5 July 1998, A48–9, Nikolakopoulou; *Vima*, 21 November 1999, A50–1, Ioanna Mandrou; *Kathimerini*, 24 August 1997, 1, K. Michailidi.

21 *Vima*, 1 September 1991, D2.

22 *Vima*, 14 June 1992, A36, G. Lakopoulou; *Vima*, 27 June 1999, A44–6.

23 *Vima*, 29 December 1996, A8; *Kathimerini*, 28 April 2000; *Kathimerini* (English Internet edition), 25 May 2001.

24 *Vima*, 3 October 1999, A1–2.

25 *Vima*, 12 March 2000, A29, Nikolakopoulou.

26 *Vima*, 3 March 1996, A21, Th. P. Lianou.

27 Konstantinos A. Lavdas, *The Europeanization of Greece. Interest Politics and the Crisis of Integration* (1997), 188; Makridimitris, *Government and Society*, 248–58, 275–7; *Vima*, 1 March 1998, A39, Nikolakopoulou; *Vima*, 5 September 1999, D29, G. Christoforidi; *Vima*, 12 March 2000, A29, D. Nikolakopoulou; *Vima*, 30 July 2000, D4; *Kathimerini* (English Internet edition), 29 May 2001.

28 *Vima*, 20 January 1991, A3, Nikolaou; *Vima*, 21 March 1993, A4, Nikolaou; Lygeros, *Game of Power*, 227; Nicholas G. Pirounakis, *The Greek Economy: Past, Present, and Future* (1997), 86–7.

29 *Kathimerini*, 11 January 1998, 4, Gianni Loverdou; *Vima*, 28 June 1998, D2, Nikolaou.

30 *Vima*, 5 September 1999, D29, G. Christoforidi.

31 Kenneth Matziorinis, 'Greek economy at a turning point: recent performance, current challenges and future prospects', *Journal of the Hellenic Diaspora* 19 (1993), 62; George Pagoulatos, 'Governing in a constrained environment: policy making in the Greek banking deregulation and privatisation reform', *West European Politics* 19 (1996), 754; Pirounakis, *Greek Economy*, 121.

32 Maurizio Ferrara, 'The "southern model" of welfare in social Europe', *Journal of European Social Policy* 6 (1996), 34; Maria Petmesidou, 'Social protection in Greece: a brief glimpse of a welfare state', *Social Policy and Administration* 30 (1996), 326–7; Dimitrios N. Venieris, 'Dimensions of social policy in Greece', *South European Society and Politics* 1 (1996), 265–6; Giorgios Provopoulos and Platon Tinios, 'Pensions and the fiscal crisis of the Greek state', in Harry J. Psomiades and Stavros Thomadakis (eds), *Greece*, 338–9; Dimitris Kioukias, 'Interest representation and modernisation policies in Greece: lessons learned from the study of labor and farmers', *Journal of Modern Greek Studies* 15 (1997), 314–5; *Vima*, 11 February 2001, B7, D. Stergiou, citing Eurostat figures.

33 Zaharopoulos and Paraschos, *Mass Media*, 75–6.

34 *Kathimerini*, 11 July 1999, 10, Gianni Loverdou.

35 *Vima*, 25 July 1999, A5, Stavrou P. Psychari.

36 *Vima*, 24 May 1998, A18, Nikolaou.

37 Kioukias, 'Interest representation', 316; *Vima*, 11 May 1997, E4, K. Papadis.

38 *Vima*, 10 January 1999, A4, Nikolaou; *Vima*, 19 September 1999, D6, Nikolaou; *Kathimerini*, 8 November 1998, 52.

39 *Vima*, 29 April 2000, B8, Ch. Korfiati.

40 *Athens News*, 16 April 2000; *Vima*, 18 July 1999, V. Chioti; Kostas Zafeiropoulos and Nikos Marantzidis, 'Electoral changes in the social base of New PASOK', *Greek Review of Political Science* 14 (in Greek, 1999), 30–46.

41 *Kathimerini*, 2 January 2000, Special Issue, Petrou Papakonstantinou.

42 *Vima*, 25 July 1999, A5, Stavrou Psychari.

43 *Athens News*, 28 February 1999.

44 Michael Spourdalakis, 'From "mass movement" to "New PASOK"', in Michael Spourdalakis (ed.), *PASOK. Party, State, Society* (in Greek, 1998), 68.

45 Constantine Danopoulos, 'Democratizing the military: lessons from Mediterranean Europe', *West European Politics* 14 (1991), 33; Panayotis Kafetzis, Giannis Mavris and Ilias Nikolakopoulos, 'The elections of 1996', *Greek Review of Political Research* 9 (in Greek, 1997), 168–207; *Ta Nea*, 10 June 1989, 3; *Kathimerini*, 4 October 1998, 20, Tasoula Karaïskaki; V-Project Research Consulting, *Public Opinion in Greece* (in Greek, 1999), 117, 121.

46 D. E. M. Mihas, 'New political formations in Greece: a challenge to its party system?' *Journal of Modern Greek Studies* 16 (1998), 54–7.

47 *Ta Nea*, 27 May 1989, 7; *Vima*, 4 June 1989, 9; *Vima*, 12 June 1994, A13; *Kathimerini*, 3 September 1995, 6; *Vima*, 24 March 1996, 1; *Athens News*, 25 April 2000.

48 Paraskevi Christofilopoulou, 'Elected prefectural government and administration in the Greek political system', *Greek Review of Political Science* 7 (1996), 132–3.

49 Makridimitris, *Government and Society*, 252, 261; Dimitrios Christopoulos, 'Clientelistic networks and local corruption: evidence from western Crete', *South European Society and Politics* 3 (1998), 12–13; *Kathimerini*, 18 May 1997, 4; *Vima*, 6 July 1997, A47; *Vima*, 24 November 1996, A42; Susannah Verney, 'Central state–local government relations', in Panos Kazakos and P.C. Ioakimidis (eds), *Greece and European Community Membership Evaluated* (1994), 174–5.

50 *Vima*, 5 November 2000, A52–3.

51 *Vima*, 4 January 1998, A40–1; *Vima*, 1 December 1996, A42.

52 *Kathimerini*, 4 October 1998, 20, K.P. Papadiochou; *Vima*, 31 August 1997, A9, P.K. Lampsia.

53 Paraskevi Christofilopoulou, 'PASOK and elected local government: organizational structure and policies', in Spourdalakis (ed.), *PASOK*, 202; Lygeros, *Game of Power*, 293, 299; Christos Lyrintzis, 'Parties and municipal elections: the restructuring of a long-term relationship', *Greek Review of Political Science* 15 (in Greek, 2000), 12–20; Rallis Gekas, 'The new relationship of the central and local government sector', *Greek Review of Political Science* 15 (2000), 77; *Vima*, 7 May 2000, A16, Dimitra Kroustalli.

54 *Vima*, 13 December 1998, A63, Michali Dekleri; *Vima*, 29 March 1998, A8, I.K. Pretenteri; Nicholas Papaspyrou, 'A farewell to judicial passivity: the environmental jurisprudence of the Greek Council of State', *Journal of Modern Greek Studies* 17 (1999), 63–84; *Economist*, 7 August 1999, 47; 2 June 2001, 54.

55 *Vima*, 31 May 1998, A50–1, Ioanna Mandrou; *Vima*, 24 September 2000, A50–1, Ioanna Mandrou; Nicos Alivizatos, *Uncertain Modernization and the Obscure Constitutional Revision* (in Greek, 2001), 72, 219–222.

56 *Vima*, 17 May 1998, A56, Ioanna Mandrou.

57 Nicos C. Alivizatos, 'The presidency, the parliament, and the courts in the 1980s', in Richard Clogg (ed.), *Greece, 1981–9. The Populist Decade* (1993), 73; *Vima*, 8 November 1992, A14, Alivizatos.

58 *Vima*, 30 August 1992, A44–5, G.N. Anastasopoulou.

59 Roi Panayotopoulou, 'Construction of ethnocentric stereotypes by the press in the case of the Macedonian issue', *Review of Social Research* 89–90 (1996), 246–7; Stephanos Pesmazoglou, 'The 1980s in the looking-glass: PASOK and the media', in Richard Clogg (ed.), *Greece, 1981–9. The Populist Decade* (1993), 101; *Vima*, 4 April, 1999, A75, K. Chalvatzaki.

60 European Commission, *Eurobarometer* 46 (October–November 1996), 46; *Vima*, 7 January 1999, A67.

61 *Vima*, 22 July 1990, A21; *Kathimerini*, 16 July 2000, 38, Fotou Lambrinou.

62 *Vima*, 31 May 1992, A56, G. Papachristou; *Avgi*, 18 August 1996, 18–19.

63 *Kathimerini*, 25 July 1999, 10, Kosta Keki; *Kathimerini*, 2 January 2000, Special Issue, 13, Petrou Papakonstantinou.

64 *Vima*, 27 June 1999, A12, anon.; *Vima*, 19 March 2000, A18, Gr. Tziova and V. Chioti.

65 Mihas, 'New political formations', 53–6; *Vima*, 15 August 1999, A6, Chioti; *Vima*, 9 July 2000, A6, anon.

66 Alivizatos, *Uncertain Modernization*, 114–15, 122–5, 222; *Vima*, 5 November 2000, A74.

67 Lavdas, *Europeanization*, 215, 244–5.

68 Stella Zabarloukou, 'Trade union movement and state intervention in Greece during the transition to democracy: a comparative approach', in Christos Lyrintzis, Ilias Nikolakopoulos and Dimitris Sotiropoulos (eds), *Society and Politics. Aspects of the Third Greek Republic, 1974–94* (in Greek, 1996), 116–17; Spourdalakis, 'PASOK in the 1990s', in Maravall (ed.), *Socialist Parties*, 177; *Kathimerini*, 4 March 2001.

69 Eleonora Karassavidou and Yannis Markovits, 'The evolution of dispute resolution, negotiation and mediation in Greece', *Relations Industrielles*, 51 (1996), 373–86.

70 *Vima*, 8 March 1998, A22, K. Papadi; *Kathimerini*, 25 July 1999, 1, 55, Christina Kopsini; *Kathimerini*, 4 March 2001.

71 *Vima*, 9 May 1993, D2, Nikolaou.

72 Theodore Couloumbis, 'The structures of Greek foreign policy', in Richard Clogg (ed.), *Greece in the 1980s* (1983), 110; *Vima*, 17 October 1999, A35, anon.

73 Lavdas, *Europeanization*, 180–4; Neil Collins and Leonidas Louloudis, 'Protecting the protected: the Greek agricultural policy network', *Journal of European Public Policy* 2 (1995), 105–6.

74 *Kathimerini*, 6 December 2000.

75 *Vima*, 15 October 2000, A42, Dimitra Kroustalli and Nikou Karagianni.

76 This information is contained in the database on diskette, which I obtained from the National Centre of Social Research (EKKE). The summary was jointly published in Greek by the Ministry of Environment and Public Works and EKKE in 1997, and entitled *Environmental Organisations*.

77 David H. Close, 'Environmental crisis in Greece and recent challenges to centralized state authority', *Journal of Modern Greek Studies* 17 (1999), 325–52; Dimitris A. Sotiropoulos, 'The ventriloquial authority: civil society and central state in the third Greek republic', in Lyrintzis *et al.* (eds), *Society and Politics*, 120; *Economist*, 20 March 1999, 59; Maria Kousis, 'Sustaining environmental mobilizations: groups, actions and claims in southern Europe', *Environmental Politics* 8 (1999), 184; *Athens News*, 4 July 1999; *Vima*, 5 December 1999, A57, Vasiliki Strati.

78 *Kathimerini*, 29 June 2000.

79 *Vima*, 20 July 1997, A35.

80 Stefanos Stavros, 'Human rights in Greece: twelve years of supervision from Strasbourg', *Journal of Modern Greek Studies* 17 (1999), 3–15; *Kathimerini*, 21 June 2000; *Athens News*, 4 May 2000.

81 Robert Putnam, *Making Democracy Work. Civic Traditions in Modern Italy* (Princeton, NJ 1993), 87–90.

82 Ronald Inglehart, 'The renaissance of political culture', *American Political Science Review* 82 (1988), 1210; European Commission, *Eurobarometer*, 'Public opinion in the European Union', no. 46 (May 1997, based on a survey of October–November 1996), 41–2. The Eurobarometer survey found that 14 per cent of Greeks admitted to not very much or no trust in their fellow-citizens. Among the 15 EU countries, there were higher percentages only in Belgium, Portugal and Italy.

83 Close, 'Environmental crisis', 333–4, 342; David H. Close, 'Environmental NGOs in Greece: the Achelöos campaign as a case study of their influence', *Environmental Politics* 7 (summer 1998), 55–77; *Kathimerini*, 12 November 2000, 72, Kl. Kontonika.

84 *Vima*, 9 July 2000, A44, Dimitri Kroustalli.

CHAPTER TWELVE

Foreign Relations, 1974–2000

The western alliance

After his return from exile, Karamanlis emphasised his intention to apply for full membership of the EEC, and lodged an application in June 1975. Although opposed by the Communist Party and PASOK, this was a popular move because of the EEC's prominent role in opposing the Junta. The fact that this was also the month in which a new constitution was voted through parliament indicated, as Susannah Verney pointed out, Karamanlis's desire to establish the external orientation of the regime at the same time as its internal structure.[1] A new and urgent attraction of membership was that the EEC was a potential source of support against Turkey – support which would not compromise national independence and domestic stability as the American connection had done. During the following four years, Karamanlis was personally responsible for overcoming the quite considerable reservations of the EEC authorities about Greece's readiness for membership, in view of the backwardness of its economy.

In response to the Turkish invasion of Cyprus in August 1974 (see below, p. 268), all that Karamanlis could do was appeal for NATO intervention, and then withdraw from NATO's military wing when the appeal was rejected. This move also expressed his desire to distance Greece henceforth from the United States. Here he represented vehement public feeling, which resulted in the assassination on 19 August of the US ambassador to Cyprus, and on 23 December 1975 (by the '17th November' group) of the chief CIA functionary in Greece. Karamanlis also announced, in August 1974, that the tenure of US military bases would be renegotiated; while the United States found it prudent to cancel the 'home port' facilities in Athens for the Sixth Fleet.

Greece's partial withdrawal from NATO broke the alliance's communications between western Europe and Turkey, and prevented the use of Greek military bases for NATO exercises. However, the significance of the Greek move was limited by the continued functioning of American bases on Greek soil, under conditions made more restrictive by a new agreement negotiated in 1975–76. The bases were placed under Greek direction; intelligence obtained from all bases was to be shared; the land-based nuclear weapons, which were now obsolete, were not to be replaced; and most of the facilities at Ellenikon air base in the metropolis were closed. Modern nuclear weapons continued to be carried on American ships and submarines which used the base at Souda Bay in Crete. Otherwise scope for military independence from the US was limited. Greece continued to depend on America for the great bulk of its military equipment and, as time showed, for mediation in periodic confrontations with Turkey. Greece also needed membership of the NATO military wing for its security; whereas America could not alienate Turkey by trying to force the withdrawal of its troops from Cyprus. So Greece accepted the inevitable by rejoining NATO's military wing in 1980, without securing a NATO guarantee of its territory. Even after the Cold War ended in the late 1980s, Greece remained locked into NATO by the need to maintain its military strength in relation to Turkey, and recently by acquiring a military role in the Balkans. On the other hand, as we have seen, Greece's economic dependence on America had declined steeply since the 1950s, in trade, investment and emigrants' remittances.[2]

While at first appealing with theatrical rhetoric and gestures to the anti-western feeling of left-wing voters, Andreas Papandreou, as prime minister in 1981–89, conducted a foreign policy consistent in essentials with that of Karamanlis. Like Karamanlis too, he conducted a personal policy which to some extent bypassed the Ministry of Foreign Affairs. A new agreement with the US was negotiated in 1983 which allowed military bases to stay, complete with nuclear weapons and spying facilities. This retreat was camouflaged by the government's announcement that the bases would close after five years, a condition not accepted by the US nor implemented by Papandreou. While the government discussed with other Balkan countries the idea of a regional nuclear-free zone, Greece remained the only one with nuclear weapons on its soil as well as in its ports. Greece remained in the military wing of NATO, and merely refused to participate in some military exercises that might jeopardise territorial rights in relation to Turkey. There was no referendum as promised on membership of the EEC, although Papandreou did negotiate somewhat more favourable terms of membership. In relations with Turkey, Papandreou was for several years more strident than the previous government. But all that changed in Papandreou's foreign policy was the tone, with a show of independence from the west and several superficial and headline-grabbing gestures, such as defence of Arab states like Libya against charges of supporting terrorism, and refusal to condemn the Soviet Union over the shooting down of a South Korean airliner. While boosting his popularity at home, Papandreou's anti-western tone had the long-term effect of antagonising essential allies, especially the United States, and had to be abandoned from 1985 as his government became dependent on EEC loans and subsidies.[3]

The acceptance in spirit by Papandreou of the EEC completed the foreign policy consensus which had been growing since 1974. Only the small and increasingly marginal Communist Party remained outside it. This was a new development. Since 1915, dissent between major political parties over the socio-political structure and dissent over foreign patrons had, as Theodore Couloumbis argued, interacted in an explosive way in a context of economic dependency and military insecurity.[4] Thenceforth, in more prosperous and secure conditions, all save the Communists agreed that Greece's future lay in growing integration in the EEC and in full membership of NATO, while maintaining friendly relations with other Balkan countries and with Arab states.

Papandreou had already discovered the EEC's value for support and leverage against Turkey. Through it he ensured the diplomatic and commercial isolation of the newly declared Turkish Republic of Northern Cyprus. His and ensuing governments also reminded other European countries of Turkey's violations of international law and human rights. Furthermore, Greece repeatedly blocked, in the 1980s and 1990s, EEC credits to Turkey; as well as Turkey's application for EEC membership when it was made in 1987 and again in 1998. The value, or apparent value, of EEC membership in these respects helps explain why Greece supported ardently the reinvigorated movement from 1989 towards EEC integration.[5] A reward for this loyalty was the broad support of EU governments, at a critical point in 1999, for Greece's position on Aegean disputes and Cyprus.

Confrontation with Turkey

Cyprus

On 14 August 1974, the Turkish invading force in Cyprus – despite the fact that a civilian government had just been restored there – advanced to seize 36 per cent of the island, forcing over 180,000 Greek Cypriots to flee their homes. The new Greek prime minister Karamanlis seriously contemplated war; but, on being reminded by military leaders that Greek defences were in no state to allow it, had to swallow the humiliation. Cyprus has been partitioned ever since. The Turkish Cypriot zone was turned effectively into a puppet state of Turkey, which was garrisoned thenceforth by Turkish forces usually about 30,000 in strength, and colonised in time by 30,000–80,000 settlers from the mainland, who occupied land vacated by Greek Cypriot refugees, and differed culturally from the approximately 120,000 Turkish Cypriot residents. In 1983 the zone proclaimed itself a sovereign state, the Turkish Republic of Northern Cyprus, which was recognised by no country except Turkey, and remained poor and dependent on Turkish subsidies. But whenever called on to persuade the Turkish Cypriots to make concessions to the Greek Cypriots, the Turkish government refused on the pretext that they were independent.

The Greek Cypriot zone, the Republic of Cyprus, became a prosperous and internationally recognised democracy. Its demands for political reunification of the island, and justice for the refugees, were supported by repeated resolutions of the UN General Assembly. Justice for refugees was also demanded in 2001 by the European Court of Human Rights. Now the state seems close to joining the EU. While its independence was thenceforth respected in full by Greek governments, it cooperated closely with them in security matters. Greek governments, having overcome the weaknesses brought about by the Junta, emphasised that further Turkish aggression in Cyprus would be a *casus belli*, and kept Greek forces there as a tripwire. In 1993 the relationship between Greece and the Republic of Cyprus was formalised as the Joint Defence Pact. The Greek Cypriots' armed forces of about 10,000 were in the later 1990s commanded by 1,000 Greek officers, and supplemented by about 1,000 Greek troops. The line between the zones of the heavily militarised island continued to be policed by a UN peacekeeping force of (currently) 2,500.

The partition of the island was so offensive to Greek feeling that it remained 'a smoldering volcano' in its effect on relations with Turkey.[6] Talks between the governments of the two Cypriot communities were periodically conducted under UN auspices; but over time the gap between them actually widened. The Turkish Cypriots were never willing to contemplate political reunification, or any transfer of territory or restitution to refugees, which were minimal demands of the Greek Cypriots. The period of greatest tension was perhaps in 1996–98. In 1996, five civilians (four Greek Cypriots and one Turkish Cypriot) were killed in different incidents along the demarcation line. In 1997–98, the Republic of Cyprus provoked Turkish threats of war by purchasing long-distance anti-aircraft missiles from Russia – a crisis eventually defused by the location of the missiles on the Greek island of Crete.

After 1974, the military threat from Turkey towered over all other dangers to Greece. The humiliating predicament remained that this threat dictated military dependence on the United States. Both Greece and Turkey tried in the long term to reduce their dependence, by diversifying their foreign suppliers and developing their own armaments industries. From February 1975 to August 1978, the US Administration imposed a partial arms embargo on Turkey, at the insistence of Congress (itself influenced by the Greek–American lobby) that Turkey be penalised for having used US-supplied arms to invade Cyprus.[7] Thereafter the normal supply of arms resumed, in the nominal ratio thenceforth of 7:10 in value between Greece and Turkey. Thus the US could, and on occasion did, exert irresistible pressure on Greece by increasing supplies to Turkey.

Although the United States repeatedly mediated so as to restore peace in major crises between Greece and Turkey, it showed undoubted partiality towards Turkey in the long run. For example, after 1978 it put no pressure on Turkey to comply with UN resolutions or international law in regard to Cyprus.[8]

The Aegean

Disagreements between Greece and Turkey over the Aegean continued. The Greek side added a fresh cause of tension after the invasion of Cyprus by fortifying several eastern Aegean islands, an action which Turkey alleged to be a violation of treaties. Turkey proclaimed in response, in 1975, the formation of 'The Army of the Aegean' equipped with amphibious vessels and poised to attack the islands.

After 1974 there were three particularly serious crises. In August 1976 and March 1987 disputes occurred over exploration activities by Turkish survey vessels over the continental shelf in the Aegean. In January 1996, Greek and Turkish warships confronted each other over ownership of two islets, Ta Imia, 3.5 nautical miles from the Turkish mainland. The islets had hitherto been claimed by Greece without challenge.

Greek air space was constantly transgressed by Turkish military aircraft from the mid-1970s onwards. The Greek government showed its confidence in its legal case on Aegean issues by repeatedly inviting Turkey to submit them to the International Court of Justice. Turkey countered that the Aegean was a special case, being a semi-enclosed sea of vital importance to both countries. Disputes could therefore be resolved only through bilateral negotiations to reach some equitable solution, for which there existed many international precedents.[9] The Greek government countered that there was nothing to negotiate about, save only for the demarcation of rights to the continental shelf.

There was a brief period of détente in 1988, after Andreas Papandreou as prime minister met his counterpart Turgut Ozal at Davos in Switzerland. The two issued a joint statement of peaceful intentions and agreed on basic procedures to fulfil them. But the old disputes started again soon afterwards.

In 1989, Turkey acquired fresh motives to dispute Greek rights. The rejection by the EEC of its application for candidate status removed an incentive to peaceful behaviour. The collapse of the Soviet bloc strengthened Turkey's position by removing a potential threat and reducing Greece's value to NATO. Meanwhile, continuing instability in the Middle East increased Turkey's importance as 'the best aircraft carrier NATO ever had' in a western diplomat's words.[10] In particular, Turkey provided the United States with air bases for use against Iraq, which was becoming, in American eyes, the chief rogue state in the Middle East. Then, in 1996, Turkey strengthened its position further by agreements with Israel for the mutual purchase of arms, cooperation against terrorism and the sharing of intelligence. In the extent and quality of its armaments and armed forces, Turkey towered over all its neighbours in the 1990s. Worse still, from the Greek point of view, Turkish military leaders retained a decisive influence on their country's relations with Greece, and stated repeatedly that Greek territory and claims in the Aegean were open to dispute. Moreover, Turkish governments found it expedient to divert public attention from economic difficulties with foreign crises.

This combination of factors seems to have been the reason for Turkey's unprecedentedly pointed challenge during 1996 to Greek sovereignty over first Ta Imia and then over other Aegean islands. In the late 1990s, Turkey's increased military superiority over its neighbours, and the unpredictable initiatives by leading members of its armed forces in the sphere of defence and foreign policy, worried American specialists in Turkish affairs.[11]

Defence

After the crisis of August 1974, military expenditure by Greece and Turkey increased greatly; but that of Turkey increased faster, so tilting the military balance further against Greece. For the next twenty-five years, the possibility of war with Turkey seemed real to Greece; even though Turkish political and military leaders have not revealed any disposition to resolve disagreements with Greece by force (as they did for a long time in regard to Cyprus before 1974), and have periodically disclaimed such an intention.[12] This apparent prospect of war with a neighbour was faced by no other European country, leaving aside the constituent republics of former Yugoslavia in the 1990s. Within Greece, the country's defence capability – in respect of population, armed forces and GDP – were matters of obvious and vital significance; while the continuance of a threat to its territory was a spur to patriotic feeling. In addition to its army, Greece had after 1974 to build up air and naval forces capable of deterring Turkish attack on eastern Aegean islands. In the 1980s, at least, it managed to maintain parity or superiority in these two types of force in the Aegean. It must always have been apparent to defence planners that Greece could not defend its territory in the event of determined attack by Turkey, and so should aim at deterrence, to be achieved by advanced technology and a high level of training.[13] All these armaments had to be paid for mainly with foreign exchange. In 1964–73, Greek defence expenditure was 5.1 per cent of GDP and 34.3 per cent of current government expenditure; in 1974–83, the corresponding figures were 6.6 and 39.2; while in the 1990s they averaged about 4.8 and 25.0. This defence burden was, proportionate to the size of Greece's economy in the 1990s, the highest in NATO, over twice the average for other EU countries, and about 50 per cent greater than Turkey's. The percentage of the labour force devoted to defence – 6.1 per cent in 1986 – was likewise the highest in NATO. With a normal defence burden, the Greek government could probably have qualified at the same time as other EU countries for entry into EMU; and could of course have spent far more on much-needed social services.[14]

The need for the burden was nevertheless accepted without question by both major parties and the great majority of the population. Opinion polls showed compulsory military service (the normal term in the late 1990s for the main force, the army, being eighteen months and somewhat longer for the air force and navy) as being supported by nearly four-fifths of the young, compared with under one-third in other EU countries. In a survey of conscripts in 1997, 45 per cent favoured armed reaction to any Turkish aggression in Cyprus. But military service could not be described as popular. One in seven conscripts suffered from some sort of depression. Until 1994 the military penal code was primitive and harsh. Many people used legal objections or pulled strings to obtain deferrals, exemptions or desirable postings; and these demands were a major preoccupation of MPs and party organisations.[15] Clearly then, governmental success in achieving peace, without making vital concessions, would be very popular.

Towards détente?

Relations between Greece and Turkey remained for the most part tense for over three years after the Imia incident in 1996; but improved abruptly after terrible earthquakes in both countries in August–September 1999. The climate of opinion in both countries was transformed as television showed Greek and Turkish rescue teams cooperating in the search for survivors under the rubble: remarkable evidence of the power of the television image.

But still more important was the revived interest of the Turkish government in détente, so as to facilitate its renewed application to the EU for candidate status. This interest in détente was reciprocated by the Greek foreign minister Georgios Papandreou junior (son of Andreas) as well as by Simitis. A move by Simitis, in December 1999, which may prove to be a turning-point in Greek–Turkish relations was at last to support Turkey's application for candidate status to EU governments at the Helsinki conference. Simitis had emphasised as soon as he became prime minister in 1996 his desire for better relations with neighbouring countries, for example publicly thanking President Clinton for America's mediation in February 1996 in the Imia dispute, and proclaiming during a crisis over Cyprus the following August that 'our restraint is our best asset'.[16] He presumably hoped in time to reduce defence expenditure, and also to create peaceful conditions attractive to foreign investors. In opposing Turkish candidacy, and blocking EU credits to Turkey in the late 1990s, Greece had only worsened relations with Turkey and intensified Turkish paranoia, while becoming isolated in the EU. As a result of Simitis's move, the blame for delaying Turkey's movement towards membership of the EU fell no longer on Greece but on the Turkish armed forces.[17] As for Turkey, it had as we saw joined the Council of Europe as long before as 1949; become an associate member of the EEC in 1963; and become united with the EU in a customs union in 1996. To the growing business community, especially in western Turkey, full membership promised more trade and investment; to politicians it promised more international influence and EU subsidies which they could dispense; and to military leaders it promised a fulfilment of the westernising, Kemalist legacy and a check on Islamic fundamentalism. Meanwhile the precarious state of the economy – necessitating recourse to the IMF – made difficult the continuance of high defence expenditure. The case within Turkey for membership of the EU is likely to strengthen still further when – as is scheduled within a few years – eleven eastern European countries are admitted.

Accordingly, at the Helsinki summit of EU governments in December 1999, Turkey duly attained candidate status. The conditions for eventual membership were forbidding, and were spelt out in the Association

Partnership Accord in November 2000: progress towards human rights and democracy (meaning in effect the withdrawal of the military from politics); increased rights for the Kurdish minority; support for UN efforts at mediation over Cyprus; and settlement of differences with Greece over the Aegean by 2004, failing which those differences would be submitted to the International Court of Justice.[18] It was also indicated that the Republic of Cyprus would soon join the EU, so leaving its Turkish Cypriot counterpart and Turkey itself outside, at the end of a long queue.

During 2000, détente between Greece and Turkey has continued, although the relationship is still strained and periodically marred by disputes. Agreements were signed, providing for cooperation concerning tourism, drug-trafficking, illegal immigration, terrorism, environmental protection, scientific and technical issues, energy sources, investment security, shipping and trade. Trade and tourism between the countries increased greatly; and to these ends – for which there had always existed great potential – governments and municipalities on both sides concluded agreements. Greek and Turkish forces cooperated for a time in NATO exercises in a way perhaps unprecedented since 1954. Turkish violations of Greek air space declined, and violations of territorial waters ceased. In April 2001, both governments announced substantial cuts in their defence spending programmes.

One worrying sign is that both sides have remained adamant on Aegean issues. The Turkish positions were indicated by the latest version of the (periodically revised) White Book of the Turkish Ministry of Defence, which became known later in April 2001. Nor have Turkish military leaders shown much inclination to stop intervening in domestic politics. Meanwhile the Greek government has been under strong pressure both from New Democracy, and from within PASOK, not to concede too much to Turkey. The government emphasised that the breakdown during 2000 of a fresh round of UN-sponsored talks between the Turkish Cypriot and Greek Cypriot governments limited the scope for rapprochement between Greece and Turkey.[19] But in what they have said and omitted to say, Turkish military and political leaders have indicated that they want the new climate to continue; and the Greek government has reciprocated.[20]

The Balkans

Relations, 1974–89

In their quest for allies against Turkey, successive Greek governments after 1974 further improved their relations with other Balkan countries, and secured their backing on the Cyprus issue. In 1984, interchange started even with isolationist Albania: the Greek government declared the frontier to be final, and it was opened for visits in both directions. Especially warm relations were established with the old enemy, Bulgaria, through an agreement in 1986 to consult in the event of threats to security. What these moves lacked was much significant practical outcome apart from mutual reassurance of peaceful intentions.[21]

Moreover relations with Yugoslavia deteriorated, after Tito's death in 1980 removed a check on nationalist propaganda by the Socialist Republic of Macedonia. In the increasingly liberal conditions of the 1980s, Greeks and foreign observers became more aware of the existence in Greece of people who still spoke slav Macedonian and had distinct cultural customs, their cause being advocated by their old ally the Greek Communist Party. Among slav Macedonians, a movement for human rights grew up which called itself the Macedonian Movement for Balkan Prosperity in 1991, but won only 7,263 votes in the elections to the European Parliament in 1994.[22]

Confrontation with FYROM
(Former Yugoslav Republic of Macedonia)

In the Balkans as in most of the former Soviet empire, the collapse of communist authority in 1989–91 ignited old ethnic tensions, which successor governments either exploited or proved incapable of managing. Particularly serious were the conflicts following the dissolution of most of Yugoslavia in 1991–92. The sudden crisis on its doorstep caught the Greek government unprepared. As late as 1992, Greek politicians had no coherent policies towards the new Balkan states, and diplomats and businessmen had few links with them. Greek governments were also handicapped by domestic instability in 1989–90, and after that by financial weakness which for some time prevented them from participating in aid to the enfeebled Balkan economies.[23]

For Greece, the outstanding obstacle to peaceful relations with the Balkans was at first the declaration of independence from Yugoslavia by the Socialist Republic of Macedonia in September 1991. To Greeks, the name Macedonia had been tolerable only so long as it applied to a part of Yugoslavia. As the name of a sovereign state, it seemed dangerous, because it appeared to imply a claim over other parts of the ancient province, which had originally been Greek-speaking and now lay partly in Greece. The new state worsened the provocation by inserting in its constitution words which might be taken to imply claims on Greek territory, and adopting on its flag the symbol of the ancient royal house. Most Greeks reacted angrily, and their feelings were expressed in vast rallies. The minority who resisted this sentiment, which included many foreign-educated intellectuals as well as the minor left-wing parties, were sometimes subjected to harassment by zealots who had sympathisers in the major parties and among journalists, the army and police. Treatment of the issue by both the tabloid and quality press was characterised by 'self-delusion, emotionalism, one-sidedness, and fanaticism' as a Greek analyst later put it.[24]

The apparent threat coincided with others, which exacerbated public sensitivities. The Turkish government was taking an alarming interest in the Muslims of Greek Thrace, and seemed to be establishing influence over an 'Islamic arc' of peoples spread across Greece, Bulgaria, former Yugoslav Macedonia, Albania, Kosovo and Bosnia. Meanwhile there were much-publicised cases of victimisation of ethnic Greeks in Albania. The Albanian government revived claims for compensation for the Albanian-speaking Muslims who had fled, or been expelled, from Greece at the end of the German occupation in 1944. Meanwhile, many people in Greece still felt that the country had some moral claim over southern Albania or 'Northern Epirus', where Greek nationalists received open support from the Bishop of Epirus and covert support from the Greek government. For fear of contacts between Turkish-speaking Muslims in Greece and those of southern Bulgaria, Greece for some time restricted border crossings with that country to one. During the civil war in Bosnia in 1992–95, the Greek government was the only one in NATO to show sympathy with Serbia by allowing, or failing to prevent, leaks in UN sanctions, so in effect encouraging the Serbian president, Slobodan Milosevic, who had become a major force for instability in the Balkans. Greek sympathy with Serbia had old origins, and was renewed by joint antipathy to Muslim and slav Macedonian aspirations. The Greek prime minister did, however, publicly reject in 1992 Milosevic's secret offer to partition the new Macedonian state. In various ways, the Greek government for about three years missed opportunities to gain influence and assist reconstruction in the post-communist Balkans.[25]

Particularly pointless was a campaign of destabilisation against self-styled Macedonia, whose survival was clearly in Greece's interest, as a buffer against possible future expansion by Albania or Bulgaria. While protesting officially against implied claims by this new state, the Greek government quickly realised that its chief complaint – the name – was untenable, while realising also that it would be suicidal to admit this inside Greece. The title proposed by the United Nations in 1993, the Former Yugoslav Republic of Macedonia (FYROM), did not meet Greek objections, but attracted international recognition and attained provisional acceptance in Greece. Andreas Papandreou characteristically outdid the New Democracy government in nationalist demagoguery. However he himself was outflanked by Antonis Samaras, who was dismissed as Foreign Minister in April 1992 because of his aggressive stance on the issue, and in June 1993 established a splinter party, Political Spring. Soon afterwards the withdrawal of support by deputies who sympathised with Samaras led to the government's fall. Then in February 1994, as new prime minister, Andreas Papandreou imposed against the state a trade embargo which lasted eighteen months, and ended with an agreement by FYROM, in September 1995, to satisfy Greek objections to its constitution and flag though not its name. By that time public excitement in Greece had largely died down, and the agreement was greeted with general relief. Greek critics of their government pointed out that the same objectives could have been attained without fuss over three years earlier. Emanating from nationalist advisers of Papandreou not the Department of Foreign Affairs, the embargo was the nadir of Greek diplomacy towards the Balkans, isolating Greece diplomatically and damaging its economic interests. As Mitsotakis admitted in 1995 of his own and Papandreou's government, 'a wave [of public feeling] grew which overwhelmed us'.[26]

Rejoining the Balkans

In other ways also, Greek policy towards the Balkans became conciliatory and constructive in 1995. Greece settled some outstanding differences with Albania. The police took decisive action against Greek terrorists operating in 'Northern Epirus' from bases within Greece; while the Albanian government relaxed somewhat its repression of ethnic Greeks. Restrictions on movement across the border with Bulgaria were reduced. Greece started to play a more active and systematic role in the Black Sea Economic Cooperation Group which it had joined in 1992. This resulted in the formation of a Black Sea Trade and Development Bank based in Salonika, and a permanent secretariat in Istanbul.[27] From 1995, commercial and military relations between Greece and FYROM developed steadily; while the movement of visitors between them surged. So declined the old isolation of slav Macedonian speakers in Greece from their relatives and compatriots across the border. Later, Greek troops assisted the reconstruction of the Albanian army after its disintegration in 1997. Greece convened a meeting of Balkan foreign ministers in Salonika in June 1997 and a meeting of Balkan heads of government in Crete the following November. The latter proved to be the first of a regular series, devoted to the development of good relations and economic cooperation. So Greece started actively to promote stability, democracy and economic recovery. It was equipped for the role by being what all other Balkan governments aspired to: an experienced parliamentary democracy, a mature capitalist economy and a member of the EU and NATO. These were facts in which Greek politicians took legitimate pride.

In developing relations with the Balkans, Greek governments were in fact following the lead taken by businessmen, who had since at least as early as 1993 been finding in these countries markets and investment opportunities. The new direction in Balkan policy was systematised by Kostas Simitis and by his successive Foreign Ministers; nor was it opposed by New Democracy. By 1996, trade with the rest of the Balkans (except for still-devastated Bosnia) was worth well over twice what it had been in 1992 and growing. Greece was now one of the largest foreign investors in Albania and Bulgaria, and a major trading partner of FYROM. By 2000, according to the Federation of Greek Industries, over 3,500 Greek companies had invested $3.4 billion in Balkan countries in the previous ten years. In February 2001, 2,535 Greek businesses have investments totalling $2.4 billion in Balkan countries. In addition, transnational companies are using Greece as a base for penetration of the Balkans, and Greek ships are carrying much of Bulgarian and Romanian trade. Central aims of the government are now to encourage and protect this trade and investment, and it is assisting the latter with guarantees. In 2000, the Greek government invited and received applications for grants totalling $326 million in 2001–5 from six Balkan countries (counting Kosovo as one), to be spent on projects in which Greek companies have a majority holding. Salonika is becoming both a base for such programmes and the main commercial centre of the Balkans.[28]

It is clear however that the economic future of the Balkans lies in association with the EU as a whole, which in 1996 was the main trading partner of nearly all the other Balkan countries as it was of Greece. Trade between the Balkans and Greece was admittedly growing, and is now said to include about one-fifth of Greek exports.[29] Meanwhile the main military force in the Balkans is NATO, in which of course the United States takes the leading role. Balkan countries' aspirations to join the EU and NATO are supported by Greece. Their admission still seems many years away, a fact which gives Greece scope in the meantime for regional leadership.

Simitis's government accepted the obligations of NATO membership to the extent of officially supporting NATO's war in April–June 1999 against the rump state of Yugoslavia (consisting of Serbia and its smaller partner Montenegro) to stop its oppression of the ethnically Albanian inhabitants of Kosovo. The Greek public nevertheless abhorred the war as great-power coercion of a traditionally sympathetic Balkan country. Milosevic was now President of Yugoslavia, but still represented militant Serb nationalism. Thereafter Greece played an independent and valuable role by pressing within NATO and the EU for a more conciliatory and constructive policy towards Yugoslavia. Greece began to support the internal opposition to

Milosevic and so exercised unique influence in Yugoslavia after his downfall in October 2000. The Greek foreign minister immediately acclaimed his successor Vojislav Kostunica as 'a good and dear friend', and has supported Yugoslavia's admission to the family of Balkan states.

The need for cooperation between other Balkan states is obviously pressing. One reason is that militant nationalism still threatens regional peace. Currently the chief threat comes from ethnic Albanian extremists encouraged by Kosovo's effective secession from Yugoslavia in 1999, and affronted by the lack of autonomy of the large ethnically Albanian minority in FYROM. The Greek government – aware of its own population of Albanian immigrants – shares an interest with most of its neighbours in promoting the democratic resolution of ethnic tensions and maintaining the sanctity of existing frontiers.

Greece has also contributed substantially to economic and military programmes for stabilisation of the Balkans. One is the Balkan Stability Pact, a programme of international aid for cross-border development projects that was initiated by many countries including the United States and the EU in July 1999, and another is the European Agency for Reconstruction directed towards ruined Kosovo, where 1,500 Greek troops now participate in peacekeeping. In August 2000, the Greek government discussed exercises by a multi-national brigade in which the Albanians, FYROM, Bulgaria, Romania and Turkey agreed to participate.

Interest in Balkan cooperation has come also from non-government bodies acting on their own initiative.[30] Balkan NGOs, organised in a federation, have taken an active role in promoting the aims of the Balkan Stability Pact, with support from the Greek government. A conference on environmental problems was organised by the Prefect of Lesbos in 1998, that was attended by, among other people, 80 Turkish prefects, professors and specialists. Another conference was organised by the Technical Chamber of Greece in Salonika in 1999 (attended by representatives of all Balkan countries) on preservation of the Balkan artistic heritage. In May 2000, the Ecumenical Patriarch of the Orthodox Church began a series of talks between representatives of different religious denominations of the Balkans (Orthodox Christians, Muslims, Jews and Roman Catholics) in order to discuss cooperation to several ends, including the promotion of peace and political stability, means of cooperation between religious groups and the reduction of youth unemployment. There were also meetings in 2000 between representatives of the film institutes, the theatrical organisations and the judicial prosecutors of Balkan countries. The growth in Greece of cultural interest in neighbouring countries is indicated by the appearance of at least two university departments of Balkan studies, and a projected department of Turkish studies in the University of Athens.

Thus the spirit of Greek policy towards the Balkans differs greatly from that of the early 1990s. What is still lacking in 2000 is an efficient administrative framework to give substance to the gestures of cooperation made by Balkan governments and NGOs. One current example is the delay in dispensation of aid under the Balkan Stability Pact. Another is the helplessness of governments to combat the monstrous, organised crime – especially traffic in drugs, white slaves and guns – which flourishes under the weak post-communist regimes and freely crosses their borders.

Notes

1 Susannah Verney, 'The political parties and entry into the EEC, 1974–9: a foreign view', *Contemporary Themes* 38 (in Greek, 1989), 63.

2 Giannis G. Valinakis, *Introduction to Greek Foreign Policy, 1949–88* (in Greek, Salonika, 1989), 217–22, 277–9; John O. Iatrides, 'Greece in the Cold War and Beyond', *Journal of the Hellenic Diaspora* 19 (1993), 25; Theodore A. Couloumbis, 'The structures of Greek foreign policy', in Richard Clogg (ed.), *Greece in the 1980s* (1983), 104–5.

3 John O. Iatrides, 'Papandreou's foreign policy', in Theodore C. Kariotis (ed.), *The Greek Socialist Experiment. Papandreou's Greece, 1981–9* (New York 1992), 132–59; Kevin Featherstone *et al.*, 'Greece and the negotiation of economic and monetary union: preferences, strategies, and institutions', *Journal of Modern Greek Studies* 18 (2000), 409.

4 'Structures', in Clogg (ed.), *Greece*, 116–17.

5 P.C. Ioakimidis, 'Greece in the EEC: policies, experience and prospects', in Harry J. Psomiades and Stavros Thomadakis (eds), *Greece, the New Europe and the Changing International Order* (New York 1993), 415–16.

6 John O. Iatrides, 'The United States, Greece, and the Balkans', in Van Coufoudakis, Harry J. Psomiades and Andre Gerolymatos (eds), *Greece and the New Balkans. Challenges and Opportunities* (New York 1999), 293.

7 Valinakis, *Introduction*, 268.

8 Van Coufoudakis, 'Greek–Turkish relations in the post-Cold War era: implications of the American response', *The Cyprus Review* 9 (1997), 11–13.

9 Tozun Bahcheli, *Greek–Turkish Relations since 1955* (1990), 139–41.

10 *Economist*, 6 June 2000, Turkey Survey, 5.

11 Thanos Veremis, *History of Greek–Turkish Relations, 1453–1998* (in Greek, 2nd edn, 1999), 162–3; *Vima*, 18 March 2001, A26, A. Papachela (citing American sources).

12 Richard Clogg, 'Greek–Turkish relations in the post-1974 period', in Dimitri Constas (ed.), *The Greek–Turkish Conflict in the 1990s. Domestic and External Influences* (1991), 17.

13 Bahcheli, *Greek–Turkish Relations*, 156; Heinz Kramer, 'Turkish relations with Greece: motives and interests', and Athanasios Platias 'Greece's strategic doctrine: in search of autonomy and deterrence', in Dimitri Constas (ed.), *The Greek–Turkish Conflict in the 1990s. Domestic and External Influences* (1991), 68, 95–6, 100.

14 Dimitri Constas and Charalambos Papasotiriou, 'Greek policy responses to the post-Cold War Balkan environment', in Coufoudakis, Psomiades and Gerolymatos (eds), *Greece*, 220; Thanos P. Dokos, 'Greek defense doctrine in the post-Cold War era', in ibid., 256–7; Nikos Antonakis, *Political Economy of Defence in Postwar Greece* (in Greek, n.d.), 103; *Economist*, 6 October 1993, 56; *Economist*, 10 June 2000, 'Turkey. Survey', 5; *Kathimerini*, 10 July 2000, citing government figures.

15 *Vima*, 23 July 1995, A37; *Vima*, 1 June 1997, A45; *Kathimerini*, 15 November 1998, 37.

16 Susannah Verney, 'Greece: a new era', *Mediterranean Politics* 2 (1997), 199; Alexander Kazamias, 'The quest for modernization in Greek foreign policy and its limitations', *Mediterranean Politics* 2 (1997), 83.

17 Veremis, *History*, 155–7.

18 Theodore A. Couloumbis, 'Greek–Turkish relations: the dawn of a new era?' *Athens News*, 18 December 1999; *Kathimerini*, 10 November 2000.

19 *Kathimerini* (English Internet edition), 29 January 2001.

20 *Kathimerini*, 10 August 2000; *Vima*, 21 January 2001, A. Kourkoula; *Vima*, 29 April 2001, Gianni Kartali.

21 Richard Clogg, 'Greece and the Balkans', in Psomiades and Thomadakis (eds), *Greece*, 427–34; Evangelos Kofos, 'Greece and the Balkans, 1974–86', in Speros Vryonis Jr (ed.), *Greece on the Road to Democracy: from the Junta to PASOK, 1974–86* (New York 1991), 115–17.

22 Loring Danforth, *The Macedonian Conflict. Ethnic Nationalism in a Transnational World* (Princeton, NJ 1995), 116–26; Victor Roudometof, 'Nationalism and identity politics in the Balkans: Greece and the Macedonian question', *Journal of Modern Greek Studies* 14 (1996), 270.

23 Axel S. Wallden, 'Greece and eastern Europe: economic relations', in Psomiades and Thomadakis (eds), *Greece*, 305–6.

24 Roe Panayotopoulou, 'The construction of ethnocentric stereotypes by the press: the example of the Macedonian issue', *Review of Social Research* 89–90 (in Greek, 1996), 250.

25 Axell S. Wallden, 'NATO, Greece and the Balkans in the Post-Cold War era', in Coufoudakis, Psomiades and Gerolymatos (eds), *Greece*, 79–80; *Vima*, 11 October 1992, A21, St. Evstathiadi.

26 Panayotopoulou, 'Construction', 260; Nikolaos Zahariadis, 'Greek policy towards the Former Yugoslav Republic of Macedonia, 1991–5', *Journal of Modern Greek Studies* 14 (1996), 320–1; Evangelos Kofos, 'Greece's Macedonian adventure: the controversy over FYROM's recognition', in Coufoudakis, Psomiades and Gerolymatos (eds), *Greece*, 379.

27 Giannis Valinakis, 'Greece and the Black Sea Economic Cooperation Group', and Dimitrios Triantafyllou, 'Recent developments in Greece's Balkan diplomacy networks', in Coufoudakis, Psomiades and Gerolymatos (eds), *Greece*, 133–4, 158–9.

28 *Kathimerini*, 3 September 2000, 55, Evgenia Tzortzi; *Vima*, 18 March 2001, B12, D. Charontaki.

29 Wallden, 'Greece and the Balkans: economic relations', and P.C. Ioakimides, 'Greece, the European Union, and Southeastern Europe: past failures and future prospects', in Coufoudakis, Psomiades and Gerolymatos (eds), *Greece*, 102, 189; *Kathimerini*, 10 November 2000.

30 *Athens News*, 7 June 2000; *Vima*, 15 March 1998, A20; *Vima*, 24 January 1999, A49; *Kathimerini*, 1 November 2000; 20 November 2000 (English Internet edition); 11 February 2001.

CHAPTER THIRTEEN

Whither Now?

December 2000 does not feel like a terminal point for this history, but rather like the middle of various intriguing developments. Where will they lead?

One question is: can the government make sufficient progress towards its goals of financial recovery and structural reforms in the economy? Its sense of triumph was short-lived after June 2000, when Greece qualified for inclusion in EMU. The government still confronted its long-term tasks, and the impression of indecision and exhaustion which it now gives can be explained by their appalling difficulty. As the opposition parties cannot convince anyone that they can do better, there is a vacuum of leadership, which is provoking a level of public disillusionment with both major parties which is high even by the standards of recent years.[1]

One difficult task for the government is to budget for a surplus from now on, which requires that revenue collection continues to rise steeply. Budget surpluses are necessary to prevent inflation, now that the government has lost control over credit policy with its entry into EMU. Surpluses are also necessary for paying off the public debt (still about 100 per cent of GDP), so as to satisfy the EU authorities, and lighten the annual burden of interest payments. According to international monitors, nominal tax rates are already so high as to constrain economic activity. The emphasis, then, must be on more efficient collection of existing taxes, for which both the government and the OECD believe that there is scope. So the government will presumably increase its efforts to bring the black economy within the tax net, at the inevitable cost of even worse relations with the majority of citizens. There is clearly scope, also, for the social insurance funds to reform their methods of collecting dues.

It does not seem that the government can achieve an overall reduction of expenditure. While it must decline in certain areas – notably the subsidisation of state enterprises – it will have to increase on a range of social services, especially education, health care and programmes to reduce unemployment and help disadvantaged groups. In addition, the government will probably have to spend more on the social insurance system merely to enable the largest funds to pay their current retirement pensions – which for most recipients are meagre by Greek standards. The government must at the same time prepare for the 2004 Olympic Games and continue an ambitious programme of rearmament.

These tasks requires a rate of economic growth for the foreseeable future (over 4 per cent) which will be high both by average EU standards in recent years, and by Greek standards in the last 20 years. Such growth might conceivably be attained, but only so long as there are no serious setbacks in the international economy. Then growth must continue after 2006, when structural subsidies from the EU are scheduled to decline sharply. In the meantime, the current account deficit must be contained in the face of intensified commercial competition from the rest of the EU and from transnational companies which have invested in it. The government is obliged to report regularly to the European Commission on progress towards all these financial and economic goals; and has accordingly submitted to it, in December 2000, a Programme of Development and Stability, which predicts growth well above 4 per cent, but is considered rather optimistic by international bodies including the OECD.

The benefits of EMU membership (particularly the major decline in interest rates), and the stimulus of preparations for the Olympic Games, improve the prospects of economic growth. But, in order to make the economy more competitive, the government must continue with much greater determination its attempts to sell state-owned sectors of the economy and to curb restrictive practices of all kinds. The former task will also yield much-needed revenue; but its accomplishment depends on the availability of purchasers at a time of slump in the stock market and limited foreign investment. The abolition of restrictive or monopolistic practices requires concessions from dozens of powerful interest groups – some of which have strong allies within the ruling party. The concessions must be secured by patient negotiation and subtle pressure – which governments have not proved good at in the past.

Examples of these vested interests will illustrate the difficulties. Trade unions must somehow be persuaded to allow employers greater freedom to sack redundant staff, and to vary working hours. A general strike on 10 October 2000 warned the government to tread cautiously in this regard. Many occupation groups must be persuaded to abandon practices lucrative to themselves but costly to the public: such as the current requirement that lawyers attend conveyancing transactions, or the current freedom of physicians to prescribe unnecessary treatment and medication. Forceful action by the government against such occupational privileges is likely to precipitate further damaging strikes. The state-owned industries and utilities – with all their legally protected employees – must be persuaded to surrender further claims to government assistance as the government sells them off, partially or wholly; and the latter task has so far proved very difficult.[2]

All these reforms are impeded by a domestic climate of social tension and economic insecurity, besides the public distrust of government that has always existed. Lower income groups are sullen because of the sacrifices which they have made in recent years. A sizeable minority of the population lives below, or just at, a standard which nowadays is generally regarded as adequate. The rate of unemployment has only just started to decline, and is still causing much anxiety: for example, a recent poll showed that one-third of the population is worried about job security.[3] These causes of discontent are reflected in fresh opinion polls showing a higher proportion in Greece than in any other EU country of people who are pessimistic about their material prospects. Increased social expenditure is therefore vital to the government's survival.

We have noted encouraging signs – especially in recent years – that the necessary structural reforms are occurring in government and the economy: state enterprises have been sold; high-technology exports have increased; labour productivity has improved in much of the economy; exporters and investors have made fresh inroads into Balkan and Turkish markets; citizen satisfaction with several public utilities has increased; consumers are paying lower prices in some sectors of the economy as a result of greater competition within them; the current boom in consumer credit is stimulating, among other things, a rapid increase in Internet usage. The tax department has greatly increased its revenue by computerising its records; and clearly the social insurance funds could do the same. But we have also noticed the persistence of various fundamental weaknesses in the economy. So the question is whether structural reforms can be accomplished fast enough.

Another question is: can Greece continue to improve its relations with its neighbours? There seems here to be some cause for reserved optimism. The improved relations with Turkey may well continue, although probably with background tension and periodic quarrels. Currently, a cause of serious dissent is the prospect that the Republic of Cyprus will be admitted to the EU without its Turkish Cypriot counterpart. However, grounds for optimism are the continuing strength of pressure within Turkey for membership of the EU, even after the stiff conditions have been confirmed. One of them is that the military abandons its interference in domestic politics and foreign policy, and another is that Turkey makes more effort to resolve its differences with Greece. Besides, as governmental finances are much weaker in Turkey even than in Greece, the economic burden of militarism there is proving unsustainable.

In the western Balkans (covered by Albania, Bosnia, FYROM and Yugoslavia with its components, Serbia, Montenegro and Kosovo), relations between national groups remain alarmingly volatile, and militant nationalism is still a dangerous force. The chief cause for optimism lies in the growing preference that most or all Balkan governments have shown – especially since the downfall of Milosevic – for peaceful external relations and consultative internal procedures, if only so that they can qualify for aid from, and closer relations with, the EU. Unfortunately this spirit among political leaders is being severely tested by Albanian nationalists in FYROM, and to a lesser extent by Montenegrin secessionists in Yugoslavia.

The Greek government, motivated especially by concern for its trade and investments, is likely to continue providing constructive regional leadership in the Balkans, by mediating between national groups and advocating the case of their governments within the EU and NATO. If relations with its neighbours do improve, it will be possible for Greece to continue expanding its economic relations with them, and eventually reduce its defence expenditure. It seems probable, also, that contacts of different kinds (governmental, commercial, diplomatic, cultural and recreational) between Greece and its neighbours to the north and east will continue to strengthen, as they have done in a remarkable way since 1995.

A broad question about Greece's internal affairs is whether the recent signs of progress towards a civic community (see above, p. 256) can be maintained. One reason for optimism is the increasing strength of counterforces to the government: parliament, local authorities, judiciary, the media, trade unions, business groups, independent administrative authorities and NGOs. Governments have no choice but to become more accountable to them, and also to show increasing respect for the law which forms the only possible framework for relations between them all. Meanwhile, the increasing vigour of NGOs seems to be a sign of strengthening civic consciousness. They form part of a more effective public opinion, which is likely to maintain pressure on governments to improve the competence and honesty of public administration. In the last respect, there are grounds for thinking (p. 241) that there has been some progress in the 1990s, although the reports by the ombudsman for 1999–2000 show that there is far to go.

Meanwhile, public expectations of the government are continuously rising, which explains in part the volume of criticism of most government-run institutions. It also helps explain the growing competition by private service-providers with government bodies in various areas, including telecommunications, health, education, air transport and banking. This encroachment by private services seems likely to continue, because they are fulfilling strong public needs.

In the Preface, I suggest that there are dichotomies which can be traced to the origins of the modern state in the 1820s. These have become especially intense in recent years; and the signs are that they will continue. Mechanisms have been established to make the public administration more efficient and impartial; but politicians and other interest groups will presumably continue attempts to penetrate and corrupt it. Fortunately, the media and opposition parties have proved increasingly keen to denounce such activities. Especially at risk of perversion are the municipalities, which have recently expanded their responsibilities, and the police, which face new challenges from masses of desperate immigrants and from criminal gangs crossing national frontiers.

The extended family, with its circle of friends and patrons, continues to have immense value for nearly everyone in the current climate of economic insecurity and political disillusionment. The symptoms of social malaise that have become widespread in developed western countries largely as a result of the weakening of family ties – for example lonely old people, homeless or fatherless children, drug addiction and suicide among youth, and various common crimes – have remained comparatively limited in Greece. The question remains whether this loyalty to the primary social unit can be reconciled with increasing respect for the public interest.

The traditional competition between modernisers and traditionalists is also intense. Governments will no doubt maintain their strenuous attempts to adopt western models of political and economic organisation. The prime minister, for example, has just announced – referring particularly to reform of public finances – that convergence with the EU demands 'a change of mentality and culture'.[4] Such a change has for a long time past been made, without government encouragement, by masses of aspiring professional people who have earned postgraduate degrees in western universities. Currently, several large firms are meeting the requirements for listing on foreign stock exchanges. Yet western ideas of various kinds have been contested vigorously in recent years by the Orthodox Church, which under new leadership has in some ways gained influence. The Church seems set to lose the battle over identity cards; but will probably fight governments over other issues, such as the religious freedom of Muslim immigrants.

The tension between modernisers and traditionalists has also been caused, in a more subtle way, by the recent renewal of contacts with other Balkan countries. As a result, the country is likely to feel a stronger affinity in coming years with these neighbours with which it shares so much of its history, and in the process will probably become culturally more tolerant and open-minded. Meanwhile, Greece will continue to blend western and

Balkan values in a unique way, having become the most westernised of Balkan countries while remaining strongly attached to its own heritage.

Notes

1   *Vima*, 17 December 2000, A15; *Vima*, 25 March 2001, A4, 6; *Kathimerini* (English Internet edition), 2 May 2001.

2   *Kathimerini* (English Internet edition), 6 December 2000.

3   *Kathimerini* (English Internet edition), 10 January 2001; *Vima*, 17 December 2000, D4, Nikou Nikolaou.

4   *Athens News*, 6 December 2000.

A GUIDE TO FURTHER READING

This bibliography is not meant to be exhaustive, and is confined to books in English.

Among the brief histories, an especially useful work is Richard Clogg, *A Concise History of Greece* (1992), with appendices including biographies of key figures, statistics and chronological tables. This covers the period from 1770 to 1990. On nationalism, Gerasimos Augustinos wrote 'Hellenism and the modern Greeks', in Peter F. Sugar (ed.), *Eastern European Nationalism in the Twentieth Century* (Washington, DC 1995). There is a historically based analysis by Andreas I. Psomas, *The Nation, the State, and the International System. The Case of Modern Greece* (Athens 1978). Nicos P. Mouzelis wrote two stimulating surveys: *Modern Greece. Facets of Underdevelopment* (1978), and *Politics in the Semi-Periphery. Early Parliamentarism and Late Industrialisation in the Balkans and Latin America* (1986). A useful reference book to recent decades is George A. Kourvetaris and Betty A. Dobratz, *A Profile of Modern Greece. In Search of Identity* (Oxford 1987). There is a thorough bibliography of works on modern Greece by Thanos Veremis and Mark Dragoumis, *Greece* (Oxford 1998). This covers books, articles and chapters, and reviews each work.

On the Balkans, there are Barbara Jelavich, *A History of the Balkans. The Twentieth Century* (1983, the second of two volumes), and Mark Mazower, *The Balkans. A Short History* (New York 2000).

On the early postwar period in Greece, there is my *Origins of the Greek Civil War* (1995), which gives special attention to the years 1943–46, but includes a survey of the prewar period and of the civil war itself. There is also the work edited by myself, *The Greek Civil War, 1943–50. Studies of Polarization* (1993), which includes my analyses of the military history of the war and of the reconstruction of the political system from 1944. Important collections of essays are contained in John O. Iatrides (ed.), *Greece in the 1940s. A Nation in Crisis* (1981); Lars Baerentzen, John O. Iatrides and Ole L. Smith, *Studies in the History of the Greek Civil War, 1945–9* (Copenhagen 1987); and John O. Iatrides and Linda Wrigley (eds), *Greece at the Crossroads. The Civil War and its Legacy* (1995). Recent research is contained in Mark Mazower (ed.), *After the War Was Over. Reconstructing the Family, Nation and State in Greece, 1943–60* (Princeton, NJ 2000).

Some of the foregoing works contain analyses of United States intervention, which is the subject of Lawrence Wittner, *American Intervention in Greece, 1943–9* (New York 1982). A well-documented study of British policy is by Thanasis D. Sfikas, *The British Labour Government and the Greek Civil War* (Keele 1994). There is also Robert Frazier, *Anglo-American Relations with Greece: the Coming of the Cold War, 1942–7* (New York 1991).

On the Communist Party, useful accounts are Haris Vlavianos, *Greece, 1941–9. From Occupation to Resistance to Civil War. The Strategy of the Greek Communist Party* (1992), and Peter J. Stavrakis, *Moscow and Greek Communism, 1944–9* (Ithaca, NY 1989).

Perceptive and still valuable accounts were written by British and American observers of events in the late 1940s. The diplomat and later historian, William H. McNeill, wrote or co-authored a series of books: *The Greek Dilemma. War and Aftermath* (New York 1947), then (with Frank Smothers and Elizabeth McNeill), *Report on the Greeks* (New York 1948), as well as *Greece. American Aid in Action, 1947–56* (New York 1957), followed by *The Metamorphosis of Greece since World War II* (Oxford 1978). There are informative works by Leften S. Stavrianos, *Greece. American Dilemma and Opportunity* (Chicago, IL 1952) and C.A. Munkman, *American Aid to Greece* (New York 1958). These generally favourable, and very informative, accounts of the impact of American intervention counterbalance several more critical works (cited above) published from the late 1970s in the aftermath of the Vietnam War. Perceptive memoirs which capture the atmosphere of the time are: *Memories of a Mountain War* (1972) by the BBC reporter Kenneth Matthews, and *The Flight of Ikaros. Travels in Greece during a Civil War* (1984) by an American student, Kevin Andrews.

On the post-civil war regime, there is John Campbell and Philip Sherrard, *Modern Greece* (1968), which is strong on politics, society and economy in the 1950s and 1960s. On an important aspect of politics from 1946 to 1985, there is Richard Clogg, *Parties and Elections in Greece. The Search for Legitimacy* (1987). On the political system in the post-civil war period, there is Keith Legg, *Politics in Modern Greece* (Stanford, CA 1969). The key figure of Karamanlis is studied, with the use of the subject's papers, by C.M. Woodhouse, in *Karamanlis. The Restorer of Greek Democracy* (Oxford 1982). On another important aspect of politics, extending to the 1980s, there is Thimios Zaharopoulos and Manny E. Paraschos, *Mass Media in Greece. Power, Politics and Privatization* (Westport, CT 1993).

Studies of relations with the United States include Yannis P. Roubatis, *Tangled Webs. The United States in Greece, 1947–67* (New York 1987); the work edited by Theodore A. Couloumbis and John O. Iatrides, *Greek–American Relations. A Critical Review* (New York 1980); and that edited by Theodore A. Couloumbis, John A. Petropulos and Harry J. Psomiades, *Foreign Interference in Greek Politics. An Historical Perspective* (New York 1976). On a related aspect of foreign relations, there are Theodore A. Couloumbis, *The United States, Greece and Turkey. The Troubled Triangle* (New York 1983), and Tozun Bahcheli, *Greek–Turkish Relations since 1955* (1990). On the European Economic Community, there is Susannah Verney, 'Greece and the European Community', in Kevin Featherstone and Dimitrios K. Katsoudas (eds), *Political Change in Greece. Before and After the Colonels* (1987). In the same book, there is a chapter by Van Coufoudakis entitled 'Greek foreign policy: 1945–1985'.

On a controversial aspect of national identity, there are many works including: Anastasia Karakasidou, *Fields of Wheat, Hills of Blood. Passages to Nationhood in Greek Macedonia, 1870–1990* (New York 1997) and Peter Mackridge and Eleni Yannakakis (eds), *Ourselves and Others. The Development of a Greek–Macedonian Identity since 1912* (1997).

Economic history is surveyed by A.F. Freris, *The Greek Economy in the Twentieth Century* (1986), Wray O. Candilis, *The Economy of Greece, 1944–66. Efforts for Stability and Development* (New York 1968) and Persefoni V. Tsaliki, *The Greek Economy. Sources of Growth in the Post-War Era* (New York 1991). Important information on the Federation of Greek Industries, and on the policy decisions arising from relations with the European Economic Community, is contained in Kostas A. Lavdas, *The Europeanization of Greece. Interest Politics and the Crises of Integration* (1997), a work extending to the 1990s. An excellent study of an important industry is Gelina A. Harlaftis, *Greek Shipowners and Greece, 1945–75. From Separate Development to Mutual Interdependence* (1993).

Among a wealth of studies of rural society, one with a strong sense of context is John K. Campbell, *Honour, Family, and Patronage. A Study of Institutions and Values in a Greek Mountain Community* (Oxford 1964). There are also Ernestine Friedl, *Vasilika. A Village in Modern Greece* (New York 1962) and Juliet du Boulay, *Portrait of a Greek Mountain Village* (Oxford 1974). Anthropological studies of urban communities are less common. One of them is Renée Hirschon, *Heirs of the Greek Catastrophe. The Social Life of Asia Minor Refugees in Piraeus* (1989). Insights on the effects on family life of movement from village to city are contained in Mariella Doumanis, *Mothering in Greece: from Collectivism to Individualism* (New York 1983). Overlapping in scope with anthropological and social studies already referred to is Jill Dubisch (ed.), *Gender and Power in Rural Greece* (Princeton, NJ 1986). Peter Loizos and Evthymios Papataxiarchis edited an important collection of articles, *Contested Identities. Gender and Kinship in Modern Greece* (Princeton, NJ 1991).

On the development of the metropolitan region, there is Lila Leontidou, *The Mediterranean City in Transition. Social Change and Urban Development* (Cambridge 1990). A study of a social group is Alec P. Alexander, *Greek Industrialists. An Economic and Social Analysis* (Athens 1964).

Trade unionism is covered in Theodore K. Katsanevas, *Trade Unions in Greece. An Analysis of Factors Determining their Growth and Present Structure* (Athens 1984), and Chris Jecchinis, *Trade Unionism in Greece. A Study in Political Paternalism* (Chicago, IL 1967).

Especially useful on social differences in access to higher education are the essays in Jane Lambiri-Dimaki, *Social Stratification in Greece. Eleven Essays* (Athens 1983).

Sympathetic studies of the Church in the post-civil war period are: Peter Hammond, *The Waters of Marah: the Present State of the Greek Church* (1956) and Kallistos Ware, 'The Church in a time of transition', in Richard Clogg (ed.), *Greece in the 1980s* (1983). Under the name Timothy Ware, the same author wrote *The Orthodox Church* (1963), much of which is especially relevant to Greece.

The military dictatorship was soon subjected to some angry but perceptive studies, including the still useful collection in Richard Clogg (ed.), *Greece under Military Rule* (1972). Later, more detached, studies include the detailed narrative by C.M. Woodhouse, *The Rise and Fall of the Greek Colonels* (1985), the analysis by Thanos Veremis, 'Greece: veto and impasse', in Christopher Clapham and George Philip (eds), *The Political Dilemmas of Military Regimes* (1984) and Constantine Danopoulos, *Warriors and Politicians in Modern Greece* (Chapel Hill, NC 1984).

For politics, society and economy after 1974, see the collection edited by Richard Clogg, *Greece in the 1980s* (1983); that edited by Kevin Featherstone and Dimitrios K. Katsoudas, *Political Change in Greece. Before and After the Colonels* (1987); and that edited by Speros A. Vryonis, *Greece on the Road to Democracy. From the Junta to PASOK, 1974–86* (New York 1991). P. Nikiforos Diamandouros wrote an especially valuable essay, 'Regime change and the prospects for democracy in Greece, 1974–83', in Guillermo O'Donnell, Philippe C. Schmitter and Laurence Whitehead (eds), *Transitions from Authoritarian Rule: Southern Europe* (Baltimore, MD 1986), 138–64.

On the major parties in this period, there is Michael Spourdalakis, 'Securing democracy in post-authoritarian Greece. The role of political parties', in Geoffrey Pridham and Paul G. Lewis (eds), *Stabilizing Fragile Democracies. Comparing New Party Systems in Southern and Eastern Europe* (1996). Also useful on party politics after 1974 is Howard Penniman (ed.), *Greece at the Polls. The National Elections of 1974 and 1977* (Washington, DC 1981). On particular parties there are: Michael Spourdalakis, *The Rise of the Greek Socialist Party* (1988) on PASOK, and Takis S. Pappas, *Making Party Democracy in Greece* (1999) on New Democracy. Michael Spourdalakis wrote on a later phase of PASOK's evolution: 'PASOK in the 1990s. Structure, ideology, political strategy', in José M. Maravall (ed.), *Socialist Parties in Europe* (Barcelona 1991), 157–86.

On the controversial attempts at radical change by Andreas Papandreou's governments in 1981–89, there is an important collection edited by Richard Clogg, *Greece, 1981–9. The Populist Decade* (1993). Other collections on the same subject are: Theodore C. Kariotis (ed.), *The Greek Socialist Experiment. Papandreou's Greece, 1981–9* (New York 1992) and Zafiris Tzannatos (ed.), *Socialism in Greece. The First Four Years* (Aldershot 1986). A longer-term analysis is Dimitri A. Sotiropoulos, *Populism and Bureaucracy: the Case of Greece under PASOK, 1981–9* (South Bend, IN 1996).

On foreign relations in about the last twenty years, there are: Panos Kazakos and Panayotis C. Ioakimidis (eds), *Greece and European Community Membership Evaluated* (1994); Harry J. Psomiades and Stavros Thomadakis (eds), *Greece, the New Europe, and the Changing International Order* (New York 1993); Kevin Featherstone and Kostas Ifantis (eds), *Greece in a Changing Europe. Between European Integration and Balkan Disintegration?* (Manchester 1996) and Van Coufoudakis, Harry J. Psomiades and Andre Gerolymatos (eds), *Greece and the New Balkans. Challenges and Opportunities* (New York 1999). On one stormy area (in the 1970s and 1980s) there is Dimitri Constas (ed.), *The Greek–Turkish Conflict in the 1990s. Domestic and External Influences* (1991). On another aspect, there is Thanos Veremis, *Greece's Balkan Entanglement* (Athens 1995), covering the period from 1975. The volume edited by Psomiades and Thomadakis includes chapters on the Greek state and on culture.

On recent economic history, there is Nicholas Pirounakis, *The Greek Economy. Past, Present and Future* (1997), besides the study by Lavdas referred to earlier. There are important social studies in Dimitri Constas and Theofanis G. Stavrou (eds), *Greece Prepares for the Twenty-first Century* (Baltimore, MD 1995).

Useful reference books to many aspects of society and the economy are the *Concise Statistical Yearbooks* published annually in Athens by the National Statistical Service of Greece, in Greek and English. There is also the work by the European Commission/Eurostat, *Living Conditions in Europe. Statistical Pocketbook* (Luxembourg 2000), and The Economist, *Pocket Europe in Figures* (2000).

Changes of government and head of state

Before 1974, it was usual for the head of state to appoint a temporary, non-party government to supervise a parliamentary election. This explains why several governments resigned shortly before an election.

1945 January. Parliament having been in abeyance since a coup in August 1936, a series of prime ministers were nominated by British representatives, under the regency of Archbishop Damaskinos, between January 1945 and April 1946.

1946 April. After the general election of March, the leader of the People's Party, Konstantinos Tsaldaris, formed a government which lasted until January 1947. Following a referendum in September 1946, George II returned as monarch. On his death in April 1947, he was succeeded by his brother Paul.

Tsaldaris was succeeded as prime minister (January–August 1947) by the non-party figure Dimitrios Maximos. His government, like its predecessor, was dominated by right-wingers, who were monarchist and strongly anti-communist, and were supported by a like-minded majority of parliament.

1947 September. Following American intervention, a short-lived government under Tsaldaris was replaced by a coalition between the People's Party and the Liberal Party, under the Liberal Themistocles Sophoulis as prime minister.

1949 June. On Sophoulis's death, leadership of the coalition government was assumed by the non-party figure Alexandros Diomedis, who remained prime minister until December.

1950 March. Following the electoral success of the centrist and Liberal Parties (distinguished by their preference for conciliation of the left, and their former neutrality on, or opposition to, the restoration of the monarchy), there was until October 1952 a series of short-lived governments, under the alternating leadership of the Liberal Sophocles Venizelos and the centrist Nikolaos Plastiras.

1952 November. Alexandros Papagos formed a government after the electoral victory of his right-wing party the Greek Rally.

1955 October. On the death of Papagos, the king chose Konstantinos Karamanlis as his successor. Karamanlis re-labelled the Greek Rally the National Radical Union, and remained prime minister until his resignation in June 1963 as the result of a disagreement with the monarch.

1963 June. The National Radical Union government was headed by two obscure prime ministers in quick succession, until it lost the general election of November.

1963 November. After election gains, Georgios Papandreou, leader of the Centre Union party which was distasteful to the king, became prime minister, but without an independent parliamentary majority.

1963 December. Karamanlis resigned the leadership of the National Radical Union, which was assumed by Panagiotis Kanellopoulos. Karamanlis chose to live in exile until July 1974.

1964 February. Georgios Papandreou's party won a parliamentary majority in a further election.

1964 March. On King Paul's death, his son Constantine succeeded him.

1965 July. King Constantine II dismissed Georgios Papandreou as prime minister. After a period of instability, Stefanos Stefanopoulos, of the National Radical Union, formed a mainly right-wing government in September with the support of 45 dissident MPs of the Centre Union.

1966 December. Panagiotis Kanellopoulos and Georgios Papandreou agreed that a general election should be held in May. They presumably agreed that the fate of the monarchy should not be an issue. The king accepted the agreement, and appointed a temporary government to prepare for the election.

1967 April. A group of officers ('the Colonels') seized power and established a military dictatorship, 'the Junta'. The regime appointed puppet governments, but power lay mainly with the military conspirators, of whom the key figure until November 1973 was Georgios Papadopoulos, and thenceforth Dimitrios Ioannidis.

1967 December. After an abortive attempt at a coup, King Constantine fled into exile.

1974 July. Military commanders overthrew Ioannidis, and appointed a civilian government, which immediately invited Karamanlis to return and become prime minister.

1974 July. Karamanlis formed a government consisting mainly of former members of the National Radical Union, which he soon re-labelled New Democracy. This won a general election in November 1974, and another in November 1977.

1974 December. Following a referendum, the monarchy was abolished. Under the new constitution of 1975, the head of state was a president elected by parliament. The first was Konstantinos Tsatsos.

1980 April–May. Karamanlis quit the leadership of New Democracy to become new President of Greece. Georgios Rallis was elected leader of New Democracy, and was appointed prime minister.

1981 October. Andreas Papandreou formed a government after his party, PASOK, won an election. He secured a second term of office by winning the following election in 1985.

1981 December. The New Democracy parliamentary party elected Evangelos Averov as leader after Georgios Rallis failed to obtain a vote of confidence from it.

1984 September. After the resignation of Averov, the New Democracy parliamentary party elected Konstantinos Mitsotakis as leader.

1985 March. Karamanlis resigned as President, and in his place was elected the PASOK nominee Christos Sartzetakis.

1989 June. Andreas Papandreou resigned as prime minister after PASOK lost its parliamentary majority in an election. He was succeeded by Giannis Tzannetakis of New Democracy, as head of a coalition government of the Coalition Party and New Democracy.

1989 November. As no party won a majority in the general election of this month, an all-party coalition government was formed under the non-party figure, Xenophon Zolotas.

1990 April. A general election was necessitated by parliament's failure to produce the requisite majority in elections for a new President. Mitsotakis, leader of New Democracy, became prime minister with a narrow parliamentary majority, which consisted of four from November.

1990 May. Karamanlis was elected President of Greece for a second term.

1993 October. After New Democracy lost its parliamentary majority in an election, PASOK returned to power under Andreas Papandreou.

1993 November. After Mitsotakis resigned as leader, the New Democracy parliamentary party elected Miltiadis Evert in his place.

1995 March. At the end of Karamanlis's term, Kostis Stefanopoulos was elected President of Greece.

1996 January. After Andreas Papandreou's resignation, Kostas Simitis was elected prime minister by the PASOK parliamentary party.

1996 June. After Andreas Papandreou's death, Simitis was elected leader of PASOK.

1997 March. Following New Democracy's second successive electoral defeat the previous October, Evert was replaced as leader by Konstantinos Karamanlis junior.

2000 March. Stefanopoulos was re-elected President of Greece.

2000 April. Simitis secured another term as prime minister, following PASOK's third successive electoral victory.

Results of parliamentary elections

The sources for this table are: Richard Clogg, *Parties and Elections in Greece. The Search for Legitimacy* (1987) and Maria M. Mendrinou, *Electoral Politics in the Greek Political System. Domestic and European Parameters, 1974–2000* (in Greek, 2000).

Date	Party	Votes (%)	Seats
1946 March	United Patriotic Camp (monarchist)	55.1	206
	National Political Union (neutral on monarchy)	19.3	68
	Liberal Party (republican)	14.4	48
	Others (mainly monarchist)	11.2	32
1950 March	People's Party	18.8	62
	Liberal Party	17.2	56
	National Progressive Centre Union	16.4	45
	Party of Georgios Papandreou	10.7	35
	Democratic Camp (left)	9.7	18
	Others (mainly right)	27.2	34
1951 September	Greek Rally (right)	36.5	114
	National Progressive Centre Union	23.5	74
	Liberal Party	19.0	57
	United Democratic Left	10.6	10
	Others (including People's Party)	10.4	3
1952 November	Greek Rally (right)	49.2	247
	Union of the Parties (centre)	34.2	51
	United Democratic Left	9.6	–
	Others	7.0	2
1956 February	National Radical Union (formerly Greek Rally)	47.4	165
	Democratic Union (centre and left)	48.2	132
	Others	4.4	3

1958 May	National Radical Union	41.2	171
	United Democratic Left	24.4	79
	Liberal Party	20.7	36
	Others	13.7	14
1961 October	National Radical Union	50.8	176
	Centre Union	33.7	100
	National Democratic Agrarian	14.6	24
	Front (left and allies)	–	–
	Others	0.9	–
1963 November	Centre Union	42.1	138
	National Radical Union	39.4	132
	United Democratic Left	14.3	28
	Progressive Party (right)	3.7	2
	Others	0.5	–
1964 February	Centre Union	52.7	171
	National Radical Union (allied with Progressive Party)	35.2	107
	United Democratic Left	11.8	22
	Others	0.3	–
1974 November	New Democracy	54.4	220
	Centre Union (with ally)	20.4	60
	PASOK	13.6	12
	United Left (Communist parties and United Democratic Left)	9.5	8
	Others	2.1	–
1977 November	New Democracy	41.9	171
	PASOK	25.3	93
	Union of the Democratic Centre	12.0	16
	Communist Party	9.4	11
	National Camp (extreme right)	6.8	5
	Alliance of Progressive and Left-Wing Forces (including Communist Party of the Interior)	2.7	2
	Others	1.9	2
1981 October	PASOK	48.1	172
	New Democracy	35.9	115
	Communist Party of Greece	10.9	13
	Others	5.1	–

1985 June	PASOK	45.8	161
	New Democracy	40.9	126
	Communist Party	9.9	12
	Communist Party of the Interior	1.8	1
	Others	1.6	–
1989 June	New Democracy	44.3	145
	PASOK	39.1	125
	Coalition Party	13.1	28
	Others	3.5	2
1989 November	New Democracy	46.2	148
	PASOK	40.7	128
	Coalition Party	11.0	21
	Others	2.1	3
1990 April	New Democracy	46.9	151
	PASOK	39.3	124
	Coalition Party	10.6	21
	Others	3.2	4
1993 October	PASOK	46.9	171
	New Democracy	39.3	110
	Political Spring (seceders from New Democracy)	4.9	10
	Communist Party	4.5	9
	Coalition Party	2.9	–
	Others	1.5	–
1996 September	PASOK	41.5	162
	New Democracy	38.1	108
	Communist Party	5.6	11
	Coalition Party	5.1	10
	Democratic Social Movement	4.5	9
	Others	5.2	–
2000 April	PASOK	43.8	158
	New Democracy	42.7	125
	Communist Party	5.5	11
	Coalition Party	3.2	6
	Others	4.8	–

INDEX